Perfecting
Women

Perfecting Women

Maulana Ashraf ʿAli Thanawi's
Bihishti Zewar
A Partial Translation with
Commentary

Barbara Daly Metcalf

University of California Press
Berkeley / Los Angeles / Oxford

University of California Press
Berkeley and Los Angeles, California

University of California Press, Ltd.
Oxford, England

© 1990 by
The Regents of the University of California

First Paperback Printing 1992

Library of Congress Cataloging-in-Publication Data
Thānvī, 'Ashraf 'Alī.
  [Bihishtī zevar. English]
  Perfecting women : Maulana Ashraf 'Alī Thanawi's Bihishti zewar :
a partial translation with commentary / Barbara Daly Metcalf.
     p.   cm.
  Translation of: Bihishti zevar.
  Includes index.
  ISBN 0-520-08093-9
  1. Women, Muslim—Conduct of life.   2. Islam—Customs and
Practices.   I. Metcalf, Barbara Daly, 1941-   . II. Title.
BJ1292.W6T4713 1990
297'.448'024042—dc19   89–30552
                                                              CIP

Printed in the United States of America

1 2 3 4 5 6 7 8 9

Contents

Preface

The *Bihishti Zewar,* written in northern India in the early 1900s, has been one of this century's most influential books. A guide for respectable women, it sets out the core of a reformist version of Islam that has become increasingly prominent across Muslim societies in the past hundred years. As a text for the world's largest population of Muslims, that of the old British Indian Empire, it has influenced countless individuals.

Among Indian reformist works, the *Bihishti Zewar* is especially important because it explicates reformist teachings for women. It presents in principle and in detail the normative rules for ritual and social life common to Hanafi Muslims then and now, and it attempts to shape a specific temperament of moderation, piety, and control. By elaborating these teachings in a particular context, it offers rich descriptions of the everyday life of the relatively privileged classes in turn-of-the-century north India, providing information on ways of thought and personal formation, as well as on family life, social relations, household management, and encounters with new institutions and inventions. Throughout, nothing is more striking than the extent to which the work treats women and men as essentially the same, in contrast to European works directed toward women at this time.

The author of the *Bihishti Zewar,* Maulana Ashraf 'Ali Thanawi (1864–1943), met the challenges of the missionaries and the westernized, his literary rivals for women's attention, asserting that he too was part of the modern age of railroads, post offices, new products, and new professions. To preach reform and to reach women required breaking out of the classic literary genres of the *'ulama*. Thanawi did so and thus played a significant role in disseminating the religious self-consciousness so characteristic of this century in India. His work has spoken with salience to large numbers of Muslims, women and men, down to the present. His work speaks to a broader audience, too, as a precious source for those interested in modern Indian social and intellectual history, in Islamic reform, and in gender and women's roles.

*   *   *

I am grateful to the Translation Grants Program of the National Endowment for the Humanities, which supported me during much of the time I worked on this project. The University of Pennsylvania cooperated with NEH in providing me with welcome leave and additional support.

Thanks to the grant, Laurel Steele, recently a U.S. Foreign Service Officer in the land of the *Bihishti Zewar,* worked on the translation as my assistant. Of her many contributions, I cherish most her unflagging enthusiasm and her conviction that the translation was a wonderful endeavor. Bruce Pray deserves special thanks for reading almost all of the translation against the Urdu and for saving me from at least some of my gaffes in translation and infelicities in English. I am grateful to him on this occasion, as I have been so often over the past twenty years, for his sterling linguistic skills and his unfailing good will. Ralph Russell first turned my attention to the *Bihishti Zewar,* and for this, as for so much else, I am grateful. Gail Minault, generous as always, provided excellent advice. I am deeply indebted to C. M. Naim for his meticulous and insightful reading of the final draft. My husband, Tom, was always ready to confer with me on the esoterica of "The *BZ*" and deserves my thanks for his constant support. My older son, Christopher, with a combination of computer skills and sound common sense, intervened to make less-than-PerfectWriter miraculously perform. Ann Devaney, in the end, took on PerfectWriter full force and produced the final version of the manuscript when I was ready to give up.

Many friends and colleagues have generously read and pondered sections of this project over the years; I particularly thank Lila Abu-Lughod, Sandria Freitag, Karen Haltunnen, Ira Lapidus, David Lelyveld, Khalid Masud, and Frances Pritchett for their help. I am also grateful to the organizers and participants of several seminars where I presented papers on this work: Thomas Laqueur, Department of History, University of California, Berkeley; Frank Conlon, South Asian Seminar, University of Washington, Seattle; Wolfgang Schluchter,

Werner-Reimers-Stiftung, Bad Homburg; Marc Gaborieau, Ecole des Hautes Etudes en Sciences Sociales, Paris; and Kay Flavell, Interdisciplinary Research Seminar, University of California, Davis. Early versions of sections of the book have been published in *Contributions to Asian Studies* (issue on Islam in Local Environments) 17, no. 1 (1982): 62–78; in *Islamic Society and Culture: Essays in Honor of Professor Aziz Ahmad,* ed. Milton Israel and N. K. Wagle (Delhi: Manohar, 1983), pp. 17–38; and in *Max Webers Sicht des Islam: Interpretation und Kritik,* ed. Wolfgang Schluchter (Frankfurt: Suhrkamp Verlag, 1987), pp. 242–255.

A Note on Translation

The Urdu of the *Bihishti Zewar* is regarded as a model of informal, conversational prose style. It represents the capacity of Urdu from the nineteenth century to appear in a wide variety of prose genres—a new development, for Urdu had been, as a literary language, a language of poetry and tales. Although Maulana Thanawi consulted the women of his family about their problems and customary practices, he did not utilize the dialect of Urdu peculiar to them, known as *begamati* Urdu.[1] Nor did he use the Arabicized and more formal style and diction he employed in his scholarly works.[2] His simple language, which at times still keeps the parallel constructions of poetry, has influenced Urdu prose stylists in the twentieth century, perhaps more than many writers consciously realize.[3] The goal of this translation has been to approximate Thanawi's fluent conversational style.

The translation is in no sense literal. Urdu has its own logic, as does any language, and can be studied for the cultural principles its structure embodies. To attempt to convey those principles in an English translation, however, simply makes for awkward language and does not in fact afford the opportunity for the serious study of the language that is allowed only by work in the original. For example, there seems to be in Urdu a priority of the object over the actor, making the passive voice very common. Similarly, actors are often acted upon: events and objects impinge on them. It would be inappropriate to replicate this structure in English, as it would be inappropriate to imitate the Urdu practice of stringing together events with conjunctions, without indicating the temporal and causal relations commonly specified in English. This use of conjunctions is a result, in part, of the lack of punctuation in Urdu until the past hundred years or so. An early twentieth-century Urdu text, moreover, typically uses only headings, with no paragraphs; thus paragraphs, lists, and much of the punctuation are added here. Urdu also uses direct discourse for reporting conversation far more than English does; I have usually rendered quotations as indirect discourse in the translation.

Urdu has certain repertoires of terms that English lacks, notably terms for expressing hierarchy. There are three ranked pronouns for the second person singular, for example; a common usage is to employ the most respectful, identical with the third person plural, when speaking of an especially revered person. Urdu uses the plural to convey respect, even when speaking of a single person (or, in a practice condemned by opponents of the Deobandis, when speaking of God). Urdu also has double and triple causative verbs to convey the delegation of actions to others. There are many examples of this in the directions for household activities in Book Ten. In general, there is a far greater range for conveying hierarchy in the everyday lexicon of an Urdu speaker. In English, you or I simply "come" or "go"; in Urdu, a worthy person conveys/takes/ brings/places his or her presence. Archaic English does not accurately represent what, in Urdu, is everyday. Some of this hierarchic language is translated literally in sample letters in Book One, where the student is being taught how to make proper discriminations.

One particular term indicating hierarchy is *hazrat,* a noun based on an Arabic root that means "presence," a term often used as a title or common noun for a respected person. Prefaced by an adjective meaning "lofty," it is used for the saintly or powerful—and was in fact appropriated by the British monarchs as they sought to invent legitimacy for themselves as emperors of India. In this text, it commonly prefaces the names of all prophets, saints, and exemplary people, male or female. It is used for the Prophet Muhammad before his proper name, before the words meaning "messenger" or "apostle," or simply in isolation. In all cases related to him, it is followed by the Arabic prayer of blessing (or its abbreviation), which is discussed below. I have left *hazrat* untranslated throughout.

I translate the Persian word for God, *khuda* (often translated as "Lord"), as "God." It is thus not distinguished from the Arabic *allah.* I make one exception to not using "Lord" for God, an exception that reflects an intriguing conundrum in translation and interpretation—the phrase Allah Miyan, translated as "Our Lord and Master" (discussed in the Introduction to the *Bihishti Zewar,* below).

Along with questions of hierarchy, those of gender require some comment. Unless there is verbal agreement, it is not clear in Urdu whether pronouns are meant to refer to a male or to a female; there is a single word for he/she, his/hers, and so forth. Because it is widely considered unacceptable in English to use the masculine forms as applicable to both sexes, I have sometimes used feminine forms when that seemed appropriate in the context of instruction for women. At other times, I have struggled to find inclusive forms: the section on rules for handling children, in Book Ten, is an example of translation guided by that concern.

Other aspects of the translation are attempts to reflect certain Islamic concepts and conventions. I translate *shari'at* as "religious law," hoping to signal that the Islamic religious law is not law in a Western sense but rather a comprehensive guide to every dimension of human life; it is not definitively codified and is valid quite apart from being administered in a court of law. I also follow a convention in English of capitalizing Prophet when Muhammad is meant, and hence Apostle and Messenger also. I capitalize Companion when referring to a Companion of the Prophet.

Muslims everywhere ideally append a pious Arabic phrase of blessing to the name of every prophet, saint, Companion of the Prophet Muhammad, or other revered person. In English, the phrase, if written, can be obtrusive; moreover, Muslims themselves often use an abbreviation in writing. And sometimes they forget. Generally speaking, I use the full phrase either the first time a name is mentioned or the first time the phrase occurs in a section of text; I usually abbreviate it thereafter. The phrases and abbreviations are as follows:[4]

The superscript sign "s" follows the Prophet Muhammad's name, standing for *salla'llahu 'alaihi wa sallam, "God's blessings and peace upon him,"* a phrase used for Muhammad[s] alone.

The superscript sign "a" follows the name of other prophets, standing for *'alaihi's-salam, "On him be peace."* Sometimes the phrase is lengthened to *"and on our Prophet also."*

The superscript sign "rz" follows the names of the Companions of the Prophet[s]. It stands for *razi'allahu 'anhu, "May God be pleased with him,"* or *'anha* (her), or *'anhum* (them), or *'anhuma* (them, dual).

The superscript sign "rh" follows the names of saints, great religious authorities, and other deceased pious persons. It stands for *rahmatu'lla'alaihi, "May God have mercy upon him."*

Translations of Qur'anic quotations, prayers, and so forth are shown in an italic bold typeface in the body of the translation, as above, to indicate that they are translated from Arabic, not Urdu. These phrases fill the conversation of the pious. As one Muslim scholar has written, "The soul of a Muslim is like a mosaic made up of formulae of the Qur'an in which he breathes and lives."[5] Some of these phrases are listed below to aid those curious about the original words and implications of these recurrent phrases.

Bi'smi'llahu'r-rahmanu'r-rahim: In the Name of God, the Merciful, the Compassionate. After the attestation of faith, this is the most used formula in Islam, including the name of God, Allah, and two characterizing terms derived from the root meaning "divine mercy." It is recited at the beginning of every act and included at the beginning of every written work in order to relate the undertaking to God and thus to sanctify it.

Alhamdu'li'llah: Praise be to God. This phrase is used constantly in everyday speech and is the complement of the phrase above. It ends an act, whereas the *bi'smi'llah* begins it.

Insha'llah: God willing. This phrase is repeated concerning events in the future that cannot be realized without divine consent.

Masha'llah: What God has willed. One uses this phrase at the end of an act or a comment as a reminder that whatever occurs comes from God; it is repeated, for example, when reference is made to one's children or personal experiences. It can be used ironically.

Astaghfiru'llah: I ask forgiveness of God; God forbid! This phrase is used when describing deplorable events.

La haula wa la quwwata illa bi'l-lahi: There is no strength or power but in God. This is also a deprecatory expression repeated when one receives bad news or hears or sees something disagreeable.

Na'uzu bi'llahi: We seek protection by God; God forbid! This phrase is most often used at the prospect of some expression of infidelity (*kufr*).

'Ufi anhu: May God forgive him. A phrase written or spoken after the name of a living person.

*Inna li'llahi wa inna ilaihi raja'un: **Truly, we belong to God, and to
him we will return**.* A phrase spoken to express sympathy upon a
death or to register sorrow or disgust when one hears something
deplorable.

It is difficult in a translation to convey the appearance of the original
pages. Urdu texts, including those for publication, are typically handwritten. Even today, readers have little taste for the machine-typed
texts that occasionally appear (and are common in Arabic and Persian). Handwriting allows the author or scribe to vary the size and
emphasis of script. I have tried to convey this variation through spac-
ing, subtitles, and occasional underscoring.

Explanatory material, commenting on the text, has sometimes been
added throughout the translation. Any such editorial interpolations are
enclosed in brackets. Urdu and other terms are defined in a glossary.
Tables of contents have been added. Bracketed headings do not appear
in the original.

The translation that follows consists of the first half of Book One as
well as most of Books Six, Seven, Eight, and Ten of the *Bihishti Zewar*.
It is based on the earliest edition available to me, that held by the
British Library and catalogued under the name Hafiz Muhammad
Ashraf 'Ali (Sadhaura, 1905). Footnotes that appear in that edition are
included here at the foot of the text pages. My own notes appear at the
end of the volume.

An Introduction to the
Bihishti Zewar

In a short time, **God willing,** *you will . . . become
a* maulawi—*that is, a scholar of Arabic. . . . You
will achieve the rank of a learned person, and you
will be able to give judicial opinions, as learned
men do. You will begin to teach Arabic to girls,
just as learned men do. . . . You will be granted
the reward equal to that bestowed on each person
to whom you have given guidance with your
preaching and opinions, teaching and books.*

Bihishti Zewar, Book Ten

*[The Prophet Muhammad] was very gentle. . . .
At night . . . he would do everything very softly, so
that no one's sleep would ever be disturbed. . . .
When he was happy, he lowered his gaze. What
young girl would have been as modest as this?*

Bihishti Zewar, Book Eight

*I have for some time . . . realized that in order to
manage women, it is absolutely necessary to teach
them the science of religion.*

Bihishti Zewar, Book One

   The *Bihishti Zewar* (Heavenly ornaments), written at the beginning
of the twentieth century, has been one of the most influential texts of
the scripturalist reform movements characteristic of Muslim societies
in the past century.[1] It strikingly represents significant changes in the
themes and emphases in Muslim religious life in recent times. Most
important, it illustrates a new concern for bringing mainstream Islamic
teachings to women—a departure from the traditional view in which
women typically were not expected to have more than a minimal acquaintance with these teachings. Women had not been regarded historically as the guardians of virtue and tradition, as, for example, they
became in Europe at this time. Rather, it was men, in the public

1

settings of mosque, court, school, and sufi hospice, who preserved and elaborated the tradition. The text itself, therefore, is part of an important cultural transformation. It is also an excellent source for a textured, detailed presentation of the major themes of Islamic reform. Moreover, because the book is directed toward women, its examples and detail provide a rich picture of everyday domestic life and of attitudes about women.

For women to act as they should, this work argues, they must be instructed. Basic to this confidence in the power of instruction is an implicit conviction that women are essentially the same as men, neither endowed with a special nature for spiritual or moral virtue nor handicapped in any way by limitations of intellect or character. This book is interesting not only for what it does but also for what it does not do, for it makes no effort to elaborate physiological or intellectual differences between women and men. The epigraphs above make this clear. There is no need for a distinctive literature for women, for example, no notion that women are more suited for literature or poetry than for anything more intellectually demanding. As the first epigraph suggests, women are best off reading Arabic texts, as men do.[2] Similarly, there is no sense that women have a specific range of feminine virtues. The second epigraph emphasizes that everyone must take the Prophet as their model, that his essential characteristics must be emulated by both women and men.

Yet the goal of reform was to create a properly ordered society in which people knew their place, fulfilled their responsibilities, and received their due. We are reminded of this in the third epigraph: central to correct hierarchy is the subordination of women to the men of their family. In principle, there is no contradiction between distinctive roles based on gender, age, and status and an essential equality of nature that is taken for granted here. The reformers also call on people to recognize the hierarchy that extends beyond humans to God, whose uniqueness, *tauhid,* is not to be compromised by human self-assertion or saintly elevation. Much of the book focuses on cultivating virtues and eliminating false religious practices.

The introduction that follows first describes the historical context of both the author and the text. It then briefly discusses the legacy of the Western stereotypes about Muslim women and suggests as a more appropriate background the *shari'at* framework in which issues related to women have historically been understood. Next, it returns to the issue of the single standard newly set for women and men, assessing its implications for women and contrasting its essential egalitarianism with contemporaneous thought about women in Victorian Britain and Hindu Bengal, as well as in modernist Islam.

The introduction next highlights a central theme of the book and of reformist thought: the high value placed on correct knowledge as a key to change. This theme reflects faith in education with a vengeance—in this perspective, if a woman (or anyone) is properly informed, she will find the truth so self-evident and persuasive that she will be transformed. An analysis of the importance of newly available print media in the elaboration and dissemination of that knowledge follows.

True knowledge is the basis of a properly ordered society, and the final sections of the introduction look at characteristics of that society, hierarchically ordered among humans and between humans and God. They also focus on the diagnosis of customary practice as the false *shari'at* that thwarts proper order and that must be abolished if the cherished goals of the reformers are ever to be met.

Ashraf 'Ali Thanawi and Deoband

The *Bihishti Zewar* was written by Maulana Ashraf 'Ali Thanawi (1864–1943), a leader of the Deobandi reform movement that crystalized in north India in the late nineteenth century. The religious leaders at the heart of that movement believed that the world they lived in was seriously awry, and they set out to reform it through the methods they held most central, namely, education of religious leaders, preaching and teaching, public debate, and—as exemplified by this text—a flood of pamphlets and books.[3] The *Bihishti Zewar* was intended to provide a basic education for a respectable Muslim woman. It rapidly became a classic gift for Muslim brides, who "entered their husband's home with the Holy Qur'an in one hand and the *Bihishti Zewar* in the other."[4]

There have, of course, been critics of the book,[5] but it has been endlessly reprinted and is found today in virtually any shop that carries works in Urdu, the learned language and lingua franca of most of the Muslims in what are now the countries of India and Pakistan. It has also been widely translated into regional languages, as well as into English for Muslims in the West. The preface to a recent English translation of the work, addressed to both women and men, makes this claim:

This is the best text and reference book on Islam and the Islamic law (Shari'ah), according to the greatest Imam with the largest following not

only in the U.K. but also in the world, Hazrat Imam Abu Hanifah. This
is [the] most widely read book after the Holy Qur'an in Urdu, Gujrati,
Bengali, Hindi, and now in English too.[6]

Thanawi, a prolific author and spiritual guide for thousands, believed,
according to his family, that on account of this book alone he would be
saved.[7]

Maulana Thanawi was an extraordinarily successful exponent of
reform. One of the second generation of Deobandi *'ulama* (and
trained in their central institution, the Daru'l-'Ulum, founded in 1867
some ninety miles northeast of Delhi), he was long active in a new
religious school in Kanpur. In his mid-thirties, he retired to his home
in a small country town called Thana Bhawan, in the Upper Doab
region of the United Provinces. There he wrote voluminously, taught,
answered letters, and counseled so many visitors that newcomers
were asked to fill out a form upon arrival. Visits were facilitated by
the newly opened railway line that passed through Thana Bhawan:
the faithful believed that the train tracks had been laid out with that
very purpose in mind.

Hundreds of written works are attributed to Thanawi, many actually written by his followers, who—in a custom known elsewhere as
well—attributed their work to the person to whom they felt they
owed everything. Maulana Thanawi was sought out for his erudition,
his passion for reform, his integrity, and his spirituality as a sufi elder;
he offered his followers a range of commitments and meanings that
were not tied to the institutions and values of the colonial state. He is
remembered as a forceful personality who insisted on directness and
frankness in all personal meetings.[8] His successors (*khulafa*), and now
their successors, continue to be influential among Muslims of the
subcontinent.

The reformist concern with women's—and men's—lives was a response to far-reaching changes in late nineteenth-century India. In
examining the stimulus for reform movements in modern India, histori-
ans have focused on the changes engendered by the colonial context:
the end of Muslim political dominance; an idiom of British rule that
encouraged religious identity; the social dislocation caused by changing
requirements for participation in governmental and economic roles;
the presence of an aggressive alternative range of cultural values; and
the growth of cities and the enlarged scale of social and economic
activities.[9] Whatever Thanawi's perceptions of the changes around
him, however, the crisis he saw was embodied in the lives of individuals, whose errors pulled them ever more deeply into entanglements

that jeopardized their own salvation, their worldly well-being, and the lives of the individuals and society around them.

Set against the sociopolitical realities of his day, a discourse of hellfire and details of correct practice and belief may seem merely escapist. But any assessment must be far more complex. The movements epitomized by Thanawi and people like him helped to spread an ethical Islam of individual responsibility, which was suitable to a more integrated and more mobile population; it also fostered self-esteem among a subject population. This religious style contributed—as did parallel movements in other communities—to a heightened sense of religious affiliation as the primary focus of social identity in a pluralistic society.[10] A text like the *Bihishti Zewar* is thus at the heart of significant sociopolitical change. All this, however, was far from Thanawi's conscious concerns as he attempted to snap a chain of cause and effect that seemed, to him, to destroy all hope for a comfortable and meaningful life in this world and bliss in the world to come.

There have been many movements broadly resembling the Deobandi in the modern period,[11] variously known by such labels as "scripturalist," "reformist," or "neo-sufi."[12] Typically, their leaders are *'ulama* educated in the classical disciplines, the heirs of the medieval legal traditions (*mazhab*) in religious law (*fiqh*), as well as the heirs of the medieval sufi orders (*silsila*) in inner knowledge and personal experience (*tariqa*). Thus rooted, this mainstream reform has flourished. Today, there are Deobandi schools throughout India, Pakistan, and Bangladesh. Although they were originally influential among the wellborn, the Deobandis now reach new groups drawn in from lower classes and from more remote provinces.[13]

The Tablighi Jama'at, an off-shoot of the Deobandis, is currently the most influential movement, in terms of numbers, among Muslims in the subcontinent and perhaps in the world. It is a missionary movement to nominal Muslims, providing instruction in basic duties. Tabligh preachers leave their homes for tours, preaching, instructing, and disseminating the tracts and publications for which they are known. Nearly one million people in each country attend the annual gatherings of the Tabligh in both India and Pakistan. The movement has spread to Southeast Asia and to Muslims in the West, even to people who are not of South Asian origin, most notably to North Africans resident in France and Belgium.[14] A translation of the *Bihishti Zewar* is now required reading for Tabligh members in Great Britain.[15] The movement may be relatively unknown, but its cultural importance in the lives of millions of Muslims, including women, who play an active part, is not in doubt.

Muslim Women and Reform

The *Bihishti Zewar* challenges widely held misperceptions and stereotypes of Islamic teachings about women. The collective European image of Middle Eastern society from the seventeenth century asserted an inherent tendency toward despotism; in this context, women's status was declared tantamount to slavery. It was believed that women were treated as objects, and they were considered virtual prisoners in their houses. This stereotype was in time overlaid with another, that of romantic eroticism, with *The Thousand and One Nights* as the canonical text.[16] Many today continue to assume that the position of women in Muslim society is the ultimate example of male oppression and exploitation.

Recent scholarship has questioned the notion that "Islam" is an immutable, independent source of beliefs and institutions and has focused instead on seeing Islam as a discursive system in which Muslims interact with shared symbols, conveyed in sacred texts and shared institutions, to produce very different cultural worlds.[17] Ethnographers have described the wide variety of patterns in Muslim women's lives—women who range from peasant field workers to enterprising traders to highly trained professionals—thus challenging the image of women as passive and secluded. Secluded women have in fact played significant roles in economic life and in family alliances and networks. The *Bihishti Zewar,* for example, both in what is enjoined and in what is condemned, gives evidence of important roles for women in exercising moral leadership, creating social alliances, and managing economic resources in the society it represents.

The Islamic discourse about women has been historically formulated within a corpus of legal texts based in the *shari'at,* the all-encompassing norms based on the Qur'an and the received example of the Prophet Muhammad (the *sunna*), communicated through sayings, or *hadis*. It has been sustained by codes of honor and shame internalized by both women and men.[18] Thanawi's goal in this work is to communicate correct teachings from the *shari'at. Shari'at* norms are realized in specific local contexts. Thus, for example, the *shari'at* urges people to marry their "like." Thanawi, writing in north India, delineates specific social categories within which marriage is possible, categories significant only to that region. The *shari'at* specifies that women be morally responsible and that men treat them fairly; the Qur'an, for example, urges fair treatment of co-wives. In recent times, the implications of that text have been variously interpreted as allowing polygamy, placing restrictions on it, or prohibiting it absolutely on the grounds that fairness is not possible.[19]

However differently realized, the *shari'at* has promoted certain themes in relation to women. Concerned with ensuring social order, the Prophet looked upon the sexual virtue of women as central. Thanawi follows the *hadis* in insisting, near the beginning of Book Six, that adultery extends beyond actual sexual relations to thought, sight, hearing, and touch. The jurists demanded that women be secluded, that even—again echoed here—their voices and jewelry not be heard, their perfume not smelled. Mainstream Islamic thought has seen licit sexuality as wholly positive but has looked with horror on deviation. As a check to deviation, control of women has been mirrored in an ideal division of space in which women were removed from public spaces, including mosques.[20]

The public was in fact the ideal domain of religion; the private, by default, was marginal. For the sufis, some of whom challenged the whole discourse on women by opting for celibacy, women were at times emblematic of the corrupt world, specifically identified with the lower soul, the *nafs* present within each person as the urge to willful and undisciplined behavior defying divine law. The sufi tradition of a love relationship as symbolic of the soul's passion for God, expressed above all in Persian poetry, also posits the beloved as irrational and beyond *shari'at* bounds, outside the public world of Islam and its guardians. Thanawi knows this tradition and explicitly condemns it.[21]

What is it, then, that the *Bihishti Zewar* seeks to reform? It is certainly not the *shari'at*. It is rather all that keeps the *shari'at* from being fulfilled—specifically, wrong attitudes about women that identify them with, or leave them enmeshed in, a world outside the straight path of Islam. Women have often, explicitly or implicitly, been deemed innocent of knowledge, *juhhal,* like children or those who lived in pre-Islamic times.[22] Thanawi and his fellow reformist *'ulama* sought to do nothing less than bring women into the high standard of Islamic conformity that had been the purview of educated religious men.

A Single Standard

As the colonial state in India took from Muslims the control of government, it ended what had been both a sphere of activity and a central symbol of an Islamic order. Muslim reformers from the eighteenth century sought to make the *'ulama* the guardians of Islam, and individuals under their guidance its bastion. For that effort to succeed, the *'ulama* necessarily had to address a far wider range of Muslims than had scripturalist reformers in earlier times. They were able to seek a wide audience because of new methods and techniques of communication that were available to them, as well as to rivals. They were also motivated by a colonial framework that created an arena for "communities," whose leaders could "represent" them.[23] The *'ulama* themselves did not act in the colonial political arena during this period, but they were part of a society whose communal idiom they saw on every side. Common knowledge assumes that identities such as "Indian Muslim" are primary and of long historical standing, but in fact they are products of recent history.[24]

The *'ulama* thus increasingly made the custom-laden private world, resting in women's hands, a central target of reform. To reform individual Muslim lives—when public institutions not only were beyond Muslim control but in some cases also challenged Islam—traditional practices of private life were made an overriding concern. As Faisal Devji has pointed out, this suggests a shift in the relative value of public and private from that held by the traditional ideal of Islamic society.[25]

Thanawi's argument, as he sought to reform women, can be simply put: women and men are essentially the same, endowed with the same faculties and equally responsible for their conduct. Both must contend with the fundamental human condition of the struggle between intelligence or sense, *'aql,* on the one hand, and the undisciplined impulses of the lower soul, *nafs,* on the other. Looking around him, Thanawi believes that women are more likely than men to be troubled by *nafs,* but, to use modern language, he finds this situation culturally, not genetically, determined. This is clear from his emphasis, discussed below, on the centrality of knowledge and on the ability of women to adhere to the standard being set for all, if only they are adequately informed. There can never be a prima facie case that women are morally inferior to men.

At the same time, they are not superior. In contrast to the Victorian notion of women's special spiritual capacity, Thanawi argued that women and the home were yet to be converted to appropriate standards. This point must be emphasized, for a special female spiritual capacity has often been wrongly read into Islamic tradition. The historical view does not, in fact, see women as "better equipped than men to be 'carriers of tradition' "—quite the opposite.[26] The argument that identifies women and the home as the locus of cultural tradition, the rock against an encroaching alien world, does appear among Muslim thinkers, but it is one constituted during and after the colonial period, not earlier.

The conclusive evidence that Thanawi enjoined a single standard of behavior for women and men was his response when he was asked to write a companion guide, directed to men, to the *Bihishti Zewar*. He replied that the existing book would serve perfectly well. He simply added an appendix, the *Bihishti Gauhar* (The heavenly gem), describing practices such as the community prayer specific to men. Indeed, the English translations of the work in use today, focusing on legal norms rather than on sample letters, the household, and so forth, give no indication that the book was once meant solely for women. It is hard to imagine a guidebook for women written in 1900 in Europe or America that could also be recommended as a proper guide for men.

Though men and women are identical in all that matters, Thanawi never questions their different social roles. Women are meant to be socially subordinate to men and to adhere to the *shari'at* standard of seclusion, when possible, inside the home. Indeed, Thanawi insists, it is reformed behavior that will instruct women—and all people— concerning their proper place and that will enhance fulfillment of their proper roles. One of the first reformist texts directed to women,[27] the *Bihishti Zewar* is not a conservative document, "the dying cry of a repressive feudal order,"[28] but the product of a modern movement that both redefined a social role for the *'ulama,* apart from the state, and challenged the received cultural tradition preserved above all by women in the home.

If the *Bihishti Zewar* can be seen to have an overriding focus in its teachings for all individuals, it is to delineate the characteristics of a reformist temperament: moderate in all things, unfailingly self-controlled, minimally engaged in social relations, and wholly absorbed in fulfillment of the religious law. There is no effort to differentiate male and female in this model.

It is risky to generalize about a "reformist temperament." But Thanawi's anxieties about human behavior, his despairing assessment of the world around him, and his convictions about the possibility of change all strike themes that resonate in other movements of religious reform, notably in major streams of Protestant thought in the sixteenth century, as well as in the reformist positions of some Hindu thinkers who were Thanawi's contemporaries in India.[29] Among all these reformers, we find images of society as a suffocating morass that entangles people in false paths. We find a confidence that unambiguous true knowledge can be realized and must be conveyed to all through education; it is the key to escape from false paths that distort relationships and priorities. We find a concern with encouraging individuals to cultivate personalities based on moderation and relentless self-control. We find as well a shared conviction that women's conduct is the key to social reform.

Women were, however, to be subservient to men. This is patriarchy, as the word "manage" in the epigraph above suggests. But the new patriarchy of the *'ulama* was not the old. Women were to enjoy the respect accorded those who had mastered true knowledge. At the same time, the *'ulama* reinforced the ideal of women remaining in their own homes, secluded from all but family and selected female friends. This central teaching constrained the potential power that could have been derived from literacy and access to the learned tradition. These limits on women's public roles would become even more significant as a public sphere of employment, education, voluntary associations, and entertainment expanded in the twentieth century.

Men's authority, moreover, now ideally reached into what had been largely a female world, the world of social and familial relationships, expressed in festive occasions and the passages marking birth, growth, illness, marriage, and death, as well as a world of distinctive traditions in piety and worship.[30] Eliminating all these customary practices meant a check on female autonomy as well as restrictions on the participation of women in gatherings and ceremonies that defined much of their social interaction and even identity. The *Bihishti Zewar,* particularly in Book Six, provides rich descriptions of that sphere in its very attempt to penetrate and modify it.

Medicine offers an example of male intrusion into a heretofore largely female domain. The medicine of herbs and amulets, the medicine connected above all with midwives and childbirth, had long been in women's hands. Parallel to the reform of the religious sciences in the late nineteenth century, however, came reform in medicine, a revival of the scientific medicine of the Greco-Arabic humoral system, which came to be seen as equivalent or even superior to the Western medical system.[31] This medicine, *yunani tibb,* was even taught as an ancillary subject at Deoband so that the *'ulama* could further serve their followers. Women were enjoined to learn its application, too, and the *Bihishti Zewar* itself, in Book Nine, includes a section summarizing *yunani* treatments.[32] Women were now to disdain the interventions of the wise women, who were dismissed as no more than quacks. The reformers sought to include women in what they saw as a higher standard of behavior, but they did so at the cost of areas of family and ritual life that had been women's domain.

Thanawi's unitary ideal of human nature and moral capacity presents a dramatic contrast to prevalent Victorian notions of femininity and masculinity. The epigraph describing the Prophet's manner suggests aspects of an ideal person who is in no sense tailored to fit a Victorian masculine standard. Ashis Nandy has recently argued that the European ideal originated, in part, in the colonial experience. The cult of masculinity in Victorian Britain, he suggests, must be seen as part of the impact of the colonial experience on the colonizers, who cast their relationship to the colonies in terms of gender as part of their implicit justification of their imperial role. Their definition of masculinity was, in turn, to shape the interpretation both of gender roles and of central religious symbols by Indian reformers motivated to share this aspect of imperial discourse.[33] But, as the brief epigraph describing the Prophet makes clear, Maulana Thanawi stood apart from such concerns.

To put Thanawi's principles in perspective, one might compare the first epigraph above to a description of an important strand in the contemporaneous European and American discourse on women, restricting female education on medical grounds:

> Because reproduction was woman's grand purpose in life, doctors agreed that women had to concentrate all their energy downward toward the womb. . . . Too much reading or intellectual stimulation in the fragile stage of adolescence could result in permanent damage to the reproductive organs, and sickly, irritable babies.[34]

Maulana Thanawi's society knew no counterpart to the pseudoscientific medical theories of the nineteenth century that posited such radical difference between women and men. In relation to education, Thanawi argued, the only difference between girls and boys was that girls, being (ideally) confined to the home, had an advantage in having more time available for learning. In nineteenth-century Europe, the hierarchic model of antiquity had begun to give way to a bipolar model insisting that genders differed in kind, not only in status.[35] No such change took place among Muslims, where Galenic theories of common human bodily and moral characteristics continued to hold sway. The Muslim reformers simply wanted to make the women of their day—in all that was important—more like educated men.

The "heavenly ornaments" of Thanawi's title, one might add, are not women themselves as adornments or ornaments of domestic life.[36] There is no notion that women are the Victorian "angel of the house," that in their protected sphere they rise to a higher and purer morality. Darwin, for example, judged women unlike men in their "greater tenderness and less selfishness" (although he hastened to link these and other traits to "the lower races and . . . a past and lower state of civilization").[37] The "ornaments" in Thanawi's work are rather a metaphor for the virtues both women and men must cultivate in themselves, the virtues that will earn them the pearls and bracelets of heaven (Qur'an 22:23). They correspond to the "treasures" one lays up in heaven, the point reinforced by the fact that the book was to become a dowry gift, a context in which "real" jewelry had been expected. Thus two of the distinctive themes of Victorian culture in relation to women—what might be called the "medical" view and the "pedestal"—must not be read into the position of Islamic reformers, with the assumption that a domestic role for women carries these notions along as inevitable baggage.

There were Indian reformers who did participate in the European discourse on women. Contrasting their position with Thanawi's is instructive. The British critique of Indian society, as early as the first decades of the nineteenth century, singled out issues related to women: child marriage, female infanticide, sati, female education, remarriage of widows. In responding to this British agenda, reformers, preeminently Bengali Hindus, sought to define a domestic sphere that provided a source of self-esteem and unity. Reacting to the colonial critique, they insisted that their social life, restored to its true form, represented a higher, more spiritual morality than that of the imperial rulers.

They set a standard for a new middle-class woman of modest dress, distinctive educational attainments, and piety that at once distinguished her from the uneducated, traditional, often lower-status Indian woman and from what they saw as the heartless, worldly European woman. She was to be nothing less than a central symbol of cherished, but endangered, Bengali culture. The woman was the center of the home, and the difference between the world and the home became the root dichotomy from which other dichotomies—notably, materialism in contrast to spiritualism, and masculinity in contrast to femininity—flowed. The masculine, materialistic world was dominated by the colonial presence; the feminine, spiritual home was seen as free. The Indian woman was to be the bastion against all that was corrupt in the West, and, weighted with new skills and a new moral role, she was also to be unlike the traditional woman, who was caught up in what were now objectionable practices.

As in Victorian Britain, a central premise of Bengali Hindu reform was that women were essentially different from men. In India, the Hindu middle-class reformers could draw on their own tradition of goddesses and saints to outdo the Victorians and imbue domestic "angels," similarly sheltered from the external world and able to cultivate tender and spiritual qualities, with divinity itself.[38] Ironically, as in the Muslim case, strands in this historical tradition, notably in the Sanskrit Vedas, had long marginalized women; far from being privileged carriers of sacred tradition, women had not even been allowed to hear the sacred texts.

The *Bihishti Zewar* differs in significant ways from the advice books for women that proliferated in nineteenth-century America and England—or in Bengal. Like them, this book sought to standardize a respectable morality throughout a large population during a period of social change; also like them, it encouraged female competence and self-confidence in a domestic sphere.[39] Unlike them, however, this work did not attempt to enhance gender differences, making women's unique self-sacrifice and dependence the key to a guardianship of morality. That guardianship was entrusted to anyone, woman or man, who honed his or her essential character to Islamic standards through knowledge and through relentless discipline and self-control.

An irony of the "new traditionalism" in Bengal is that the reformist program, while purporting to be starkly anti-Western, took its parameters from the Western critique. The same is true for Muslim "modernists," those who—in contrast to the *'ulama*—interacted with Western values and institutions. In fact, however, the concern with women's education among the first generation of the "westernizers" at Aligarh owed much, as did their entire program, to a grounding in the reformist milieu of the *'ulama,* with whom they shared an opposition to customary practice. Many moved on to apologetics and to defense of "true" Islam against Western criticism.[40] They also began to see women as both helpless and spiritual. Iqbal's poems, for example, place women above book-learning and consider education potentially harmful to the special feminine qualities that inspire men.[41]

Abul A'la Maududi, the founder of the Islamist Jama'at-i Islami,[42] similarly espoused a "dualistic view of humanity," rendering women passive and submissive but endowed with a special spiritual capacity.[43] But one should not assume that this Jama'ati emphasis, making women the central symbol of a properly ordered Islamic society, is part of a long tradition.[44] Thanawi, closer to the historical tradition, was egalitarian in respect to human nature. Moreover (despite the use of the *Bihishti Zewar* by the late Zia ul Haq, the Islamizing president of Pakistan),[45] Thanawi never saw his teachings as part of state policy: he enjoined self-control, not state control over others, which is a modern phenomenon rather than part of a long tradition.

For all this, Thanawi's effort was emotionally charged. In a portrayal that is especially notable in a work predicated on the importance of control and self-control, the *Bihishti Zewar* clearly represents women as always on the verge of moving out of control, of displaying excess, of spilling over—in where they go, what they buy, how much they talk, what they eat. Thanawi implies that most women must struggle more than men to attain the discipline and self-control that are the heart of his teachings. Women are shown as the victims of custom, but also as its perpetrators.

No section highlights this vision more than the colorful vignette set out in Book Six, in which women cast aside all restraint and gad about day and night to drop in on someone or participate in some ceremonial gathering or another. A seemingly innocent event brings endless sin and disorder in its train. The author identifies no fewer than thirty-two sins in these imagined outings and warns that these are only a few of those actually committed! The trips are morally corrupting, becoming occasions for pride, extravagance, financial pressure on the husband that might lead him to sin, financial dealings that are beyond the law. Immodesty and mingling of the sexes occur at every turn. Envy, ingratitude, and greed are coupled with gossip and backbiting as the women talk among themselves. The porters are likely to be abused, as is the hostess, who is invariably saddled with extra guests. The reformist standards of outward observance of the *shari'at* and inward moral purification and self-control could not be more challenged.

Much as he insisted on women's potential and on the variety among women, Maulana Thanawi described the women's behavior he saw as largely uncontrolled and emotional. In the depiction of the outing in Book Six, in the treatment of good women in Book Eight (where their virtues are marveled at), and, most explicitly, in Book Ten's list of twenty-nine points on the shortcomings of women (most related to lack of proportion and self-control), Maulana Thanawi depicts women as having suppressed *'aql,* the intelligence or sense on which a good life depends. Even literacy for women, a key reason the *Bihishti Zewar* was written, seems problematic when Thanawi imagines the possibility of women breaking through seclusion to indulge in illicit correspondence or reading heaven-knows-what in novels. The conviction that women are essentially the same as men, different only in hierarchy and hence in role, seems precarious at best, given what appears to be persistent breaking with the role that women should, by nature, fervently accept.

The anxiety over women's behavior suggests that women are seen as an extension of men: in women, men see the lack of control they most fear in themselves. As noted above, women have been associated with the *nafs,* or lower soul, both as a stimulus to male lack of control and as a metaphor.[46] The regional culture, moreover, when called into question, as it is particularly in Book Six, can also be equated with *nafs,* as a dark unruly world, less disciplined and less ordered than the principles represented by Islam.[47] Thus the emotional intensity associated with the end of custom and the establishment of the *shari'at* can be understood. In opposing custom, the reformers at once call into question their own propensity for deviation and reject intimate aspects of their own lives associated with women and home.

Yet Maulana Thanawi did hold, in principle, to the insistence that because women are in essence like men, they should be educated like men. In later editions of the *Bihishti Zewar* (summarized in the translator's introduction to Book Eight), he takes issue with those who hold that women are intrinsically weaker in character than men. Thanawi did, after all, write the *Bihishti Zewar.* For him, it is central that Muslims—all Muslims—develop the personal characteristics and acquire the learning that will permit them to worship God as they should and to live their everyday personal and social lives with ceaseless scrutiny. He believes that women are, in the end, every bit as capable as men of the moral discipline he enjoins. He believes that women's interests—like those of all people—will be enhanced when Muslims acknowledge one another's rights and respect one another's places, as they come to know the place of all humans in relation to God. He does *not* seek to enhance sexual differences—essential physiological or moral differences—that burden women, as we would see it, with either silly little heads or hearts of gold.

Readers of this text will no doubt ask, in the light of their own social norms, whether women lost or gained by the influence of scripturalist reform. Clearly, many Muslim women have seen their interests, usually understood as closely linked to those of their families, served by teachings of the sort set forth here. Not only were they assured of divine blessings, but they were also offered the clearly empowering skills of literacy and rationally organized principles of behavior. In some specific legal areas, moreover, they gained rights provided in Qur'anic teachings that enhanced women's autonomy in relation to property and marriage. Such skills and standards often proved a source of status for them within the family and for the family as a whole. Against this, of course, reformed women lost a separate sphere of female activity. They accepted the authority of male specialists. They took as their ideal female seclusion in the home. They did all this in the confidence that they could, with effort, achieve the same standards and merit the same rewards as any man.

Maulana Thanawi and the Importance of Knowledge

At the beginning of the *Bihishti Zewar,* Thanawi firmly sets his sights on the positive. The heart of his message is education in doctrine, behavior, and character. Thus he exhorts women to become educated, and he summarizes for them in considerable detail the fundamental religious obligations in worship and in social relationships on which all else rests. Women *can* change. In the poem on "true jewelry" (with which Thanawi begins and ends this work), it is the faculty of intelligence or sense (*'aql*), theirs to deploy, that crowns all as the "head fringe" and that responds to the authoritative guidance of good counsel and the Book as earrings; they make possible the fruits of good works, symbolized by the remaining jewelry.

Thanawi clearly believes that his fellow Muslims have brought trouble on themselves by straying from the teachings of Islam; they have distorted their true nature, the nature that lives in harmony through Islam. Their lives have become vapid, offensive, consumed with concern for worldly goods and a good reputation, plagued by frustrated social relationships. All of this results from what Thanawi—unlike most women and men of his day—sees as a single cause: ignorance that accepts customary practices. Those customs, in an inexorable sequence, drag people into what Thanawi frequently describes as a prison. His pedagogic technique is to begin with instruction in what is right; only correct knowledge can break the chain that creates its own bondage.

The privileged position given to correct and certain knowledge was part of the heritage of most learned Muslims of Thanawi's time, though reformers like himself gave it particular emphasis. The first key aspect of this knowledge is that it is absolute, outside the knower, revealed by God for all time. Concerning what is essential, there is no need for interpretation, no possibility of legitimate disagreement. Anyone who fails to accept the core of correct knowledge, identified as Islam, either has failed to understand it or is in deliberate rebellion against God. (This is an understanding, I might note, that the non-Muslim researcher encounters today in conversation with those who continue this view of the self-evident validity of Islam.)[48] If Thanawi can only get people's attention and provide them with the information they need, reform will—or should—necessarily follow.[49]

The authority for this correct knowledge is the revealed text of God's direct word, the Qur'an, and the *sunna,* the practice of the Prophet that makes manifest the teachings of the Qur'an, as conveyed in the *hadis.* Thanawi turns to these two sources to begin his work. He first quotes a Qur'anic verse: "O believers, save yourselves and the people of your households from the fire whose fuel is people and stones." Nothing could more strongly emphasize the seriousness of his teachings. The second verse points to the key to salvation: "Remember what is read in your houses of God's verses and wise teachings." The *hadis* confirm this, echoing each verse. The first recalls the Judgment: "Every one from among you is guardian of my words, and every one is liable to be questioned about that guardianship"; the second points to prudent behavior: "It is a duty incumbent on every Muslim man and every Muslim woman to acquire knowledge." There is no distinction of gender in this most important of all responsibilities.

The Qur'an is, in principle and in different ways, important to all Muslims. But it is the reform movements that focus on the content of the revealed sources. Academically, their leaders have studied and taught Qur'an and *hadis* (*manqulat*), at the expense of the so-called rational sciences (*ma'qulat*), understood as representing the exercise of mental effort upon the original texts. Thanawi's fellow *'ulama* of the Deoband school, for example, were *hadis* scholars above all. They discouraged the speculative disciplines such as logic and philosophy that had first flourished in the eighth to tenth centuries (stimulated by interaction with Greek culture) and had received renewed impetus in eighteenth-century India through the curricular reform of the *dars-i nizami*.[50]

In his list of correct beliefs in Book One, Thanawi refers implicitly to the great questions that exercised the minds of Muslim philosophers. Many concerned the nature of God's unity and the status of his attributes—essential or contingent, created or uncreated. Thanawi asserts God's complete omnipotence and self-sufficiency and closes off discussion with his seventh point: "As for the statements about these attributes reported in many places in the Qur'an and *hadis*, entrust their meaning to God, for he alone knows their truth. We, without undue explication, believe with certainty that whatever their meaning, they are right and true." Other philosophical issues confronted the intractable questions of predestination (*qadr, taqdir*), human agency, and the existence of evil. In point eight, Thanawi writes: "There are many mysteries concerning the creation of evil that no one knows." A generation earlier, Delhi intellectuals had debated questions such as whether an all-powerful God could lie and whether God could create another prophet like Muhammad.[51] Thanawi would have none of this.

The focus on scripture made for certainty. The *Bihishti Zewar* is filled with references to *hadis* and Qur'an, including a consolidated list of one hundred one key *hadis* in Book Seven, many of them repeated elsewhere in the work. What is given in Qur'an and *hadis* is beyond question. In the twenty-seventh point of his list of beliefs, Thanawi writes: "Faith is lost . . . from considering any of these matters false, or from picking out faults or making jokes about them." Nor, he notes in the next point, is there any legitimacy in "bend[ing] the text to one's own purpose."

The second key aspect of this knowledge is that it is not only certain but also comprehensive. The knowledge embedded in Islam encompasses all dimensions of human concerns. There are no alternate models to explain various aspects of a person's life: no religious model using constructs such as "body" and "soul"; no political model speaking of "the will"; no psychological model using terms such as "ego" and "id," or "anima" and "shadow"; no medical model using the language of a distinctive science. Islam offers a single language, and a scholar like Thanawi can move from a discussion of religious practice to psychological development, to social organization, to medicine. There is no knowledge more basic or more important.

Third, this knowledge is not sought for its own sake. It is worse to know and not act upon this knowledge than not to know at all. The fourth story from the *hadis* included in Book One describes the horrific punishment facing someone who knows the Qur'an and fails to remember it. The point is reiterated in various lists and in the summaries of *hadis*. True knowledge must be acted on and shared. Moreover, as the theory of personal development implicit in Book Seven makes clear, correct knowledge and correct behavior are reciprocal: if one knows, one acts; as one acts, one's knowledge is deepened. Book Seven, informed by principles that resonate throughout the sufi tradition, makes clear how knowledge must be embodied. It analyzes the bases of human emotions and vices and lays out a program for building character, insisting on each person's potential for personal change.

Thanawi's stylistic technique is to show that people base their actions and beliefs on false understandings. In Book Six, for example, he categorizes customs by the degree to which they are misconstrued as legitimate. He sets up irony upon irony, showing that people believe one thing when in fact their judgment is radically wrong. He also organizes his argument to show the slippery downward slope of error, an argument begun on the very first page of the work. Lack of knowledge begins the descent. Women's ignorance of the religious sciences is not, as we might say, academic: "faulty belief leads to faulty character, faulty character to faulty action, and faulty action to faulty dealings that are the root of the disquietude of society." As the emphasis on knowledge makes clear, however, women's error is not inherent but susceptible to change.

Knowledge and Printed Books

What makes Thanawi's focus on correct knowledge so distinctive is that, in company with the other reformers of his day, he is concerned not only with scholarly reproduction of the received tradition but also with communicating the essence of this tradition to all persons, including women in the home. This concern takes its urgency and its potential from the newly available facilities for printing, an availability that shapes the centrality given to bookish learning in Thanawi's argument. The medium, in that sense, permits the message.

It is difficult to imagine the popularization of systematic teachings on correct belief and practice without the religious publications that began to be widely available in the late nineteenth century. Printed works had been crucial to the early nineteenth-century reform movement; they had been circulated very widely because they were used as texts for oral presentation in what was largely an illiterate society.[52] Only when written texts provided a detailed standard of religious learning could that detailed standard be made the goal. By the late nineteenth century, printed books were increasingly available. One contemporary follower has appreciatively written of Thanawi himself: "The number of pages of his published work exceeds the number of days of his life."[53]

Maulana Thanawi's generation saw the spread of lithographic printing, which had been introduced in north India only decades before. Old people still remembered the situation earlier in the century, when religious education depended on precious manuscripts, and teaching took place only in learning circles, as aspiring scholars moved from master to master and fragmentary texts passed hand to hand.[54] Printed books were central to the transformation of religious education in the late nineteenth century, as formally organized religious schools began to spread. But change in education was not limited to change in the education of the *ulama*.

The availability of books marks the transition from what one scholar has called an "esoteric" paradigm, in which knowledge depends on a hierarchic relationship of personal transmission, to a "rationalistic" paradigm, in which education is in principle available to all.[55] The latter paradigm carries with it a new concern for understanding, as opposed to rote learning alone. One can contrast the education linked to the *Bihishti Zewar* with what had earlier been standard education for girls. An autobiography of a Muslim woman born at mid-century, one Bibi Ashraf, describes her learning (along with other girls of the family and a maidservant) to vocalize the Arabic of the Qur'an in order to be able to read it aloud, an important ritual activity. She was also taught needlework.[56]

Thanawi's "Second Essay" at the end of Book Ten offers a contrast to Bibi Ashraf's education: here, the author urges the teacher using this vernacular work to elicit the lessons from the girls, having them figure out as much as they can on their own. The girls should always repeat the lesson in their own words, he writes, and if there are two or three of them, they should ask each other questions. The teacher is to teach only what the girls can grasp. The teacher should also explain the subject and intervene if the girls act contrary to what they are taught. This is far from technical reading aloud in an unknown language or rote memorization of fixed texts. Not only Bibi Ashraf's education but primary education everywhere has often stressed authority and rote.[57] Maulana Thanawi's remarkably effective method was innovative, as indicated by the lists of instructions he included. It was, no doubt, the product of his concern that girls actually learn their lessons in order to follow what was taught.

Print changed the roles of teacher and learner, allowing learning to take place independently—as Bibi Ashraf, with purloined ashes for ink and a cousin's schoolbook, demonstrated. Nevertheless, the *Bihishti Zewar* reiterates throughout the need for a teacher, even though printed works were available.[58] "It is absurd," Thanawi writes, "to think that Muslims can dispense with *'ulama.*" Thanawi specifically addresses this issue in Book Ten, where, as he prepares to end the work, he worries that the young women he has taken this far may now be set loose on the various readily available publications of the day. To try to continue his influence after a reader has finished the *Bihishti Zewar,* he draws up lists to shape what is to be read next. The Deobandis themselves taught women of their own families, in contrast to families like Bibi Ashraf's, who either hired female teachers or depended on older women in the family.[59] Thanawi reminds his readers of the importance of consulting the learned, whether one is reading a book of medicine or of spiritual discipline; the risks of education without masters are too great. The issue is not limited to women gaining education independently. One of the major changes of this century has been the breakdown of the monopoly on religious education held by the *'ulama* when the secularly educated—for example, in the Islamist movements—claim authority, without *madrasa* education, in the interpretation of sacred texts.

Although it was intended to teach literacy, the *Bihishti Zewar* has flourished in a largely nonliterate society. The *Bihishti Zewar* carries with it—in its repetitiveness and lists, for example—characteristics of an oral world.[60] Again and again, the reader is urged to make oral presentations based on the various books, by reading aloud to those in the household who cannot read themselves, whether family or menials or guests.[61] Thanawi even envisions a wife sharing this work with her husband, lest there be an imbalance in their knowledge.

The *Bihishti Zewar* was intended for an oral, public world. It was to be read aloud, discussed openly, taught in groups. The image of reading in this society is primarily formed by the recitation of the Qur'an, the first goal of any education. Injunctions on the importance of reading aloud from the Qur'an recur throughout the *Bihishti Zewar*. In creating his list of proscribed reading in Book Ten, Thanawi perhaps intended to discourage not only the content of the works listed but also the privacy of reading silently, of creating a private world of one's own inner voice by losing oneself—a terrible image, in Thanawi's view—in books like novels.[62] Thanawi, to be sure, also condemned oral reading and recitation that he associated with corruption and excess: the nightlong *musha'ira* of the poet, the mourning *majalis* of the Shi'a, and the storytelling sessions of the *dastango*.

As print shaped the popular dissemination of religious teachings and an entire style of religious education, it also fostered the sectarianism that was such a central characteristic of religious change in this period. Printed works made room for internal debate and the honing of sectarian differences, perhaps promoting divisiveness, but also advancing the extent to which religious issues became part of a public world. The importance of an oral debate was often found less in the event itself than in the formulaic presentation of the event in published, pamphlet form. "Pamphlet wars" were carried on among Muslims and with outsiders, with response stimulating response.[63] The role of Protestant missionaries in such exchanges, with their commitment to certain knowledge of the Bible and their interest in debate, seems to have reinforced—or, perhaps, in the case of some Hindus, actually to have created—a response in kind.[64]

The *Bihishti Zewar* competed with missionary publications and with the publications of those associated with the movement in favor of Western education. The latter often shared some of Thanawi's concerns (most important, the education of girls and the disapproval of customs), but they did not disseminate detailed legal guidance. Unlike

Thanawi, they typically sought, and often got, patronage from the government, which was concerned with developing what it considered beneficial literature in Urdu, including literature for women.[65] Other reformers also competed for women readers. The Begam of Bhopal, for example, princess of a protected state, had come under the influence of the Ahl-i Hadis. Veiled completely, she traveled widely to encourage the education of girls and also wrote the popular *Tahzibu'n-niswan,* on religious guidance for women. (Despite the difference in legal principles, Maulana Thanawi expresses admiration for her work in Book Ten.) Books for women were also written by the so-called Barelwi *'ulama,* one titled the *Sunni bihishti zewar.*[66]

Texts like the *Bihishti Zewar*—produced in printed form, meant for a new kind of education, and avowedly competing with other viewpoints—nevertheless resemble in some ways their predecessors, the Persian works of deportment (*adab*), which were intended for popular instruction in this cultural area. A recent analysis of two of these works shows that they cover much the same range as the *Bihishti Zewar:* tenets of the faith, requisite religious duties, hygiene, family relations, useful knowledge, stories of the prophets, virtues and vice and their consequences at Judgment. They include lists of good advice and are divided into separate parts.[67] Intended for a male audience, they were read aloud in the home, in mosques, and in teahouses; they too appear in printed form.

But the *Bihishti Zewar* differs from these and other *adab* texts in significant ways. First, it is written in colloquial Urdu, a mark of its late nineteenth-century origin and of the fact that it was meant to be pondered carefully and understood. Second, far from reproducing and disseminating the received culture, it is critical, avoiding what are deemed superstitious teachings, for example, and ecstatic poetry. Its legal teachings are more detailed, and they are presented systematically, with the aid of rationalized lists of principles. And, finally, the *Bihishti Zewar* was written for women, not men. There is no discussion of public life, the ethics of rulers, or service to the king. Gone too is the conventional misogyny of the earlier texts, with warnings of female infidelity and checklists of desiderata for a bride. The classic texts of Persian *adab,* the *Qabusnama* of the eleventh century and the *Akhlaq-i nasiri* of the thirteenth, were widely read in India for the edification of the male elite and specifically discouraged instruction in writing for women; the latter work discouraged reading as well.[68] In the reformist climate of the *Bihishti Zewar,* women, far from being discouraged, were seen as key. Maulana Thanawi and his fellow reformers thus utilized a new medium to reach a new audience with what was in fact a new message.

Women and Hierarchy

At the heart of the message was a concept of appropriate hierarchy in every domain. Muslims needed to know their place in relation to God and in relation to one another. Women's place was defined by being Muslim, by gender, and by class, all factors that were shaped in significant ways by the particular cultural and historical context. As Muslims, the reformers insisted, women were equally addressed by the message of revelation and were individually responsible for—and capable of—securing their own salvation.

Women were, however, regarded as socially subordinate to the men of their families. Following the Qur'an, Thanawi lists women among men's possessions. Following the *hadis,* he identifies dominant women as a sign of the Last Day. Women, he says, must not dress like men and must not claim superiority over men (for example, in a ritual inversion that was sometimes part of the marriage festivities described by a horrified Thanawi). He quotes a *hadis* asserting that women are the greater number of those assigned to hell.

In Book Four, Maulana Thanawi argues that ingratitude toward a husband is as much a sin as ingratitude toward God. A woman is to follow her husband's will and whims in all things, to seek his permission on all issues, to call the day night if he does.[69] A woman is expected to be responsible for her husband's happiness and to respond to his mood: "She holds his heart in her hand." "Never think of him as your equal, never let him do any work for you. . . . If he comes to you and begins to massage your hands or feet, stop him; you would not let your father do this service, and your husband's rank is higher than your father's." A woman's power, Maulana Thanawi claims, is in her submission. He describes a woman in Lucknow whose husband is a scoundrel; she never complains, and she even sends out food for him to eat with his women from the bazaar. When God orders him to cease his bad conduct, Thanawi insists, he will become her slave.

Women in this subordinate niche, however, were entitled to rights (*huquq*) that the reformers believed had been obscured by custom. Custom had deprived widows, for example, of the right to remarriage, condemning them in most cases to a life of penury and dependence. Custom also often denied women their rights to inheritance and the

marriage portion (*mahr*). Custom subjected women to extreme inconvenience, physical discomfort, and financial exploitation.

Reformist teachings, moreover, provided women with literacy and
numeracy, keys not only to religious knowledge but also to better management of their domestic roles, to their personal advantage, and to the
advantage and status of their families. The reformers also taught systematic principles (as seen in the list at the end of Book Six) against which all
custom should be measured; the presentation of Galenic medicine, for
example, was meant to replace both charms and the folk medicine of
midwives. To be able to think and reason methodically—not simply to
know discrete cures or practices—contributed to a kind of cultural em-
powerment for women. Early Islam strengthened women's legal and
economic position, and the reformists, inspired by that period, sought to
do the same. When challenged by modernists, Thanawi's heirs insisted
that they alone sought women's authentic "rights."

There was, of course, considerable variability in the actual authority
enjoyed by women in different families. A particular opportunity for
an enhanced role for women was presented during this period by the
absence of male family members who were posted away from home
because of work. The sample letters in Book One suggest the new
pattern of husbands and fathers being away from home, as do many
literary works of the time, including Bibi Ashraf's life story and the
novel *Mir'atu'l-'arus,* discussed in Book Ten. This pattern was a stimulus to the writing of the *Bihishti Zewar,* which was intended both to
provide women with the skills they needed in this situation and to
encourage them to act correctly and demonstrate self-control. The
Qur'anic verse printed on each title page refers to a woman's responsibility in her husband's absence. As in the case of women today whose
male relatives migrate to cities or to the Gulf, women in charge of a
household could assume more roles and responsibilities than had earlier been the case.

Women were nonetheless subordinate to their husbands and to
other senior men of their families. In a highly stratified society, however, privileged women were superior to inferior men. Maulana
Thanawi did not challenge the basic structure of that society. Its pervasive characteristics, part of both the Muslim and the Indic heritage, are
implicit in his teaching of letter writing and forms of address, in his
emphasis on civility, and in his injunctions concerning arranging marriage partners and dealing with servants. The *'ulama* themselves were
from families who typically claimed foreign descent, understood to be
a claim to superior status. By the late nineteenth century, it was likely
that most of these families owned some land, had some members em-

ployed in government or princely service, and perhaps were engaged in some kind of trade. It was to such families that the *Bihishti Zewar* initially spoke.

The women in these families ideally remained secluded from all but their close kin and particularly from all men, except their closest relations; it was intended that the women would stay at home.[70] Even so, they were responsible and powerful within their families and within their society. A woman in such a family had heavy responsibility for the family's social and material resources. The importance of managing social relations, including alliances defined by marriage and gifts, is evident in Book Six; and the technical skills required to run a household where primary products had to be processed and stored are evident in Book Ten.

The wellborn of both sexes had considerable authority over those of lower birth. The *Bihishti Zewar* assumes that the women it addresses deal with menials. Part of its goal, in fact, is to clarify hierarchic relations, so that people get and receive their due, moral and material—among family members, with retainers, and toward the poor. Women may in principle be subordinate to men, but they are certainly not subordinate to inferior men in this hierarchic society.[71]

Maulana Thanawi did not question the existence of social hierarchy. He did deplore an excessive emphasis on lineage, especially if it distracted one from personal responsibility. He also criticized snobbery toward women who had been brought into a family from outside (marriage within the family was preferred), especially if the newcomer was regarded as being of low birth (of a *ghatiya jagah*). In Book Four, he accepts the *shari'at* injunctions that like should marry like.[72] Although he recommends that occupational groups marry among themselves—weavers with weavers, tailors with tailors, and so forth—he modifies the conventional marriage categories of those who claimed respectable birth (the *ashraf*): the *saiyid*s, descendents of the Prophet; the *shaikh*s, descendents of the Companions and converts not identified with service castes; Mughals; and Afghans or Pathans, these two being descendents of medieval rulers. Although each of these four groups is further divided into hierarchically ranked endogamous units, Maulana Thanawi asserts that all *saiyid*s and all *shaikh*s are equal for the purposes of marriage; similarly, the Mughals and Pathans could marry each other. These looser categories give him more scope to insist that real nobility, *sharafat,* depends more on character than on birth.

Following Hanafi law, Thanawi points out that status is determined not only by birth but also by a family history of being Muslim, not being destitute, and not being insane. But the greatest source of status, he insists, is piety. By this measure, he ventures, even the poor could in fact be superior. He argues that manual labor deserves respect. English education, whatever worldly achievement it allowed, is viewed as a threat to piety. Parents are warned to weigh piety heavily, on the grounds that an impious person, by definition, would thwart hierarchy: failing to render God his due (*haqq*), a man could hardly be expected to give his wife her due.

The *Bihishti Zewar* was used from the beginning by those making claims to enhanced respectability. Over time, it has been read by populations distant from the heartland of Muslim cultural and political dominance (evident from its translation into languages such as Pashtu) and by groups at various (and lower) levels of the social hierarchy. As in Europe, print culture has disseminated elite norms.[73] Group emulation of the ritual and social practices of the wellborn has historically characterized social mobility in the subcontinent, a process described in some contexts as "sanskritization," to suggest the extent to which upwardly mobile groups aspire to be included in the ritual and rules of Sanskrit texts;[74] the term "ashrafization" has been coined to describe the parallel process among Muslims. Participation in normative religion and education is a mark of respectability, made more possible by printed texts such as the *Bihishti Zewar*.

The reformists' insistence that women should receive religious education, justified by the teachings of pristine revelation, went against conservative opinion of the time, however. Maulana Thanawi at one point in his text answers an imaginary critic, an older woman who, in her disapproval of religious education for girls, asks, "Do you want to teach them to read and write to turn them into *maulawi*s, like men?" Maulana Thanawi answers that this is indeed his goal but insists that education can at the same time enhance a girl's domestic role. Central to that role is knowledge of her place in relation to other human beings and to God.

Tauhid and Allah Miyan

The apex of the hierarchic pyramid is God himself. Thanawi holds that his fellow Muslims, through their adherence to customary practices, have compromised what should be the chief end of their existence: the lived expression of their belief in *tauhid,* the unity of God, who is above all. The opening list of correct beliefs makes this clear. Other powers have been raised to gods: saints, *imam*s, and masters who do not intercede for their followers but themselves answer prayers. Believers trapped in routines of elaborate ceremony, of self-devised customs tied to sacred times and sacred places, think that their own strategies can secure desired ends; custom controls God. The demands of custom lead to moral corruption—pride, extravagance, indulgence, license. Custom supplants the correct occupation of Muslims, namely, relentless attention to the requirements of the *shari'at* that affirm the primacy of God.

The God of *tauhid* is described in Thanawi's list of beliefs in Book One, in his unity, self-sufficiency, omnipotence, timelessness, and creativity; "no one can know the subtlety of his being." The first practice sentence for the reader learning to write is "Fear God." The torment of hellfire for those who do not show this fear is a thread running through the entire work.

What is the relation of a person to the judgment of this God? Can God's favor be earned? And how can one know if it has been earned or not? The balance between works and grace, a problem for both reformist Christianity and Indic *bhakti,* is evident here as well. To suggest that the believer can earn God's favor through good works defies the common sense of those whose standard is the perfect law of the *shari'at* and the perfect example of the Prophet. Moreover, it limits the absolute power of a God who is not bound by any human action. If God is all-powerful and knows what is ordained, what power of choice does the human actor have? And what of reward? Is reward to be found in this life, a prosperous existence the confirmation of righteousness? Or does an inscrutable God make no such evident confirmation, perhaps even visiting those he loves with special trials?

These issues are not explicitly raised in the *Bihishti Zewar,* a work intended for a popular audience. Elsewhere, the Deobandis interpret illness and misfortune, for example, as meaningful visitations from God. Whatever complexity one may understand intellectually, however, emotionally and temperamentally Thanawi's emphasis is on human responsibility and human capacity to choose the good and receive divine reward, not only in the afterlife but also in the immediate world of everyday life. This tidy expectation of reward may seem psychologically and morally facile, but it is true to the urgency of Thanawi's message.

The God of such interactions is at once the awe-inspiring God of formal doctrine and the God of predictable human responses, the stern and demanding father, Allah Miyan. This title for God is an unusual one, apparently unique to Urdu, with no equivalent in languages such as Arabic or Persian.[75] To call Allah "Allah Miyan" is to make him comprehensible and familiar, to anthropomorphize the Absolute, as

Muslims have characteristically sought to avoid. The term *miyan* means "lord" or "master" and is an everyday word in Urdu. It is used in a familiar way of saying "husband and wife" (*miyan-biwi*); as a title appended to a given name, often becoming part of that name (Ahmad Miyan); as a title for older menials (as *bare miyan*); and as a term of affection for children. The term imputes human emotions to God and renders him familiar, as do English phrases like "the dear Lord" or "the good Lord."

This term underscores a theology posited on the notion that human behavior is decisive in the relationship to God; it is that behavior that secures his approval or elicits his anger. Thanawi writes in the ninth point of his list of beliefs in Book One: "Allah Miyan is angry with works of sin and happy with works meriting reward." The phrase is used to cajole the reader into good behavior, as a parent cajoles a child: "Say your prayers and make Allah Miyan happy." Allah Miyan, moreover, is depicted as demonstrating his happiness concretely and materially on the believer's behalf.

In Book One, Thanawi retells four dramatic stories from the *hadis*. In the original *hadis* compilations, the first three are organized to illustrate issues related to *zakat,* the requisite tithe. Injunctions to charity are at the very heart of the earliest Qur'anic ethical teachings: Muhammad fervently inveighed against oppression by the rich, the hardness of heart, and the contempt for the poor that Islam sought to end. To give charity is to acknowledge one's dependence on God, to cultivate humility, to free oneself of the trammels of greed. In the stories told here, the rewards of charity are shown as marvels, physically realized and embodied. In the first story, beneficent rain miraculously falls on the person who is just, the man who gives one-third of his crop to charity. In the second story, well-being is the direct gift of God, a gift that can literally disappear when the recipient shows hardness of heart. In the third story, most marvelous of all, a denial of charity, even with the best intentions, turns the hoarded meat into a stone. This transformation turns out to be a blessing to the Prophet's household, for had the meat been eaten, the heart of the eater, not the meat, would have become the stone that callousness to the poor represents.

The physicality or materialism of reward and punishment almost suggests an autonomous physics of cause and effect. Book One concludes with two lists, the worldly losses and worldly gains caused by sin and virtue, respectively. A sinner is, the list notes, a person who lacks sense and is defective in knowledge. She therefore is agitated at the thought of God, lacks the grace of repentance, and loses even the ability to distinguish sin. God holds her in contempt, the Prophet reproaches her, the angels decline to intercede on her behalf. But that is not all. Beyond these rather abstract effects, she herself deteriorates socially and physically. She is agitated in the presence of the righteous, and her relationships are disrupted. Her heart, intriguingly, becomes physically weak, and the weakness spreads to her whole body. There is no perplexity here about how the evil flourish. Instead, it is the sinner who has insufficient income, whose crops fail, and who sees the beneficent rain fall not on herself but on the godly. The karmalike sense of inexorable recompense goes beyond one's life, as illustrated in the denunciation of dancing at the beginning of Book Six: the person who organizes dancing is responsible for the sin of every person involved; if any guest emulates the host, the host bears the sin for that; and on and on. The same point is made in the seventh *hadis* quoted in Book Seven.

The one hundred one *hadis* presented in that book, selected by Thanawi from the thousands available, are chosen to illustrate the promise of reward and the threat of punishment. At least half specifically mention heaven or hell. Others describe acts of merit and acts of sin. Often, the punishments or rewards suggest a kind of poetic justice: a person who acts in order to be spoken well of will have her faults spoken of at Judgment (number three); a person who looks around during a prayer may have her sight taken away (number twenty); the person who unjustly encroaches on another's land will be yoked with all seven divisions of the earth (number thirty-five); whoever exposes the faults of a fellow Muslim will have her faults exposed (number forty-six); whoever reproaches someone for a fault will commit the same fault before she dies (number forty-eight); God will help the work of a person who helps the work of a fellow Muslim (number fifty-five); an eavesdropper can expect molten lead in her ears at Judgment (number sixty-two); a backbiter's crime is rendered literal, and she will be forced to eat carrion as she once "ate the living" (number seventy-two). The appended morals in some cases stress punishment and reward or note particular examples of sins prevalent in Thanawi's milieu.

The physicality of sin is also dramatically represented in two vivid and unforgettable images in these *hadis*. The nineteenth *hadis* calls on the believer to perform the prayer carefully and wholeheartedly. If she does not, the prayer is black and lusterless. "The prayer itself says, 'May God destroy you as you have destroyed me,' until it reaches its special place acceptable to God. Then, wrapped like an old cloth, it is struck against the face of the worshipper." The sixty-seventh *hadis* denounces curses: "A curse directed at another person rises toward heaven, whose doors are closed. Then it descends to the earth, which is also closed. Then it wanders right and left and, when it finds a place nowhere, arrives at the person cursed. If that person deserves to be cursed, fine. If not, the curse falls upon the curser." These selections culminate in three ringing calls to remember Judgment. In the last, the Prophet weeps "until his blessed beard was wet with tears. . . . I swear by that Being in whose power is my life that if you knew what I know about the afterlife, you would flee to the wilderness and place dust on your head." The book then continues with the portents of the final days and the powerful and evocative description of Judgment itself.

Each woman has the power to choose. In the beliefs listed in Book One, point nine is clear: "Almighty God has given will and understanding to his servants so that by their own will they can do works of sin and works meriting reward." The central theme of Book Seven, on human formation, argues a theory of the potential for right action inherent in every human being and sets out techniques for developing that potential. But God is a God of mercy. When the dead gather before him, hungry and thirsty, distraught because of the heat, Muhammad will be able to intercede, and Judgment will begin. When the scale is set and each person's account taken, all prophets, scholars, saints, martyrs, memorizers of the Qur'an, and virtuous people will intercede again: "Whoever has the tiniest manifestation of faith in their hearts will be taken out of hell and sent to paradise." We learn too (especially in the concluding section of Book Six) that others can contribute to the balance of good deeds for the dead by praying to God to assign the merit for their acts of piety not to their own record but to the records of those who have gone before.

As for reward in this life, the major argument insists that the good will receive tangible reward now, although a minor strand acknowledges that the just do in fact suffer. A *hadis* suggesting the redemptive power of suffering for those who are faithful creeps into the collection in Book Seven (number ninety-four). Similarly, the stories of exemplary women in Book Eight are filled with cases of terrible hardship endured by people who are good. Suffering then serves as an occasion for the righteous to learn and to manifest the litany of virtues celebrated in these stories: chastity, trust, gratitude, courage, patience in adversity, discrimination, unworldliness, selflessness, forgiveness, and love. There is, in the end, no simple correlation of virtue and worldly comfort. But Providence is always there. Either the virtuous are rewarded on a later occasion, or it is assumed that they receive their reward in the world to come.

Shari'at and the Bondage of Custom

The goal of the *Bihishti Zewar* is to set out the teachings of the *shari'at,* whose fulfillment merits reward. To make those teachings understood, Maulana Thanawi describes in detail the network of custom that, in the reformers' view, had done no less than create an alternate *shari'at* of its own. The real *shari'at,* ordained by God and perfectly congruent with human nature if properly understood, is the road that leads to individual and social harmony and well-being. The false *shari'at* of custom is its opposite. Far from being authentic and natural, it is the product of human willfulness and artificiality. It too is a road—not the straight road of *shari'at* but the convoluted dead end of *bid'at,* the reprehensible innovation that is the negative counterpart of the *sunna* toward which the *shari'at* leads.

Roughly the first half of the *Bihishti Zewar* (following the introduction) leads the young female reader through extraordinarily detailed teachings on the religious law. Precisely because they are normative Hanafi teachings, these are the sections emphasized in the existing English translations used by women and men; they are as relevant for Muslims today in the United Kingdom or South Africa (who may know only English) as they were for the north Indian Muslims of Thanawi's day. These sections contain some discussions of important local issues, such as specific marriageable categories. But, overall, little of this legal material reflects its immediate environment. As I explain below, these sections are not translated here, in part because of their availability in English elsewhere.

The organization of the teachings on religious law follows the conventional division of books of *fiqh,* first presenting those issues that define the relations between the believer and Allah—the acts of obedience or worship known as *'ibadat,* including ablution (ritual purity is required for the prayer), the canonical prayer, the fast of Ramazan, the tithes of *'ushr* and *zakat,* and the *hajj* pilgrimage to Mecca. This is followed by discussion of issues involving relations among humans, *mu'amalat,* also ordered by divine decree. Book Four covers family law, including marriage, divorce, adoption, and inheritance. Book Five deals with commercial transactions, important even for housebound women, who handled their own finances and the finances of the family; Islamic law has always treated women as legally autonomous.

The rules for ritual worship, one might note, set norms for the ordinary believer that would mark extreme piety in many other traditions. The believer is expected to rise before dawn to pray; to punctuate the day with additional prayer; to keep an absolute daytime fast for a full month, even in the long, hot days of summer, if Ramazan falls then; and to undertake, if possible, the *hajj* to Mecca at least once in a lifetime.

The rules of *fiqh,* which systematically present the *shari'at,* are highly logical and rational, and Thanawi covers them in exhaustive detail. For example, the discussion in Book Two of bathing the dead includes not only elaborate details of exactly how the bath is to be done but also all possible contingencies, in all logical permutations and combinations: what to do if proper water is not available; if one is able to bathe the corpse only once and not three times; if no male is available to bathe a male, or a female to bathe a female; if the deceased died of drowning; if only parts of the body were found; if it is not clear that the deceased was a Muslim; if the deceased was non-Muslim but a relative; if the deceased was a corrupt person or a rebel or an apostate; if the deceased was a stillborn baby or a fetus (at a variety of stages) or died in the process of birth; and so forth. Issue after issue is explored in similar detail.

Conventional wisdom might expect that Islamic reform, like Christian reform, would see a diminution of concern with ritual. In fact, the opposite is the case. If one looks at Muslim social experience in this century, a reformist emphasis on ritual has had an impact rather like that of Islamic teaching in the period of the Prophet. It has moved believers from parochial ties, cultural and religious, to a common standard of practice (and ethics) that has provided a basis for community in the new urban and international contexts of modern life. Ritual serves, moreover, in an Islamic perspective, to provide the sine qua non, the requisite framework, for all spiritual life. As Book Seven demonstrates, religious law alone gives structure and shape to the inner life; the two domains are not separable. It is not possible to argue that one can focus on good works or the spirit of the religion and not bother with "meaningless" ritual. The notion of "mere ritual" is alien to mainstream, and particularly to reformist, Islam.

A recent study argues that Islamic ritual is essentially "reformational," a quality that can of course be obscured but that, in a context of reform, can assume central importance.[76] The ritual is not priestly, but popular, and it depends on individual initiative. It is not confined and hedged about by notions of magical efficaciousness. It spills over into much of daily living, shaping an entire month of everyday activity or, in the case of the tithe, cleansing in principle all of one's wealth, for *zakat* on ill-gotten gains would be unworthy. Many of the rituals are associated with particular prayers of ethical import, for example, the sacrifice at Mecca, which reminds the worshipper that God is the giver of all and that the poor require charity. All of the core rituals have a dimension that is involved in creating community: the joining together for prayer, the shared experience of the fast, the charity involved in the tithe, the gathering of the community at Mecca. But normative ritual—unlike custom, with its proliferation of notions of sacred time and space and its concerns with magical efficaciousness—lends itself to the kind of interior religion that can be practiced in any setting and that is widespread in many traditions during periods of geographic and social mobility, like the recent past.

One can imagine, moreover, the sense of mastery that access to the information on ritual and daily life, presented in convenient form, would provide for a woman and the authority such knowledge would give her in whatever society she found herself. We need not see such obligations as primarily constraining or restricting. The ideal of the *shari'at* gives rhythm and pattern to life, a marking of events and seasons with divinely instituted actions and responses. Islamic teachings are understood as being as natural to humans as their cycles and habits are to the rest of creation.

In Thanawi's tradition, to be natural is not to be unfettered but rather to be like the animals and plants and inanimate objects of nature, in the sense of following ordained cycles and habits. For humans, those cycles and habits are the revealed religious law, which they choose either to follow or to thwart. A normal person, Maulana Thanawi explains, therefore hates sin just as she hates what goes against her nature (*tabi'at*). Thanawi can explain the existence of custom only by concluding that a curtain has fallen over people's reason. People today, he says, are like children whose intelligence has not been developed and who are misled into eating the sweets that make them sick. Intelligence, or sense, if properly cultivated, in this tradition does not provide an autonomous authenticating source. It means reasoned discrimination of the law of God, so that what one knows by sense one also knows by correct knowledge of *shari'at*.[77] The reasonable, the natural, and the divinely revealed thus coalesce.

The term "custom" does not describe trivial or minor practices that are peripheral to social and personal life. Custom infiltrates all aspects of life, just as the *shari'at* is meant to do: it shapes human relations; it colors all life-cycle and calendrical ceremonies; it structures the believer's relationship to God, the saints, and the dead. But, in Thanawi's view, custom is not at the heart of the natural and divine order; rather, it is the product of human willfulness and speculation, leading people not to their authentic selves but to distorted shadows of what they are meant to be. The possibility that customary practices are integrative and functional (as I discuss in the Translator's Introduction to Book Six) is wholly irrelevant to Thanawi.

In discussing custom, Thanawi uses to perfection the literary device of irony. Even the three subdivisions of Book Six play on setting up the point of view of the readers, only to show how very far off the mark it in fact is. The subdivisions are based on ascending degrees of popular approval. The first section examines those customs that all Muslims deem sinful but inconsequential. The second section, the longest, describes those customs wrongly regarded as legitimate. The final section lists practices considered not only legitimate but actually deserving of reward. One might expect the customs to be organized by origin, for the period during which the book was written saw a deepening attempt by reformers on both sides to eliminate the mixing of practices now labeled "Hindu" or "Muslim." Indeed, Maulana Thanawi, more often than reformers who preceded him in the nineteenth century, does at times point out that a particular custom is borrowed from the Hindus. Other customs might have been identified as the product of Shi'i influence or corruptions in sufi practice. But focusing instead on skewed understandings is consistent with Thanawi's overriding theme: knowledge is the source of all else, and people will recognize true knowledge if only their minds are clear and the case is properly made. Thanawi wants to expose each category of custom as being far different from what it is popularly understood to be.

Thanawi systematically runs a single ironic metaphor through his discussion: he calls custom itself a *shari'at* and juxtaposes the vocabulary of the sacred law with the self-devised law of customary practice. Nothing could better show the vacuity of customary practices than presenting them in the language of the *shari'at,* which they in fact destroy. When cast in these terms, the distance between foolishness and truth is presumably even more apparent. Customary gifts and dues are consistently referred to as being a *farz-i wajib,* a necessary obligation. A woman makes an intention (*niyat*), as she is required to do as a prelude to a ritual act, before the most trivial of undertakings. Thanawi often describes how customs are considered more important and more a source of pride than are the rituals of the faith.

Maulana Thanawi writes ironically about the shares given to the female singer and to the barber's wife as being more of an obligation than the tithes of *zakat* and *'ushr.* In another reversal, he insists that the practice of "showing the face" during the marriage ceremony has been turned into a religious duty and that anyone who does not do it is regarded as shameless: "They act as shocked as if a Muslim had 'turned infidel'!" The practice of putting rice pudding in the bride's hand, he says, is more important than whether the girl has ever in her life had the grace of the canonical prayer. Muslims have created an alternate law and reversed all categories. During the marriage festivities, "all sins and immodesty become 'legally permitted' (*halal*) and proper," he concludes.

The misconstrual of these customs is highlighted in one of Maulana Thanawi's particularly striking passages, in which he discusses the custom of keeping the new bride immobile in her husband's home. Only if someone happens to make arrangements for her does she read the canonical prayer. Mocking this as the practice of an alternate school of law, he writes, "In the 'law school' (*mazhab*) of women, there is no permission for her to arise or to ask anyone else to make preparations for the prayer [or even] for her to move here and there." Such a juxtaposition—*mazhab* and no prayer—makes its own point.

Nearly as striking as the use of legal vocabulary to describe custom is the use of Sanskrit-derived vocabulary to describe this counter-*shari'at.* This is a *man-gharat,* a self-devised *shari'at;* the details of ceremonies are *man-samjhautiyah,* self-devised schemes or rationalizations. Urdu draws, of course, on both a Sanskrit and a Perso-Arabic vocabulary, typically emphasizing the latter in documents of a religious nature. In using these Sanskrit terms to describe this "*shari'at,*" Thanawi subtly suggests how far from *shari'at* it actually is. The range of Urdu vocabulary allows for other ironic usages: referring, for example, as Thanawi often does, to customary ceremonial visitations as *a'o bhagat* ("O come, *bhagat* [a Hindu holy man]"), an ironic term for hospitality.

The central metaphor of custom as a reversed *shari'at* is supplemented by detailed descriptions of other kinds of reversal. Thanawi is horrified by the confusion he sees on every side: social roles are confused, things that are not sacred are treated as if they were; obligations that are sacred are ignored; saints and holy men are elevated while God is not given his due. A hierarchic society of reciprocal obligations, of expected material and personal exchanges is in his view being subverted. Thanawi envisions this society (discussed in more detail in the Translator's Introduction to Book Six) as nothing less than a prison. He refuses to agree that people take up these practices voluntarily, and he repeatedly insists that people are compelled to do so, acting no more voluntarily than the victim who submits to the thief's gun. As he describes the ensnarement of the hapless husband of a corrupt wife in Book One, the entrapment of porters who are beaten and abused in the section on women's outings, and the solitary confinement, or "black hole," faced by a new bride, he makes clear his feelings that the reversed boundaries of custom, far from making life meaningful and joyous, in fact destroy what life should be: "Sinful deeds and worry about reputation can become a noose around your neck."

The depth of Thanawi's feeling is measured not only by the disapproval—even contempt—with which he presents custom but also by the confidence and serenity with which he presents the example of a life ceremony, a wedding, properly observed. Although he insists that description of a contemporary reformed wedding should not be necessary for anyone who has followed his argument, he offers a vignette of a wedding recently performed. Insisting that this was the kind of wedding any respectable family could take pride in—not the wedding of *maulawi*s or dervishes or of people so poor they had no choice—he describes the circumstances and episodes, from the engagement to the settling in at the groom's home. In this wedding, boundaries are clear: people are where they should be, time is organized normally, money is spent appropriately. There is "peace and calm" throughout; there is "no tempest." It is hard not to be moved by Maulana Thanawi's evident feeling and sincerity: "There was a luster and sweetness [to this wedding] that words cannot describe. With God's grace, all who observed it were happy."

It is perhaps not an exaggeration to suggest that Thanawi saw custom in much the same way that sixteenth-century Protestant reformers in Europe saw the indulgences and other corruptions of the Roman church—as a distraction from pristine teachings. In both cases, reformers regarded history as having followed a downward course, with the present being an especially low point and the only hope a kind of cyclical return to original teachings. The Christian reformers asserted that the church, in its emphasis on works at the cost of faith and grace, had distorted the image of God and had placed the church, not God, in control of salvation. Thanawi similarly identified custom as an attempt to control God, in this case through public display, auguries, omens, soothsaying, and charms that took the place of fidelity and trust. Custom is, therefore, *shirk,* the joining of partners to God. Saints and *imam*s, instead of being exemplars, guides, and intercessors, become themselves the rivals of God. Custom is personified for Thanawi as a monster whose tentacles reach everywhere: "Bravo, O Custom, how mighty you are! May God banish you from our land!"

To banish custom, the reformers must control women. *"Righteous women are devoutly obedient and guard in their husbands' absence what Allah would have them guard."*[78] Women are capable of righteousness and obedience, but they must be guarded by men or by their own disciplined will to prevent the irresponsibility or disgrace to which they may otherwise succumb. Enlightening women strikes deeply into personal relations and the patterns of everyday life. Powerful themes coalesce, themes of control and self-control and of distance from the very world that gives one birth.

The changes Maulana Thanawi urged were significant, both in his time and in regard to such critical issues as literacy, which is even today far from being attained. Thanawi certainly never questioned women's domestic role. Indeed, in standing up to those who accused him of thwarting hierarchy—or of turning girls into *maulawi*s, like men—his defense was that only an educated girl could fulfill her role properly, know what is owed to herself and to others, and know her proper relation to God. Nothing inherent limited her from developing intellectual skills or from cultivating the highest ideals of moral virtues.[79]

The urgency in defining woman's place—with all its ambiguous implications—was part of an attempt to stabilize a correct hierarchy in all areas. In a period of alien rule and disruptive change, the reformers were driven to establish boundaries for belief and behavior that would ensure order among humans and between humans and God. Women were to be subordinate to men, children to their elders, the humble to the great: deference on the one side, right-dealing and protection on the other. Proper hierarchy had to extend from earth to heaven. No one should assert her status to defy divine law. No one should exalt holy men or *imam*s to equal God, Allah Miyan, the great elder who must also be pleased.[80]

Maulana Thanawi wrote as someone troubled by the world around him, troubled not by change per se but by change that threatened the cultivation of proper Islamic lives in a society properly ordered. He saw himself, as did other reformers of his day, as one in a chain, stretching over the centuries of those who call Muslims—now, explicitly, Muslim women as well as Muslim men—back to the model of Prophetic life, the model from which fallible humans so frequently stray.

*   *   *

The *Bihishti Zewar* remains an instrument of that call. It is very much a living document, annotated, enlarged, modified, and commented on by successive generations of scholars and publishers. At the simplest level, such sections as the explanation of the workings of the post office are not frozen in time but have been brought up to date in new editions. New problems have been raised: for example, the form of salutation to be used for teachers in secular schools in independent India. There has been over the years ever greater refinement in setting an Islamic norm; Persianate salutations in letters have given way to simple Islamic ones. In general, the editions are increasingly annotated. Much of the annotation provides a scholarly apparatus, a citation of Qur'an, *hadis,* and other texts characteristic of all the writings of the *ulama* in the contentious atmosphere of internal Muslim debate in this century. Although I have translated the earliest available edition, I have indicated in notes some later emendations.

The detailed history of the impact of this work—and of other works like it—remains to be written. As noted above, however, the audience of the *Bihishti Zewar* has also changed. Once a document for the privileged families who supported the reformist movement, over time it has been read by the more humble and the more remote. Currently, in English translation, it is a document for Muslim migrants to the West and for their children who no longer know Muslim languages. Parts of the work are now little read. No fewer than four recent translations into English, for example, are notable for emphasizing the legal injunctions and giving little attention to those sections that were primarily meaningful in the context of turn-of-the-century Muslim India.[81]

This emphasis is sensible, given the audience of these translators, but the resulting editions omit material that is rich in content for those concerned with religious change, social history, and women's studies— material that is offered in the translation that follows.

I

Book One of the *Bihishti Zewar*

Translator's Introduction to Book One

When Maulana Thanawi put pen to paper to begin this monumental work, he crowded the early pages with every kind of argument he could make to convey the seriousness with which he regarded literacy and religious education for girls. He began with quotations from the ultimate authorities, the Qur'an and the *hadis* of the Prophet, reminding his readers of eternal judgment and the responsibility of every Muslim to acquire knowledge. He related his own experience and his observations on what lack of education meant in the lives of individuals and families. He recounted the serendipitous events of finding a patron for the book and having a poem appear, just as he was about to start writing, that would make his point with the charm and the "sweet delight of successive lumps of sugar."

In this introductory section, Maulana Thanawi sets out the basic principles that inform the work as a whole. Women may need "to be managed," as he says here, but they can learn, he insists, by discipline and the exercise of their will to be the kind of Muslim all persons, men and women, ought to be. Adorned with the faculty of *'aql* (intelligence), the "ornament" most celebrated in the poem he approvingly quotes, women can follow sage advice and sacred teaching to triumph over their base instincts (*nafs*) and display their accomplishments in the other ornaments: good deeds as a necklace, a strong and able arm as a bracelet, skill in handicrafts to adorn the hand, insight to guide the feet.[1]

Thus convinced, the pupil is presumably ready for the hard work ahead. Maulana Thanawi moves directly to provide the keys to the girl's ability to read: his primer, sample sentences, and orthographic rules. The sample sentences, moreover, are not arbitrarily chosen: Maulana Thanawi missed no occasion to reiterate his arguments, and the practice sentences are filled with the lessons he wanted his readers to learn.

Once the reader has mastered basic reading and writing, she is to move immediately to a practical use of her skills: reading and writing letters. The sample letters bring alive the domestic setting of the *Bihishti Zewar,* a world of close relations among women, naughty and obedient children, and a concerned but absentee (and reformist) father. The letters are addressed to the members of a circle of close relatives, who were the only people to whom a respectable girl would write. In their rhetorical style, the letters also suggest the importance of hierarchy, with appropriate salutations listed, to be used according to the addressee's relationship to the writer.

The importance of knowing these titles is evident in a charming vignette included in a life history of Bibi Ashraf (1840–1903), a young Muslim woman who, against all odds, taught herself to write in the mid–nineteenth century. In her final years, she published her story in a new Urdu journal for women, recounting an anecdote concerning her role as scribe for the women of her family:

> I knew only one way to address someone [*alqab*] and used that form all the time, regardless of the age and relationship of the addressee. One lady had me write letters to her husband. This was the way I addressed her husband on her behalf: "Dear young man, light of my eyes, comfort of my life, pupil of my eye, may your life be long!" I used these same words in all her letters. Finally, the husband wrote back: "I can fully understand your letters, for their language is just like your own speech. But tell me this, where did you find this strange scribe who knows only one way to address people?"[2]

Anyone who reads Maulana Thanawi's discussion of letters will understand what Bibi Ashraf had done wrong!

The content of the letters makes clear the reformist concern for preserving women's honor and enhancing family status. Maulana Thanawi placed great emphasis on the fact that literacy would enhance a woman's standing and the standing of her family. In one letter, he adopts the persona of an individual named 'Abdu'llah to set out six reasons in favor of educating girls. First, he writes, an educated woman will be able to speak elegant and correct Urdu, an incontrovertible mark of respectable status. This was and is a society that delights in a well-turned phrase; the letters themselves illustrate the refinement and polish that are valued. Second, Maulana Thanawi points out, an educated woman, in contrast to the "illiterate and ignorant," knows how to perform the prayer and fast correctly. Scripturalist religion is thus a mark not only of salvation but also of respectability. Third, an educated woman can manage her household and accounts effectively, to everyone's benefit. Fourth, she is able to raise children of good character and behavior. Fifth, she knows how to fulfill her hierarchic obligations within the family. And, finally, she can guard her modesty and the family's honor by not being forced to take family business to outsiders.

A dutiful daughter named Khadija writes to her father "that the skill of reading and writing is wealth indeed." A family that can train its children—including its daughters—demonstrates that it possesses resources, that it has the moral capacity to exercise a sustained adult discipline upon children, and that it has made a profitable investment, as shown by the educated children that emerge.[3] These points are illustrated in other letters, where the illiterate are shown as hapless and foolish and the literate as accomplished and deserving respect. Maulana Thanawi covers possible objections that he is distorting status: he includes a letter reminding a niece that, however important reading and writing may be, they are not enough and that honor (*'izzat*) also depends on properly deferential behavior.

After presenting the letters, Thanawi returns to citing the sort of authority with which he began the work. In this case, he recounts four vivid stories from the *hadis* accounts of the sayings of the Prophet. They again underline Thanawi's serious tone by recalling the importance of obedience and the cultivation of moral virtues, on the one hand, and the awesomeness of the divine presence and future judgment, on the other. The final story of terrifying punishments is meant to represent the ultimate sanction against laxity and sin. It also pictures the Prophet in his role on behalf of humankind: he belongs in the most wondrous of heavenly homes but remains on earth to convey to others what they must know.

Having reminded his readers again of why religious knowledge is so important, Thanawi turns to serious detailed instruction, by summarizing in six statements much of what he will teach, in greater detail, in later portions of the work. The first statement is on beliefs (*'aqa'id*), a classic way of beginning compendia of the law (*fiqh*). The longest of the statements, it serves to express the urgency felt by reformist Muslims concerning adherence to absolute and correct belief.

The next three statements are graded lists of what must be avoided: one covers points of complete infidelity and polytheism; the next, reprehensible innovation and deviation; the last, "mere sin." Much of the agenda set out here had been articulated in the earliest nineteenth-century efforts at reform, those of the *Tariqa-yi muhammadiyya* of Saiyid Ahmad Barelwi and Maulana Isma'il Shahid. The most famous work of that movement, the *Taqwiyatu'l-iman*, written in the 1820s, focused on many identical concerns about the purification of Islam through the rejection of non-Islamic customs, which were attributed either to the deviations of sufis and Shi'a or to imitation of the unbelievers. Among the points of infidelity (eight through twelve, for example) was behavior reflecting the belief that sufi *pir*s could intuitively know their followers' thoughts and could accurately foretell the future. The Deobandis insisted that only God—not the saints and not even the Prophet—had such knowledge of the unknown (*'ilmu'l-ghaib*). They also denied that the saints could directly intervene in the course of worldly events. They opposed undue veneration of the Prophet's family, the sin of the Shi'a, and all participation in the customs of the Shi'a. The final two statements catalogue worldly losses and gains that result from sin and obedience, respectively, illustrating the immediacy of punishment and reward.

In this first book, Maulana Thanawi provides what was considered sufficient for literacy: an alphabet and some rules. He also—through argument, a poem, letters, and lists—persuades the reader of the necessity of applying herself to the lessons presented. He continues with material not translated here on religious ritual (in Books One through Three, beginning, for example, with fifty dense pages on the ablution), followed by sections on marriage and family (Book Four) and on business transactions (Book Five). The translation will resume with Book Six, which expands in great detail on the customary practices whose evil has already been signaled here.

*Righteous women are devoutly obedient and guard in their husbands'
absence what Allah would have them guard.*

A pamphlet meant to instruct women and girls in the
way to act on this Qur'anic verse

Heavenly Ornaments

Book One

A discussion, by section, of everything that women need to
know about beliefs, legal points, ethics and social behavior,
child-rearing, and so on

Compiled by the Reverend Hazrat, Sun of the Scholars,
Crown of the Learned,
Maulana Hafiz Muhammad Ashraf 'Ali Sahib

Published at the direction of
Janab Maulawi Muhammad Yahya Sahib, Dealer in
Religious Books, Gangoh, District Saharanpur

Printed at Bilali Steam Press, Sadhaura, District Ambala

Contents of Book One

The First Book of the
Bihishti Zewar

I. [Introductory Comments]

All praise to God, who declared in his Book: "O believers, save your-selves and the people of your households from the fire whose fuel is people and stones."

And Almighty God declared: "Remember what is read in your houses of God's verses and wise teachings; and praise and blessings on your messenger Muhammad, God's blessings and peace upon him."

He is the elect of the prophets who declared: "Every one from among you is guardian of my words, and every one is liable to be questioned about that guardianship."

And the Messenger, God's blessings and peace upon him, also declared: "It is a duty incumbent on every Muslim man and every Muslim woman to acquire knowledge."

And praise descend on his family and his Companions who learned and taught his virtues and his ways.[1]

Here I, Ashraf 'Ali Thanawi Hanafi, contemptible and worthless as I am,[2] declare my purpose in writing this work.

For many years, I watched the ruination of the religion of the women of Hindustan and was heartsick because of it. I struggled to find a cure, worried because that ruin was not limited to religion but had spread beyond to everyday matters as well. It went beyond the women to their children and in many respects even had its effects on their husbands. To judge from the speed with which it progressed, it

47

seemed that if reform did not come soon, the disease would be nearly incurable. Thus I was ever more concerned.

Thanks to divinely granted insight, experience, logic, and learning, I realized that the cause of this ruination is nothing other than women's ignorance of the religious sciences. This lack corrupts their beliefs, their deeds, their dealings with other people, their character, and the whole manner of their social life. Their faith is barely spared, for they speak many words and commit many deeds that verge on infidelity. Beyond that, their words, their thoughts, and their style of behavior take root in the hearts of the children whom they nurture in their very laps. So the children's religion is ruined, and their daily life grows vapid and tasteless. The reason is that faulty belief leads to faulty character, faulty character to faulty action, and faulty action to faulty dealings that are the root of the disquietude of society.

As for the husband, if he is like his wife, the two together grow even more corrupt.[3] They can expect a desolate afterlife, and desolation is likely in this life, too, for the end of such corruption is mutual contention. If instead there is some rectitude in the husband, the hapless fellow is subjected to life imprisonment. For him, his wife's every act is a source of distress; for her, his every counsel is annoying and offensive. If he cannot put up with her behavior, the result is dissension and distance between them; if, on the contrary, he is resigned to her, his prison is bound to be bitter. It is this ignorance of the religious sciences that brings his daily life to ruin. Look at some examples:[4]

If his wife engages in backbiting, she makes enemies. Inevitably, someone is hurt.

If she spends money on wasteful ceremonies in order to get attention and status, she changes wealth into poverty.

If she makes her husband angry, he either expels her or deliberately neglects her.

If she puts up with everything from her children, they wind up ill trained and ill bred. Watching them, a person could pass a whole lifetime in grinding sorrow.

If she wants riches and jewelry, she cannot get enough to keep up with her desires. She spends her whole life in frustration.

Thanks to this ignorance, many such causes of corruption inevitably spring up. Because the cure of each thing is its opposite,[5] the cure for all this is clear: sure knowledge of the science of religion.

I have for some time, therefore, realized that in order to manage women, it is absolutely necessary to teach them the science of religion—

even if it must be through the medium of Urdu.[6] With this in mind, I looked over the existing Urdu books and pamphlets and found them insufficient to alleviate the need.[7] Many books were simply unreliable and wrong. The style of several others, which were reliable, was not sufficiently simple to be intelligible to women. Moreover, they covered subjects that were irrelevant. In contrast, I found other books, written for women, that were so thin that they fell short in covering the requisite rules and points of law. I therefore came up with the idea of writing a book, particularly for women, whose style would be very simple; it would be composed of the sum of all necessities of religion and would exclude those injunctions that are necessary only for men. It would be just the right length, so that reading only this volume would obviate the need for other reading on everyday religious obligations. Obviously, the whole scope of the religious sciences cannot be contained in one book. It is absurd to think that Muslims can dispense with *'ulama*.[8]

For many years, this idea ripened in my heart, but because of various considerations, particularly a lack of time resulting from other pressing tasks, there was no chance to begin. Finally, in A.H. 1320 [1902–1903], taking God's name, I did begin as best I could. And, with God's grace, there appeared at the same time the first contributions to support the publication of the book. Almighty God provided the co-operation of the director of the Surati Women's Madrasa in Rangoon, Seth Sahib,[9] as well as help from the late daughter of Janab Maulana 'Abdu'l-Ghafar Sahib Lakhnawi, *God's mercy on her*,[10] who was married to Hakim 'Abdu's-Salam Sahib Danapuri.[11] With their contributions, this promising undertaking began. May Almighty God accept it. Let us see who will take part in the future. The book has been attributed to this worthless person, but in truth its "finest flower" is my beloved relative Maulawi Saiyid Ahmad 'Ali Fatahpuri, *may the peace of Almighty God be upon him with instructions and benefactions. May the reward of Almighty God be upon him, and the best of rewards on me and on all Muslim men and Muslim women.*

Now, *what God has willed,* this book—may it be protected from an evil eye—includes not only most of the obligations but even the niceties of religion;[12] and, beyond that, it deals with many obligations of everyday life as well. If anyone reads it with understanding from start to finish, she should be the equal of a middling *'alim*. Moreover, its style is so simple that greater simplicity is clearly beyond our power. Those matters that are not usually necessary for women, such as the rules relating to the Friday prayer, to 'Id, and to leadership of prayer, are excluded. Only two kinds of injunctions are set out: first, those that are necessary for both men and women; and second, those that are specifically for women. In the latter cases, however, the rules for men are given in marginal notes so that they might also profit and avoid error. With a view to making it unnecessary to search out another book, the alphabet is provided here at the beginning. It is based on the pamphlet "Tarkibu'l-haruf" (The shape of letters), written by my revered maternal uncle Makhdumi[13] Janab Mamun Munshi Shaukat 'Ali Sahib, *may his life be protracted.*[14] As soon as a girl has finished the Glorious Qur'an,[15] she can begin this book.

The name of the work is meant to appeal to women. It is called *Bihishti Zewar* (Heavenly ornaments) because real ornaments are none other than those perfections of religion thanks to which one shall receive ornaments to wear in heaven. In the words of Almighty God: *"Gardens of Eternity will they enter; therein will they be adorned with bracelets of gold and pearls."*[16] And in the words of the Messenger of God, *God's blessings and peace upon him: "The jewels of the believer will reach as far as the water of ablution reaches."*[17]

Because it is impossible at this point to make a correct estimate of the length of this work, and because waiting to finish it would delay a worthwhile endeavor, it seems appropriate to divide the work into several separate books. This both facilitates publication and gives the reader heart, so that she will be able to say, "Now I have read one book; now I have read two books"; and so forth. Moreover, it gives scope for writing as much as seems necessary. Also, if a girl is already familiar with the subject matter of some of the books from reading other works, those books can be de-emphasized in instructing her. Similarly, if for some reason there is a pressing need to teach a particular subject, it is easy to give it precedence.

Book One is in your hands. Pray to Almighty God that you may master it quickly and well. By the proofs of Qur'anic verses and *hadis* cited above, it is required of men that they set their wives and daughters to study this work; and it is required of women that they learn it and direct the attention of their progeny, especially their daughters, to it as well. My heart will be joyous when those matters that are in my mind are assembled and printed and when I may see with my own eyes that this book is generally included in the instruction of girls and talked of in house after house. The future is in the power of the grace of the Truth, eminent is his glory and majesty.

At the time I was to write this introduction, I caught sight, in the paper *Nūrun 'Ala Nur,*[18] of a poem with the same name as this work and making the same point. To my heart, this seemed auspicious, and I fancied ending my introduction with the poem for the delight of my readers, especially young girls, who would then be more favorably inclined toward the subject of the work. If this poem were at the beginning of every section of the work, it would offer the sweet delight of successive lumps of sugar. Here it is:[19]

The True Jewelry of Humanity

A little girl asked this of her mother dear:
"Tell me about all jewelry; since I am unclear

Which pieces are good, this make known to me;
And which of them are bad, that too explain to me

So that of good and bad I can the difference tell;
With your blessing, then, to me the secret tell."

The mother then replied, with love, "O Daughter mine,
To this word on jewelry an attentive heart incline.

Jewelry of silver, gold—people may call it fine.
In it put not your trust—never, Sweetheart mine.

The glint of silver, gold, is only a thing to see.
Four days of silvery light, and then dark night will be.

It is required of you the kind of jewelry to want
From which good faith and life, my dear, may never want.

Good sense, dear, always be the head fringe you put on;
Sense is the means by which your work gets done.

If you earrings wear, ears of attentiveness, dear,
And your earrings' little bells: good counsel [*nasihat*] for you to hear.

And the pendants that hang down tell the heart to bow down too.
If act on them you will, good fortune swift to you.

Earrings of the upper ear always cause you pain,
Put in your ears the Book, good counsel yet again.

And if some jewelry you need to put upon your neck,
Good deeds, my beloved, be the chain upon your neck.

The yield of the strength of your arm, the bracelet of your arm be,
With your success in that, you will merry and joyful be.

All of the jewelry of the arm, none of it serves an end;
The ability of the arm, O Daughter, that does serve an end.

More than jewelry of the hand, cherished is handiwork fine;
Handiwork is the skill toward which everyone does incline.

What will you do, O my dear, with anklets that ring away?
O Daughter, a nuisance like that just simply throw away!

The best <u>jewelry for the feet</u> is surely the light of insight
That on the path of good you remain, sure-footed, aright.

If gold and silver jewelry be not on the feet—no fear—
If from the path of right your feet never slip, O my dear."

II. [Learning to Read]

[THE ALPHABET]

[The next seven pages of the text, omitted here, present the Urdu alphabet as well as examples of joining letters. (Urdu letters, like the Arabic from which they are derived, change shape depending on their position—initial, medial, final—in a word.)]

THE NAMES OF THE DAYS

[In the text, the Persian names are given in larger script and the Hindi names are in smaller script below them (here in parentheses), suggesting that the latter would be more familiar, although the former would have been used by the more educated. The first day is Saturday.]

Shamba (Sanicar)   Chahar-shamba (Budh)
Yak-shamba (Itwar)   Panj-shamba (Jum'arat)
Du-shamba (Pir)   Jum'a
Sih-shamba (Mangal)

THE NAMES OF THE MONTHS

[Only the names of the Muslim lunar months are given here and are thus presumably preferred; later, in Book Ten, other local calendrical systems are also presented.]

Muharram   Rajab
Safar   Sha'ban
Rabi'u'l-awwal   Ramazan
Rabi'u's-sani   Shawwal
Jumada'l-awwal   Zi-qa'd
Jumada'l-ukhra   Zi'l-hij

PRACTICE SENTENCES

[These are meant to be used for practice in reading, but their content is also of interest. Many of the injunctions derive from traditions of the exemplary sayings and behavior of the Prophet—sometimes amended, as when the more common "Heaven is at the feet of your mother" is expanded to include the father, too. The first four imperatives are in the direct (*tu*) form; the rest are in the familiar (*tum*).]

Fear God.

Do not sin.

Perform the ablution and pray.

The person who performs the canonical prayer is beloved of God.

The person who does not perform the prayer is far from mercy.

Oppress no one.

The supplication of the oppressed is readily accepted.

It is very bad to tease any animal or bird for no reason or to beat a dog or cat.

Obey the word of your mother and father.

Consider a beating from them to be an honor.

Serve them with your heart.

Heaven is at the feet of your father and mother.

Never answer them back with an argument.

Listen quietly to whatever they may say in anger.

Annoy them in nothing.

Act respectfully before your elders.

Treat those younger than you with love and affection.

Consider no one contemptible.

Regard yourself as less than everyone else. To consider yourself great is very bad.

It is a great sin to make fun of other people, to call attention to them, or to pick out their faults.

Eat with your right hand.

Drink with your right hand. The devil eats and drinks with his left hand.

Drink water in three gulps.

Cool your food before eating it. There is no blessing in very hot food.

Whatever you say, say the truth.

To lie is a great sin.

Always greet your elders when you arise in the morning.

Read the Noble Qur'an after performing the prayer.

Memorize your lesson carefully.

Do not always want to be playing and jumping.

Do not take an oath on every matter. To take an oath frequently is very bad.

Put away your book carefully.

Do not ridicule someone because her appearance is bad. To God, beauty and ugliness are the same.

Do not be naughty, and you will not be beaten.

Clean your nose with your left hand.

Clean yourself with your left hand after defecation.

When entering a toilet, put your left foot inside first.

When leaving, put your right foot outside first.

Place your shoe first on your right foot, then the other on your left foot.

[The next two sections, "Special Rules for Certain Letters of the Alphabet" and "The Use of Certain Pronunciation Signs Called Motions and Rests," are omitted here. They cover the nasal, aspiration, vowels, elision, glottal stops, and so forth.][20]

III. On Letter Writing

If you plan to write a letter, first ascertain whether the person addressed is older than you, younger than you, or your equal. The words used in a letter should match the rank of the person. A letter from an elder is called *wala nama* (an eminent letter), *sarfaraz nama* (a letter conferring distinction; literally, a "head-raising" letter), *iftikhar nama* (an honoring letter), *karamat nama* (a letter of generosity), *e'zaz nama* (an honoring letter), *sahifa-yi 'ali* (a lofty epistle), *sahifa-yi garami* (a precious epistle).

Do not use *ap* [the respectful second-person plural] for a person who is extremely superior to you; instead, use *anjanab* (sir, "that place of refuge"), *janab-i 'ali* (exalted sir), *janab-i wala* (eminent sir), *hazrat-i wala* (your eminence, eminent sir, "the eminent presence"), *hazrat-i 'ali* (your highness, lofty sir). For example, if you intend to write "Your letter came," write *janab wala ka sarfaraz nama aya* (the honor-bearing letter of your eminence came). And instead of "came," write *sadir hu'a* (was issued) or *musharraf farmaya* (conferred honor, nobility).

Letters from younger people are *masarrat nama* (a joy-bringing letter) or *rahat nama* (a comfort-bringing letter).

The letters of equals are *wala nama* or *karamnama* (a letter of generosity or kindness).

As an example, if you write a letter to your father, write thus: "Respected father, sir, the *qibla* and *ka'ba*[21] of your offspring, *may your lofty shadow*[22] *never vanish*. After salutation with endless respect and veneration, I beg to submit to you that your eminent letter arrived. I derived great satisfaction from ascertaining the well-being of your blessed constitution."[23] After that, write whatever you want.

The section up to *"may your lofty shadow never vanish"* is called "titles" (*alqab*). The section of greetings and supplications is called "respects" (*adab*). The section after that, in which you write whatever you wish, is called the "content" (*mazmun*) of the letter.[24]

TITLES AND RESPECTS FOR ELDERS

For a Father

1. Respected father, sir, the *qibla* and *ka'ba* of your descendents, the object of service from your dependents,[25] *may your lofty shadow never vanish*. After salutation with endless respects and exaltation, I beg to submit . . .

2. Respected father, sir, the *qibla* of both terrains and the *ka'ba* of both domains, *may your lofty shadow never vanish*. After respects and salutation with endless veneration and exaltation . . .

3. Respected father, sir, revered and honored by your offspring, *may your lofty shadow never vanish*. After salutation with endless veneration, I beg to represent that . . .

4. Respected father, sir, my *qibla* and *ka'ba, may your lofty shadow never vanish*. After respects and salutations, I beg to submit that . . .

5. My *qibla* and *ka'ba, may your lofty shadow never vanish*. After salutation, I beg to submit that . . .

For a Paternal Uncle

1. The *qibla* and *ka'ba* of your scions, the object of service by your minions, *may your lofty shadow never vanish*. After salutation and endless veneration, I beg to submit . . .

For a Maternal Uncle

    1. Respected uncle, sir, venerated and honored by the lesser, *may your lofty shadow never vanish* . . .
    2. Respected uncle, sir, served and exalted by the humble, *may your lofty shadow never vanish* . . .

For a Mother

    1. Respected mother, madam,[26] served and venerated, *may her shadow never vanish* . . .
    2. Respected mother, madam, venerated and exalted, *may her shadow never vanish* . . .
    3. Respected mother, madam, venerated and honored, *may her shadow never vanish* . . .

To an Elder Sister

    1. Venerated and honored sister[27] . . .
    2. Venerated and exalted, *may her shadow never vanish* . . .

To an Elder Brother

    1. Respected brother, sir, venerated and honored, served and exalted, *may your lofty shadow never vanish* . . .

    The titles used for the father are also used for a paternal grandfather, maternal grandfather, father's elder brother, mother's brother, and father-in-law.
    The titles used for the mother are also used for a mother's sister, mother's brother's wife, maternal grandmother, father's brother's wife, and such elder relatives. In place of "mother, madam," write "aunt, madam."
    As far as possible, do not engage in correspondence with your husband's younger or elder brothers. Do not cultivate familiarity with them. If some necessity should befall, then write and address them as "Respected brother, sir."
    The "respects" for all elder relatives are the same.

TITLES AND RESPECTS FOR YOUNGER RELATIVES

For a Son, Grandson, Nephew, and So On

1. Most prosperous, light of the eye, comfort to my life, settler of joy and fortune, *on him the peace of Almighty God.* After supplication for prolongation of life and advance in rank, may it be set out . . .

2. Light of my life, piece of my liver,[28] may his life be prolonged. After supplication for length of life and obtainment of joy in both worlds, may my happy opinion be set out . . .

3. Child tied to my heart, of my liver a part, may his life be prolonged. After copious supplications, may it be set out that . . .

For a Younger Brother

1. Brother dearer than life, *may the peace of Almighty God be upon him.* After supplication, may it be set out . . .

2. Brother equal to life, *may the peace of Almighty God be upon him.* After supplication of felicity and good ways, may it be set out . . .

For a Younger Sister

1. Dear sister, light of the eye, most virtuous, *may the peace of Almighty God be upon her.*

2. Auspicious sister, may her life be prolonged.

Respects for all are the same. Then write whatever you like.

TITLES AND RESPECTS FOR A HUSBAND

1. My lord, may you prosper! After greeting and desire for meeting, I beg to submit . . .

2. Confidant of secrets, companion, my consoler of sorrows, may you prosper! After longing greetings, it is humbly represented . . .

3. Knower of secrets; breath-sharer, play-sharer; may you prosper! After greetings and desire for meeting, I beg to submit . . .

TITLES AND RESPECTS FOR A WIFE

1. Confidante of secrets; breath-sharer, play-sharer; may you prosper! After expression of my longing and desire for our meeting, may it be set out . . .

2. Light of the dwelling and adornment of the lodging, may you

prosper! After expression of longing for our meeting, may it be set out . . .

3. Companion of my afflicted life, mitigator of the sorrows of my dejected heart, may you prosper! After longing for meeting, may it be set out . . .

[EXAMPLES OF LETTERS]

A Letter to a Father

Venerated and honored by his offspring, *may his shadow never vanish.* After salutation with endless veneration, I beg to submit that for some time no ennobling epistle has issued from your eminence. Thus everyone here is anxious and worried. We hope that you will honor us by quickly communicating to us that your blessed constitution is well.

My dear sister, entitled Zubaida Khatun,[29] through the grace and generosity of God, is well. Yesterday she completed her reading of the Glorious Word. Now would you kindly send some Urdu book for her that she can set to reading? The book *Ta'limu'd-din* (Instruction in religion), which you sent me, is excellent.[30] All the ladies are looking for it. So please send four or five more copies.

For the rest, all is well. Please let us know soon that you are well, so that we shall no longer be anxious but may rest content. My obeisance. End.

The petition of respect of Hamida Khatun from Allahabad, 13 Muharram, Monday.

A Letter to a Daughter

O piece of my liver, my good omen, light of my eye, comfort to my life, Mistress Khadija, *may the peace of Almighty God be upon her.* After praying for thy[31] long life and progress in learning and skill, may it be set out that for some time no letter of thine has come, so that my heart has been anxious. But the day before yesterday, the joy-bringing letter of your elder brother arrived. I was content when I ascertained that you were well.

From this letter I also learned that you have no enthusiasm for reading and writing and that you are scarcely putting your heart into your lessons. I also learned that several women talk about your reading and writing, saying, "What is the point of teaching girls to read and write? They should be taught sewing, cooking, *chikan* embroidery,[32] things like that. Do you want to teach them to read and write to turn them into *maulawi*s, like men?" It seems that the chatter of these people has made you discouraged, and you have done little work. O my daughter, do not be caught up in the talk of these foolish women. You must realize that no one could want your best interests more than I do. Hold fast to what I tell you. Their talk is completely foolish.

Every woman should at least be able to read and write Urdu. There are great benefits in this; and in ignorance of reading and writing there is great harm.

The first great benefit is that educated women speak clearly. I have heard many illiterate women say *sabab* for *sawab; surwa* for *shurba; qabutar* for *kabutar; dahez* for *jahez; jukham* for *zukam,* or even *zukham.* Women who are literate laugh at them and mimic them. With reading and writing, this flaw completely disappears.

Second, educated women perform the prayer and fast correctly; their religion and faith are put in order. Illiterate women, in their ignorance, do many things so that their faith is lost, and they do not even realize it. If, God forbid, death should come when they are in such a state, they will have to burn in hell like the infidels; salvation is impossible. With reading and writing, this dread possibility disappears, and faith grows strong.

Third, educated women manage their homes well. This is the special responsibility of women. They personally keep their eyes on books and household accounts at every moment.

Fourth, they raise their children well. Little children stay mostly with women; and girls stay only with their mothers. The habits and conversation of a literate woman will be good. Her offspring will learn from her example. From their earliest age, the children will be of good character and well behaved, because every minute their mother is teaching and reproving them. Look how valuable this is.

The fifth benefit is that when a woman has learning, she knows every minute the proper status of her mother, father, husband, and other relations; and she will fulfill her obligations (*huquq*) to them, so that both her worldly life and her afterlife will be in order.

Finally, a serious disadvantage of not knowing how to read and write is that an illiterate woman must reveal household matters to outsiders—or else keep them to herself, with resultant harm. Women's matters are often ones that affect the women's honor, but at times must be revealed to a mother or sister who may not be nearby. In this case, a woman must either be immodest and have a letter written by someone else or, alternatively, say nothing at all and cause great harm.

There are, in addition, thousands more benefits from learning and many more disadvantages in not learning. How much longer must I go on? Just remember my advice; do not in any way shirk your reading and writing. With many prayers for you. End.

The writer: 'Abdu'llah, from Banaras, 25 Ramazan, Friday.

An Answer to This Letter, Sent by the Daughter

O *qibla* and *ka'ba* of your offspring, *may your lofty shadow never cease.* After salutations and respects, I beg to submit that the issuing of your lofty epistle bestowed felicity. Your welfare being ascertained, everyone was content. May Almighty God always keep your auspicious self fixed over our heads.

What your eminence wrote in relation to the reading and writing of this servant was very beneficial. It is certainly true that I had become disheartened on account of people's talk. Now, since the day your epistle arrived, I have put my heart into my reading, and I have even begun to write a little. What you said is absolutely right, and there *are* countless benefits in this. Those women who do not know how to read and write lament continually and ask themselves why they never learned.

The day before yesterday, the wife of the *peshkar*[33] who lives in our neighborhood got a letter from her maternal uncle. Nowadays, there is no man in her house. The poor creature wandered around imploring everyone to read the letter or have it read, saying, "How is my aunt? I know that she is doing poorly." So she was truly in a state. The letter came in the forenoon; it lay all day with no one to read it. After sunset, she came to me, and I read her the news. Only then she settled down. Since then, the point has stuck with me that the skill of reading and writing is wealth indeed and that ignorance is often the source of great trouble.

I also realized that there are five women among our kinfolk (*biradari*) who are well educated. Everyone honors them wherever they go. Whenever someone commits something that is against the *shari'at* or observes some false custom at a wedding, they interrupt it, insist that it stop, explain what is wrong, and give advice. All the ladies keep quiet and set their ears to listen. The ladies consult them if they have some question. *All* the ladies ask them first, and everyone praises them on and on.

I will surely put my heart into learning to read and write. I have become very enthusiastic on my own. You pray to Almighty God, too, that he may grant me this wealth.

For the rest, all here is well.

With great respect. End.

Your maidservant Khadija, *may she be forgiven,* from Saharanpur, 28 Ramazan, Tuesday.

A Letter to a Brother's Daughter

Light of my eye, comfort of my life, Mistress Sadiqa, *on her be the peace of Almighty God.* After supplication for you, may it be set out that your joy-bringing letter arrived. I was content when informed of your state.

It made me very happy to learn about your reading. May Almighty God give abundance to your age and quickly grant you the fruit of your work. On the day when you write me a letter with your own hand, I shall dispatch five rupees for sweets.

I give you one more bit of advice. I have heard that you are somewhat saucy and do not have regard for the respect due anyone. I felt grieved at hearing this, because a person's honor does not derive only from being able to read and write. Until you learn to have regard for *adab* (civility), people will not love and cherish you. Along with reading and writing, it is necessary, above all, for boys and girls to learn civility, for with civility a person is dear to the heart of everyone and everyone seeks to please that person. A person of civility is a person of good fortune. As someone once said: *Ba adab ba nasib; be adab be nasib* (With civility, good fortune; without civility, bad fortune). Now I shall tell you what civility is and why you must behave in accordance with it.

You should greet anyone superior to you in age and relationship with great veneration. Never let an indecent word come out of your mouth in front of such a person.

Do not play or joke around with your equals in front of an elder.

If an elder calls you, answer in a very soft voice; and when given something, respond with a salutation.

Listen with close attention to whatever advice an elder gives. When she speaks, do not interrupt her.

Never sit in a place higher than where she happens to be sitting.[34]

Never call an elder by name, but rather call him or her by the relationship to you. Indeed, use a long form of that title, as: *khalu jan* (auntie dear); *phuphi aman* (auntie mama); *nanaji* (dear grandfather); *appa jan* (dear big sister).

If your elders speak sharply to you in anger, you must never answer back. Disappear and say nothing.

The name of all this is civility, and it is of great importance for all people. End.

Muhammad Wajid Husain, from Faizabad.

TITLES FOR AN EQUAL

If you are to write to an equal, first include the titles for equal rank: O most bounteous to me, may you prosper . . . ; My kindred kindly friend, may you prosper . . . ; My gracious friend, may you prosper . . .

Then offer your respects: After grateful salutation and desire for meeting, I beg to submit . . .

Then write the content of the letter, keeping in mind not to be too expansive, as when you write to elders, and not to be too brief, as when you write to younger relatives. On every point, keep equality in mind.

TWO EXAMPLES OF ADDRESSES

1. Place: City of Lucknow, Quarter Aminabad. Near the house of Hakim 'Abu'l-Ghani Sahib, Assistant Tahsildar, To the service of him of eminent rank, the respected *darogha*, my *qibla* and *ka'ba*, Wahidu'z-Zaman Sahib, *may his lofty shadow never vanish.*

2. Place: Faizabad, the market. By the shop of Liyaqat Husain Sahib, Goldsmith. To the attention of him prosperous in joy and good ways, Munshi Muhammad Sa'idu'd-Din, *may the peace of Almighty God come upon him.*[35]

IV. Numerals

[The next two pages, omitted here, provide a chart of the cardinal numbers from one to one hundred.]

V. True Stories from the *Hadis*

THE FIRST STORY

Hazrat Messenger of God, *God's blessings and peace upon him,* recounted this story:

Once, a man came to a deserted place where he suddenly heard a voice in a cloud, telling the cloud to water the garden of a certain person. The cloud moved and rained down heavily on barren ground.

The man then followed the water, which had gathered into a channel, until he came upon someone standing in a garden, directing the water with a spade. He inquired of this person: "O Servant of God, what is your name?"

The person answered with the name spoken in the cloud and asked in turn: "O Servant of God, why do you inquire about my name?"

He answered, "I heard a voice in that cloud say your name and tell the cloud to water your garden. What do you do that deserves this?"

He said, "I shall tell you only because you have asked. When my crop is ripe, I give one-third of the harvest in charity, put aside one-third for myself and my children, and invest one-third in the garden."

*Moral: **Praise be to God.*** Such is God's mercy that help from the unknown furthers the work of those who obey him, even without their knowing it. Surely it is true that if a person belongs to God, God in turn belongs to that person.

THE SECOND STORY

Hazrat Messenger of God, *God's blessings and peace upon him,* once recounted this story:

Among the Bani Isra'il, there were three men: one was a leper, one was afflicted with scalp disease, and one was blind. Almighty God wished to test them, and, to do so, he sent an angel.

First, the angel went to the leper and asked, "What is your greatest wish?"

He replied, "I wish that I might have a good complexion and beautiful skin and that this evil that makes people shun me and refuse to let me sit near them might disappear."

The angel passed his hand over the leper's body, and, lo, his skin was clear and his complexion beautiful.

Then the angel asked, "What sort of goods would you most like to have?"

He answered, "A camel."

So the angel gave him a pregnant she-camel and said, "May Almighty God give you increase of it."

Then the angel went to the man with scalp disease and asked, "What is your greatest wish?"

He replied, "I wish that my hair would grow in and that this evil that makes people shun me would disappear."

The angel passed his hand over his head, and, lo, his scalp was healed and grew good hair.

Then the angel asked, "What sort of goods would you most like to have?"

He answered, "A cow."

So the angel gave him a pregnant cow and said, "May Almighty God grant you increase of it."

Then the angel went to the blind man and asked, "What do you need?"

He answered, "I need Almighty God to restore my sight so that I might again see other people."

The angel passed his hand over the blind man's eyes, and Almighty God restored his sight. Then the angel asked, "What sort of goods would you most like to have?"

He answered, "A goat."

The angel gave him a pregnant goat.

The animals of all three men bore young, and in a short time the area was filled with the camels of the first, the cows of the second, and the goats of the third.

Then the angel, at the order of God, came in the same fashion to the leper and said, "I am a poor man; all the goods I needed for my journey have been used up. Today I have no recourse for my return travel other than God and then you. In the name of that God who bestowed on you a clear complexion and fine skin, I ask of you one camel that I may ride on it and reach home."

The man answered, "Be gone! Get away from me! I have other people to take care of and nothing left for you."

The angel then said, "I think I recognize you. Weren't you that leper whom people shunned? Weren't you very poor until God gave you so much?"

He replied, "Ha! Very good. Well, in fact, this wealth goes back several generations in my family."

The angel said, "If you lie, may God make you as you were before."

The angel then went in the same way to the man who had had scalp disease and asked him the same question and got the same kind of answer. The angel again said, "If you lie, may God make you as you were before."

Then the angel went in the same way to the blind man and said, "I am a traveler and have ended up with no goods. Today, except for God and then you, I have no recourse. In the name of him who restored your sight, I ask for one goat that I might use it to complete my journey."

The man replied, "Of course. I was blind, and Almighty God,

through his mercy alone, granted me sight. Take whatever you like and leave whatever you like. Upon God, I deny you nothing."

The angel said to him, "Keep your goods. I need nothing. I was sent to test you, as I have. God is pleased with you and displeased with the others."

Moral: You must reflect on the cost suffered by the first two men for their ingratitude. They lost all their blessings, and they became as they had been. God was displeased with them, and they were deprived of salvation in this world and the next. The third man, however, because he was grateful, won great reward. He kept his blessings; God was happy with him; he reaped satisfaction and joy in both this world and the next.

THE THIRD STORY

Once Hazrat Umm Salama,[36] *may God be pleased with her,* was given some meat. God's Messenger[s] liked meat very much; and Hazrat Umm Salama[rz] therefore told her servant to keep the meat on a shelf in case he wanted it. Meanwhile, a beggar came and stood at the door and called out, "Send something out to me, in the name of God. God will bless you."

From within the house, she answered, "May he bless you also."

This reply meant that she had nothing to give him. The beggar left.

Then God's Messenger[s] arrived and asked Umm Salama if she had anything for him to eat. She replied that she did, and she instructed her servant to fetch the meat for him. The servant went and saw that there was not even the name of meat—only a stone.

The Prophet[s] declared, "The meat turned into stone because you gave nothing to the beggar."

Moral: Reflect on the fact that this misfortune of the meat turning into stone happened because of a refusal to give in the name of God. Any persons who make excuses to beggars but themselves eat will be eating a stone whose effect is a stony heart that is increasingly hard. Because of God's great mercy and generosity to the people in the household of the Prophet[s], he physically changed the appearance of the meat so that they would be saved from the ill effects of using it.

THE FOURTH STORY

It was the excellent custom of God's Messenger[s] to read the prayer at daybreak and then to attend to his friends and companions, asking if any among them had had some dream in the night. If they had, he would offer an interpretation of the dream. Once, following his custom, he asked if anyone had had a dream, and all replied that they had not. He then declared:

I had a dream last night in which two men came to me and clutched my hand. They led me toward a sacred place, where I saw two men, one seated and one standing. The man who was standing had iron tongs in his hand with which he was tearing the other man's cheek off completely to the nape of his neck; then he did the same thing to the other cheek. The first cheek was then restored, and the man began again. I asked the two men who were leading me what was happening, but they told me to move on.

We moved on until we came to a man who was lying down. At his head stood another man with a huge, heavy rock in his hand. He dashed the rock on the head of the man who was lying there. The rock rebounded and fell far away. While he went to retrieve it, the head of the first man was restored to its previous state, and the second man began again. I again asked the two men who were leading me what was happening, but again they told me to move on.

We moved on until we reached a cave shaped like an oven, wide at the bottom and narrow at the top, with fire burning inside. It was filled with naked men and women. When the fire rose to the top, they all rose with it and almost came out. Then, when it settled, they too went to the bottom. I again asked the two men who were leading me what was happening, but again they told me to move on.

We moved on until we reached a river of blood. One man stood in the middle; another stood on the bank, surrounded by rocks. Whenever the man in the river came toward the bank and tried to get out, the man on the bank hit him in the face with a rock with such force that he fell back to his original place. This happened again and again. I again asked the two men who were leading me what was happening, but again they told me to move on.

We moved on until we reached a green and verdant garden. An old man, surrounded by children, sat under a big tree. Another man sat near the tree, fanning a fire. The two men took me up into the tree, where a very fine house had been built in its midst. They led me inside. I had never seen such a house. It was filled with men, old and young, and women and children. They then took me farther up, where there was a house even finer than the first. They led me inside it also, and again it was filled with young and old.

I finally said to the two men, "You have led me about the whole night. Tell me at last what all this has meant."

They answered, "The man whose cheek was being torn was a liar who told lies that spread throughout the whole world. They will keep doing this to him until the Day of Judgment.

"The man whose head was being crushed was a man to whom Almighty God gave knowledge of the Qur'an. In the night, he slept, oblivious; in the day, he failed to act on what he knew. He will continue thus until the Day of Judgment.

"The persons in the cave of fire were adulterers.

"The person in the river of blood was a usurer.

"The old man under the tree is Hazrat Ibrahim, *peace be upon him*. The children around him are children who died young. The man blowing the fire is the guardian of hell. The first house you entered is the house of ordinary Muslims; the second house, the house of martyrs."

They then revealed that they were Jibra'il and Mika'il[37] and instructed me to look up. I lifted up my head and saw a white cloud. They told me that was my house. I asked them to leave me so that I could enter it.

They said, "Your life remains unfinished; it is not completed. Only if it had been completed could you have entered your house."

Moral: You must know that the dreams of the prophets are divine revelation. All these events are true. In this *hadis* many points are clear: first, the harshness of the punishment for lies; second, the fate of a learned man who does not act on what he knows; third, the punishment for adultery; fourth, the punishment for usury. May God keep all Muslims safe from these deeds![38]

VI. On Beliefs

[Maulana Thanawi now lists the fundamental beliefs (*'aqida;* pl. *'aqa'id*) of a Muslim. He uses language that is simple and somewhat repetitive, preferring everyday Hindi words to erudite Arabic, even for technical terms such as "worship" (*pujna*), "partner" (*sajhi*), and "singular" (*nirala*). Although the Deobandis often use the plural of respect characteristic of Urdu when speaking of God, here, because he is identifying doctrine, Thanawi uses the singular. Only in point nine when God is anthropomorphized as Allah Miyan does he revert to the plural. The various points emphasize both God's power and human responsibility for right action and belief. The opening beliefs distinguish Muslims from people of other religions. Points seventeen to twenty-one distinguish Muslims from those who follow "false sufis." Points twenty-four and twenty-five distinguish them from the Shi'a, who give precedence to the Prophet's family. The final points on the Day of Judgment and heaven and hell make clear the reformists' conviction that their teachings are, literally, matters of life and death.]

1. The whole world was at first uncreated, but then it came into existence through the creation of Almighty God.

2. God is One; he needs no one. He gave birth to no one. He is born of no one. He has no wife; neither is anyone his equal.

3. He has always existed and will always exist.

4. Nothing is like him; he is different from all else.

5. He is alive. He has power over everything. Nothing is outside his knowledge. He sees everything. He hears everything. He speaks, but not as we speak. What he wishes, he does; no one stops him. It is he who is worthy of adoration. He has no partner. He is kind to his servants. He is a king. He is free of all faults. It is he who saves his servants from all calamities. It is he who has dignity.

5[*sic*]. He is great. He is the creator of all things. No one has created him. He is the forgiver of sins. He is powerful. He is the giver of great bounty. He provides for all daily needs. He gives little to whomever he wants; he gives much to whomever he wants. He puts down whom he will and raises whom he will. He dignifies whom he will and disgraces whom he will. He is just. He is forbearing and patient. He knows the value of worship and service. It is he who accepts supplications. It is he who is all-embracing. He is the ruler of all. No one is his ruler. No work of his lacks wisdom. He fulfills the needs of all. It is he who brought forth all, and it is he who will bring forth again on the Day of Judgment. It is he who gives life, and it is he who kills. All know him through his signs and qualities; no one can know the subtlety of his being. He accepts the repentance of sins; he punishes those deserving punishment. He is the one who gives guidance. Whatever happens in the world is through his order alone. Without his order not a mote can move. He neither slumbers nor sleeps. He does not weary from guarding the whole world. It is he who sustains all things. He has thus all good and perfect qualities; there is no harm or evil in him; there is no fault in him.

6. All his qualities have always existed and will always exist. None of his qualities can ever disappear.

7. He is free of the attributes of created beings. As for the statements about these attributes reported in many places in the Qur'an and *hadis,* entrust their meaning to God, for he alone knows their truth. We, without undue explication, believe with certainty that whatever their

meaning, they are right and true. This is best. You may perhaps give the statements some appropriate meaning to make them understood.[39]

8. Almighty God has always known what good and evil there is in the world before it happens; he brings it into being in accordance with his knowledge. This is called predestination or *taqdir*. There are many mysteries concerning the creation of evil that no one knows.

9. Almighty God has given will and understanding to his servants so that by their own will they can do works of sin and works meriting reward. But the servants have no power to create any work. Our Lord and Master is angry with works of sin and happy with works meriting reward.

10. Almighty God requires of his servants no task that they are incapable of performing.

11. Nothing is required of God. Whatever kindness he may do is his grace.

12. Many messengers of Almighty God have been sent to show his servants the straight path. All of them are free of sins. Only God knows fully how many of them there have been. In order to show their authenticity, Almighty God revealed many new and difficult acts through them that other people cannot do. These acts are called miracles (*mu'jiza*). Among the prophets, Hazrat Adam, *on whom be peace,* was the first, and Hazrat Muhammad, the Apostle of God, *God's blessings and peace upon him,* is the last. The rest were between them. Among them, many are very famous, such as Hazrat Nuh[a], Hazrat Ibrahim[a], Hazrat Ishaq[a], Hazrat Isma'il[a], Hazrat Ya'qub[a], Hazrat Yusuf[a], Hazrat Da'ud[a], Hazrat Sulaiman[a], Hazrat Ayyub[a], Hazrat Musa[a], Hazrat Harun[a], Hazrat Zakariya[a], Hazrat Yahya[a], Hazrat 'Isa[a], Hazrat Ilyas[a], Hazrat Alyasa'[a], Hazrat Yunis[a], Hazrat Lut[a], Hazrat Idris[a], Hazrat Zu'l-kifl[a], Hazrat Salah[a], Hazrat Hod[a], and Hazrat Shu'aib[a].[40]

13. Almighty God has not told anyone how many messengers have been sent. Therefore, believe as follows: We believe in those messengers whom we know and also in those whom we do not know.

14. The rank of some among the messengers is higher than the rank of others. The highest rank is that of our Messenger, Muhammad the Chosen[s], and after him no new messenger can come. Until the Day of Judgment, he is the messenger to all people and *jinn*.

15. Almighty God took our Messenger[s], while he was yet awake and in his body, from Mecca to the Baitu'l-muqaddas (Jerusalem),[41] and from there to the seventh heaven and beyond, to wherever God wished. He then brought him back to Mecca. This is called the *mi'raj*.

16. Almighty God brought forth some creatures from light and hid

them from our sight. They are called angels. Many works are entrusted to them. They never do any act against the order of God. They do whatever task they are set to do. Among them, four angels are very famous: Hazrat Jibra'il[a], Hazrat Mika'il[a], Hazrat Israfil[a], and Hazrat 'Azra'il[a]. Almighty God made some creatures from fire, and they, too, do not appear to us. They are called *jinn*. Among them, some are good and some are bad—all kinds. They also have offspring. The most famous of the evil *jinn* is Iblis, who is Satan.

17. When Muslims worship faithfully, avoid sin, do not love the world, and obey the Messenger[s] in every way, then they are friends of God and the beloved of God. People like this are called saints (*wali*). Sometimes they accomplish deeds that are impossible for other people. These miracles are called *karamat*.

18. No *wali*, whatever high rank that person may reach, can ever be the equal of a prophet.

19. However beloved of God they may be, *wali*s are bound to the *shari'at* as long as their senses and consciousness last. They are not excused from the canonical prayer or the fast or any other act of worship. It is not correct for a *wali* to commit any sin.

20. Whoever is against the *shari'at* cannot be a friend of God. If anything amazing appears by the action of such a person, it is either magic or the work of that person's lower soul (*nafs*) and of Satan. It should be rejected.

21. Many mysteries are made known to the saints either while they are awake or while they sleep: these are "openings" (*kashf*) or "illuminations" (*ilham*). Accept them as true if they are in accordance with the *shari'at*, and reject them if they are against the *shari'at*.

22. God and the Messenger[s] have told their servants all points of religion (*din*) in the Qur'an and the *hadis*. Now it is not proper to innovate; such novelty is called *bid'at* (reprehensible innovation). *Bid'at* is a very great sin.

23. Almighty God has revealed many long and short books from heaven, through Jibra'il[a], to many messengers, so that they could provide religious teachings for their different communities. Four of the books are well known: the Torah of Hazrat Musa[a], the Psalms of Hazrat Da'ud[a], the Gospel of Hazrat 'Isa[a], and the Glorious Qur'an of our Apostle[s]. The Glorious Qur'an is the final book. Now no other book will again descend from heaven. The order of the Qur'an will run until the Day of Judgment. Erring people have greatly changed the other books, but Almighty God has promised to guard the Glorious Qur'an. No one can change it.

24. Any Muslim who saw our Apostle[s] is called a Companion. The

Companions have many great qualities. One must love them and be well disposed to them. Any talk of a quarrel or fight among them must be considered as forgetfulness and not as evil on their part. Four were the greatest of all. Hazrat Abu Bakr Siddiq, *may God be pleased with him,* who sat in the place of the Apostle[s] after him and managed all religious affairs, is called the first caliph. He is the best of the whole community. After him, Hazrat 'Umar[rz] was the second caliph. After him, Hazrat 'Usman[rz] was the third caliph. And after him, Hazrat 'Ali[rz] was the fourth caliph.

25. The rank of the Companions is so high that the greatest saint cannot reach a rank equal to the lowest rank of a Companion.

26. The offspring of the Apostle[s] and his wives are all worthy of veneration. Among the offspring, the greatest rank is held by Hazrat Fatima[rz]. Among the wives, Hazrat Khadija[rz] and Hazrat 'A'isha[rz] are greatest.

27. Correct faith requires the recognition that all matters relating to God and the Messenger[s] are true, and it demands belief in all of them. Faith is lost from doubting any matter concerning God and the Messenger[s], or from considering any of these matters false, or from picking out faults or making jokes about them.

28. It is false religion to deny the evident meaning of the Qur'an and *hadis* and to bend the text to one's own purpose in devious ways.

29. If sin is judged to be legitimate, faith is lost.

30. If one recognizes that he or she has committed a sin, however great a sin it might be, faith is not lost, but it does become weak.

31. It is infidelity to be without hope or fear of Almighty God.

32. It is infidelity to ask others about the unknown and to put faith in them.

33. No one other than Almighty God knows the unknown, although the prophets know some things through revelation; the saints, some things through openings and illuminations; and the common people, some things through signs.

34. It is a great sin to call someone an infidel or to curse that person. One can, to be sure, call down curses on tyrants and liars generally. It is not a sin to say a person is cursed whom God and the Messenger[s] have cursed by name or announced to be an infidel.

35. When a person dies—either after the burial or, if there is no burial, wherever the person may be—two angels, one of whom is called Munkir and the other Nakir, come to the dead person and ask, "Who is your lord, and what is your religion?" They ask about Hazrat Muhammad, the Messenger of God[s]. A dead person who is faithful answers correctly and is given all kinds of comfort. The angels open a window

in the direction of heaven, from which come cool breezes and fragrance. The dead person sinks into pleasure and sleeps. But a dead person who is without faith and is unable to reply to the questions suffers great harshness and torment until the Day of Judgment. Almighty God excuses many from this trial. All these things are known to the dead; we do not see them. It is as if a sleeping person saw all kinds of things in a dream and the waking person sitting nearby knew nothing of it.

36. After they have died, people are daily shown their future abode, every morning and every evening. A person going to heaven is shown heaven and thus given good tidings. A person going to hell is shown hell and thus given increased sorrow.

37. Supplication on behalf of the dead person and charity given in the dead person's name earn reward for that person. This gives the dead person great benefit.

[Points thirty-eight to forty-nine concern the Day of Judgment. This subject is treated in great detail in Book Seven, and the section is thus omitted here.]

*   *   *

VII. [Sins: Listed According to Grievousness]

At this point, in order that people might avoid them, it seems appropriate to describe the many false beliefs, bad customs, and great sins that often occur and that harm faith. They include acts of complete infidelity and polytheism, acts that verge on infidelity and polytheism, others that are reprehensible innovations, and, finally, some that are mere sin. The point is that all of them must be avoided. Once they have been described, we will then discuss briefly the harm done by sin in everyday life, in contrast to the profit earned by obedience. People do take account of what causes harm or profit in their everyday concerns, and hence they might find the resources to perform good deeds and to abstain from sin.

ACTS OF INFIDELITY AND POLYTHEISM

1. To like infidelity.[42]
2. To consider matters of infidelity good.

3. To cause another to do some act of infidelity.

4. To regret your faith for any reason: "If I were not a Muslim, I would have gotten such and such."[43]

5. Upon the death of your children or someone else, to say in sorrow such things as, "God had only him to kill," "God should not have done this," "No one does such evil as you have done."

6. To consider any order of God and the Messenger, *God's blessings and peace upon him,* to be bad; to find fault with it.

7. To deprecate any angel or prophet; to impute fault to them.

8. To believe that any elder or *pir* has certain knowledge of everything about you at every minute.

9. To ask news about the unknown from a Brahmin (*pandit*) learned in astrology or a person dominated by *jinn;* to have a fortune told and consider it to be true; or to see an omen in the speech of some elder and impute certainty to it.

10. To call on some holy person from afar and to believe that person will hear.

11. To believe that someone other than God is responsible for all your profit and loss.

12. To demand fulfillment of your wishes from someone other than God; to ask that person to grant you livelihood or offspring.

13. To fast in the name of some revered person; to prostrate yourself before that person; to set an animal free or sacrifice it in that person's name; to make a vow in a revered person's name; to circumambulate a grave or building; to give precedence to some custom or to the word of some revered person over the order of God; to bow or to stand like an image before that person; to sacrifice a goat on a sacred tumulus; to slaughter an animal in someone's name.

14. To make offerings to *jinn,* ghosts, departed spirits, and so forth in order to set them free.

15. To worship the umbilical cord of a child in order to ensure the child's life. To slaughter a goat or other animal.

16. To appeal to anyone other than God for help.

17. To respect or venerate any place as equal to the *ka'ba.*

18. To pierce a child's ear or nose in order that the child might wear a nose ring or earring in the name of some venerated person.

19. To tie a coin on a child's arm or a string on a child's neck in someone's name.

20. To put a wedding wreath on a child; to allow a child to grow a pigtail (*choti*); to have a child wear a garland of colored strings.

21. To have a child dress as a *faqir* [perhaps to avert the evil eye].

22. To give children such names as 'Ali Bakhsh (granted by 'Ali),

Husain Bakhsh (granted by Husain), 'Abdu'n-Nabi (slave of the Prophet[s]), and so forth.[44]

23. To attach the name of some elder to an animal and then treat the
animal with respect.

24. To believe that the affairs of the world derive from the influence
of the stars; to inquire about auspicious and inauspicious dates and
days; to seek omens; to consider any month or date ill omened.

25. To repeat the name of some elder as your daily discipline.

26. To say: "If God and the Messenger[s] wish, such and such will be
accomplished."

27. To swear on someone's name or head.

28. To keep pictures, especially to keep and venerate a picture of an
elder for its auspiciousness.

REPREHENSIBLE INNOVATIONS, BAD CUSTOMS, AND BAD DEEDS

1. To hold fairs with great to-do at graves; to light lamps at graves;
for women, to go to graves; to offer shawls to cover the grave; to build
a permanent monument at a grave; to revere graves excessively in
order to please elders; to kiss or lick *ta'ziya*s or graves; to rub their dust
on your face; to circumambulate them; to prostrate yourself; to perform the canonical prayer in the direction of graves; to make offerings
of candies, pudding (*halwa*), sweetcakes, and so forth; to keep *ta'ziya*s
and flags and salute them or offer them *halwa* and cake.

2. To consider anything too pure to be touched (*achuti*). To refuse
to eat *pan,* apply henna or black powder to the teeth, remain with men,
or wear red clothes during the month of Muharram.

3. To refuse to let men eat food offered in the name of Fatima (*bibi
ki sahnak*).

4. To consider observation of the third and the fortieth days after a
death to be an obligation.

5. To regard a second marriage for a woman as a fault, despite
there being a need for it.

6. To perform all family customs in marriage, circumcision, the
ceremony initiating a child's studies (*bi'smi'llah*), and so forth, even
though there may not be adequate resources; especially, to take loans
in order to put on musical performances and display.

7. To observe the customs of Holi and Diwali.[45]

8. To say "Your servant" or some other such greeting instead of
salam [an Islamic greeting]; or to merely touch your hand to your head
and bow.

9. To go before brothers-in-law and cousins unceremoniously, or to come before any other marriageable person.[46]

10. To sing while bringing pitchers from the river; to listen to music and singing; to have *domnis*[47] dance; to rejoice in watching them and give them gifts.

11. To take pride in your lineage; to consider descent from some elder sufficient for salvation; to taunt someone about a deficiency in his or her lineage; to consider any legitimate occupation contemptible.

12. To praise anyone excessively.

13. To make foolish expenditures and engage in foolish acts during a wedding.

14. To perform the customs of the Hindus:[48] to dress the groom in a fashion opposed to the *shari'at;* to put a wreath on him and tie a string on his wrist;[49] to put henna on him; to set off fireworks; to make wasteful decorations; to call the groom in among the women, and for the women to come in front of him and peek out at him; for mature sisters-in-law or other such women to come and flirt with him; to play at *chauthi;*[50] to gather around where the bride and groom are lying together in order to overhear them and peek at them, and, if someone finds out something, to report it to others; to have the bride sit in isolation[51] and to force her to be so overly modest that the canonical prayer is missed; to put on airs by fixing the marriage portion at a very great amount.

15. Upon a death, to cry aloud and weep in sorrow; to beat your face and breast; to recount the event and weep; to smash water pitchers; to have washed whatever clothes have touched the dead body; to refuse to use pickles in the house for a year; to observe no occasions of joy; to mourn afresh on special dates.

16. To spend all your time on adornment and decoration; to consider a simple style a fault; to place pictures in the house; to use boxes of gold and silver for *pan* and essence or a silver or gold needle for collyrium; to wear very fine clothing or jingling jewelry; to wear a *lahnga* (skirt); to go into gatherings of men, especially to see *ta'ziya*s and to go to fairs; to adopt the style of men; to tattoo the body.

17. To keep the nocturnal religious feast of women (*khuda'i rat*); to make spells (*totka*).

18. To use wall or ceiling hangings solely for adornment.

19. To embrace or be embraced by marriageable men at the time of departure or arrival from a journey.

20. To pierce the ear or nose of a boy in order to prolong his life; to have a boy wear a nose ring or earring; to have him wear silk clothing

or safflower-dyed or saffron-dyed clothing; or to have him wear a necklace or an anklet or any other jewelry.

21. To feed a baby opium in order to make it cry less.

22. To feed a person the milk or meat of a tiger during a sickness.

There are many more such customs; those above are given as examples.

SOME VERY GRIEVOUS SINS

1. To assign partners to God.

2. To shed blood unjustly. Some women who have no offspring perform spells during another woman's confinement so that her baby will die and they will have children instead. This counts as bloodshed.

3. To torment your parents.

4. To commit adultery.

5. To use the wealth of orphans unjustly, as when many women take control of all the wealth and property of their husbands and squander the share that should belong to small children; to fail to give girls their share of inheritance.[52]

6. To accuse a woman of adultery on a slight suspicion.

7. To oppress anyone.

8. To speak ill of people behind their backs.

9. To despair of the mercy of God.

10. To fail to fulfill a promise one has made.

11. To be unfaithful to a trust.

12. To forsake any duty to God, particularly the canonical prayer, the fast, the pilgrimage, and the tithe.

13. To read the Noble Qur'an and then forget it.

14. To lie, especially to swear a false oath.

15. To swear an oath by anyone other than God; or to swear in this manner: "At the time of death may I be deprived of the attestation of faith," "May my end come without belief."

16. To prostrate yourself before anyone other than God.

17. To miss the canonical prayer without legitimate excuse.

18. To call any Muslim an unbeliever or faithless; or to say, "May the wrath of God fall on him," "The curse of God," "The enemy of God."

19. To listen to someone's accusations and complaints.

20. To steal; to take interest; to rejoice in the high cost of grain; to set a bargain and then insist on giving less.

21. To sit alone with a marriageable male.

22. To gamble. Many girls and women play round pebbles with bets and other games that are also gambling.

23. To like the customs of the unbelievers.

24. To say that food is bad.

25. To watch dancing and listen to music.

26. To fail to give advice, even though one has the capacity to do so.

27. To shame or humiliate someone through buffoonery.

28. To search out someone's faults.

VIII. [The Impact of Islam on Everyday Life]

WORLDLY LOSSES CAUSED BY SIN

1. To be deprived of knowledge.

2. To have your livelihood decline.

3. To be distraught at the thought of God.

4. To be distraught before other people, especially good people.

5. To confront difficulty in most of one's affairs.

6. To lose cleanliness and purity of heart.

7. To become weak at heart and often in the whole body.

8. To be deprived of obedient devotion.

9. To face a shortened life.

10. To lack the grace of repentance; to quickly lose from your heart an awareness of the evil of sin.

11. To be despicable in the opinion of Almighty God.

12. To be cursed by others because of the harm your state causes them.

13. To be deficient in sense.

14. To be cursed by the Messenger of God, *God's blessings and peace upon him.*

15. To be deprived of the supplication of the angels.

16. To suffer deficiencies in your crops.

17. To lose modesty and a sense of honor.

18. To lose an awareness of God's greatness in your heart.

19. To lose your blessings.

20. To be encircled by calamities.

21. To have Satanic forces fixed over you.

22. To remain worried at heart.

23. To have the attestation of faith fail to come to your lips at the time of death.

24. To despair of the mercy of God and therefore to die without repentance.

WORLDLY GAINS WON THROUGH OBEDIENCE

1. To have increased livelihood
2. To have an abundance (*barkat*) in everything.
3. To have all difficulty and worry be far removed.
4. To have your intentions be realized with ease.
5. To have a life of joy.
6. To have rain.
7. To have all kinds of evil forestalled.
8. To have Almighty God as your benefactor and helper.
9. To have the angels ordered to keep your heart strong.
10. To have true honor and respect.
11. To have high rank; to be loved in everyone's heart.
12. To have the Qur'an as a cure on your behalf.
13. To gain an even better return to replace any loss in wealth.
14. To receive an increase in blessings day by day.
15. To have increased wealth.
16. To have satisfaction and comfort remain in your heart.
17. To have this benefit reach the next generation.
18. To receive visions of the unknown in this life.
19. To have the angels sound glad tidings and give you words of blessing at the time of death.
20. To have increased life; to be spared poverty and hunger; to secure more blessing in whatever is lacking.
21. To have the anger of Almighty God disappear.[53]

Book Six of the *Bihishti Zewar:*
A Discussion of Custom
by Category

Translator's Introduction to Book Six

In Book Six, Maulana Thanawi describes in vivid detail the customs (*rasm,* pl. *rusum; riwaj; dastur*) that he feels have so distracted his fellow Muslims from the straight path of Islam, entangling them in practices ruinous to both their worldly and their spiritual lives.[1] He shares this concern with a long tradition of reformers who have periodically attempted to cleanse the Islam they see around them of what appear to be corruptions.

Thanawi does not shape his argument as one might expect, by identifying the origin of the customs as non-Muslim (although that point is periodically adduced). Instead, he is concerned with ascertaining what is legitimate in light of the *shari'at.* The *shari'at,* he argues, sets the standards for a society of individuals committed to order, moderation, just dealings with one another, and piety toward God—all of which are thwarted by the intransigent and pervasive error he identifies on every side. He places his hope, as always, in showing people that they have misunderstood, that their knowledge is incorrect. "When you understand" is his persistent refrain: "When you understand the sinfulness of this nonsense, you can act to make this bane [of custom] evaporate from Hindustan. . . . May all now be again just as it was in the blessed time of Hazrat^s, *God's blessings and peace upon him.*"

Reformers like Thanawi saw custom as thwarting the ordered and bounded life ordained by the *shari'at*. He begins his first section, on customs deemed sinful but trivial, with discussion of dancing, keeping pet dogs, setting off fireworks, and playing games. All of these activities are notorious for spilling beyond control: dancing leads to unchecked license; dogs are impossible to control; fireworks can explode in one's face; games involve chance and seduce one from all else. Two other practices cited here—keeping images and trimming a male's hair to allow a tuft—are preeminently associated with Hindus; to imitate non-Muslims is to defy boundaries of the most basic sort. The various customs also threaten control in that the harm of a single occasion goes on and on, like an example that, once set, is repeatedly emulated. Beyond this, these introductory subjects set out the kinds of problems Maulana Thanawi finds characteristic of custom throughout: they set up false obligations, waste money, lead to wrong financial dealings, encourage display and ostentation, mix men and women, and risk physical harm. In short, they defy the *shari'at* in point after point.

The text demonstrates remarkably well the style of argumentation and the form of logic characteristic of reformers steeped in the traditional sciences. The key to reasoning is to measure every practice systematically against the norms of the *shari'at*. Thanawi's rationalizing style is especially evident in the two lists he provides in this book, one after the discussion of the customs of marriage and a second at the conclusion of the book. With these principles, all bolstered by the citation of *hadis,* and in some cases by citations from the Qur'an as well, the reader is in a position to deal with the seemingly endless and diverse customs that appear to characterize everyday life. Most of these customs mark rituals of the life cycle and are grouped in the second section as "customs considered legitimate." Again, Maulana Thanawi is concerned to break the balloon of false knowledge: "People think that there cannot possibly be any sin in men and women gathering to eat, drink, and exchange gifts. . . . What is there that could possibly be against the *shari'at*?" What there is, he finds, is not merely an occasional minor fault. By his count, he identifies nine errors in the circumcision, five in the *bi'smi'llah,* eight in the engagement, and an astonishing total of some three hundred errors in the marriage!

Most of the time, most Muslims, like others, take their practices and beliefs for granted. At times of heightened self-consciousness and cultural redefinition, however, those Muslims educated in the classical tradition bring the *shari'at* to the fore to evaluate what is properly Islamic and what is not: Maulana Thanawi examining everyday life among Muslims in the north Indian countryside; legislators in Punjab debating customary inheritance law; Malay courtiers troubled by royalty who keep Dalmatians as pets—all share a characteristic mentality in making moral assessments in the light of the *shari'at,* across a wide variety of places and times.[2]

Fiqh, the body of jurisprudence that systematizes *shari'at,* developed in the historical law schools, makes reference to Qur'an and *hadis* decisive. The importance of these sources is evident here in how frequently they are quoted. No argument beyond the Prophet's own experience is really needed in matters such as the remarriage of widows, for example. The learned in this tradition also reason on the basis of *ijma',* the opinion of the learned, in addition to the two textual sources (although the former is only implicit in this work). Finally, these scholars also reason by analogy, seeking what Hanafi scholars call the *haqiqa,* the true essence, of any action in order to find its status in the light of sacred teaching. Thanawi's endless, often ironic exposures of the real implications of behavior are an example of that kind of reasoning. Whatever people may say or even believe their motive is in carrying out some custom, he shows that the reality behind the custom is ostentation or superstition or some other motive whose status is plainly condemned in the *hadis:* "The sinfulness of these customs," he says, "is not so subtle or obscure."

Custom per se is not condemned. Muslims in all geographic areas recognize some practices that are not explicitly sanctioned in Islamic scripture; other practices may not even be noticed. Anything not evidently objectionable—and that assessment can change over time—can be incorporated as a defining feature of a Muslim community. The incorporation of custom is seen in the recognition that certain practices can be legitimated in Islamic law as *'urf* or *ada.* Some legal traditions even adduce jurisprudential principles of "social good" (*istihasan*) or "expedience" (*istislah*) to sanction certain local practices. Thus rules governing inheritance in parts of India long followed customary rather than *shari'at* practices. Thanawi does not adduce explicit jurisprudential principles in this work, which was meant for such a general audience; rather, his argument is simple and direct, reinforced by quotations from sacred authority. At times, he adds references to intelligence or sense (*'aql*). These references lead to the same conclusions he deduces from his citations of the *shari'at* and from his references to nature; all three confirm the same essential truth.

In condemning many customary practices, the reformist *'ulama* were in accord with more westernized reformers as well as with Hindu reformers who raised similar issues within their own community. Indian reformers across the board condemned extravagance and conspicuous consumption; Maulana Thanawi, for example, urged families to give newlyweds land or a business rather than squandering their wealth on weddings. They discouraged detailed rituals that tied people to being present in particular places at particular times. They denounced what they saw as superstition. Customary practices in turn-of-the-century India, as in seventh-century Arabia, not only were theologically suspect but also were not congruent with societies moving toward more mobile, urban, and larger-scale organization. The reformers fostered a religious style based on rational principles and dependent on individual moral choice and responsibility; they denounced the religion of holy men, charms, and anything they saw as smacking of mediation or magic.

This did not mean that they withdrew from participation in social and family life. The heart of society in this area was the family (*kunba*) and the extended group of intermarrying kin (*biradari*). The reformers directed their followers to fulfill the obligations of a hierarchic, patriarchal society in which the rich and the poor, the older and the younger, the male and the female each sustained obligations to the other and exchanged deference from the one in return for protection from the other.

The family rituals and ceremonies that form the heart of this book do not, however, in Thanawi's view, foster those obligations. They distort proper hierarchy. They make adults act like children and the powerful mistreat the weak. They distort relations between men and women. Maulana Thanawi is appalled at the mistreatment of servants, such as the palanquin bearers whose wages are not fixed and who are forced to work. He is scathing in denouncing the hardships imposed on young brides. He is scandalized by the groom who tells his new wife, "I am your slave," and "You are the lioness, I am the sheep." He disapproves of the teasing that goes on between the groom and his new sisters-in-law. He sees Hindu notions of pollution keeping the father away from his natural position with his new baby and his wife. Custom distorts the proper relations of Muslims to unbelievers, Thanawi insists, both by emulation of non-Muslim behavior and by such practices as giving gifts to untouchable Hindu *bhangi*s instead of to the deserving Muslim poor. The prohibition on the remarriage of widows, a customary prohibition of the Hindus and an example of the powerful abusing the weak, drew Thanawi's special wrath on many grounds.

The subject of the remarriage of widows comes up throughout the entire work. Those responsible for widowed women, he argues, fail in their responsibility. They not only prevent these unfortunate women from remarrying but also fail to look after them properly. Midway through this book, Thanawi brings all his arguments to bear. He points out the human problems when widows are mistreated: "Have you no pity for widows today? Doesn't your heart grieve at the sight of their condition? Their lives are ruined, and they are brought down into the dust." "By the *shari'at* and by sense," he argues, the second marriage must be like the first. The *sunna* could not be more clear, he points out, for all the wives of the Prophet except 'A'isha had been married before. He claims that the prohibition is unique to Hindustan and that the wellborn are emulating high-caste Hindus. But this point is not central, and on another occasion he insists that even if readers deny their borrowing and say they have devised the custom themselves, it is no less wrong. At its heart is greed and—the reality of custom after custom—the pursuit of false honor.

It is not honor and family interests that Maulana Thanawi opposes; rather, he argues against what he sees as pursuit of status and reputation on false grounds. In one paragraph in the section on the remarriage of widows, he runs through a veritable vocabulary list of words related to honor in order to mock the assumption that such remarriages, practiced by the Prophet himself, were not worthy: "Has your respectability (*sharafat*) risen above [that of the Prophet's wives], so that your honor (*'izzat*) is spoiled by doing what they did . . . ? Will this cast a slur upon your honor (*abru*)? . . . [You must rid] your heart of undue concerns with honor (*nang o namus*). You must put custom on the shelf." False notions of honor are at the heart of almost every practice cited here. But Maulana Thanawi insists that real honor is to be found elsewhere. "In fact," he claims, "experience has shown that obedience to Almighty God brings you an even better reputation and greater honor"; fear of dishonor must never stand in the way of correct behavior.

Customs thwart not only proper worldly order but also the order that extends from this world to the other. Ignoring the teaching of the Prophet who follows divine command demonstrates disrespect that threatens correct belief. Such disregard for sacred hierarchy is particularly evident in the third and final section of this book, which identifies practices believed to be not only legitimate but actually deserving of reward. Each practice is related to some ceremonial or religious observance, good in itself, but now overlaid with "foolishness." As Maulana Thanawi often ironically calls custom a *shari'at* of its own, a self-devised *shari'at,* here he calls these practices a *tariqa,* a way of piety—but a self-devised *tariqa.*

Concerning the custom of performing *fatiha* for the dead, for example, one should simply assign the credit for carrying out a good deed, such as reading the Qur'an or feeding the poor, to the benefit of the dead person. The late nineteenth-century memoir of Bibi Ashraf quoted her grandmother's advice, given to her as a child when her mother had just died:

> Now, you must stop your endless weeping. For if you don't, your mother will greatly suffer and be angry with you. On the other hand, if you wish to please your mother, there is nothing better for you than to read something in her name and offer her the reward for that reading. . . . Those seven sections of the Qur'an [that you know], you should read them every day. Then raise your arms to God and say, "I give their reward to my mother's soul."[3]

But such straightforward behavior was not characteristic, Thanawi writes.

Typically, he claims, people plaster the floor with mud, set out food, including *pan* and water, and only then do they have a Qur'anic reading. In short, they create a *chauka* (the ritually clean area spread with mud and cow dung where Hindus cook and eat their food) and then proceed to invite and feast the dead person. Many believe that food cannot be given in charity without the efficaciousness of the reading of sacred words. At the least, Thanawi warns, this is an unnecessary elaboration and a distraction from normative observances. At worst, it is intended not to transfer benefit to the dead but to invoke powerful figures, who transform the food, to come to one's aid. It suggests a magical efficacy, alien to normative Islamic rituals. All this is nothing less than *shirk,* the assigning of partners to God. The numerous ceremonies related to death, as Thanawi describes them, also share the familiar sins—misspent money, elaboration of ceremonies on particular dates, the quest for status, the errors of women's gatherings—that distort other life-cycle rituals.

Finally, Maulana Thanawi reviews the calendrical celebrations that punctuate the year. He urges that the practices deemed required for their observance be diminished: preparing *siwaiyan* (sweet noodles) and giving gifts at 'Id; a particular distribution of parts of a sacrificed animal; the necessity of sweets at a *maulid* or at the Shab-i Barat; the fast of 27 Rajab; and the *sharbat* and *ta'ziyas* of Muharram. He points out many objectionable features of the events, most of them familiar from earlier discussions of parallel practices. Having begun this book with what were seemingly innocent peccadilloes, Maulana Thanawi is now describing acts considered to be sources of material and spiritual favor—only to show, notably concerning ceremonies related to the dead, that they are the most serious sins that any Muslim, any human, can commit.

Evident throughout the description of these customs—but of no interest to Thanawi—are clues that the customs in fact form part of a pattern of structured relationships and values that integrate north Indian society. He notes from time to time that a particular custom has a meaning for Hindus, but he never addresses the possibility that it might have meaning for all the inhabitants of this area, Hindu and Muslim both. From his descriptions, we can elicit details of what appear to be three important social institutions: *ne'ota,* the system of delayed reciprocity; *bhat,* the practice of gifts to daughters and sisters; and *jajmani* (although this term is not used), the hierarchic patronage relationships of material, ritual, and service exchange. Shot through all these institutions are concerns for auspiciousness, attempts to control the outcome of an event for the good. All are part of organizing structures of local society in north India, as described by ethnographers throughout this past century.

The practice of delayed reciprocity has been central in defining relationships beyond the immediate household and in providing resources for families in times of ritual or emergency need.[4] As described in the custom of *vartan bhanji,* in the Punjab, those invited to participate in some occasion are expected to bring a cash gift, slightly larger than the one they last received, which then sets up an obligation for the recipient to provide a gift to the giver on some future occasion. Information about and control of these gifts appear to be largely in the hands of women and are a source of prestige and power for them within the family. The appropriate discharge of these obligations determines much of a family's status and its resources in time of need. The term used for an invitation of this sort is *ne'ota,* and it is regarded as a *haqq,* an obligation for the recipient.

Maulana Thanawi has no interest in how this practice functions to create social bonds or to cushion the financial needs caused by those occasions of which he largely disapproves. He suggests that this custom had its origin as *in'am,* spontaneous gifts given out of happiness, but that now these gifts are wholly objectionable. He condemns this custom—as he does virtually all customs—on the grounds that it is illegitimate to require something that once was optional. He identifies the only purpose and intent (*niyat* and *maqsud*) of the practice as pride. He points out that *ne'ota* violates specific *shari'at* rules that prohibit extracting gifts by force and taking illegitimate loans. He insists that gifts on these occasions must be recognized for what they are, namely, loans that are repaid ceremonially instead of by the requisite norms for repayment. According to the *shari'at,* loans must be repaid as soon as possible. But in this case, if a person tried to fulfill her *haqq* on the day following her receipt of a gift, the payment would be refused. Thus the giver, the recipient, and the people of the house are all equally implicated in sin.

Thanawi also condemns customary gifts to daughters and sisters (*dhyani*). On occasions such as a childbirth or circumcision, the maternal side of the family gives gifts, known as *bhat,* which are considered the due of the daughters and sisters. Maulana Thanawi recognizes the place of such gifts in the Hindu system and condemns them, both for being Hindu and for replacing the legitimate *shari'at* system of inheritance.

In the same way, the custom of giving gifts to menials during the course of ceremonies is identified as meaningful to Hindus but simply illegal for Muslims. These gifts were presumably part of patron-client reciprocity (*jajmani*), in which services were rendered in return for periodic gifts from patrons.[5] In speaking of the primacy of gifts to the barber at weddings, Maulana Thanawi writes, "This is the custom of the Hindus. In their usage, the powers of the barber are very great, and therefore he is highly valued. Ignorant Muslims have divested him of these powers but fix wages for him that are usually unjust." Elsewhere, he mocks the custom by conflating it with *ne'ota:* "Why not give? The elders of this Sir Barber gave a 'loan' to the ancestors of this unfortunate party, and now these poor folks are repaying it. Otherwise, their ancestors will be obstructed from entering heaven! *There is no strength or power but in God!*" The barber and his wife dominate the ritual action of the wedding. The seeming contradiction of their low status but privileged role is the kind of confusion Thanawi deplores.

The gifts given to the menials are variously termed *chattis thaniyah, purota, neg, rit,* and *berghari.* Maulana Thanawi identifies this last term, the gift given to the bearer, as a Hindi word; thus it is not only wrong in itself but also a violation of order, because of its origin. He sums up these payments with a proverb: "In a marriage, nothing but an account book of seed," that is, the record of transactions so emphasized on this occasion. These payments violate the legal requirements of both gifts and wages. A gift is an *ihsan,* a kindness, to be given spontaneously and when one has the means. Wages, in contrast, must be fixed in accordance with the specific job and set in advance to avoid their being *ijara-yi fasid,* a corrupt recompense.

All three of these institutions—*ne'ota, bhat,* and *jajmani*—involve gifting relationships. In a recent study of the dominant caste (Hindu Gujar) in the Deoband area, Gloria Raheja argues that, beyond the redistribution entailed in such gifts, the gifts (*dan*) transfer the inauspiciousness often generated in life processes. Thus the husband's sister (*dhyani*) who is given a gift at the breast washing removes danger to the mother; it is her obligation to take this gift. Raheja notes as current among the Gujars many of the exchanges described here, including the gifts of grain and clothes to the midwife, the *chatti* to the husband's sister, grain to menials, and coins circled over the groom's head.[6] The feeding of meat to birds of prey and the offerings made at crossroads are also, as Thanawi points out, attempts to displace inauspiciousness. This concern is evident in the many customs involving married women (*suhagan*), who are particularly auspicious in Hindu thought, and in the practice of sending a wife to her natal home on what are considered inauspicious calendrical observances.

In Thanawi's opinion, all these acts are doubly foolish. First, they jeopardize one's pure dependence on God alone. Second, they don't work. In speaking of the custom of seating a child on the lap of a new bride in order to ensure her fertility by a kind of parallelism, he asks, "But what happens? Even with all this, many women remain childless their whole lives." "Repent," he adds, "repent!"

Maulana Thanawi knows that he is up against the most deepseated and pervasive practices of his community. Commenting on something as fundamental, to him, as the illegitimacy of women's outings, he writes, "It is lamentable that in all Hindustan this rule is nowhere acted upon, and the custom is not even considered improper." Nevertheless, with every argument he can muster, from divine wrath to catching cold from *sharbat* at weddings, he insists that custom must be abandoned. No worldly consideration is to stand in the way. He urges an entire kinship group to act together, but if that is not possible, individuals or families should, as far as they can, act alone, confident that the benefits of doing so will be sufficiently self-evident that one good example will inevitably spread.

As discussed in the general introduction above, these reforms were advanced at the cost of what had been a sphere of activities involving primarily women. In the context of the reformers' lively concern with a correct interpretation of Islam, that sphere had to give way. In British India, many Muslims—men and, increasingly, women too— were stimulated to be concerned with creating religiously informed, highly self-controlled, and responsible individuals. To this end, they inveighed systematically against many customarily sanctioned cere- monies and observances as violations of scripture; as occasions for frivolity, if not licentiousness; as risks to physical well-being; and as distractions toward family involvements that interfered with the cor- rect, all-important relationships to the Prophet and God. The kinds of tensions, the forms of argument, the attention to normative symbols, and the process of change involved in this debate in north India are ones that have been periodically characteristic of Muslim reform across regions and throughout history, nowhere more evident than in the recent past.

Righteous women are devoutly obedient and guard in their husbands' absence what Allah would have them guard.

All praise to God and prayer that the
pamphlet be of profit

Heavenly Ornaments

Book Six

The delightful composition and fascinating compilation
of Janab Maulana Maulawi Hajji
Muhammad Ashraf 'Ali Sahib Thanawi

Published at the direction of the most contemptible
Muhammad 'Abdu'llah Siddiqi

Printed at the Matba'-i Mujtaba'i, Lucknow

Contents of Book Six

In the Name of God, the Merciful, the Compassionate

The Sixth Book
of the *Bihishti Zewar:*
A Discussion of Custom by Category

I. Customs Deemed Sinful But Inconsequential

The first section of this book deals with customs that are recognized as sins even by those who follow them.* People judge these sins to be so minor as to be of no consequence. The section covers many diverse practices, including the use of music and dancing at weddings, setting off fireworks, keeping children's hair long and uncut, keeping images, and owning pet dogs. Each practice is described separately.

ON DANCING AT WEDDINGS

There are two kinds of dancing at weddings. The first is the performance of harlots, called *randi,* which is set up in the men's quarters. The second, arranged for the women, involves vagabond singers, known as *domni*s[1] and *mirasin*s, who dance by displaying and moving their hips and waists. Both kinds of dancing are forbidden and illegitimate.

Everyone knows what sin and evil the dancing of harlots entails. All the men look at unrelated women.[2] That is adultery of the eyes. They hear the sound of the women singing and talking. That is adultery of the ears. They talk with these women. That is adultery of the tongue. If the hearts of the men are drawn to the harlots, that is adultery of the

---

* From *Islahu'r-rusum* (The reform of customs) and other works. [See Book Ten, "The Names of Several Worthwhile Books," item 29.]

93

heart. Those men who are most shameless lay hands on them. That is adultery of the hands. They walk up to them. That is adultery of the feet. Some even engage in fornication. That is actual adultery. The noble *hadis* makes the point very clearly that such seeing with the eyes, hearing with the ears, and walking with the feet are just like committing adultery and fornication. To commit a sin openly is considered even more evil in the *shari'at*. The noble *hadis* says that whenever immodesty and obscenity spread among a people and they begin to misbehave openly, then such plagues and other illnesses as never happened to their ancestors will surely spread among them.

If dancing is this evil, just think how sinful the people must be who arrange for dances or demand dancing from the future in-laws. In fact, the one person who arranges such a gathering accrues as much sin as all that accrues separately to each of those invited to sin. Imagine, for example, that a hundred people come to the gathering. This single person commits the total amount of sin that all of the guests commit individually, added together. The one person who arranges the gathering has the sin of the full hundred. But that is not all. If any guest emulates the host and puts on a similar gathering, the first host will acquire the sin of the later gathering also. Even after death, as long as the chain keeps going, the sin will keep accruing to the first person's record of deeds.

Moreover, the musicians play various instruments such as the *tabla* and *sarangi* with great enthusiasm at these gatherings.[3] That, too, is a sin. Hazrat Apostle of God, *God's blessings and peace upon him,* declared: "My Provider ordered me to destroy these instruments." Now, what kind of sin is it to encourage something that Hazrats himself sought to destroy?

The worldly harm for a woman in all this is that often her husband or bridegroom develops an interest in one of the dancers and withdraws his heart from his wife or bride, causing her to weep her whole life long. The real calamity is that women consider all these arrangements necessary for their reputation and regard failure to observe this custom as a disgrace and the mark of a lackluster wedding. Pride in sin—indeed, judging failure to commit the sin to be a disgrace—destroys faith. Just look at the enormity of this sin!

Many people say that the bride's family will not accept a restriction on music and dance and that they therefore feel compelled to keep the custom. You should ask them, then, if they would be prepared to put on dancing dress and dance themselves! Would they dance in order to ensure the wedding? Aren't they more likely to react with anger and forget all about the bride?

It is the moral duty of a Muslim to hate anything forbidden by the *shari'at* with the same hatred that is directed against something that goes against one's own nature (*tabi'at*). There should be no concern about whether the marriage will take place or not. You should give a clear answer in matters that go against the *shari'at* and refuse a marriage if dancing is required. You should not participate in dancing or even look at it.

Now, as for the dancing arranged for the women, you should consider it equally illegitimate, whether there are drums and other instruments or not. Books forbid the performances of monkeys—isn't it much worse to have people dance? Moreover, the men of the house sometimes catch a glimpse of the dancing, with all the evils described above as the result. Sometimes the dancers sing, and their voices reach the men outside. The men who hear women sing are committing a sin, as are the women responsible for the singing.

Some women put a man's hat on the head of the dancer. It is a sin for a woman to look or act like a man, and equally a sin to make a woman do so. Musical instruments are evil, as just explained above, as is singing. Often, people try to find a young *domni* with a beautiful voice who sings love songs. Unrelated men may well hear her, and, again, it is the women of the house who are to blame. Women's hearts may also be corrupted by her songs. In any case, the women are caught up in the music all night, night after night, and many of them will miss the morning prayer. This is another reason why such music is forbidden. In short, all the dancing and music that goes on today is sin.

ON OWNING PET DOGS AND KEEPING IMAGES

Hazrat Apostle of God[s] declared that the angels of mercy do not enter any house where there are pet dogs or images. The Prophet[s] said that Almighty God's greatest wrath will be for those who make images. He also declared: "The accumulation of merit is diminished each day by a fraction[4] for anyone who keeps a dog for anything other than guarding the cattle, guarding the fields, or hunting."

And it says in another *hadis* that by "fraction" our Lord and Master means an amount equal to Mount Uhud.[5]

These *hadis* make it clear that it is forbidden to make or own images and to keep pet dogs. Avoid both practices completely. The *hadis* make it clear, for example, that girls and women should not make dolls with faces or order them from the bazaar, nor should they order clay or sugar toys for their children, as many do. Stop your children from doing this! Break the toys! Burn the dolls! Likewise, many children keep puppies. Parents should stop them, and, if the children do not obey, the parents should be harsh with them.

ON FIREWORKS

Setting off fireworks and firecrackers on the Shab-i Barat or at a wedding involves many sins. First, it is a waste of money. The Noble Qur'an calls spendthrifts the brothers of Satan. Another verse declares that Almighty God does not love those who waste their wealth; that is, he is disgusted with them. Second, you run the risk of burning yourself or setting your house on fire. To place your life or goods in such danger is in itself an evil in the *shari'at*. Third, fireworks are often made out of paper on which something is written. Any writing deserves respect. It is forbidden to use paper with writing on it for fireworks; the writing may even be verses of the Qur'an or *hadis* or names of the prophets. Now just tell me if it is not an outrage to treat such paper with disrespect! You must never give your children money for such things.

ON CHESS, CARD GAMES, KITES, AND *CHAUSAR*

Chess is strictly forbidden in the *hadis;* cards and *chausar* are like chess and therefore also forbidden.[6] Players' hearts get so absorbed in these games that the players are good for nothing else; they neglect both their worldly concerns and their religious concerns. Surely this is very bad! Kites[7] are exactly the same. In the case of kites, moreover, boys have been killed falling off roofs while chasing kites. You must be firm in never letting your children play such games or giving them money to do so.

ON SHAVING BOYS' HAIR IN THE MIDDLE

It is written in the noble *hadis* that the Apostle of God[s] forbade *qaza'*. The meaning of this word in Arabic is that you should not shave the head in one place and leave hair in another.[8]

II. Customs Considered Legitimate

Most, if not all, of the customs performed from the time of birth to the last dying breath not only are bad but also have spread like wildfire among otherwise rational and perceptive people. People think that there cannot possibly be any sin in men and women gathering to eat, drink, and exchange gifts. If there is no dancing, frivolity, or music, what is there that could possibly be against the *shari'at* and therefore needs to be stopped?

The only explanation for this delusion is that a veil has fallen over people's sense ('*aql*), because these customs have become so common. Sense simply does not penetrate to these wrongs and subtle evils. People are like innocent children who think sweets are good for them because the sweets taste good and are brightly colored. Children see no harm in eating sweets. Parents know the harm and therefore intervene. Children regard those who want the best for them as their enemies!

In fact, the sinfulness of these customs is not so subtle or obscure. People actually find the customs frustrating and would prefer that they not exist. But because they are the custom, everyone observes them willingly. Not a single person has the courage to simply give them all up. On the contrary, if you tell people to refrain, they get upset!

The following sections explain the evils of each custom. When you understand the sinfulness of this nonsense, you can act to make this bane evaporate from Hindustan like camphor. It is required of every Muslim man and woman to take courage in eradicating all these foolish customs and to attempt with heart and soul to see that not one custom remains. May all now be again just as it was in the blessed time of Hazrat, *God's blessings and peace upon him,* when everything was done with utter simplicity and straightforwardness! All good women and men who make an effort to restore this situation will get great reward. The noble *hadis* says that whoever revives the way of the *sunna* after it has disappeared will get the reward of a hundred martyrs. Since all of you are involved in carrying out these customs, if each one of you makes the least effort, *Almighty God willing,* you will very quickly have some effect.

ON THE CUSTOMS CARRIED OUT UPON THE BIRTH OF A CHILD

1. It is considered necessary that whenever possible the first child should be born at the house of the bride's father. Often, in following the rule of sending the expectant mother there near her time, people fail to consider whether the woman is able to travel or not. She may fall ill, or the pregnancy may be harmed. She may be so debilitated that both she and the child end up paying for the journey for a long time. Knowledgeable people say that children's diseases often result from carelessness during pregnancy. This custom harms both mother and child.

In addition, to stringently require what is in fact unnecessary is to make a new *shari'at* on your own, especially when you believe that doing otherwise will be inauspicious or will give you a bad name. Belief in omens is clear polytheism, because only God causes benefit or harm. It is polytheism when something other than God is considered inauspicious or the cause of harm. The noble *hadis* denies that there is such a thing as a bad omen. It also identifies charms and spells as polytheism and attributes fear of ill repute to false pride. The Glorious Qur'an and the noble *hadis* clearly prohibit false pride. Sinful deeds and worry about reputation can become a noose around your neck.

2. Before the birth, women often place some grain and one and one-quarter *paisa*s in a winnowing basket or sieve in the name of the Solver of Difficulties.[9] This is blatant polytheism. It is also customary to fill an expectant mother's lap with seven kinds of dry fruit and nuts placed in a bag. This can take place either early in the pregnancy or later, during the fifth, seventh, or ninth month. The women cook *panjiri* and *gulgula* and stay awake all night.[10] (This custom is not performed for a woman whose first child has died.) It is considered a "requirement," like it or not, and it is taken as an omen—whose evil you have just read about. Women also place a sword or knife near the woman giving birth, to protect her against evil. This is, again, a polytheistic charm.

3. After the birth, women of the household, along with the women of the family (*kunba*), gather something together as a *ne'ota* and give it to the midwife. They do not hand it to her, but instead they place it in a piece of broken pottery. Is it rational to put something in a shard of pottery instead of in someone's hand? Even if the gift is handed over properly and not put in a pot, we might well ask why it is given at all. It is not known when this custom was invented, and we are thus not able to figure out its original rationale. Perhaps the hearts of all the relatives were happy and each gave something as a gift (*in'am*) out of joy. What is certain now, however, is that—joy or not, desire or not—everyone has to give.

Many of the women of the family may be impoverished or indigent. They are sent invitation upon invitation. If they do not come, it is held against them all their lives. If they come, they must arrange to bring an eight-*ana* or a four-*ana* coin. If they do not, they are shamed and disgraced among the women. So they have to go and come back, having been forced to give! What an outrage to invite a person and loot her! Instead of feeling happiness, many feel greatly put upon. You yourself be fair in judging this. How is it legitimate for the recipient or the people of the house to make others give money in this way?

The intention of the giver is simply to secure her own reputation. The noble *hadis* says that whoever is clad in the vestment of pride will be dressed by Almighty God on the Day of Judgment in the garb of opprobrium. This refers to the punishment for wearing clothing solely for the sake of people's opinion, but it is clear from this that it is not legitimate to do anything with such a motive. The specific motive in this case is that those looking on will say, "Such and such a person gave so much." Otherwise, they will taunt her and say that she is such a miser that she will not give even a copper.[11] "She came empty-handed and sat there like a stump. What was the point of her coming?" So much for the sin of the giver.

As for the recipient, the noble *hadis* says that "the property of any Muslim is not legitimate if taken without complete consent." Thus if someone gives under constraint or with aversion, the recipient sins in taking her gift. Even if the giver is a well-to-do, prosperous person and there is no compulsion, her purpose is still to put on airs. The noble *hadis* reports that the Apostle of God[s] forbade accepting the invitation of anyone who offers food out of pride. It is forbidden to eat the food of such a person or, by extension, to accept her gifts. So the recipient herself does not escape from sin. As for the people of the house, those who issue insistent invitations are the cause of sin and are sinners themselves. It is quite an invitation that invites everyone to sin!

This custom of invitation, common in other gatherings as well, presents another serious sin. Whatever is given becomes in effect a loan to the recipient. But to take a loan without necessity is forbidden.* A debt, moreover, must be repaid as soon as possible. Here, on the contrary, it is required to wait for an occasion at the giver's house when the repayment can be presented. If a person wanted to reciprocate immediately, no one would accept the gift. This is also a sin, for a person is obligated to repay loans as soon as the means are available and is not obligated to repay if the means are lacking. In this case, however, whether a person has the means or not, she takes a loan, or pawns something, or frets until she finds some way to get the money she needs. Surely, in all three principles, the *shari'at* has been opposed. The custom of invitation as current today is not legitimate. Take nothing from anyone; give nothing to anyone. Such an approach secures you comfort on the one side and the contentment of God and the Apostle[s] on the other!

* Considering the *ne'ota* a debt is in Shami 6:512, in the edition printed in India with commentary. [This reference presumably cites Makhul al-Shami (d. 112/730), a Syrian scholar of *hadis*.]

To make it an obligation to distribute raw sugar or *batasha* at the time of the first call to prayer spoken into the baby's ear is to step completely outside the boundaries of the *shari'at*.[12]

4. The barber's wife fills her skirt with grain and circulates among the family to give a greeting on the baby's behalf. All the women give her more grain. This custom has all the same motives and intentions described above, and on these grounds this custom also should be abandoned.

5. All those members of the lower orders associated with the house are given their due, which is called *chattis thaniyah*.[13] Among the menials are servants. There is no harm in giving something to them as their due or as a gratuity. It is best, however—no, required—that you give with respect to your means. You should not borrow, let alone feel compelled to take out a loan with interest. You may feel you must sell your land and garden or take a mortgage. If you do any of this, you will indeed be sinful. You would be motivated by a desire to secure your reputation and honor, or you would be taking a loan without need, or you would be paying interest because of false pride. Each of these actions is a sin equivalent to taking interest.

Some of the menials are not servants but rather are wholly useless to you. They render you no service; they are fit for nothing; they are wholly unnecessary. They are present to make more demands than creditors do. Like it or not, you have to pay them. Here are the same evils and sins of giving and taking discussed above; there is no need to repeat it all again. If you give to menials who have no legitimate claims, you do so out of kindness, as a gift. But it is forbidden to be compelled to do a kindness. That, however, is what happens when you have to give, like it or not, out of fear of ill repute. If you keep such a custom, you are encouraging a forbidden practice. To encourage something forbidden, and to make it a custom, is itself forbidden. You must stop these practices completely.

6. The sisters of the family (*dhyani*) are given something called *dudh dhula'i*.[14] Here we are again. You think the payment is required, and you give it, no matter what. Even if you give it willingly, you do it for the sake of your reputation and to gain a flush of pride. All the evils noted above are present. Moreover, because this is a custom of the Hindus, apart from everything else, it is a practice analogous to that of the infidels. Therefore it is not permissible. Consider it a general rule that any custom is forbidden if it has become so obligatory that, willing or unwilling, you are constrained to observe it. Not observing it entails concern for honor and esteem, whereas observing it is for your own

status. A good understanding of this rule makes many other matters clear to you automatically.

7. The dishes *achwani* (a gruel) and *gond panjiri* (a strengthening preparation of gum and *panjiri*) are distributed within the immediate family and among the kinfolk. This, again, involves the faults of concern with fame and honor, of bad intent, and of considering customs more important than the canonical fast and prayer. People are so likely, moreover, to belittle *panjiri* that they had better seek forgiveness! It costs the hosts of the occasion a fair amount, yet no one thinks much of it. How is such a waste of grain legitimate?

8. The barber carries a letter with the news of the birth to the bride's home or to her in-laws. There, he receives a gratuity. It is worth considering the value of sending a special person for a job that can be handled by a simple postcard. Whether there is anything to eat in the house or not, Mr. Barber's "debt," which, God forbid, is greater than the debt owed God, has to be paid. Here are those same twin evils of desire for good reputation and pressure to give. This custom, too, is illegitimate.

9. All the women gather again for the ritual bathing, after forty days (*chilla*). They eat together, and the family members, or extended kin, are sent rice and milk at night. Well, now, why should you cheerfully swallow their high-handedness? Their house is just two steps away, yet they must eat here. Remember the proverb: "Like it or not, I am your guest." On the guests' side is high-handedness; on the household's side are, once again, the same motives of gaining a good reputation and escaping reproaches and taunts. Either reason is sufficient for forbidding the custom. The distribution of rice and milk is also plain foolishness. Why should adults and old folks drink milk with a baby? Once again, the practice is tainted with the poison of giving greater importance and prestige to a custom than to the fast and the prayer— along with encouraging fear for honor and reputation based on carrying out customs. This custom, too, is improper.

10. Throughout these forty days, the new mother completely neglects her prayers. Even the most faithful adherents are careless. The *shari'at* requires the new mother to bathe immediately when her bleeding ceases. If she feels that bathing will be harmful, she can perform the ablution with sand and resume the prayer. To omit the prayer even one time without excuse is a grave sin. The noble *hadis* says that whoever knowingly omits an obligatory prayer has left the faith. It also says that such a person will be in hell, along with Pharaoh, Haman, and Qarun.[15]

11. The *chhuchhak* is prepared for the new mother to bring back from her father's house to the in-laws' house. In keeping with the family's means, it includes outfits for the whole household, *panjiri* for the kinfolk, and items such as jewelry, vessels, and outfits for the new mother. When the bride first comes to the in-laws' house bearing the *chhuchhak,* all the women come to examine it. They do not leave until they have had a meal. How can any of this be legitimate, when the custom is understood as more important than an obligatory duty and is so obviously performed for the sake of name and reputation? How can any custom so filled with pride and display be legitimate? It is often common for the mother's side to send such gifts as *khichari* (mixed pulse and rice), chickens, goats, and clothes, under the name of *chati* (the sixth day). This also entails undue concern with one's reputation, lack of choice, and some concern for auspiciousness. It is also forbidden.

12. The new mother's clothing, bedding, and shoes are all considered the right of the midwife. Often, the mother must endure some hardship because of this requirement: just keep shuffling along in the same old shoes![16] How can she have a comfortable bed when in four days it will be snatched away? This practice exemplifies all the evils described above.

13. To regard the new mother as polluted (*najas, chhut*); to sit apart from her; to consider it unthinkable that she share food (just imagine!); to refuse to drink from the vessel she has touched until it is washed and polished—to think of her, in short, as an untouchable *bhangan*—this is all foolishness and stupidity.

14. It is also common not to let the husband of the newly delivered woman come near her until she is ritually pure or at least until she has been bathed on the sixth day. It is considered inappropriate and very bad if he does so. This rule often causes a great deal of harm and trouble, because the husband cannot even approach his wife and therefore can do nothing, no matter how necessary. Is this rational? Sometimes, something very pressing comes up, the kind of thing he cannot tell anyone else. Even if there is nothing particular, he may just long to see his child. The whole world can see the child, and he cannot! This is nonsense. What a wonderful child has been born that the husband and wife must stay apart! Is there no limit to this irrationality?

15. The child is often put in a winnowing basket or is pulled along in a basket, ostensibly in order to secure a long life. This is also a superstition and completely illegitimate.

16. The mother is often taken out to see the stars on the sixth day. After she is bathed and dressed in fine, expensive clothes, her eyes are covered, and she is brought to the courtyard of the building at night

and made to stand on a platform. The women uncover her eyes, so that her first glance falls on the stars of the heavens and she sees nothing else. These are nonsensical and foolish customs. Is it not irrational to make a normal person blind, to say nothing of the sin of seeking an omen? In many places, they have the new mother count a large number of stars, and then they feed her and seven married women (*suhagan*) from a tray containing every kind of food. They believe that they will thus ensure that no food will ever harm the child. This custom is also forbidden.

17. On the sixth day, the woman's relatives give the husband a suit of clothes. It is wrong to require something so precisely, as described above.

18. It is considered necessary to bathe the new mother three times: on the sixth day, on the "small *chilla*," and on the "large *chilla*." In the *shari'at,* there is the simple rule that the mother should bathe when her bleeding ceases, whether it happens after two or three days or after forty. But now these three baths are considered obligatory. Is this complete opposition to the *shari'at* or not? Many people say that they bathe the woman to make her feel clean and pure and that otherwise she will feel dirty. This statement is completely false. If the motive is cleanliness, she should wash whenever she wishes. Why should you insist on specific times, like the fifth day, the tenth day, or the fifteenth? What can be the point of this? It is nothing but a custom, with no justification at all. The truth is that the woman does *not* bathe when she wishes and *does* bathe when required, even if she and the baby are harmed. To top it all off, worst of all, when the bleeding does stop, she does not bathe until the right time comes. Now tell me, is this clearly sin or not?

At a boy's birth, it is *sunna* to bathe him, to have the call to prayer said in his right ear and "*allahu akbar*" in his left, and to have a pious elder chew some date, of which a little bit is applied to the baby's palate. All else is false custom, including the provision of sweets for the person who calls the prayer, if providing them is regarded as an obligation. The customs are foolish, devoid of sense, and forbidden.

ON THE CUSTOMS OF SHAVING THE BABY'S HEAD

It is worthy of reward to sacrifice one goat for a girl and two for a boy; to distribute the goat's meat, either raw or cooked; to distribute silver equal in weight to the baby's hair as charity; and to apply saffron to the baby's head after it is shaved. Beyond this, the foolishness that has been devised for this occasion (*'aqiqa*) must be seen.

1. The kinfolk and the immediate family gather on this occasion and place gifts of money in a cup or, often, in a winnowing basket containing some grain. This money is considered the right of the barber. The money is understood to be a loan to the master of the house, to be repaid when the donors in turn have some similar occasion. You have learned the error of this above.

2. The sisters and others also take their "due," which, if you want the truth, is not their due at all. This custom resembles the practices of the unbelievers. It is wrong for other reasons as well, the most obvious being the motive for giving. Many people clearly lack the means to give and find giving a burden. They give nonetheless, because otherwise they would be put to shame. People would slander them. They are constrained to give. This is affectation and false pride, and it is forbidden to spend wealth in such a way. Just think about the implications of putting someone under an obligation that becomes such a burden. The recipient sins, because a gift should be given only as a kindness; to use high-handedness to secure a kindness is forbidden—and this custom is certainly high-handed. If a person does not give, she will be slandered, disgraced, and made infamous throughout the whole family. Even if someone gives freely, her motive for doing so surely is her own good reputation. The Qur'an and *hadis* clearly prohibit this.

3. There is also the vice of distributing *panjiri,* a practice contrary to sense, as discussed above, and one meant to secure a good reputation, a motive that is forbidden.

4. Among the adverse effects of adhering to these customs is that the ceremony may be delayed because people lack sufficient resources. It is then performed contrary to what is legally desirable. In some places, it is held only after several years.

5. Some people sacrifice the goat at the very moment the razor is placed on the baby's head. This is sheer nonsense. In the *shari'at,* it is correct to sacrifice either some time before shaving the head or immediately after shaving, as long as both acts are done on the same day.

6. To consider it necessary to give the head of the goat to the barber and the thigh to the midwife is also nonsense. It makes no difference what part you give. What is the profit of fabricating a self-devised *shari'at* of your own? What harm is there in giving some meat other than the leg?

7. Many people consider it evil to break the bones of the sacrificed animal. They also consider it necessary to bury the remains of the animal. This attitude is simply without foundation. It is just as wrong as the customs observed when the child's teeth fall out and *ghunghni* is distributed among the family. To omit this is considered more of a fault

and an evil than the omission of an obligatory duty. Similarly, the custom of feeding *khir* (rice pudding) to a six-month-old child, who from that day begins eating solid food, is regarded as necessary, like it or not. You have learned the evil of such customs above. Another common custom is that when nursing stops, women gather to offer congratulations. Like it or not, you have to entertain them and distribute dates among the kinfolk. This kind of gathering is just as wrong as it always is. In many places, there is one more custom, even worse than all the others. The women fill a virgin jug with water and place in it an uneven number of dates. They have the child reach in and pick out dates, and they claim that the child will insist on nursing for the same number of days as the number of dates picked out. This is both an omen and a claim to knowledge of the unknown. Its sin is evident.

Women consider it necessary to gather for the customary annual celebration of the birth. Like it or not, you must cook food and tie a ring on a special cord.

They also gather for the "flash of the spear," when down starts to grow on a boy's face. They apply ground sandalwood paste to the mustache with a silver rupee and *siwaiyan* (thin noodles), so that the mustache will grow long like *siwaiyan*.[17] All these are charms, whose evil you already know.

ON THE CUSTOMS OF CIRCUMCISION

People have also devised foolish customs for this occasion (*khatna*) that are absurd and irrational.

1. It is altogether against the *sunna* to send a man around with a letter to invite people to assemble for this occasion. Someone invited a Companion of Hazrat Apostle of God[s] to a circumcision, and he refused to go. When people asked why, he answered that in the time of Hazrat Apostle of God[s] they had neither gone to circumcisions nor invited people to them. This *hadis* makes clear that it is against the *sunna* to gather people for anything that does not require being made public. There have come to be many such customs that require considerable preparations.

2. These customs often cause so much delay that the boy matures before the circumcision takes place. Hence, besides the delay, there is the additional objection that everyone sees his body (even though it is forbidden for anyone except the circumcisor to see it). This sin is a result of the custom of summoning people by invitation.

3. We have already mentioned the harm caused by the disgraceful custom of setting out a cup into which the invited guests put money.

4. The maternal side gives cash and clothes. This, in common parlance, is called *bhat*. The real point of this gift has to do with the fact that when a Hindu father dies in Hindustan, the daughters receive no share at all from his wealth. Ignorant Muslims have imitated the Hindus, or, if you wish, they did not imitate them but invented the practice themselves. Either way, it is wrong. How is it legitimate to deny—indeed, to suppress—the right of any claimant as established by God and his Apostle[s]? Because the family has deprived the girl of her inheritance, they give her some gifts as compensation to satisfy her on different occasions and festivals. Thus everyone convinces themselves that she has no claim on anyone. In elaborating this custom, there is either imitation of the unbelievers or oppression. Both these sins are forbidden.

The third sin is that same unbounded compulsion in which the maternal relatives, whether they have the means or not, must make a thousand exertions, take loans on interest, or pledge some belonging to get the necessary cash. On a pledge, nowadays, one may pay interest with cash or not pay interest at all; but in the latter case, the crop of the mortgaged land is taken by the creditor. That in fact is interest; and to take or give interest is, of course, forbidden. Yet, whatever happens, all the preparations must be made. You judge yourself whether it transgresses the *shari'at* to prepare for an unnecessary, indeed a sinful, matter with a more wholehearted commitment than is likely for any obligatory religious duty!

The fourth sin is the desire for status and the display of pride, whose prohibition was discussed above. Many say that to treat their relatives well is an act of obedience and merit that cannot possibly be sinful. But if their only concern were good and kind treatment of their relatives, they would have given gifts, quite apart from all these fixed restrictions, whenever they had the means and their relatives had the need. In fact, relatives may be starving, and no one even asks about them. Only on these customary occasions, for the sake of reputation and honor, do they speak of good treatment and kindness.

5. In many cities, there is the curse of lively music, dancing, and merriment, either on the day of the circumcision or on the day of the bath to mark the recovery. In some places, singers perform. I have described the illegitimacy of this custom above and, *God willing,* will continue the description of its evils and ills below. You should abandon all these sins and absurdities. When the child has sufficient strength to endure the circumcision, just summon the barber quietly and have it performed. When the child is well, have him bathed. If you have the means and are not making it obligatory every time or acting with desire for recognition or fear of reproach, then offer food to a few good

friends or poor people who are nearby, asking God to grant the boy health and well-being. Do not do this at every circumcision, for fear it may become a custom.

ON THE CUSTOMS OF THE *BI'SMI'LLAH* UPON BEGINNING SCHOOL

Among these illegitimate customs is that of the *bi'smi'llah,* which people carry out with elaborate preparations and a high sense of obligation. It has the following errors:

1. First, people have, on their own, fixed the event to occur when the child is at the age of four years, four months, and four days. This precision is simply unfounded and nonsensical. People consider this scheduling so necessary that they disallow variation, no matter what. Illiterate people consider this a matter of the *shari'at;* they thus disturb belief and distort the rule of the *shari'at.*

2. The second error is the fixed requirement of distributing sweets. You must provide sweets, no matter what you have to do to get them. Anyone who does not is disgraced and despised. This has been discussed above. The custom, moreover, is intended to win recognition and gain public congratulations.[18]

3. Many well-to-do people have the child taught reading from a silver slate with a silver pen and inkstand. To own and make use of silver objects is forbidden. To have something written with them, and then to have it read out, is also forbidden.

4. Many people dress children on this occasion in clothes that are forbidden by the *shari'at*—in silk or embroidered clothes or in clothes dyed red with safflower or saffron. This is a sin.

5. People believe that menials and girls of the family (*dhyaniyan*)* are owed a due more pressing than any act of religious obligation. The evil of this attitude has been discussed above. This custom should be stopped.

Teach children the *kalima,* the attestation of faith, as soon as they begin to talk. Then take them into the presence of some pious elder and have the *bi'smi'llah* said. In gratitude for this blessing, if your heart wishes, you may give some charity, but do it secretly, without any feeling of compulsion, only as your means permit, and from a desire to do some good. Never give charity with any kind of display. All the rest is hypocrisy. People of the house often teach a prattling child to say, "*Abba,*" "*Amman,*" "*Baba,*" and so forth. How much better if, instead, you teach the child to say, "Allah, Allah"!

---

* Sisters and so forth.

Ceremonies held upon the completion of the child's study of the Glorious Qur'an are similar. Again, people set unnecessary requirements, such as inviting guests and distributing outfits of clothing, done only to achieve recognition. The evils of this have been discussed above.

ON WOMEN GATHERING FOR CELEBRATIONS

The women of a family gather for many celebrations, including those described above as well as many others. All described here are illegitimate.*

Celebrations aside, whenever women have a whim, they just think, "I have not seen so and so for ages!" Someone gets sick, and off they go to see her. They may hear of some occasion of celebration, and off they go to offer congratulations. Some women are so free that they set out at night without even summoning a palanquin! Worse yet, as soon as night falls, they think of travel! To go out on a moonlit night is even more shameless. The point is that it is wrong for women to leave their homes and go about here and there.

At most, it is permissible for them to visit their parents or other close relatives, and then only once or twice a year. Beyond that, to go out imprudently, as is the custom, is simply illegitimate, whether it is to the home of relatives or someone else and whether the occasion be a wedding or a condolence, visiting the sick, offering congratulations, or joining the wedding procession from the bridegroom's house. It is not proper to go out for a wedding at all, even if it is at the home of close relatives. A husband who gives permission is guilty, and so is the wife. It is lamentable that in all Hindustan this rule is nowhere acted upon, and the custom is not even considered improper. Indeed, it is regarded as legitimate, although it is the source of so many sins. Now that you know the practice to be wrong, you must wholly repent. This is the injunction of the *shari'at*. Here follows a list of the evils of going out.

When the news spreads among the kinfolk that such and such a ceremony is set in such and such a house, every wife starts thinking about a costly new outfit. Sometimes she asks for money from her husband; sometimes she just summons a cloth merchant on her own and shops on credit or takes a loan with interest. She refuses to accept her husband's objections if he says he does not have the means. The

---

* This point is clearly discussed in the compendium of Shami in the chapter on expenditure (*nafaqa*), p. 665, and in the chapter on *mahr*, p. 320, of the edition printed in India.

outfit is obviously made just for showing off. In the *hadis* it is written that a person who dresses to show off will be dressed on the Day of Judgment in garments of ignominy. Thus a woman commits one sin.

To spend money with this motive of showing off is to waste it. The evil of such waste has already been discussed in the section above. This is a second sin.

To make demands on a husband beyond his means, without necessity, is to cause him vexation. This is a third sin.

To summon the cloth seller and to converse unnecessarily with a strange man to whom you expose half your arm, decorated with bangles and henna, as you handle the cloth—all this is to violate a proper sense of modesty. This is a fourth sin.

To take a loan on interest is to pay interest. This is a fifth sin.

To make inappropriate demands on a husband may lead his good resolve astray. He may be tempted to deprive someone else of rights or to take a bribe so that he can fulfill demands that cannot be met by legitimate means. This sin takes place because of the wife. To be the cause of this is the sixth sin.

Often, a woman purchases gold and silver edging or fillets of brocade for her outfits. Out of ignorance or carelessness, she may pay interest on the purchase, because she does not understand the complexity of buying silver and gold and things made out of them. (This has been discussed in the previous book on buying and selling.)* This is the seventh sin.

Women do not regard an outfit made for one wedding as adequate for another wedding. A woman needs a new outfit for each occasion, for fear that the other women may taunt her for having only one outfit and arriving in the same dress. Thus all the sins are repeated again. To keep on committing a sin is a sin. This is the eighth sin. So much for preparing the clothes.

Now, thoughts turn to jewelry. If a woman has none, she wheedles a loan of someone else's jewelry and displays it as her own. This is a form of lying and deception. The noble *hadis* says that those who falsely display something as their own are like a person who wears two garments, one of lies and one of deceit. From head to foot, that person is wrapped in lies. This is the ninth sin.

The jewelry may jingle so much that everyone's eyes are riveted on it as the wearer enters. The noble *hadis* forbids jingling jewelry, because Satan is present in every sound. This is the tenth sin.

* There is a very clear description in *Safa'i-yi mu'amalat* (Purity in transactions). [See Book Ten, "The Names of Several Worthwhile Books," item 14.]

Now comes the matter of conveyance. Either the woman orders her servant to fetch a palanquin, or a palanquin is sent from the house where the gathering is to be held. Then the lady suddenly thinks of bathing. There is some delay in preparing water and *khali* (a cake of mustard seed oil for washing hair). Then there is further delay in "forming the resolve" to bathe.[19] In all this delay, she fails to say her prayers. No matter! Or she disrupts something else important. No problem! In fact, such disruption occurs daily upon the occasion of the bath of these grand ladies (*bhalamanus*). If the prayer is missed or read at a disapproved time, that is the eleventh sin.

The bearers of the palanquin, the *kahar,* are summoning the lady at the door, and from within the woman is shouting curses in return. To dismiss someone or to curse them without cause is tyranny and sin. This is the twelfth sin.

Now, with great difficulty, and muttering, "God, God," the lady is ready. She has the bearer move away and seats herself. Many ladies are so careless that they let their hem hang out of the palanquin, or leave the curtain open on one side, or reek so much of perfume that its sweet smell hangs about them on the road. That is to display beauty before strangers. The noble *hadis* says that any woman who goes out of her house wearing perfume in such a way that its odor reaches others is very bad. This is the thirteenth sin.

Now she arrives at her "intended destination."[20] The bearers put down the palanquin and move aside. She descends without hesitation and enters the house, not even thinking whether some strange man might be in the house. Frequently on these occasions she will encounter a stranger, and their eyes will meet. Women lack the common sense to first make inquiry. Not to inquire when there is a strong likelihood of possible sin is the fourteenth sin.

Now she has arrived at the house. She greets the women of the house. Fine, for many do not even take the trouble to speak but simply place their hand to their forehead in greeting. The *hadis* says that this style of greeting is forbidden. Some say the word "*salam,*" simply "*salam.*" That too is against the *sunna.* One should say, "*As-salamu 'alaikum*" (***"Peace be upon you"***). Now just look at the responses:

"Keep cool!"[21]
"May you live long!"
"Remain a beloved wife (*suhagan*)!"
"Long life!"
"May you bathe in milk and enjoy grandsons!"
"May your brother live long!"
"May your husband live long!"

"May your children live long!"

It is easy to count off the names of the whole family but difficult to say *"As-salamu 'alaikum,"* which in fact subsumes all the other prayers. Always to oppose the *shari'at* is the fifteenth sin.

Now the "congregation" has gathered, and everyone settles down to gossip, complaining of this one, engaging in backbiting about that one, slandering the other, reproaching someone else. All this is completely forbidden and prohibited. This is the sixteenth sin.

In the midst of the conversation, each lady strives mightily to make sure that her dress and her jewelry are seen by all. She exhibits them with her hands, her feet, her tongue—in short, with her whole body. This is blatant pretension, which is very clearly prohibited in the Qur'an and the *hadis*. This is the seventeenth sin.

Just as every lady is showing off her paraphernalia of pride to the others, she is in the same way trying to see everyone else's. If she finds another to be inferior to herself, she judges the other woman contemptible and herself exalted. Many so swell with pride that they refuse to speak with their inferiors. Such clear pride is another sin. This is the eighteenth sin.

If the lady sees a woman superior to herself, she becomes envious, ungrateful, and greedy. These are the nineteenth, twentieth, and twenty-first sins.

Often, in this storm of worthless preoccupations, a woman lets her prayers fly by or, at best, offers them late. This is the twenty-second sin.

Often, women pass on these worthless practices to others who see and hear them. This is the twenty-third sin.

It is also common on such occasions for women not to bother going into a closed room to keep secluded from the boy who brings the water. They simply tell him to cover his face and avoid looking at anyone. What of his faith and religion? No one shows any sense of shame or modesty if he happens to look at them out of the corner of his eye. He does, of course, because he can see everything through the cloth he puts over his head. Otherwise, how could he go directly to fill the earthen jugs and pots with water? Deliberately to remain seated in a place where strange men can see you is forbidden. That is the twenty-fourth sin.

The grown sons of many ladies, boys of ten or twelve years of age, wander about indoors. Out of civility, nothing is said to them, and everyone passes before them. That is the twenty-fifth sin, because to act civilly toward someone in contravention of the *shari'at* is a sin. A woman is to keep secluded from a boy as soon as he becomes mature.

Now the time has come to eat. A real tempest arises because each woman has brought with her four or so hangers-on. She feeds them well, taking no account at all of the means and honor of the people of the house. This is the twenty-sixth sin.

Now, after finishing, when it is time to go home, they all hear the sound of the palanquin bearers and run to the door like Yajuj and Majuj,[22] one on top of the other. All are crushed at the door, trying to be the first to get a ride. Often, the bearers themselves are trapped and meet the women face to face. This is the twenty-seventh sin.

Sometimes, two ladies are loaded into one palanquin and the bearers are not told, so that the women will not have to pay one *paisa* more. This is the twenty-eighth sin.

Then someone loses some possession. On no grounds at all, she accuses someone else of taking it and may even grow harsh. This often happens at weddings. This is the twenty-ninth sin.

Often, the men of the house giving the ceremony stand at the door facing in toward the house and glance in at the women, either because they are careless or because they are in a hurry—and often deliberately to peek. Seeing them there, one woman will turn her face; another will stand behind someone else; a third will lower her head a little. So this is seclusion, to continue sitting happily in view! This is the thirtieth sin.

The women consider it a "duty" and a "source of blessing" to see the spectacle of the groom's procession and to attend the bridegroom. It is just as illegitimate for a woman to display her body to an unknown man as it is for her, with no real need, to look at him. This is the thirty-first sin.

Finally, after returning home, for days the woman continues to tear to pieces and find fault with the women who came and those who put on the ceremony. This is the thirty-second sin.

There are even more faults and sins in women's gatherings. How can something be legitimate that entails such innumerable ills? To abandon these customary gatherings is absolutely necessary.

ON THE CUSTOMS OF THE ENGAGEMENT

The customs observed for an engagement (*mangni*) entail a veritable storm of indiscretion. Some of the customs are listed below.

1. When the engagement is arranged, the barber arrives with a letter and is fed *shakarana,* a dish made of sugar, rice, and ghee, made by the bride's family. This custom reflects the excessive compulsion noted above. If an obligatory duty is put off, fine—but this custom must not be put off. There may be nothing in the house except beans

and bread, but somehow you must make this dish, for fear there will be no engagement. ***There is no strength or power but in God!*** This is the first error. If you do not have the ingredients on hand, you must take a loan, although unnecessary loans are forbidden. The *hadis* gives strict warning against taking loans like this. This is another sin.

2. When the barber finishes eating, he puts a hundred rupees, or whatever the girl's family gave him, onto his tray. Someone from the boy's side removes one or two rupees, returns the rest, and divides the one or two rupees among the menials. Well, here is something to think about. Everyone understands that only one or two rupees will be exchanged, so why bring a hundred? Most people have to take a loan with interest to carry out this custom. This of course is condemned in the *hadis*. That aside, the only possible motive for this is pride. If, however, everyone knows that no more than one or two rupees are at stake, there can hardly be glory or status in taking along a hundred or even a thousand rupees. It would be a matter of status only if the onlookers believed that all the money would be handed over. As it is, this is nothing but a childish joke. People do it out of pride. Even the most intelligent people, those who teach reason to others, are caught up in this unreasonable custom! The heart of this custom is a sin, namely, pretension. Pretension aside, the deed itself, as we have just explained, is worthless frivolity and hence wholly wrong. The noble *hadis* says that the value of a person's Islam lies in forsaking meaningless things: absurdities and frivolities are therefore against the will of the Prophet[s]. Interest may also be involved, and the sinfulness of that is well known. This custom involves many sins.

3. The girl's family gives the barber some clothes, along with more cash. He then repeats the comedy, displaying a hundred rupees but giving only one or two. Custom is indeed a strange thing, for however irrational it may be, even the rational are not ashamed to observe it. The evils of all this have already been described.

4. Before the departure of the barber, all the women gather and the singers perform. A description of the evils of women's gatherings has been given above; a description will be given below of the ills of singing during the ceremonies of marriage (*byah*). In brief, it is not legitimate.

5. When the barber arrives at the groom's house, he sends the groom's outfit of clothing, along with the money, into the house. After the outfit is displayed from house to house among the kinfolk, it is returned to the barber. Just judge for yourself whether the intent can be proper when cheers attend the display of every item. Surely the intent at the time of making the outfit is to avoid criticism. This prac-

tice encourages pretension and frivolous expense, which are clearly prohibited in the Qur'an and the *hadis*. The pity of it is that often, despite all this preparation, the onlookers dismiss the outfit, like those who disdained the bird who gave up its life for the meal! Typically, the most arrogant will pick faults and deprecate the outfit the most. Pretension, worthless expense, backbiting—all this, thanks to this custom.

6. The bride's family then sends sweets, a ring, a handkerchief, and an amount of money called *nishani* (a mark [of approval]). They collect money by means of *ne'ota*. This again involves the ills of pretension and frivolous expense. The specific ills of *ne'ota* have already been discussed.

7. The barber and the palanquin bearers who bring the sweets are dismissed after the barber is given an outfit of clothes for himself and the bearers receive some turbans and cash. The leading elderly ladies of the family distribute the sweets from house to house among the kinfolk and then eat at the bride's house.

Everyone knows that the palanquin bearers are not told in advance what wages they will receive, nor is any consideration given as to whether they go willingly or under pressure. No matter if they ask to be excused because of some business or because they are sick or their wives or children are sick. Those who send for them give them a good beating with a shoe if they have the strength, or else they order someone more powerful to do it for them. They extract the work from the palanquin bearers on this occasion—indeed, most of the time—by force. This is nothing but tyranny and sin. Tyranny is often punished in this world, and it is judged a sin in the afterlife, too. Not to fix wages is also illegitimate. This sin is the direct fruit of sending these gifts.

Who does not know what affectation is involved in giving out sweets? Moreover, the women get so preoccupied that they let their prayers fly by or, at best, offer them in a rush. This is against the *shari'at*. People at each urging are expected to refuse the sweets or to take only one at a time. Whatever they do, they are encouraging and sanctioning a pretentious custom.

This custom conflicts with the *shari'at*. It is best to give it up completely. A simple postcard or a conversation can propose a wedding. The second party can make inquiries as necessary and send back a postcard or simply a verbal assurance. Thus the engagement is settled. No matter if people claim that the customs are necessary to confirm the contract. In the first place, expedience does not justify a sin. Moreover, we see that in spite of all this foolishness, if one side does not wish to go through with the marriage, no one can do anything anyway.

8. The following customs are often observed at the time of the

betrothal. The boy's guardian is summoned to place items such as a coconut, dried fruit, *pera* (a sweet made of curd), and *batasha* in the lap of the bride and to put a rupee in her hand. The girl's family, in exchange for this, gives money to the extent of their means. This entails many faults. First, to call a strange man into the house for this purpose is wrong, even if he stands behind a screen. Second, the custom represents the kind of act involving auspiciousness that is not legitimate according to the *shari'at*. Third, the onlookers determine whether the coconut is good or rotten, and in this they find an augury that the girl's fortune will be good or bad. The polytheism of this kind of reprehensible practice has already been discussed. Fourth, the custom involves compulsion and concern with pride, whose evils also have been discussed before. In short, there is no custom of this sort that is free of sin.

ON THE CUSTOMS OF MARRIAGE

The biggest occasion upon which one opens up one's heart, spends lavishly, and performs countless ceremonies is marriage, which should not be called "bliss" (*shadi*) but "ravage" (*barbadi*)! And what ravage and ruin, of religion and of worldly matters both! The customs observed during the marriage are as follows:

1. The very first is that the men of the bride's family gather to write a letter fixing the date of the wedding. They give it to the barber and send him off. They consider this custom so essential that the barber must go even if it is the rainy season, even if there are rivers and streams on the way in which one fears he may *really* be sent off! They simply are not satisfied with a letter in the post or with someone more trustworthy who may be going that way. They must send the letter by the barber's hand. To consider a matter so necessary when it is not considered necessary in the *shari'at*—indeed, to consider arranging it as more necessary than something that is legally required—judge that yourself. Isn't that making it equal to the *shari'at,* and, if that is the case, shouldn't one give it up?

The requirement of assembling the men is also wrong. It is false to say that they gather for consultation. The poor fellows ask themselves what date they should write, knowing that it has been set during the real consultation within the house. Consultation should be sought as it normally is, by asking a few sensible people for advice. Why is it necessary to summon people from different houses? People who cannot come may send their young sons instead. Well, what arrow can *they* shoot in this consultation? None at all. These are just rationalizations (*man-samjhautiyah*). Why not admit that this is just a custom? The error and the need to abandon such a custom have been discussed. All elements of this custom are against the *shari'at*. Custom also requires the letter to be in red and edged with trimmings. This aspect involves that excessive compulsion whose evil and whose illegitimacy have been described so many times above.

2. Meanwhile, inside the house, the women of the family gather and confine the girl in a corner. This is called "sitting the girl on a *manjha* or a *ma'iyun*."[23] Etiquette calls for the girl to be seated on a low platform, for ointment (*butna*) to be placed on her right hand, and for her lap to be filled with puffed rice and *batasha*. Rice and sweets are also distributed among those present. From that day on, the women continually rub the girl with ointments. They distribute fried sweet flour balls (*pindiyan*) among the kinfolk. This custom involves much foolishness. The first objection is to the requirement of seating the girl alone. Whether it is hot, whether it is stuffy, whether all the doctors and physicians of the world say that she will get sick—whatever—this obligation must not be missed. This entails the evil of strict adherence to set customs. If there is apprehension about her getting sick, then there is the further sin of causing harm to a Muslim, a sin in which, *as God wills,* all the kinfolk are implicated.

Second, what need is there to seat her on a low platform? Will she not be just as clean if the ointment is applied while she sits on the floor? The illegitimacy of such unnecessary requirements has now been pointed out. Third, placing the ointment on her right hand and filling her lap with puffed rice and sweetmeats seem to be some kind of omens or superstitious acts. If this is so, it is polytheism. What Muslim does not know that that is opposed to the *shari'at*? And there is compulsion. The requirement of distributing puffed rice and *batasha* is all evident and unnecessary constraint, affectation, and false pride. Fourth, there is the gathering of women, the root of all those excesses that have been described above. In many places, there is also the rule that seven married women gather to place the ointment on the bride's hand. You have already heard such superstition described as polytheism. There is no objection if the ointment is rubbed on the girl's body out of concern for cleanliness and softness. But then you should simply rub it on in an ordinary way, without being held to a particular custom, and be done with it. Why stretch it out like this?

Many women give reasons for siding with this custom. Some say that when the girl goes to her in-laws, she will have to sit in one place with her head bowed for several days; thus they "sit her on a *manjha*" to let her get used to it, so that she will not be overly troubled there. And many ladies declare that because rubbing on the ointment makes the body clean and fragrant, there is a risk of harm if the girl goes about.[24] These are all thoughts of the devil and rationalizations. If applying the ointment is the only concern, then why do the women gather, putting the ointment in her hand, filling up her lap, and all the other nonsense? The goal of cleanliness does not need all this confusion.

It is also wrong for her to act like a corpse before her in-laws; this will be discussed below. Thus anything done to encourage and sustain such behavior is illegitimate. Even if this were not the case, I still maintain that although a person bears whatever befalls her, you should just think about what you are doing. Up until now, the girl has wandered all over the whole house. How can she suddenly just sit in one corner? To be sure, she will sit quietly for a day or two when she goes to her in-laws and will have a couple of days of discomfort there. But here she is made to endure ten or twelve days of imprisonment! Finally, even if she is not permitted to go out for fear of misfortune, at least let her come into the courtyard or go onto the roof! *Why* put her in a corner where she suffocates and from which she cannot stir even to get food and water? These are all self-devised absurdities.

3. When the barber takes the letter fixing the date of the wedding and goes to the house of the groom, the women of the family gather and prepare two trays of *shakarana,* one for the barber and the other for the female singers. The barber's tray is sent outside, and all the men gather to offer the *shakarana* to the barber, watching him while he eats. The singers meanwhile sit at the door and sing obscenities. First, it is a sin to make all this a requirement. Second, it is a sin to give wages to the women at all, let alone to reward them for singing obscenities— itself a sin. The noble *hadis* declares such singing the mark of a hypocrite. This is the third sin, in which all those who hear are implicated, because whoever participates in a sinful gathering is also a sinner. Fourth, it is a sin to consider the men's gathering necessary, for in fact it is not. Nor is it clear why so many elders have to help the barber in eating the *shakarana*! The fifth sin is the gathering of the women; you already know the sinfulness of this.

4. After the barber from the bride's family eats the *shakarana,* he places one or two rupees on the tray, as his master has instructed him, and these are divided half and half between the bridegroom's barber and the singing women. The singing women take the second tray of *shakarana* off to their house intact. Then another batch of *shakarana* is made for the women and is distributed among them. This too entails affectation, pride, and unnecessary compulsion. It is therefore completely against the *shari'at.*

5. In the morning, the men gather to write the answer to the letter. They give the barber from the bride's side a very fine and costly outfit, along with a large sum of money, one or two hundred rupees. Here again transpires the same absurd pretense that took place before: they put out a hundred rupees, of which he takes only one or two. Not only is this affectation and foolishness, but it is also an occasion for taking loans on interest. This is a separate sin, which has been thoroughly described above.

6. The barber then returns to the home of the bride, where the women have already gathered. The barber gives them his outfit to be displayed in the house and among the kinfolk. This obviously involves the evils of the women's gathering, of ostentation, and of pride in displaying an outfit.

7. From this day until the date of the wedding, the bridegroom is also rubbed with ointment. The women of the families gather at the groom's house to prepare the *bari* (gifts of clothing and so forth) and at the bride's house to prepare the *jahez* (dowry). In the midst of this, any guest who comes from the other family's house, whether invited or not, has his or her fare paid. This encourages the gathering of women and provides another instance of unnecessary compulsion. To pay for travel, whether one wishes to or not, is the crowning blow and is done simply for the sake of ostentation and glory. It is a kind of compulsion forced on those who have come to think it obligatory. Such ostentation and compulsion are obviously against the *shari'at*.

An even worse story is that of the bridegroom's gifts and the bride's dowry, which are great and weighty pillars of the festivities. Both are legitimate in origin and were once even laudable. The groom's gifts (*bari* or *sachaq*) are essentially gifts from the groom (or the groom's family) to the bride (or the bride's family); and the dowry essentially reflects kindness and good treatment toward one's offspring. As custom has developed, however, both have degenerated to the point that their intent is neither to give a gift nor to do a kindness. They are meant to secure a good reputation and to demonstrate obedience to custom. This is why both the bridegroom's gifts and the bride's dowry are announced with display and proclamation. The groom's gifts are sent with great fanfare and ceremony, and the various items are in fact specified so that certain kinds of utensils, for example, are considered necessary. They are openly displayed in a fixed place. A true gift would be sent simply out of love, in an ordinary way, whenever and whatever, without any concern for custom or publicity. The items of the dowry are also fixed so that certain items are required. All the kinfolk—although in some places only the family and household—are expected to see the dowry. The day for such visiting is fixed. If an ordinary gift, inspired by generosity and kindness, had been intended, it would have been given as available. No one would have taken on the burden of a loan to pay for it. To carry out these two customs, however, people often become debtors, even if they have to pay interest or even sell or mortgage their property. The custom thus involves all the familiar sins of unnecessary compulsion, display, desire for fame, and foolish expenditure. On these grounds, it is illegitimate.

8. One day before the arrival of the groom's party (*barat*), the groom's barber, bringing henna, and the barber of the bride's family, bringing a suit of clothes for the groom (*naushah*), set out from their respective places. This is called the day of the nuptial canopy (*mandha*). The women of the groom's family gather at his house and prepare the bride's outfit. They are given puffed rice and *batasha* as wages for sewing. All the menials are given their presents of food (*purota*) for each job. Here again is an occasion that is unnecessarily required and that encourages the gathering of women, from which evils flow.

9. The bride's family gives some gratuity to the barber when he arrives with the outfit. Then the barber's wife takes the outfit to display it from house to house among the kinfolk. That night, the women gather and dine. Obviously, the intent behind displaying the outfit is nothing other than ostentation; and you have already learned the "blessings"[25] of gatherings like this. On this occasion, again, there is a fine assembly of sins.

10. Early in the morning, the groom is bathed and dressed in a splendid outfit. His old outfit, along with the shoes, is given to the barber, and the "right of the *sihra*" (the bridal veil of strands of flowers) is distributed to the menials. The outfit often includes items of clothing that are opposed in the *shari'at*. And since the custom of the *sihra* belongs to the infidels, it is without doubt a sin to give its name to this "right"; it imitates a custom of the infidels. This, too, is against the *shari'at*.

11. The bridegroom is now summoned to enter the house and is made to stand on a platform. The sisters tie on the *sihra* and claim their due. The women of the family pass some coins around the groom's head and give them to the menials. No precautions at all are taken when the groom comes into the house. Even women who observe seclusion most strictly are all decked out. They stand right in front of the groom, under the impression that on this occasion he is too embarrassed to look at anyone. Well, is this outrageous or not? In the first place, why do they think he will not look? Boys have different personalities, and nowadays many are mischievous. *He* may not look, so why

are *you* looking at him? It is in the *hadis* that God curses both the person who looks and the person who is looked at! In short, the bridegroom and the women are all involved in sin. Placing the *sihra* on the groom's head is another custom contrary to the *shari'at,* because it is a custom borrowed from the infidels. The noble *hadis* says that whoever imitates any people is in fact one of them. As for the quarreling and struggling to claim one's so-called due, it is forbidden to force anyone to give you something. Beyond that, to take something from someone in return for a sin is to add insult to injury. Passing coins over the groom's head is a charm, which the authentic *hadis* says is polytheism. All this is from head to foot a collection of practices opposed to the *shari'at.*

12. Now the groom's party sets out. This procession is also considered a great pillar of the wedding festivities. Sometimes the groom's people, sometimes the bride's, make insistent demands to have it. Its real motive is ostentation and nothing else. The custom began, understandably, to protect the bride and groom, and their possessions and jewelry, at a time when the roads were not secure and were frequented by plundering bands (dacoits) and robbers. A few men would therefore certainly go along from the house for protection. Now there is neither that necessity nor any other excuse. There is no motive but pride. Often, moreover, fifty people may be invited to go, but a hundred will show up. First, to go to someone's house without an invitation is forbidden. The noble *hadis* says that any person who goes to a feast uninvited goes as a thief and leaves as a robber. It is the same crime as robbery and plunder. Second, the host is dishonored. It is another sin to disgrace someone else. This leads to mutual intransigence and unpleasantness that affect people's hearts all their lives. Because discord is forbidden, whatever causes it is also forbidden. These foolish customs are not at all legitimate. Then, on the road, the ignorant coachmen begin to gallop without sense or need and cause hundreds of dangerous accidents. It is evident that involving oneself in such danger without need is in no way legitimate.

13. The bridegroom at this point goes off to one of the city's well-known sacred tombs to make a cash offering before rejoining the wedding party. What the ignorant believe about this custom is nothing less than polytheism. Even if some particular enlightened persons are free of pernicious beliefs, they should avoid the practice, because it encourages those who are ignorant and contributes to the growth of a bad custom.

14. The barber who brings the henna to the bride receives a gratuity. The groom's people then calculate the amount they in turn will

have to give to the menials, reckoned as eight times the amount of the gratuity. Again we have the sin of compulsion. The menials know how much was given and figure out how much they will get out of this. This custom is forbidden, because it is a sin to force or compel someone to give. The method of reckoning is also forbidden, because what leads to sin is also sin.

15. Some henna is applied to the bride, and the rest is distributed. This is another example of compulsion, because any opposition to doing it is considered a fault. For this reason, again, this practice exceeds the limits of the *shari'at*.

16. The women gather at the house of the bride on the day the groom's party arrives. You have learned above the many distasteful aspects of gatherings like this.

17. Gifts (*purota;* that is, *neg*) are distributed for each job that is done. For example, the barber digs a hearth for the cooking pot; he asks for a *purota* and is given some grain with a lump of raw sugar on a tray. In the same way, a price is extorted for each and every job, however small. It is fine to give gifts to servants, but why must there be this pretense of pay for each job? You should give them their wages in a lump sum calculated as their due for service. The real root of this practice of repeated giving is that old desire for recognition. You should give money either as a gratuity or as wages. If it is a gratuity given out of kindness, then taking it by force is forbidden; and if taking by force is forbidden, then giving is too. If, however, you call this payment wages, you must fix the amount first and announce it. To keep workers ignorant of what they will earn is dishonest compensation, and it is forbidden.

18. Upon the arrival of the groom's party, the animals are given grass and fodder, and the drivers of hired conveyances are given clarified butter and raw sugar. Often, the coachmen raise such a storm on this occasion that the people of the house are disgraced. The person responsible for this disgrace is the one who has brought along too many people in the bridegroom's party. It is evident that to be the cause of something evil is evil.

19. The groom's party then settles down. The groom's gifts (the *bari*) are opened in front of the kinfolk on both sides. Now the time has come for the ostentation and self-aggrandizement that lie behind the gifts. The custom is therefore forbidden.

20. Many items are required as part of the *bari:* a fine suit of clothes; a ring; jewelry for the feet; a special basket of cosmetics, perfumes, a comb, and ornaments specific to this occasion (*suhag pura*); oil; tooth blackener;[26] a container of collyrium; *pan;* puffed rice;

and other unnecessary items. The same number of small earthen pots are included as there are outfits in the *bari*. It is evident that all these absurdities involve the excessive compulsion whose opposition to the *shari'at* has been described so many times. Of course, ostentation and self-aggrandizement are now the life of these customs. There is no need for me to stress that.

21. Menials of the bride's people arrive, bearing trays to carry off the *bari*. Each places one item on his head. This just shows that the whole point is ostentation! Even if there is only enough for one person to carry, there will be a whole caravan, so that everyone can see the procession from a distance! This is a fine stew of putting on airs and pretenses!

22. All the men of the family go along to the women's quarters with the groom's gifts. People are often very careless on this occasion. The men go right into the house and face unveiled women directly. I do not know how it happens that on this day all sins and immodesty become "legally permitted" and proper.[27]

23. The fine suit of clothes and some other items in the *bari* are set aside, but everything else from the *bari* is sent back. One of the groom's men puts it all in a box. If the gifts are going to be sent back anyway, why bother to send them in the first place? It is just the same display and ostentation! Since it was certain that all this would be returned, what value can it have? In fact, people who are aware of these things know it is likely that many of these items were borrowed from someone and will be returned as soon as they arrive back home. And you can be sure this happens often. In short, all these absurdities are against the *shari'at* and against sense, too. Yet people are still stupefied by them!

24. The bride's family places a rupee or one and a quarter rupees on the trays of the *bari*. This is called the "*changir* (tray) of the *bari*," and it is the right of the groom's barber. A female singer then goes to the groom carrying a cord and is given a small gratuity of one or two *ana*s. This is, again, an unnecessary requirement and a gratuity given under compulsion. I do not know what claim Madame Singer has, or for what absurdity the cord is intended.

25. The groom's party is summoned inside the bride's house for the signing of the wedding contract, the *nikah*. Not bad—they are finally given a reprieve from their wait! Often, there is such delay because of the absurdities preceding the *nikah* that the whole night is given over to them. From missing sleep, one person gets sick; another has indigestion; yet another, overcome by weariness, goes to sleep and misses the morning prayer. If there was *one* thing to cry about, one would cry; but

here, from head to foot—what can I say? May Almighty God grant mercy!

26. Then the water bearer brings water. He is given one rupee or one and a quarter rupees, called *berghari*. Like it or not, giving this gratuity is a duty greater than giving the canonical alms! How can one not give? This is an outrage, first, because it is simply forbidden to compel someone to give a gratuity. The meaning of compulsion is not limited to being beaten with staves and sticks and being robbed. It is also compulsion when people who do not give will be disgraced. The claimants insist on their due and may even start to quarrel, so the poor soul gives for the sake of honor and pride. All this compulsion is forbidden. *Berghari,* moreover, is a term used by the Hindus, so it seems that this custom has been learned from infidels. This is a second violation of proper order (*zulmat*).

27. After this, a musician (*dom*) comes to stir the *sharbat* and is given one and a quarter rupees. The sugar for the *sharbat* comes from the house of the bride. The gratuity is, again, given in error, because it is compulsory. Of what use is the musician? To be sure, the musician is very fit and appropriate for stirring the *sharbat,* because his hand creates a source of pleasure in playing all that music and his *sharbat* gives yet more pleasure to those who drink. The crowning blow is that however cold it may be, the *sharbat* must still be drunk, even at the risk of catching a cold. There is no limit to this irrationality either.

28. Then the *qazi* is called to read the *nikah.* This is one matter, alone among all these absurdities, that is good and in accordance with the *shari'at.* Even here, however, the Reverend Qazis are often unacquainted with the legal points of performing a marriage, so that the ceremony is undoubtedly improper and the couple commits fornication all life long. Some *qazi*s are so greedy and covetous that, out of greed for a rupee or two, they toss off the marriage however requested, whether it is a proper wedding or not. Whether the dead go to heaven or to hell, *they* at least will have gotten their sweets and cake. You must therefore take great care that the person reading out the wedding contract either is himself a learned man or is someone who has been thoroughly prepared through inquiry of a learned man.

Before the wedding, some people summon the groom into the house to eat items such as sesame seed from the bride's hand, which they pull out from under her veil. Think about the immodesty involved in needlessly exposing the bride's hand to the groom before the marriage. May God save us!

29. If dates have been brought by the groom's people, they are distributed about or grabbed up. Otherwise, the *sharbat*—whether the

weather is hot or cold! Besides the objection of undue compulsion concerning the *sharbat,* how can it be legitimate to provide the means for people to fall ill, as invariably happens at some times of the year?

30. Now the barber of the bride's family washes the hands of the groom and receives one and a quarter rupees for "washing the hands." To give this was once a gratuity and a kindness. Now, however, the givers and the recipients both consider it an obligatory right, or *neg.* It is therefore forbidden, because it is forbidden to exert compulsion in a kindness, as explained above. If you say the money is due for service, it should be the responsibility of the bride's family, for he is their servant. What does this have to do with the groom's people, who are guests? Besides being against the *shari'at,* how can it be rational for guests to pay the wages of your servants?

31. *Shakarana* is sent from the house for the groom and is distributed to all the party on plain plates. Here again is an unnecessary requirement and an example of false belief—in this case, that it is inauspicious not to make the *shakarana.* This same belief is in fact present in most customs. It is polytheism. The noble *hadis* says that bad omens and inauspiciousness have no base in reality. But what the *shari'at* has declared baseless, people have made into a bridge to stand on. Is this opposition to the *shari'at* or not?

32. Afterward, all members of the groom's party eat and go off. A bed is sent for the groom, prepared at the house of the bride's family. What a time to send the bed, when the groom has gotten all stiff and sore lying on the ground the night before! Now some ointment has come. Now he can make a claim, when before he was a stranger. Good people,[28] even if he was not the son-in-law, he was at least an invited guest! After all, both sense and the *shari'at* make a rule of hospitality for a guest, do they not? The other members of his party are still superfluous, and even now no one has inquired of them. Gentlemen, they too are guests.

33. One and a quarter rupees are given to the barber who brings the bed. So it seems that the bed has come for the sake of this abuse! God forbid! It reflects compulsion in giving a gratuity.

34. Late at night, all the boys of the groom's party join in and eat the tray of *shakarana* sent to them. Even if the poor things have indigestion, the people giving the celebration carry out their customs. Making *shakarana* was discussed above, where it too was noted as being against the *shari'at.*

35. The barber who brings the tray is given one and a quarter rupees. Why not give? The elders of this Sir Barber gave a "loan" to the ancestors of this unfortunate party, and now these poor folks are repay-

ing it. Otherwise, their ancestors will be obstructed from entering heaven! *There is no strength or power but in God!*

36. In the morning, the untouchable *bhangi* from the groom's party play the drum (*daf*) at the home of the bride's family. This drum came with the groom's party. Basically, the drum is legitimate, because the *shari'at* allows it as a means for making the wedding well known. Now, however, it is clear that it is played to display pomp and glory and pride. Therefore it is illegitimate and deserves to be checked. There are a thousand other ways of making the announcement. Nowadays, people get together for everything, and talk spreads on its own in every village. This is quite enough. If, along with the drum, however, there is the oboelike *shahna'i,* the music is in no case legitimate.[29] The noble *hadis* describes its evil and clearly prohibits it.

37. An untouchable from the bride's side picks up the dung of the horses of the groom's party, and the untouchables of both sides receive an equal *neg* for collecting the dung and cleaning up. Now, what is the advantage of this sharp deal? When each gets the same amount, why not give to your own menials? To have both give for no good reason is again the sin of compulsion.

38. The singing woman from the bride's people comes to feed *pan* to the groom and, in accordance with common practice, goes off with her presents (*purota*). He *must* give her a gratuity. Rob the poor fellow today, so that he cannot go off with anything saved, but rather will be more in debt! Remember that all this is a form of compulsion.

39. The wife of the barber braids the bride's hair and takes the comb away in a cup. She is given something called "tying up the hair" or "grinding the sweet cake (*pura*)." Why not give? Poor thing has a loan from everyone else! Here is more of that same compulsion.

40. The bride's people prepare a list of gratuities for the menials and give it to the groom's people, who then either distribute the amount themselves or give it in a lump sum to the bride's people to distribute. Of course, this also involves the compulsion whose prohibition has been described over and over. Some people say, "Sir, these servants work their whole lives in the hope of occasions like these." The answer is that they should get paid for their service by the people they serve! It is absurd for them to be in service to certain people but paid by other people!

41. The groom is called into the house. At this time there is a complete lack of seclusion. He is asked many immodest questions, whose sinfulness and indiscretion are evident. There is no need for description. In many places, the groom is asked to say to the bride, "I am your slave," and "You are the lioness, I am the sheep." God forgive

us! Almighty God has declared the husband the chief of the wife, yet they make him the slave and obedient servant. Just tell me, is this custom against the Qur'an or is it not?

42. If things are done with great modesty, those within the house send for the bridegroom's handkerchief, which is used to collect money given in response to his "greeting" (*salami*) from invited guests. The money is then given to the groom. The sin of these gifts has already been discussed.

43. From this money, a sum as great as eight *ana*s is given to the singing woman and the barber's wife. The fortieth share (*zakat*) due our Lord and Master is not such a duty! The tithe (*'ushr*) on agriculture is not so obligatory! But extracting the share claimed by these two is a duty to exceed all duties. How foolish is this compulsion! At least the barber's wife is a servant. Of what use is the singing woman? Who is she, that she gets a share everywhere? As someone once said, "In a marriage, nothing but an account book of seed." Perhaps her share is considered her due for the service of singing and playing. But when singing and playing are forbidden, as has been clearly described, how can it be legitimate to pay her, or to have someone else pay her, for that? Moreover, this cannot be her fee, as it would be if the people of the house had summoned her for a celebration and paid her. Here, to the misfortune of the guests, it is collected from them under pressure. Those who do not give are disgraced, made contemptible, blamed, and reproached.

Why are such songs and such claims not declared forbidden? Many people have the misapprehension that singing is legitimate at a wedding, because they fail to see all its attendant ills. These singing women sing melodies, and that, in our school of law, is forbidden in itself. Their voices reach to the ears of strange men. It is a sin for unrelated men to hear such voices, especially because the singing women are often young. This causes still more harm, for the hearts of those who hear are not pure to start with and will be more impure yet from hearing the songs! People sometimes play the small drum (*dholak*), whose presence is an open sin. If people spend the whole night in this business, they are likely to miss the morning prayer. Finally, the words of the songs are often opposed to the *shari'at*. How can having someone sing such a song be right?

44. When the meal is finished, all the items of the dowry are brought into the common gathering. Each item is displayed, and a list of the jewelry is read out. Now, tell me, is this complete and unadulterated ostentation and show or not? Besides this, how shameless to display women's clothing to men! Many people think they show great

religiosity by not displaying the dowry but keeping it locked up in boxes. They prepare only a list of the goods. But surely this is also ostentation! People see the groom's party bringing boxes. Some also ask to see the list and set themselves to read it. Even then, the gifts are opened among the guests gathered at the groom's house and shown to them. The only way to avoid all this is not to send the dowry, but to show all the items to the girl and entrust them to her at some convenient time. When she wishes, she can take them along, either all at once or a few at a time.

45. One and a quarter rupees are placed on the tray of the dowry as *neg* for the menials. Please recall the point concerning compulsion in gratuities.

46. Now the day of the girl's departure has come. A curtained sedan or palanquin is placed before the door, and the bride's father, brothers, and other relatives are called to the house to place their hands on her head. All this time, men and women are passing in front of each other, which is, of course, a sin.

47. The girl's relatives bid her farewell and seat her in the palanquin. Then they raise up cries and wails against all sense. It is possible that some are upset about her leaving, but most of them weep just to fulfill a custom, so that no one can say that their daughter was a burden to them or that they are glad to be rid of her. This false weeping is deception, which is against both sense and the *shari'at* and is a sin.

48. In many places, it is the rule for the groom to carry the bride in his arms and place her in the palanquin. He does this in view of everyone. If he is weak, his sisters and other relatives help him out. This custom offends propriety and modesty. The women, moreover, are often right at the front, having arranged this just to watch the show. Sometimes the bride turns out to be heavy; when the groom cannot hold her, she slips from his arms and is injured. This custom also is illegitimate.

49. In one corner of the bride's scarf, cash is tied; in the second, a knob of turmeric; in the third, a nutmeg; and in the fourth, rice and a leaf of grass. These are omens and charms, which are not only irrational but also polytheistic.

50. A small basket of sweets is placed in the palanquin. Their use will be described below, and the foolishness and the need to prohibit this custom will then be clear.

51. At first, the palanquin is lifted up by bearers from the bride's side. At this point, the groom's people begin to scatter coins (*bakher*) that they have passed over the bride's head. If this custom is understood as a good omen meant to save her from all calamities falling on

her head, then it is harmful to belief. At the very least, the custom is observed out of concern for one's reputation. In either case, it is evil. Those who snatch the shower of coins are untouchable *bhangi*. Thus you cannot say that you are acting out of charity, for if you were, you would have given to the poor and needy. It is a foolish and misplaced expenditure to avoid the deserving and give to the undeserving. People are injured by this custom, some because of the crowd and some because they are hit by the coins. This is yet another evil.

52. A handful of coins is given to the bearers as the share due all the menials. Recollect here, too, the illegitimacy of compulsion.

53. Coins are scattered until the party arrives outside the city. The bearers then put the palanquin down in some garden, take their *neg* of one and a quarter rupees, and go off. This is another example of a compulsory gratuity.

54. The relatives of the bride, who until now had stayed with the palanquin, take leave to depart. Thereupon the members of the groom's party remove the basket of sweets and begin a mad scramble. Again, we have a custom wrongly required. Moreover, there is often such a lack of propriety that an unrelated man will stick his hand into the palanquin blindly to get the basket, unconcerned that the curtain might open or that he might touch the hand of either the bride or the barber's wife. Some of the more proper relatives of the bride or groom then fly into a rage and denounce the men, and often the matter escalates. Nevertheless, no one forsakes this dismal custom. All this contentiousness is acceptable—but giving it up is not acceptable. *Truly, we belong to God, and to God we do return.*

55. When the bearers come to the first stream along the way, they put down the palanquin and insist on their due before crossing. This due is at least a rupee, which they call "bearing across the river." This again is a forced gratuity.

56. When they reach the house, the bearers do not put the palanquin down until they receive a gratuity of one and a quarter rupees. If this is a gratuity, then why this compulsion? And if it is wages, then it should be like wages and paid accordingly. To fix the time and to force someone to pay involve carrying out a custom about which one must say, yet again, that it is wrongly required.

57. In some places, it is also customary that some young relative of the groom comes and stops the palanquin, saying, "Give me my due, or I will not let the palanquin into the house!" Yet more compulsion!

58. Before the palanquin arrives, the women daub smooth a small place in the courtyard and use flour to make a design like a house. The

palanquin is first put down there. The women have the bride place her toe on the design before she is taken inside. This involves not only a custom wrongly required but also endless omens. It resembles customs of the infidels. It is also a misuse of grain. For all these reasons, this custom is illegitimate.

59. When the bearers put the palanquin down and go off, the sisters do not let the daughter-in-law get out until they have gotten their due. Often, they close the door, which is the same as saying, "Until our fee is given, we will not let the bride enter the house." This too is coercion in forcing a gift.

60. After this, the sisters summon the groom and stand him next to the palanquin. This is, again, a custom wrongly required, and it is also a kind of omen that entails error in belief. Often, women in seclusion stand right in front of him without any discretion.

61. Women bring ground sandalwood and henna to place a *tika* mark on the bride's right foot and abdomen. This is openly an amulet and a form of polytheism.

62. They give oil and the bean *mash* as charity to the sweeper's wife and sprinkle oil on the four feet of the palanquin. The malady of corrupt belief is responsible for this foolish deed!

63. They ask the goatherd for a goat. They give it back to him as charity, along with some *neg* of a few *ana*s, after placing the money over the heads of the bride and the groom. What a foolish act this is! If they bought the goat, when did they pay for it? If this is buying it— well, buy away at such a price! If they did not buy it, the goat remains the property of the goatherd. How can you give someone else's property in charity? It is like the proverb: "The shop of the confectioner and the *fatiha* of Grandfather."[30] Then the sponsor of the "charity" is the goatherd! That is very fit. From head to toe, this deed is foolish and completely contrary to the principles of the *shari'at*.

64. They help the daughter-in-law out, bring her to the house, and seat her on a jute mat facing the direction of prayer. Seven married women together place a little rice pudding in the right hand of the daughter-in-law. One of the wives licks it off with her tongue. This custom is nothing but omen and oracle together, whose result is to corrupt belief. Facing the direction of prayer is certainly a matter of blessing, but not when its point is only to act on foolishness like this, which is considered more important than if the bride never in her whole life had the grace of the canonical prayer! If, in fact, she is more strongly compelled to carry out this custom than to carry out a legal duty, for fear of a bad omen, then this is indeed transgressing the limits

of the *shari'at.* The custom is not legitimate. In some places, at this point, the groom picks up the bride. The evils of this have already been described.

65. The rice pudding is served on two dishes, one of them for the singing women. (Splendid, O Singer, you show up everywhere!) The other is for the barber's wife. This is accompanied by a gratuity of at least five half-*ana* coins. This is all attachment to custom and foolishness.

66. After this, one hundred or one hundred fifty pounds of rice pudding are distributed among the kinfolk. Besides compulsion, there is nothing in this but ostentation and pride.

67. The face of the daughter-in-law is then uncovered. First, her mother-in-law or the eldest woman of the family looks at her and gives some money as "showing of the face," collected by one of the bride's people. There is such severe compulsion that one who does not have this "showing of the face" payment can never, ever look the other women in the face. Such a heavy burden of blame and reproach is put on her that she can in no way remove it. This custom is set among obligatory acts that clearly transgress the limits of the *shari'at.* Nor can one find any rational reason why the bride should have to put her hands over her face or, rather, her face in her hands. Why is that a duty?—indeed, such a duty that if she does not do it, she is known among all the kinfolk as shameless, immodest, and without pride. They act as shocked as if a Muslim had "turned infidel"! Just tell me, is this a transgression of the limits of the *shari'at* or not?

In their modesty, many—indeed, all—brides miss their canonical prayers. If a bride's companions find an occasion to have her read the prayer, fine. Otherwise, in the "law school" (*mazhab*) of women, there is no permission for her to arise or to ask anyone else to make preparations for the prayer. For her to move here and there; to speak; to walk; to eat; to drink; to scratch, if she begins to itch; to stretch, if she wants to stretch or yawn; to lie down, if she begins to get sleepy; to involuntarily begin to void or excrete (do not even mention this, for in the school of these women it is "forbidden")—this is all infidelity. On this account, the bride gives up food and drink for two or three days beforehand, so there will be no need of voiding or excreting—acts that would be condemned by all. God knows what crime this poor oppressed creature has committed, that she should be imprisoned in such a harsh black hole! Just consider whether or not this is causing trouble to a Muslim for no good reason! How can it be permissible? Remember, moreover, that the bride has committed the sin of missing prayer. In fact, all the other women, thanks to whom these customs are established, have committed the same sin. One must check all this foolishness. In some cities, there is the further foolishness that all the men of the family look at the face of the bride. *God forbid!*

68. After all the women have looked at the face of the daughter-in-law, they seat a child in her lap. They feed him some sweets, then carry him off. More foolishness and omens. But what happens? Even with all this, many women remain childless their whole lives. Repent, repent! What wrong notions these are!

69. After this, they pick up the daughter-in-law and seat her on a bed. The barber's wife then washes the toe of the bride's right foot and is given the rupee or eight-*ana* piece tied in the corner of her scarf (*dupatta*) as the "washing of the toe." This too is some kind of charm.

70. After the bride's arrival, the women prepare two plates of *shakarana*, one for her and one for the barber's wife, who has come with her. At this time, the married women gather again. They put a few bits of the dish in the daughter-in-law's mouth, just to tantalize the poor thing. Then all gather together and eat the *shakarana* themselves. Splendid, splendid! (*Shabash!*) All these customs appear to be charms.

71. Then the wife of the barber on the groom's side washes the hand of the wife of the barber on the bride's side, who then, in accordance with her master's instruction, gives some money as "washing of the hand" and begins to eat. Here again is a custom wrongly required and the evil of compulsion in giving a gratuity.

72. While she eats, the singing women sing obscenities. (God's curse on the wretches!) They get a gratuity (*neg*) from the barber's wife. *As God wills!* To hear obscenity upon obscenity, and, on top of that, to have to pay! There is no limit to this ignorance, either. *God be my refuge!*

73. When the dowry is opened, one outfit of clothing is given to the barber's wife, who has come along, and an outfit is distributed to each sister. Bravo! What fine compulsion! "Whether you like it or not, I am your guest." If someone says this is not compulsion, because everyone accepts it, the answer is that everyone knows that if they do not accept it, they will be thought contemptible. In what sense is this acceptance? Accepting compulsion is like the acceptance of a person who is being robbed and sits quietly or that of someone whose wealth is being snatched by a tyrant but who does not speak up out of fear. Such acceptance does not make property lawful. In many places, it is also customary that the dowry contains purses and sashes and hold-alls that the sisters divide among themselves and share with the daughter-in-law.

74. Nighttime is for solitude. Some shameless women, however, peek in and spy on the couple. According to the *hadis*, these women deserve reproach.

75. In the morning, the sheets and bedclothes from the night are examined.[31] This is a shameless act. An even worse offense is that in some places the barber's wife circulates the bedding throughout the whole family. To make someone's secret known is completely forbidden, especially in such a private matter. Everyone knows how shameful this is, but at the time, alas, it does not seem intolerable to anyone. God save us!

76. Between the afternoon and the post-sunset prayers, the hair of the daughter-in-law is set loose. The singing women sing and are given one and a quarter rupees or five half-*ana* coins known as "filling the part" or "undoing the hair."[32] Again, we have a custom wrongly required, as well as illegitimate payments.

77. The day after the arrival of the daughter-in-law, her relatives come by cart with some sweets. The name of their visit is *chauthi,* "the fourth."[33] Here is compulsion again. Moreover, the practice is a custom of the infidels, and acting like them is forbidden.

78. The brother and other male relatives of the daughter-in-law are called into the house and sit with the daughter-in-law in a separate room. Usually, some of the men who are included are not legally prohibited in marriage. Yet no one acts with discretion in this matter or recognizes how great a sin it is—and a dishonor as well—to sit alone in a room with those marriageable men, particularly now, when the girl is beautifully adorned. They give the daughter-in-law some cash, feed her some sweets, and present to the household the outfit of "the fourth," along with some oil, essence, and expenses for the menials. All this enters again into customs that are wrongly required!

79. When the barber comes to wash everyone's hands, he takes as *neg* a sum that may be as little as four *ana*s or as much as one and a quarter rupees. He then helps everyone wash their hands. This indispensable "moral obligation" also has no bound. All the rights owed to God and his creatures may be suspended, but in this self-devised right—which, if you ask the truth, is a wrong—what chance is there of the slightest deviation? You first get an advance and discharge your debt to him, and only then do you think about eating. God forgive us! You take the cost from the guests, then feed them. This custom is the work of the enemies of sense! Here is a false requirement, exceeding the bounds of the *shari'at,* and compulsion in giving a gratuity.

80. When it is time to eat, the singing women who come along for "the fourth" sit at the door and sing their obscenities and claim their *neg.* May God deal with you as you deserve! The givers and the takers are just alike. They won't give the needy even a cracked cowrie, no matter how the poor beg and supplicate, but they hear the obscenities

of these base-born singers and bestow rupees on them. Bravo, O Custom, how mighty you are! May God banish you from our land!

81. On the next day, the daughter-in-law departs, wearing the outfit of "the fourth" and taking back with her the sweets that have come from her house. *As God wills!* Well, what is gained by sending these sweets and then taking them back? Perhaps they were sent to bring the auspiciousness from that auspicious house. You must realize that you abandon your sense in adhering to this custom—quite apart from the sin of an unnecessary requirement.

82. The groom goes along with the daughter-in-law. At the time of her departure, the same four items are tied into the corners of her scarf that had been tied there when she came. This is evidently a charm, and foolishness as well.

83. When the bride arrives and starts to get out, the barber's wife washes her right toe and claims the rupee or eight-*ana* piece tied into the bride's scarf. This is the same charm noted before.

84. When the groom goes into the house, his sisters-in-law hide his shoe and claim at least one rupee in the name of "hiding the shoe." Splendid! So they steal, and in return they get a reward! In the first place, the *hadis* forbids this kind of pointless joke of stealing someone's belongings. Second, such joking encourages familiarity. To create this kind of relation or tie with an unrelated man is against the *shari'at*. To consider this reward your necessary right is to exercise compulsion and to exceed the bounds of the *shari'at*. Sometimes people do not hide the shoe, but they still demand the reward.

85. Worse than this is "playing the fourth," a custom current in some cities. There is no asking what degree of immodesty and dishonor there is in this! Those husbands whose wives join in "playing the fourth" and who, in spite of knowing about it, do not control and forbid it become nothing less than tame cuckolds[34] and emulators of the infidels. Besides all this, people often wind up with injuries that leave them very uncomfortable. This is a separate sin.

86. When the groom arrives, the barber washes his right toe and claims a payment of about one rupee. The other menials are paid their due within the house. All this involves charms and false requirements. On all these occasions, the due owed the barber is considered greatest. This is the custom of the Hindus. In their usage, the powers of the barber are very great, and therefore he is highly valued. Ignorant Muslims have divested him of these powers but fix wages for him that are usually unjust, because there are no legal grounds for them.

87. Now it is time to eat. The groom sits down coolly. He listens to a thousand supplications and all kinds of flattery, but he will not lift his

hand until he is given some money. When he gets his "right," then he will eat. God be praised! Is it rational to be given fine food and then to ask for the "sinking in of the teeth"? This custom, like the others, shares the ills of compulsion in kindness and ostentation in giving. It too is illegitimate.

88. After a few days, the groom's people again take away the bride and groom. This custom is called *bahora*[35] and repeats again the customs that took place on "the fourth." All the sins of "the fourth" are repeated.

89. Women then come from the home of the daughter-in-law to take her back again, and they bring dried dates along with them. Again, a custom wrongly required!

90. These dates are distributed among all the kinfolk. That same ostentation and pride!

91. When the bride leaves, she in turn takes dates with her. That same excessive compulsion!

92. And when her party arrives at her father's house, the dates are distributed among the kin. Pride and ostentation again!

93. Afterward, the bride returns to her father's house on the Shab-i Barat or during Muharram. In which verse or *hadis* is this required? The reason for it is simply a supposition, based on ignorance, that Muharram and the Shab-i Barat, *God preserve us,* are inauspicious. Therefore, people hold it inappropriate for the bride to be at the house of the groom during those times.

94. Ramazan is the same. As 'Id approaches, the family sends a conveyance for the daughter-in-law. In short, whatever observance is one of sorrow, hunger, and grief—such as Muharram, which is considered a time of grief and sorrow; Ramazan, in which people are obviously hungry and thirsty; and the Shab-i Barat, which the common people call *jalta balta,* burning and being consumed—these are all the father's share. But on 'Id, which is an observance of joy, the bride should be at her new home. *There is no strength or power but in God.*

95. The bride's people send some one hundred fifty or two hundred fifty pounds of goods such as sweet noodles, flour, and dried fruits. They also give the bride and groom clothes, along with some cash (called ghee)[36] and some sweets. This is considered such a "necessary duty" that it must not be missed even if people have to take a loan on interest. It is obvious that this is exceeding the bounds of the *shari'at.*

96. For a year or two after the wedding, the daughter-in-law is sent off at every departure with sweets, cash, outfits, and the like from both sides. There are also fine feasts among the relatives. These are punitive feasts—this whole troublesome business is solely for avoiding disgrace

on the one hand and securing fame and honor on the other! Moreover, everyone takes account of reciprocity and equality. Sometimes the guests feast only after making complaints and demands. For a few days this politesse,[37] true or false, is carried on. Afterward, no one even inquires after the others! All those who were enjoying the festivities and those who were purveying false hospitality have now gone their own ways. Now if some real calamity strikes, they must just bear with it. If only the amount of money that had been wasted had been spent to buy some property for the young couple, or if some business had been started, how much peace of mind there would have been! All this misfortune results from adhering to these customs.

97. Sweets from both sides are distributed in both families, just for the sake of ostentation. If the sweets are not sufficient, then you provide them from your own house. This, too, is like having a fine imposed.

98. In some places, there is the custom of *kangna bandhna,* "tying the bracelet," which is forbidden because it is a custom of the infidels.[38]

99. In some places, they carry out the custom of *arsi-mushaf,* "the mirror and the Book."[39] This custom is disgraceful and infamous, against sense and against the *shari'at.*

100. In some places, there are preparations for fireworks. This is done wholly from pride and is a waste of wealth. It is clearly prohibited.

101. In many places, English or Indian instruments are played. They are forbidden in the *hadis.* In some places, there is dancing, whose prohibition has already been described in the first section.

102. Many dates, months, and years are considered unlucky. For example, people do not marry in the eighteenth year. This belief is completely against sense and against the *shari'at.*

103. In some places, the dowry includes silver legs on the bed, a silver holder for collyrium, silver needles, cups, and so forth. Using these items is forbidden, for the *hadis* clearly prohibits it. Giving these items is also forbidden, for it promotes something forbidden.

[A Summary of the Sins; Their Scriptural Denunciation and Reform]

More than one hundred points have been discussed. Some describe one sin; some, two; some, four or five; some up to thirty-two! If you calculate an average of three sins in each point, the entire marriage celebration has a total of more than three hundred sins. How can anyone speak of good and blessing on an occasion that opposes more than three hundred teachings of the *shari'at*? In summary, these customs are filled with the following sins:

1. Wasting wealth.
2. Inordinate pride, shown in conspicuous display.
3. Undue compulsion.
4. Resemblance to unbelievers.
5. Taking a loan on interest or without genuine need.
6. Taking a gratuity or gift of kindness under compulsion.
7. Lack of seclusion.
8. Polytheism and harm to belief.
9. Missing the canonical prayer or performing it at a disapproved time.
10. Promoting sin.
11. Encouraging sinful acts and considering good what is clearly denounced in the Qur'an and the *hadis*.

Here are some examples of scriptural denunciation of these sins:

Almighty God declared, "Do not waste wealth. Without doubt, Almighty God does not love those who waste wealth" [7:31]. In another place, he declared, "Those who waste wealth are the brothers of Satan, and Satan is ungrateful to his God" [17:27].

The *hadis* says, "The Messenger of God⁵ declared, 'Almighty God will make a show of anyone who acts out of ostentation. That is, he will show forth that person's disgrace. He will speak of the faults of anyone who acts in order to be spoken of.' "

The Pure Qur'an says that no one should exceed the limits given by Almighty God [2:229]. This makes it clear that whatever is not necessary according to the *shari'at* should not be considered necessary. Adhering to a practice excessively is evil, because that goes beyond the divine limits.

The noble *hadis* says that the Messenger of God⁵ condemned those who take interest and those who pay interest. He declared both to be equal in sinfulness. The *hadis* also gives many warnings and prohibitions about taking loans. Loans, if not necessary, are a sin.

The noble *hadis* says that no gift of property is legitimate unless given with a willing heart. It is therefore clearly forbidden to take anything with any kind of force, constraint, or pressure.

The noble *hadis* says, "May God condemn anyone who looks and anyone who is looked at." This proves both the evil of breaking seclusion and the prohibition against going about openly, for the one who looks is cursed, as is the one who comes forth without proper caution.

For a man to see an unrelated woman and for a woman to see an unrelated man are both sins.

Who does not know the evil of polytheism? The *hadis* says that the Companions of the Messenger of God[s] did not consider the omission of any act to be infidelity, except for the omission of prayer. Missing prayer is therefore an obvious evil, rendering a person's faith defective and flawed.

Almighty God declared, "Do not assist another in committing sin and oppression" [5:3]. The *hadis* says that you are a believer indeed when your heart is happy to do good and heavy to do evil. To consider sin good and to adhere to it are clearly to destroy belief itself.

The *hadis* gives particularly strong warnings about the customs of the Age of Ignorance. The Messenger of God[s] said, "Almighty God hates three people most; he declared one of them to be the person who comes into Islam but wishes to cling to the customs of the Age of Ignorance."[40]

There are many more *hadis* besides these that we will not cite further. It is, then, a duty and an obligation for every Muslim, and a matter of faith and sense, that when the evil of these customs is made clear by the *shari'at* and by sense, everyone should take courage and bid farewell to such practices and not fix their sights on the desire for a good name and the fear of dishonor. In fact, experience has shown that obedience to Almighty God brings you an even better reputation and greater honor.

There are two methods of checking these customs. One is that all the kinfolk (*biradari*) should agree that all this foolishness will cease. The second is that, if no one joins you, you should simply abandon the customs yourself. Seeing your example, other people will imitate you, because everyone suffers the consequences of this nonsense. In this way, *Almighty God willing,* in a short time the general effect will spread. The reward of doing this will redound up to the Day of Judgment, even beyond death.

Many people say, "Well, sir, those who have the means will continue to carry out the customs, but those who do not will not." The answer is that it is not legitimate for those with means to sin either! When the sinfulness of these customs has been proven, there cannot be permission for them simply because people have the means! In addition, when those with means carry out the customs, the poor people among the kinfolk will certainly do so too, in order to protect their own honor. It is therefore a matter of necessity and proper order that everyone should abandon these customs.

Many people say that if these customs are checked there will be no occasion for social mingling. The answer is, first, that no one can justify sin on the grounds that it encourages social intercourse. Moreover, gatherings do not depend on custom. Without the compulsion of custom, one person may go to another's house, or invite someone to visit, or entertain someone, or treat someone well, as is the custom among friends and acquaintances. Is this not possible? Indeed, love and affection are not the real purposes of these customary gatherings, and there is often sorrow, wrangling, complaint, renewal of old grudges, searching for faults in the hosts, seeking their abasement, and many other faults like these. Because custom requires this kind of exchange and entertainment, there is no happiness or joy either for the givers, who must take up a kind of forced labor, or for the recipients, who consider it all their due. Where is the pleasure? You must stop all this foolishness.

For an engagement, a verbal promise is enough. There is no need of the barber, of an outfit, of a token, of sweets. When both boy and girl are of marriageable age, fix the date for the wedding orally or by letters, and summon the groom. It is enough for a sponsor and a servant to accompany him. There is no need for a *bari* or for a groom's party. Immediately after the wedding, or after the groom has stayed as a guest for a day or so, send him off and, in keeping with your means, send along whatever essential and useful items you wish to give as dowry, without showing them to others or announcing them. Alternatively, you can give the gifts to the couple at your own house. There is no need of outfits for the in-laws, no need of the *bahora* on the fourth day. Whenever they want, the bride's people can extend an invitation to the couple; whenever there is an occasion, the groom's people can extend an invitation. Each should give to their own servants in accordance with their means, not each to the other's. To bury your face in your hands is not a necessity; and scattering coins is a foolish extravagance. If you have the means, give to the poor in thanksgiving. Take no loans for anything.

The *walima* feast, given by the groom's side, is lawful but should be done with pure intentions and minimally, not with pomp and pride, for that kind of *walima* is not legitimate. The *hadis* call such a *walima* "a very corrupt meal." It is not legitimate to either participate in or provide an ostentatious *walima*. A pious person should neither carry out these customs nor participate in gatherings where they take place, but should clearly refuse to have anything to do with them. Satisfying the kinfolk and family is of no use before the displeasure of Almighty God. Almighty God grant all Muslims such grace!

On Fixing an Excessively Large Marriage Portion

Among these illegitimate customs is that of fixing an excessively large marriage portion.[41] This is against the *sunna*. The *hadis* says that Hazrat 'Umar, **may God be pleased with him,** declared: "Beware! Do not fix a large marriage portion. If it had been a matter of honor (*'izzat*) in this world and of piety before God, then surely your Apostle[s] would have been most worthy. Yet I do not know that the Messenger[s] married any wife or married off any daughter with more than twelve ounces (*uqiyat*) of silver." In some traditions, the amount given is twelve and one-half ounces, which in our reckoning is about one hundred thirty-seven rupees. Some people say that a large marriage portion is fixed so that the husband cannot leave the wife. This excuse is, in fact, completely foolish. Whoever wants to leave leaves, whatever may happen. Whoever does not leave simply out of fear of the demands of the marriage portion does worse: he neither divorces his wife nor keeps her with him. He puts her in midair—neither here nor there. What is one able to do to them? These are all foolish excuses. The truth is that people set a large marriage portion out of pride, to show off their splendor. It is forbidden to do any act, even if it is legitimate in itself, for the sake of pride. So what can we say about something that is itself against the *sunna* and disapproved? It is even more forbidden, even more evil. In keeping with the *sunna,* one should fix a portion like that set by Hazrat Apostle[s] for his wives and daughters. If a person wants to set it higher, then it should be set in keeping with that person's means and not above.

On the Marriages of Wives and Daughters of the Prophet[s]

The Marriage of Hazrat Fatima Zahra[rz]

Hazrat Abu Bakr Siddiq[rz] and Hazrat 'Umar Faruq[rz] each expressed a desire for this great treasure. Hazrat[s] demurred on the grounds of her young age. Then Hazrat 'Ali[rz] came to him shyly and asked for her himself. God's approval came immediately to the Prophet[s], and he accepted the request. This episode makes it clear that all the current foolishness surrounding the engagement is senseless and against the *sunna.* Just a verbal message and a verbal answer are sufficient. At the time of their marriage, the age of Hazrat Fatima[rz] was fifteen and one-half years and the age of Hazrat 'Ali[rz] was twenty-one years. As this shows, it is not good to put off the marriage beyond this age. Moreover, the ages of the bride and groom should be compatible. It is best for the groom to be somewhat older than the bride.

Hazrat^s said, "O Anas, go and invite Abu Bakr, 'Umar, 'Usman, Talha, Zubair, and a group of the Medinans." (There is therefore clearly no harm in inviting those closest to you to the wedding gathering. This has the value that the wedding is then known to have taken place. There should, however, be no special efforts or arrangements. Those few people who are close should simply gather informally.) When all the people invited were present, and Hazrat^s had read a sermon, he performed the wedding. (It is thus clearly against the *sunna* for the father to wander around hidden from view. It is in fact best for the father himself to perform the marriage of his daughter.)[42] A marriage portion of four hundred *misqal* of silver was fixed. The reckoning of the value of this portion has already been discussed. (Setting a sky-high marriage portion is thus clearly against the *sunna*. The portion of Fatima is enough and is a source of blessing. If someone does not have the means, even less is fitting.) The Prophet^s took a tray of dates and distributed them to those present. He then sent Hazrat Fatima^rz, along with Hazrat Umm Aiman^rz, to the home of Hazrat 'Ali^rz.

O sisters, look! This is the "departure" (*rukhsati*) of the princess of both worlds. No bustle or blunder, no sedan or palanquin, no scattering of coins. The Prophet^s did not have 'Ali^rz pay the expenses of the menials or feed the family and *biradari*. It is required that we follow our Apostle^s, the chief of both worlds, and not reckon that our honor is greater than his. *We seek refuge in God from this.*

The illustrious Hazrat^s then went to their house and asked Hazrat Fatima^rz for water. She brought water in a wooden cup. (It is therefore clearly against the *sunna* for new brides to commit such excesses of modesty that coming and going and doing any work with their own hands are considered faults.) Hazrat^s put his saliva into the cup and told Hazrat Fatima^rz to turn her face toward him. He sprinkled her blessed breast and blessed head with a little water. Then he prayed, *"O God, I give the offspring of these both into your shelter and away from the cursed Satan."* Then he said, "Turn your back toward me," and he sprinkled some water between her shoulders and offered the same prayer. He asked Hazrat 'Ali^rz for water and did the same with him, except that he did not sprinkle water on his back. (It is appropriate to do this with the bride and groom together, for this is a cause of blessing. In Hindustan, there is the erroneous custom of keeping seclusion between the bride and groom, despite their marriage.) He told the couple to go to their house, with a blessing, in the name of God.

There is a tradition that Hazrat^s on the day of the marriage went to the house of Hazrat 'Ali[rz] after the afternoon prayer, spat his blessed saliva into a vessel of water, and recited the verses, *"Say, I take refuge in the God of the Heavens"; "Say, I take refuge in the God of Mankind."*[43] Then he blessed them and told Hazrat 'Ali[rz] and Hazrat Fatima[rz] to drink the water, one after the other, and to perform the ablution. He prayed for the purity of both, for the continuance of love between them, for blessedness in offspring, and for good fortune. He then told them to go and rest. (It is a source of blessing for fathers today to perform this act if the son-in-law's house is close.)

This was the dowry of the chief of all women: two Yamani shawls in the style made of silk and cotton; two small quilts stuffed with linseed hulls; four large cushions; two silver upper-arm bracelets; one little blanket; one bolster; one cup; one grinding mill; one leather water bottle; and a water vessel, that is, an earthen pitcher. In some traditions, there was also a bed. O women, you should take account of three things in a dowry. The first is that it should be minimal and not exceed your means. The second is that it should include only things that are of immediate need. The third is that there should be no announcement or proclamation of what is in the dowry, because it is given simply out of kindness to your children. What need is there to show it to anyone else? These three points are proven by the action of Hazrat[s], just described.

Hazrat[s] divided the work of the couple so that outside work was the responsibility of Hazrat 'Ali[rz] and housework was the responsibility of Hazrat Fatima[rz]. It is not clear why the wellborn ladies of Hindustan object to the chores of the household.

Then Hazrat 'Ali[rz] gave the feast of the *walima,* which included the following items: cooked bread of several *sa'* of barley, some dried dates, and some *malida* (a cake made of bread crumbs, butter, and sugar). *Sa'* in terms of a *ser* is one *chhatank* above three and one-half *ser.*[44] So this is the manner of *walima* by the *sunna:* to entertain those closest to you, minimally, as practical, and without formality or pride.

The Marriages of the Wives of Hazrat[s]

The marriage portion of Hazrat Khadija[rz] was five hundred *diram,* or camels of this value. Abu Talib[rz] took the responsibility for it. The marriage portion of Hazrat Umm Salama[rz] was some useful item worth ten *diram.* The marriage portion of Hazrat Juwairiyya[rz] was four hundred *diram.* That of Hazrat Umm Habiba[rz] was four hundred *dinar,* provided by the emperor of Ethiopia. The marriage portion of Hazrat Sauda[rz] was four hundred *diram.* The *walima* of Hazrat Umm Salama[rz] was some dish made from barley. At the *walima* of Hazrat Zainab[rz], daughter of Jahsh, a goat was slaughtered, and the people were fed meat and bread. At the marriage of Hazrat Safiyya[rz], whatever the Companions had available was gathered, and that was the *walima*. Hazrat 'A'isha Siddiqiyya[rz] said that, for her marriage, no camel or goat was sacrificed—just a cup of milk came from the house of Sa'ad bin 'Ubadah, and that alone was the *walima*.

A Recent Example of a Wedding Held
in Accordance with the *Shari'at*

The following account is provided for people who hear about the evil of customs and ask how they can in fact carry out a wedding without them. The discussion above on fixing a modest marriage portion offers a start to carrying out a wedding properly. The subsequent accounts of the weddings of the wives and daughters of the Apostle[s] offer examples. This should suffice for a person of understanding. Nonetheless, many people say, "Sir, *that* time was different. Show us something done today." Little is accomplished by mere words!

Here, however, is an account confirming that a proper wedding is possible nowadays, too. Moreover, the example I give is not of a family of *maulawi*s or *darwesh,* nor of a poor person, nor of a person of low standing (*choti qaum ka*). Both sides—*as God wills!*—are people who eat and drink well, manage their worldly affairs well, and are of well-born and honored homes. For this reason, no one can say, "It is different for *maulawi*s and *darwesh.*" Or, "They had nothing to spend anyway and had no choice but to follow the *shari'at.*" This account will dispel all such suspicions.

The marriage took place this year in a country town of District Muzaffarnagar. The bride's people were in one town, the groom's people in another. For some time, there had been great resolution in the hearts of both sides. Then, at a certain point, Almighty God directed both to listen to the order of the *shari'at,* expel all reservations from their hearts, and make preparations in keeping with the order of the Messenger[s]. No barber was sent to fix the date of the wedding, bring the henna, or deliver an outfit. Nor was the barber involved in any other custom. Women from outside the household did not gather to rub ointment on the bride; instead, the women of her own family rubbed and massaged her. Neither side invited guests, nor did they even inform their near and dear. They simply fixed the date by letter five or six days before the wedding.

An elder brother accompanied the groom. The legal guardian of the bride had agreed to the wedding by means of a letter written to him. A servant came along to help, as did a young nephew, in case a message had to be sent into the house. Because this child did not merit seclusion, he could deliver the message with no bother. These few people alone got into a hired oxcart on a Friday and arrived at the bride's house. They brought the bride's outfit with them. The groom wore clothes from his own house. When they arrived, they sent word to people they knew, informing them that the marriage would take place after the Friday prayer.

Shortly before the Friday prayer, the outfit for the groom was sent out from the house. He put it on and went off to the congregational mosque. After the Friday prayer, there was a brief sermon describing the errors of customs. Every person present for this sermon understood its point. After the sermon, the marriage was solemnized, and dates were distributed both inside and outside the house. They were also sent to the houses of those who could not come. Everything was completed before the late afternoon prayer. After the post-sunset prayer, the groom's people were fed fine food at the usual time. After the night prayer, the same kind of sermon was delivered for the women. It had a great impact on them, too. Everyone went to sleep on time, in peace.

On the next day, very early, the family placed the bride in a small oxcart and bade her farewell. A woman relative went along for company, as did the barber's wife, in case she was needed to help. The cart was part of the dowry, and no one bothered about using a sedan or palanquin. The dowry was left behind. The bride's people distributed gratuities to their servants. The groom's people did not receive money as "greetings." Instead of scattering coins passed over the bride's head, the family sent money to mosques and to the homes of the poor. At noon, the party arrived at the groom's house. The bride missed no canonical prayer. The women who came to see the bride did not have the "showing of the face" money taken from them. On the next day, the family ordered fine sweets from the market and prepared both hot and cold food, which was sent to such appropriate recipients as their friends and acquaintances, the poor, and respectable students. No one was invited to the house. No one came from the bride's side for the custom of "the fourth day."

On the third day, the bride and groom returned to the bride's home, remained a week, and then returned to the groom's home. At this time, they took with them some items of dowry, leaving some behind for another occasion. On this occasion, the bride did, as it happened, ride in a sedan. The groom's menials were given as gratuity more than they usually get by custom.

Thus the marriage took place with peace and calm. There was no trouble for anyone; there was no tempest. I myself participated in this wedding from start to finish. There was a luster and a sweetness to it that words cannot describe. With God's grace, all who observed it were happy, and many of them resolved to celebrate weddings in the same style. Afterward, there was another marriage in the same family, and it was even more simple. If it is not possible to emulate the second wedding, at least follow the example of the one you have just read about here. May Almighty God grant his grace. *Amin*, O God of both the worlds!

On the Marriage of Widows

Among current nonsensical customs is the idea that the marriage of widows is evil and disgraceful. The wellborn are especially ensnared in this error. By the *shari'at* and by sense, the second marriage is like the first, and to consider them different is baseless and foolish. This idea has become fixed only through association with Hindus, and it has been reinforced by greed for property. It is a matter of faith and sense that you should perform the second marriage without hindrance, just as you do the first. There is no reason for your heart to shrink at the second marriage if it has not done so at the first. Women have acquired such bad habits that, quite aside from themselves remarrying or encouraging others to do so, they hold in contempt any servant of God who reverently places the order of God and the Messengerˢ to her head and eyes and remarries. They ridicule her in conversation. They laugh at her. They denigrate her. In short, they never converse without showing spite toward her. To consider remarriage a fault is a great sin, nothing less than risking infidelity. It is, after all, infidelity to consider the order of the *shari'at* a fault and to degrade and denigrate those who follow it.

It is worth considering that all the wives of our Apostle, the Messenger of Godˢ—Hazrat 'A'ishaʳᶻ aside—had been married before. Indeed, each had been married once or twice previously. Then what? *We take refuge in God! We take refuge in God!* Will you call these women evil? Repent, repent! Has your respectability (*sharafat*) risen above theirs, so that your honor (*'izzat*) is spoiled by doing what they did and what God and the Messengerˢ ordered? Will this cast a slur upon your honor (*abru*)? Will your nose be cut off? Just say outright that in your opinion it is dishonorable to be a Muslim! Just remember that until you expunge this thought from your heart and recognize that the first and second marriages are identical, your faith is unsound. You must make every effort to eradicate this erroneous idea. The only effort that will be effective is to rid your heart of undue concerns with honor (*nang o namus*). You must put custom on the shelf and make God and the Messenger⁵ happy by immediately marrying off widowed women. If they refuse, encourage them through persuasion and pressure. In any way that you can, see that they marry. You must realize that their refusal is only an outer refusal, resulting from custom. If there were no custom, no one would refuse.

This fault will remain in your heart until you take action and encourage opposition to the custom. The *hadis* says that "whoever makes current and spreads my abandoned practice will receive the reward of a hundred martyrs." Both those who make an effort to encourage the remarriage of widows and those widows who remarry to please the Messenger⁵ and destroy a false custom will have the reward of a hundred martyrs. Have you no pity for widows today? Doesn't your heart grieve at the sight of their condition? Their lives are ruined, and they are brought down into the dust.

III. Customs Considered Properly Religious and Deserving of Reward

ON *FATIHA*

To begin by defining the *fatiha,* it is a way of transferring reward to the dead. Its legal essence is that one does a good deed and transfers its reward to someone else by praying: "O God, give my reward for this to so and so." For example, a person may, in the way of God, distribute food, sweets, money, or cloth and then pray to God to assign the reward for the deed to someone else. Or a person may read a section or half a section, or a chapter or half a chapter, of the Glorious Qur'an and transfer the reward for reading to someone else. The reward may be transferred at any time in one's life, not necessarily on the day the good deed was done. This much is declared in the *shari'at.*

But look at what ignorant people have done and the complications they have devised! First, they daub a small place with mud and place food on it. They may set out water and *pan* along with the food. They have someone stand in front of the food, read out some Qur'anic chapters, and transfer credit to the dead, name by name. This self-devised procedure entails the following errors:

1. The basic error is that ignorant people believe that credit is not transferred unless the practice is done precisely as described. They therefore go around trying to cajole someone to perform the *fatiha* for

them, and until it is done they will not distribute the food. Now, how can they transfer the reward for distributing the food before it has even been given out? Women sometimes invite an unrelated man into the house to perform the *fatiha*. That is not permissible acccording to the *shari'at*.

I myself have seen what happens when credit is meant for several deceased people whose names the reader cannot remember. He is ordered to say "hun" when he finishes reading. The donor then has him repeat each name, one at a time, and believes that each person named will get credit and that whoever is not named will not. However, the owner of the food, not the reader, has the power of transferring the credit. Nothing happens if the reader invokes a name. The donor can, in fact, give the credit to whomever she wants and withhold it from whomever she wants. All this results from a fault in belief.

Many ignorant people say that credit can be transferred without the Qur'anic reading. They explain that the chapters are read out so that double credit can be transferred, one for the food, a second for the reading of the Qur'an. This raises the question of why people insist on the reading at the same time the food is given out. They could transfer the credit of a Qur'an recitation given earlier that day. They could transfer the credit of a previous reading of a whole or half section of the Glorious Qur'an—or indeed of the whole Qur'an—if there is no reading then. They could distribute the sweets first and read the Qur'an and transfer its credit later. But no one will ever accept these options, nor will anyone come for the food or sweets if they are offered separately. Nor will they accept the reader sitting at some distance from the sweets to do the reading. In fact, the very arrangement of having someone else perform the *fatiha* is flawed, because the credit for reading the Qur'an belongs to the reader. The organizer actually gets credit only for distributing the sweets. What high-handedness! Just because the owner transfers some credit, the reader must also transfer some credit!

2. People who believe in the customary *fatiha* feel that there is no need to give the food as charity. They eat the food themselves when a *fatiha* is held for an elder or for Hazrat Messenger, ***God's blessings and peace upon him***. If they do distribute sweets for the eleventh or some similar occasion, then to whom do they give them?[45] They send them to some Nawwab Sahib, Tahsildar Sahib, Peshkar Sahib, Thanedar Sahib, friends and acquaintances![46] We have never seen or heard of all the sweets being given to the poor and needy. The customary belief seems to be that the credit is transferred by the mere reading and bestowal of credit. The belief is wrong and a sin, because the food itself is not

given—only its credit—and, contrary to belief, the food does not reach the person on whom the credit is bestowed. The only reward is for the recitation of the chapter or two. Now, if this was the aim, why the useless trouble of sweets and food? For nothing, you claim to have done a big favor for these people![47] You may claim to have given sweets to *faqirs*—but how many did you give? You gave sweets to five or ten *faqirs* at most, and what of that? You meant to get and assign credit for all the sweets you bought. If you expected credit only for a few sweets (*jalebis*), why do you speak of the whole amount? In truth, you handed out the sweets not as charity but as an offering of an auspicious gift. Indeed, if you distribute the food as charity, no one will take it—but will be offended and take it amiss. As far as today's custom is concerned, it is completely foolish and pointless.

3. "All right, we accept that after the *fatiha* the food should be given to the needy." How can you assign the credit before distributing the food? You will get your reward only after you feed the poor. How can you transfer credit to the unfortunate deceased before you have gotten it yourself? This custom has no basis at all.

4. Many people believe that the food itself reaches the dead. They therefore set out water, *pan,* maybe even a water pipe (*huqqa*) along with the food. "After eating, where will they find water?" "They need *pan* so that their mouths will feel pleasant." God help us! Even ignorance has reached its limit. They also believe that they should use in the *fatiha* whatever the person liked in life. Thus there should be *fatiha* using milk for a small child. I remember well one occasion at a *fatiha* on a Shab-i Barat when an old woman set out several sparklers, because the dead person had liked fireworks so much. Now, just tell me, is that false belief or not?

5. Some people believe that the souls of the dead are present at this time. This is the point of burning camphor and fragrance. Not everyone thinks this.

6. People have fabricated on their own the restriction of performing the ceremony on Thursday evening, whereas the *shari'at* holds all days the same. To consider Thursday the special day for *fatiha* is to change a rule of the *shari'at*. A related sin is the belief that the spirits of the dead return to their homes on Thursdays. If they receive reward, fine; if otherwise, they return empty-handed. All this is false, and to believe it is a sin. To fix one date as deserving more credit also reflects a sinful belief.

7. Common people are often in the habit of taking a small amount of food, placing it on a tray or cloth in front of themselves, and offering *fatiha*. Now, do they mean to get and transfer credit only for this small

amount of food or for all food? Surely they intend to transfer credit for all of it, not for only that bit of food! Then why have the *fatiha* given over only a small amount? By your rule, only the credit of the tray should be transferred, and the rest of the food is wasted and worthless. If you say that it is not necessary to place all the food in front of you, that just the intention is enough, then what is the need of placing food on the tray at all? The intention itself should be enough. Is this— repent, repent!—to show a sample to the Supreme Truth? "Please look, this is the kind of food that is in the pot; please bestow the reward of giving it on such and such." *We take refuge in God from this!*

8. If it is necessary to place food in front of you to transfer the credit, why do you not read *fatiha* over cloth, grain, and other items given in charity? And if that is not necessary, why do you do it for food and sweets and consider that necessary?

9. And why daub the ground?[48] Was it clean or dirty? If it was dirty, it did not become clean from daubing but became dirtier, for before it was dry and you could set cups and plates directly on it. Now the vessels will get dirty. And if it was clean, then daubing was unneces- sary. Daubing in fact creates, so to speak, a "square" (*chauka*) of the Hindus. *We take refuge in God.* They seat the dead in a square and feed them. *There is no strength or refuge but in God.* For a *fatiha,* in which there are even more elaborate arrangements, the hearth and other areas are daubed as well. The implications are exactly the same.

10. People think that everything used in a *fatiha* for saints (*buzurg*) should be brand-new. Virgin jugs and vessels should be brought out and filled with water fresh from the well; they should not even be touched by water stored in the house. The vessels are not to be handled at all, and no one is permitted to eat or drink from them. The tray is thoroughly washed before the sweets are put out. Everything in the house, except these few items, is regarded as impure. This is all very strange, quite against sense. If everything is in fact dirty, why do you ever use it? If it is not dirty, why do you need to go to all this bother? The rule in the *shari'at* is that it is legitimate to give to a *faqir* whatever it is legitimate for you to eat yourself. Once given, it is then legitimate for you to assign the credit of the gift to someone else. Is all this other nonsense illogical or is it not?

You may say, "Sir, that is a great court;[49] these are saints. We must send things there with great care." First of all, Almighty God has no respect for external care and cleanliness; he takes into account only what is permitted (*halal*) and what is good (*taiyib*). If the money spent on the occasion was acquired through forbidden means, then you may take a thousand precautions, but all will be in vain. If the money was acquired in some good and permissible way, then all these restrictions are worthless; the offering is acceptable if it is given just in an ordinary way. Second, if you believe that this offering is being sent to the court of the saints, your belief is forbidden and polytheistic. The point is to give the food for the sake of God, not to send it to the saints themselves and give for their sakes. If you hold a wrong belief, the food itself becomes forbidden!

Consequently, when your intention is to give charity for the sake of Almighty God and to transfer the credit for the gift, give just as you give other things in the way of God. Do not engage in all this foolishness. For example, you certainly do not wash money that you give to a *faqir.* You should prepare and distribute this food in exactly the same ordinary way that you give to the poor such things as grain or bread cooked for the family. That food goes to the great court, namely, to Almighty God, and this does, too. How can there be a difference? Just think! In these customary practices, if you think about it, you are exalting the saints above Almighty God. As for the deficiency in the heart of one who thinks that some of the food goes to the court of the saints and some to the court of God, that is something else. It is open polytheism.

11. Worse than this is the custom of offering the *fatiha* separately for each holy person. This is for our Lord and Master; this, for Muhammad Sahib[s]; this, for our Revered Lady.[50] Clearly, the intent is to give only so much to our Lord and Master and only so much to the others. Well, who can doubt that this is polytheism? *I ask forgiveness of God, I ask forgiveness of God!* The evil and polytheism of this are clearly stated in the Glorious Word, and you must repent of them. Simply give everything for the sake of God, and transfer the credit to whomever is intended. To crown it all, people perform the *fatiha* of ordinary deceased people together, but they hold separate ceremonies for saints and important people. The meaning of this is that ordinary hapless folk are weak, so that all can be honored in one observance with no harm. But important people, if the *fatiha* is done jointly, will begin a free-for-all and grab what they can! *There is no strength or power but in God!*

12. There is also the restriction that in the *fatiha* for our Revered Lady, the food should be covered, because she kept seclusion. Her food therefore should not be displayed in front of unrelated people, either. The foolishness of this is self-evident.

13. There is also the restriction concerning the food of the *fatiha* of our Revered Lady, as well as the food of the *sahnak,*[51] that men cannot eat it. After all, if they were to eat, wouldn't they come face to face with her? Nor can every woman partake—only a clean, pure, good

woman should eat. Nor should she who has remarried have a share. The Glorious Qur'an itself declares a wrong practice like this to be evil.

14. People carrying out the *fatiha* also err in considering the elders and saints of God able to relieve their ills and solve their problems. These people perform *fatiha* and give offerings (*niyaz*) so that the elders will help them. They expect their needs to be fulfilled, offspring to be granted, wealth to increase, and their children to live long. Every Muslim knows that this kind of belief is pure idolatry. God save us! You must completely forsake these customs and habits. If someone intends to transfer credit, she must transfer it in the simple and straightforward way instructed in the *shari'at,* as we described it above. You must forsake all this foolishness. Without restrictions of custom, give to the needy whatever is bestowed on you and is available. Then transfer its credit. You can apply what you have learned here to the celebrations of *giyarhwin, sahmani, tosha,* and so forth.[52] Many people make offerings at graves. This is completely prohibited, and the food offered is not legitimate. You should neither eat it yourself nor give it to someone else to eat, because whatever you should not eat yourself should not be given to others.

15. Many people send shawls and covers to tombs and make an oath that if their wish is fulfilled they will offer *fatiha*. It is forbidden to offer shawls. The belief with which it is done is polytheism.

The ignorant have also devised many customs against the *shari'at* in relation to charity and alms. Many of the ignorant give meat to birds of prey as an offering to free themselves from sickness. They typically believe that the illness sticks to the meat, which should then not be eaten by another person. The *shari'at* does not sanction this belief at all; indeed, it is completely against the *shari'at*. Another custom is to order an animal from the market and set it free. People think, "We have freed a life for the sake of God, so our Lord and Master will set our invalid free from all trouble." The *shari'at* does not sanction this either, and to believe in such an unsanctioned practice is a sin in itself. One outrageous custom, even worse, is to put something to eat or drink at a crossroads. This is entirely a custom of the infidels. It is forbidden to act in the manner of the infidels, and when, along with that, there is false belief as well, there is the risk of polytheism and infidelity. Those who follow this particular practice think that someone is being troubled by some *jinn* or ghost or *pir* or martyr, who will be made happy by an offering in his name and will therefore cease making trouble. This is worship (*puja*) of something created, and its polytheism is clearly evident. The custom entails the additional sins of the waste of one's goods and inconvenience to travelers.

People have fabricated yet another false belief along these lines. They will, on many occasions, set apart as charity something such as oil or the pulse *mash* and give these items, if possible, to the untouchable *bhangi*. In the first place, the *shari'at* does not sanction specifying a particular food for charity, and to specify something without sanction is a sin. Second, it is opposition to the *shari'at* to ignore needy Muslims and give to a *bhangi*, because the *shari'at* gives precedence to the right of a Muslim. Moreover, people do this because they believe that the illness they seek to cure sticks to this charity and that the food, for this reason, must be given to dirty and impure people who will eat up this misfortune. This belief is wholly unsanctioned, and to believe such a thing without sanction is itself a sin. For all these reasons, you must give up these methods of charity and take up the straightforward way of giving to some needy person, quietly, whatever Almighty God has made available. Realize that this will make Almighty God happy and that he will remove trouble and affliction by his blessed power. To do more than this not only is useless but is in fact a sin.

Women have devised another custom of preparing sweets such as *gulgula* to take to the mosque and place right in the facing arch or pulpit. The women are often accompanied by music as they go. The evil of such absurd practices is evident, and they are only examples of many. In fact, a woman's going to the mosque is itself forbidden. When it has been forbidden for women to go to the mosque for prayer, the act of taking the sweets, on top of going, is truly objectionable. Many of the women are young; many are wearing jewelry; many have a lamp in their hands as if to say, "Look at my face, too!" In the same way, many women go to the mosque to make a vow or offer supplications or give salutations of respect. All this is against the *shari'at*. You must repent of this. Sit at home and distribute whatever is to be given, and offer whatever supplication is to be made.

ON THE CUSTOMS CARRIED OUT UPON A DEATH

First, upon a death, women greatly delay the arrangements for washing and shrouding the body. Somehow, their heart does not want the dead person to leave the house. The Apostle[s] strongly insisted that there should be no delay in the funeral procession.

Second, they send along some grain or money with the procession, to be given as charity at the grave. This is done primarily to gain a name, for which no reward is received at all. The poor and needy remain unfed; it is the professional beggars who take all this away with them. To earn reward, you must give secretly whatever there is to be given, offering it to those who are very needy, to the crippled, to the respectable poor, or to people who are pious and good.

Third, it is often the custom to give away the possessions of the dead person, such as clothes and the Qur'an, for the sake of God. You must understand very clearly that the *shari'at* specifies that, when someone dies, all those who receive a share in the inheritance are the owners of every possession of the dead person, whether large or small, and they become joint proprietors of all these things. How, then, can it be right for one or two people to give someone else the belongings of the other proprietors? If all the proprietors give permission, but one of them is a minor, it is still not right to give anything away, because the permission of minors has no standing. Nor is it legitimate, even if all the proprietors are adults, if they give permission under the pressure of other people's opinion. On the occasion of a death, you must first ask a scholar about each person's share of the inheritance, so that you can divide it according to the *shari'at.* Then all the heirs are in charge of their own shares and can do what they want; they can give them to whomever they want. Of course, if all the heirs are mature and all give permission gladly, then it is right to give things away without dividing everything first.

Fourth, on many fixed dates, or a little before or after, food is cooked and divided among the kinfolk and fed to the poor. They call this *tija, daswa, chaliswa* (the third day, the tenth day, the fortieth day), and so on. In the first place, the motive is not proper; all this is done for the sake of reputation. When this is the motive, what can be the reward? In fact, it is the opposite of what is desired—sin and a curse. In many places, women carry out these customs after taking a loan, although everyone knows that to become a debtor without necessity is wrong in itself. It is also a sin to make regulations about ceremonies even more binding than the order of the *shari'at.* Often, these customs are carried out with the wealth of the dead person, in which the orphans have a share. Spending the money of orphans in works worthy of reward is not right. Spending it in works of sin is even worse. Of course, you may give away whatever is available to you from your own wealth, as long as you give it secretly and offer it to the poor. Such charity is accepted by Almighty God. Many people specifically send sweet rice, or sometimes oil, to mosques; some send milk after the death of children, because the child drank milk. The *shari'at* does not sanction these customs, and fabricating new ways on your own is a great sin. Such a sin is called *bid'at* (innovation) in the *shari'at.* The Apostle[s] said, "*Bid'at* is error and leads one to hell."

Many women believe that on these dates, on Thursdays, and on the

Shab-i Barat the souls of the dead return to their houses. There is no foundation for this in the *shari'at*. Why should they come? Whatever reward is transferred to the dead reaches them wherever they are, so what is the need for them to wander about? Anyway, if the dead person was good, a dweller in paradise, why would the soul leave that place of springtime to come here? If the dead person was evil and a dweller in hell, why would the angels let that person leave to take a trip and escape torment? This notion is wholly illogical. Even if you see these notions written out in some book or another, you must not believe them. A book not sanctioned by a respected scholar is not to be trusted.

Fifth, women frequently gather at the home of the deceased and think that they are sharing in the sorrow of the house. In fact, they often get there and busy themselves with *pan* and betel nut. If these are in short supply or slow to come, they go about singing for their whole lives that in such and such a house they did not get a bit of *pan*. Some eat there, too, no matter how close their own house is. They just go to the house and settle in, sometimes for a full month. Now, tell me, have these women come to share in the sorrow, or are they dumping more sorrow on others? Because of these foolish women, there is trouble and worry beyond limit to the people of the house. They had trouble to start with; now they have even more. It is like the saying: "To be beaten on your head, and have your house looted, too!" Many do not even talk about the deceased. Instead, they sit in groups of two or three and tell tales of everything in the world; they even laugh and are gay. They come wearing showy clothes, as if they had come to partici- pate in a wedding. Well, what is the heavenly or earthly good of the presence of such foolish people? Some really wish the bereaved well and do share in their sorrow to some extent, but no one shares in the real way of sharing sorrow, namely, to comfort the bereaved, to coun- sel patience, and to settle their hearts. Instead, they embrace them and begin to weep. Some put on a phony face of sorrow—but there is not even a tear in their eyes. Some recall their own buried dead but place a burden of obligation (*ihsan*) on the household. Even those who weep with a sincere heart—how are they good? In the first place, they call out the deceased's name and weep, which the Apostle⁵ strongly for- bade, even cursed. Second, their crying brings a still greater burden to the hearts of the members of the household and sprinkles salt on their wounds. They grow more distraught and cry even more. What forbear- ance they had is gone. These women, far from instilling patience, on the contrary increase agitation. What is gained by their coming? The truth is that no one comes to share the sorrow of the bereaved; they gather to avoid reproach.

How can women gathering together be legitimate when the occasion encourages so many faults? Many of the women come from a distance, arriving in oxcarts and staying on as guests for several days. They dump on the household the burden of providing grass and feed for the oxen, as well as the glad hand (*a'o bhagat*) for themselves. Whatever sorrow the bereaved may have, they are expected to provide all hospitality for these guests, even if they have absolutely nothing to eat in the house, and despite the fact that it is in the *hadis* that a guest must not cause strain to the household. All this is to strain the bereaved even more! Many of the guests bring along a band of children besides. The children ask for food as many as four, even eight times a day. One demands butter and sugar; another cries for milk. All the arrangements for this fall on the household, and for a long time, too.

This is especially the case if the woman of the household has become a widow. The women make a first assault right at the time of the death, and a second, similar attack when the period of *'iddat* has passed.[53] They call this *chah mahi* (six months), and they say that they have come "to take her out of *'iddat*." Someone should ask them if the *'iddat* is a cell and if they will grab the hands and feet of the widow and pull her from it. She comes out of *'iddat* when four months and ten days have passed. If she was pregnant, *'iddat* ends when the child is born. What need is there for such foolishness on this occasion? Everyone in the world gathers. Often, the expense of all this storm is paid from the property of the deceased. All the heirs have a claim on this property, yet many may live elsewhere and may not give their permission to spend it. Or some may be minors, whose permission has no validity in the *shari'at*. Remember, whoever has spent this wealth is responsible for it and will have to repay the claim of all the heirs. If someone makes the excuse that the widow's share was not sufficient to cover the expenses, the answer is, "Well, if everyone's shares were not sufficient, then what would you do? Is it right to rob the neighbors?" In short, those who spend money on this storm are sinners. And because this expenditure takes place on account of those who come, they are sinners, too.

Thus, what is desirable is that those men and women who are close by should come briefly to give comfort and counsel patience—and then leave. There is no need for them to come again. It is wrong to fix a particular date for them to come. Whenever one has a chance to come, one may come. There is no harm if those who are distant come because they believe that otherwise the bereaved will remain disconsolate. They must, however, pay the cost of their travel themselves. And if they come only to avoid reproach, they should not come. They can offer their condolences by letter.

Sixth, it is the custom that food for the bereaved should be sent first of all from the house of close relatives. This is all well and good. But even in this, people have made erroneous additions. These must be avoided. First, people are motivated by reciprocity: those who received food must now send food back. They take this notion to such extremes that even if they lack means and someone else is happy to send the food, they still doggedly insist that it will come from them. The only reason is that they do not want to be blamed for having eaten but not reciprocated. Such pressure is itself forbidden, the more so if the person has to take a loan. Give up this pressure. Whichever relative has the means should send food. In the same way, such pressure forces relatives at some distance to send food—and to quarrel to do so—even when there are relatives nearby, all to avoid disrepute. Stop this pressure. Another evil is that relatives send much more food than is necessary. People with very distant connections then gather at the house of the deceased to eat. The only persons who need food are those who are so overcome with trouble and sorrow that they cannot even keep the fire on the hearth lit. Guests think they needn't bother to eat the food cooked in their own house. In fact, they should go home to eat or order food sent to them from their own house. Relatives also commit the fault of preparing fancy dishes. You must give this up. Prepare a modest amount of simple food and send it to the house of the bereaved.

Seventh, many women give something to one or two *hafiz* and have them read the Qur'an, in order to transfer credit to the deceased. In many places, they have the attestation of faith and the Qur'an (in sections) read over chick-peas. Because these *hafiz* read the Qur'an out of greed for money, chick-peas, and food, they get no credit themselves. When they get none themselves, how can they transfer it to the deceased? The whole undertaking is utterly worthless. Some people do not do the readings out of greed, but out of concern for propriety and a sense of obligation. These, however, are also worldly motives and bring no credit. The only person who is sure to give credit is one who reads for the sake of God and does not do so at a fixed, customary place or time.

ON THE CUSTOMS OF NOBLE RAMAZAN

1. An evil custom during Ramazan is that women will summon a *hafiz* inside the house to have him recite the Glorious Qur'an during

tarawih, the supererogatory night prayers.[54] There is no harm in this if two conditions are met: first, that the *hafiz* is a near relative and is heard only by women of the household itself; and, second, that the *hafiz* himself offers the required *namaz* in the mosque before coming to the house. Nowadays, it is common to be careless about this. An unrelated *hafiz* is often summoned into the house, and, although there is a curtain before them for name's sake alone, the women, who are quite careless, begin either to talk with Hafizji or to call out among themselves. Hafizji hears. Since when is it correct to let an unrelated man hear your voice without necessity?

2. Whoever recites the Qur'an makes his voice as beautiful as possible. The melody of some voices is so good that the hearts of the hearers surely incline toward the reader. In this circumstance, how wrong it is for the melody of the voice of an unrelated man to reach the ears of the women!

3. Women of the whole neighborhood gather day after day. First, it is forbidden for women to set their feet outside their house without necessity. This is not a necessity, for the noble *shari'at* does not require the supererogatory prayer to be read in congregation. To go out is bad—and to do so daily is even worse. Coming home is especially dangerous, for it is late at night, and the streets and alleys are empty and deserted. In such a situation, it would not be surprising if, God forbid, a person was robbed or her honor impaired. To put yourself into such difficulties without thinking is against sense and against the noble *shari'at.* Many women go out wearing anklets, earrings, and so forth, making it even more likely that they will come to harm.

Our custom of noble Ramazan is that women prepare special food for breaking the fast of the fourteenth day and consider it a matter of credit. But to consider as credit something that is not declared a matter of credit by the *shari'at* is a sin in itself. So you must also give this up.

Another custom is observed when a child first keeps the fast.* No matter how poor the family is, no matter if they have to take a loan or go begging, they consider the vexatious custom of "breaking the fast" a necessity. It is a sin to consider necessary what is not deemed necessary by the *shari'at.* Therefore you must give up this unnecessary requirement!

---

* Many ignorant people consider it unnecessary to keep the fast until they have observed the custom of "breaking the fast"; they thus justify not fasting. This is all foolish. Ja'far 'Ali, *may God pardon him!* [Presumably, this note was added by the scribe.]

ON THE CUSTOMS OF ʿID

First, women consider it absolutely necessary to cook *siwaiyan* on ʿId, but the *shariʿat* does not require it. If your heart wishes to, you may cook it; but do not consider it creditable to do so. Second, the requirement of exchanging gifts with relatives' children and sending food to relatives' houses—and with this, keeping account of reciprocity and taking loans when you are needy—is foolish and a bother as well. Therefore, abandon all these customs.

ON THE CUSTOMS OF BAQR ʿID

First, exchanges on Baqr ʿId have the same faults as they do on ʿId. The rules for them are those you have just read. Second, a sacrifice on this day is legally required for many people who in fact do not perform it. This is a sin. Third, people have, on their own, fixed the idea that the head of the animal sacrificed is the right of the water carrier and the foot is the right of the barber. This is a foolish custom and against the *shariʿat*. Give happily to whomever you wish.

ON THE CUSTOMS OF ZI-QAʿD AND SAFAR

Ignorant women call Zi-qaʿd "*khali*" (empty) and consider that month inauspicious (*manhus*) for weddings.[55] This belief is a sin, and you must repent of it. They call Safar "*tera tezi*" and also consider it inauspicious.[56] In many places, they cook *ghunghni* on the thirteenth of that month, distributing it to be protected from inauspiciousness. All these beliefs are against the *shariʿat* and are sin. Repent!

ON *MAULID* DURING RABIʿUʾL-AWWAL OR AT ANY OTHER TIME

In many places, women observe the noble *maulid*, the birthday of the Prophet.[57] As practiced today, the observance entails these sins:

1. When a woman serves as reader, her voice can often carry beyond the door. It is wrong for her voice to be heard by an unrelated person; it is even more likely to cause evil because she is reading poetry.

2. When a man serves as reader, he will obviously not be related to all the women but in fact will be unrelated to many. The current custom is to read verses of poetry expressively; the women thus hear the singing of a man, which is forbidden.

3. The books and pamphlets discussing *maulid* are often filled with false traditions. To read them or hear them is a sin.

4. Many people believe that the Apostle[s] honors the gathering with his presence; for this reason, they stand up in the middle of the ceremony, when his birth is mentioned. There is no argument for this in the *shari'at,* and to consider as certain whatever is not proven in the *shari'at* is a sin. Some do not believe that he is present, but they nevertheless consider standing so necessary that they reproach anyone who fails to do so. If you tell them that standing is not required in the *shari'at* and that in fact they should not stand when there is a *maulid,* they cannot bear it. They imagine that without standing the observance is simply not a *maulid.* To consider something necessary that is not necessary in the *shari'at* is a sin.

5. The distribution of sweets or food of some kind is compulsory. The participants consider its omission a disgrace and a cause of displeasure to Hazrat[s]. It is evil to consider something required that is not so specified in the *shari'at.*

6. It grows late while the ceremony is being held or the sweets are being distributed. Often, the time is short for the canonical prayer. This too is a sin.

7. Even if one is free of erroneous beliefs and avoids sinful practices in the observance, one should still avoid this custom, because it may encourage the ignorant to carry it out. Whatever is legally optional and may cause the ignorant to stray must be given up. Therefore, do not carry out *maulid* in accordance with current custom. When you want to recite the events of the life of Hazrat Apostle[s], take a reliable book and read it to yourself or to a few people of the house or to people who have come to visit and happen to be there. And if you intend to transfer the credit of some good deed to the soul of Hazrat Apostle[s], do so by giving to the poor on some occasion other than the birth observance. No one is forbidding you to do good works—only avoid impropriety.

ON THE CUSTOMS OF RAJAB

Common people call this the month of the fast of Maryam and consider it good to keep a fast on the twenty-seventh, believing that they thus gain credit for a thousand fasts.[58] There is no foundation for this in the *shari'at.* If your heart wishes to keep a supererogatory fast, you may. God Almighty will give you whatever credit he wishes. But do not on your own determine that a fast on this date is worth a thousand or ten thousand fasts. In many places, women cook *tabaraka* bread in this month.[59] This also is a fabricated custom that has no authority in the *shari'at* and promises you no credit. To consider it a religious undertaking is simply a sin.

SWEETS ON THE SHAB-I BARAT; *SHARBAT* AND *KHICHARI* ON MUHARRAM

The only authentic aspect of the current observance of the Shab-i Barat is the belief that the fifteenth eve and day of this month have great value and great blessing. Our Apostle[s] encouraged staying awake during this night and fasting during the day. On this night, he honored the graveyard of Medina with his presence and prayed for forgiveness for the dead. Therefore it is in accordance with the *sunna* to give something to the dead on this date, whether by reading the Noble Qur'an, by distributing food, by giving cash, or by praying for their forgiveness, as he did. Anything else is just nonsense, especially all the fuss that people make about having *halwa* and offering *fatiha* in a special way and setting up all kinds of strict rules. You have already read how wrong these practices are, and you have been told that it is wrong to turn something legally optional into a requirement that is subject to excessive rules.

You should realize that the rules concerning observances during Muharram are much the same. The one essential practice according to the *shari'at* is based on the saying of the Messenger of God[s] that whoever abundantly feeds the people of their house on this day will have blessing in their livelihood for the whole year. It certainly is acceptable to cook enough food in the house on that day so that some can be given, for the sake of God, to the needy and poor. To do anything more than this entails the evils you have already heard described. For example, women fancy that they should distribute *sharbat,* in the belief that they are actually distributing it to the thirsty martyrs of Karbala. Only the credit of your giving charity on their behalf reaches the martyrs, not the *sharbat.* In terms of the credit transferred, cold *sharbat* and hot food are the same. What else can the rule requiring *sharbat* mean, other than the false belief that it slakes the martyrs' thirst? Such false belief is itself a fault.

Ignorant people arrange for fireworks on the Shab-i Barat and *ta'ziya*s on Muharram. The evil of fireworks has been set out earlier, in the first book. And as for *ta'ziya*s, what could be more wrong than arranging for them, accompanied as they are by behavior that is complete sin and polytheism according to the *shari'at*? People make offerings to them; they bow their heads before them; they dangle petitions in front of them; they read elegies; they cry and wail; they play instruments next to them. They consider the place of burial a place of pilgrimage. Men and women pass among the *ta'ziya*s without seclusion. Canonical prayers are neglected. Who does not know the evil of all this? Some people may not engage in all this foolishness but may only read accounts of martyrdom. Remember that this too is clearly forbidden if there are false traditions in the accounts. Even if the traditions are authentic, it is still not right to read the accounts, for the only point in reading them is to hear them and weep. Such deliberate cultivation of weeping in a time of trouble is forbidden in the *shari'at*. It is also a sinful innovation to give up colored clothes and ornaments during the days of Muharram, to appear as one engaged in mourning and lamentation, or to dress your children in special clothes.

GATHERING TO VIEW RELICS

People, women among them, gather at places where some relic (*tabarruk*) is known to be—the revered robe or perhaps a hair of the Apostle[s] or of some other elder, for example. Sometimes the relics are brought to someone's house. The first objection to this is that the relics are not always authentic. That aside, even if the relics are authentic, the gatherings themselves are wrong. Many of the evils of gatherings were described above in the discussion of the gatherings of women at weddings. Noise, lack of seclusion, and sometimes the singing that all the women hear (in this case, singing by those viewing the relics)—everyone knows these to be bad. It is correct to go to see relics only if you go alone and do nothing against the *shari'at*.

Concluding Comments

An even fuller description of customs is available in a book called *Islahu'r-rusum* (The reform of customs).[60] The points that follow, however, can serve as a guide. If you will keep them in mind, you will be able to evaluate all customs and avoid being misled.

It is a sin to consider permissible whatever the *shari'at* has declared not permissible.

It is a sin to consider something necessary and to do it as a rule or for the sake of earning a good name when it has been declared permissible but not necessary by the *shari'at*.

It is a sin to consider something a matter of credit when this is not so declared in the *shari'at.*

It is a sin to consider necessary something declared a matter of credit but not necessary. And if you do not consider it necessary, but do not give it up out of fear of people's reproach, it is also a sin.

It is a sin to consider anything inauspicious.

It is a sin to fabricate something without the sanction of the *shari'at* and to put your trust in it.

It is a sin to pray to anyone other than God or to consider anyone else the source of profit and harm.

May Almighty God save you from all these sins!

The End
June 1911 *'isawi*[61]

Book Seven of the *Bihishti Zewar:* On Comportment and Character, Reward and Punishment

Translator's Introduction to Book Seven

In the title of Book Seven, Maulana Thanawi uses the words *adab* and *akhlaq,* words whose conventional English translations—courtesy, etiquette, deportment—barely hint at the richness of their meanings in Muslim societies. In his rules for teaching this material, given at the end of Book Seven, the author implicitly signals those rich meanings by describing this as an essay that deals with *tasawwuf,* usually defined as sufism, Islamic mysticism, or the cultivation of inner religious experience. The juxtaposition of the English words "courtesy," from the title, and "mysticism," from the rules for instruction, suggests that the import of the terms must be explained: *adab* and *akhlaq* clearly imply more than external polite behavior; *tasawwuf* implies more than emotional or intellectual experience apart from everyday experience.

At stake here are central notions about inner and outer life and their inherent inseparability. Mainstream sufism is firmly bounded by the religious law; its seekers know that identity with the Prophet depends on emulation of his life and that the vision of God cannot be hoped for apart from righteousness. In this book, we find what is in many ways the very heart of the *Bihishti Zewar:* an ideal of virtuous character, a theory of the construction of the person, and a guide to personal development. It is, in the end, a vision of the well-formed person that sums up all the rest and that is the foundation of the movement toward reform.[1]

In principle, the Islamic tradition has always held that all Muslims are capable of moral development; moral perfection is not assumed to be limited only to religious specialists set apart from ordinary life, as it was in the Christian monastic tradition. Indeed, Muslims have insisted that spiritual development is possible only through full experience of that ordinary or everyday life. The sufi tradition in particular developed the notion that the most perfectly realized person of any era might be anyone—an artisan, an unkempt *faqir,* a woman—and would be known only to God. This teaching has taken on special significance in the modern period, as reform movements have spread the teachings of moral perfection to all segments of society. An emphasis on personal development seems to have been especially strong in the Indian subcontinent, where the loss of political power was early and complete and where Muslims have defined themselves in the presence of two alternative cultural traditions.

The hallmark of the ideal is self-control and discipline, qualities that orient the believer to unfailing fidelity to religious obligations and to rigorous moderation and restraint in all personal encounters. It is critical to the idea of reform to believe that achievement of this ideal is in fact within every woman's and every man's reach. Correct knowledge, as always, is first, followed by repeated practice in correct behavior; the inherent faculty of *'aql,* sense or intelligence, must be freed from confusion and distraction so that it can be used to make correct choices.

The role of this rational faculty is to suppress the *nafs,* the willful or carnal soul. *'Aql* is the faculty of moral discrimination shared with the angels; *nafs* is shared with the animals. The very process of discrimination gives human life its value, as each person learns to distinguish the boundaries of the *shari'at* and to wage the true jihad, which is the struggle to lead one's life within these boundaries. As set out in Book Seven, this can be done by repeated correct behavior, by self-devised punishments, and by internal debates with the *nafs,* that distanced part of one's self that always tends toward carelessness and indulgence. Islamic thought has used a variety of concepts and terms to conceptualize the person: the focus on the dyadic *'aql/nafs* formulation and the definition of the propensity to corruption as *nafs* (a term that in other contexts can, for example, be used for the reasoning faculty) seem particularly widespread in Thanawi's time.[2]

Ideally, for Maulana Thanawi, personal development—honing reasoned commitment to a righteous life and eschewing the demands of self-indulgence and self-will—should take place in the context of a relationship with a morally superior spiritual guide. Books are helpful, but books alone, Thanawi explains, can never be as effective as teaching by a person whom one reveres and who offers an exemplary model. Thanawi denies that the spiritual effect (*tasir*) or charisma (*baraka*) of a holy man is demonstrated through magic; rather, this power transforms the hearts, minds, and behavior of those touched by the presence of a holy man. Thanawi here lists guidelines for identifying a good master and for following him. Thanawi and his tradition hold, however, that right living is so coherent with a human's intrinsic nature that, once seen, it will be embraced on its own merits, even without external guidance or sanction.

The argument gains force by detailing the ultimate sanction: Thanawi presents prophetic *hadis* describing punishment and reward, followed by an evocative account of Judgment and the Final Day. The complete title of Book Seven includes two pairs of words: the first, *adab* and *akhlaq;* the second, *sawab* and *ghazab*. Each of these four nouns is a two-syllable word with the second syllable marked by a long *a;* the shared sound subtly suggests the profound connection of each pair with the other.

In striving for *sawab* (reward) and seeking to forestall *ghazab* (punishment), the *nafs* plays a central role in this book, particularly in the little dramas presented as conversations to be held with that willful element, which is ever present, sitting, as Thanawi says, "in [one's] own lap." Evil is always memorable. But another element is present, too, evident here and throughout the *Bihishti Zewar*, which does not fit into the logical pairing of opposites, *'aql* and *nafs*. Containing both the opposites, this element seems to stand for a conception of wholeness— the heart. Seemingly used interchangeably, the terms *qalb, dil,* and *ji* are, respectively, Arabic, Persian, and Hindi in origin, the linguistic universalism suggesting the comprehensiveness the term "heart" is meant to convey; in all three cases, the meaning spills over to "self," "mind," and "soul." The notion of heart draws not on the philosophical tradition, as does *'aql,* but above all on the world of sufism. Thanawi's own definition of *tasawwuf* is "reform of the heart." It is the heart whose disposition, in the end, shapes everything else. The quest for the good is not abstract or philosophical; it is an entire way of being in the world. *'Aql* and *nafs* are not so much separable faculties as orientations of the whole personality and the whole person.

The heart sums up the comprehensiveness of significant human experience. The teachings set out here concerning human behavior and human transformation include all domains of life and all aspects of the personality—intellectual, emotional, and physical. The heart underlies all. It is the heart that inclines one to action; it is the heart that must be put into prayer or Qur'anic reading; it is the heart whose weakness one fears as a result of sin. One obeys the master out of love, so that the disciple's "heart wants to act as he teaches." In one of the very first lines of the *Bihishti Zewar,* it is his heart that Maulana Thanawi speaks of as he contemplates—"heartsick"—sin on every side. The heart is not mere feeling but the essential impetus and coloring implicated in all else.

Toward the end of Book Seven, Thanawi, following a *hadis* of the Prophet declaring that "there are something over seventy matters related to the faith," lists seventy-seven points involving belief, behavior, and character. The first thirty are listed as "related to the heart." They include fundamental tenets of doctrine, which are seen not as issues of the intellect or ratiocination but as points to be felt and embraced. Thus, for all the emphasis on knowledge, knowledge turns out to be apprehended not by the mind but by the seat of feeling that brings doctrine to realization. The points related to the heart go on to identify the dispositions of the well-tuned heart: love for God and for the Prophet, action in all things out of pure intent, and fear. They include the virtues extolled throughout: hope, modesty, gratitude, fidelity, patience, humility, mercy, contentment, and trust. They also include distance from the vices of pride, deceit, envy, anger, ill will, and absorption in the world. These are the foundation for everything else.

The next seven points are "related to the tongue"; recitation of the *kalima* and the Qur'an, acquisition and teaching of knowledge, intercession, *zikr* (recollection of God through repetition of his name), and abstention from all forms of sinful and idle chatter are not matters of the mind but are physically embodied. The final forty points are "related to the whole body" and cover a wide range of forms of worship (*'ibadat*) and human interaction (*mu'amalat*), down to removing obstacles on the road. The whole of one's being is involved. The image is clearly not that of a soul as the real self, inhabiting a material and corrupt body; rather, the whole being is material and subject to physical change.

Book Seven begins with a sampling of rules for amendment of *'ibadat,* the main subject of Books One through Three of this work. Directions are given for ablution and prayer, *zakat,* the fast, and Qur'anic reading, with a brief mention of the importance of steadfastness in time of sorrow, a detailed list of prayers (*du'a*) appropriate on various occasions, and a mention of the danger of ill-advised oaths and vows. Each point of *'ibadat* is noted as an *'amal,* an "act," a word often used for charms and incantations. Its use here points to worship as the truly efficacious act.

The subject then turns to amendment of *mu'amalat,* treating business dealings, marriage, and kind and thoughtful behavior. These subjects recall the detailed discussions of Books Four and Five, not translated here. The third section, on amendment of habits, *'adat,* continues the discussion of everyday behavior with teachings on table manners, dress, and such subjects as visiting and conversation. The term *'adat,* often used to define non-Islamic custom, is not used that way here. Rather, each good daily habit, listed as an *adab,* is part of a Muslim life. All three lists repeat teachings that have been discussed elsewhere. This is pedagogically useful, of course; it also reminds anyone who may not have read the earlier books of the importance of these subjects, and it makes clear the centrality of the *shari'at* to "matters of the heart."

The fourth section explicitly focuses on amendment of the heart, *dil,* the simple Persian word signaling a lack of parallelism with the domains of the three previous sections, each of which was defined by an Arabic plural: *'ibadat, mu'amalat, 'adat.* This fourth section turns to the process that makes reform in the other areas possible: the removal of vice and the cultivation of virtue. Discussion of the *nafs* is subsumed under the rubric of the heart. Key to the instruction for effecting moral change in the heart is the importance of physical effort. This is clear from the first injunction to eat little—an effort that promises purity of heart, a love of supplication, the extinction of rebellion in the *nafs* coupled with a discomfort that keeps the *nafs* mindful of God's wrath, a disinclination to sin, physical lightness in one's nature that allows energy for actions such as night prayer, and, finally, tenderheartedness toward the humble and the hungry.

Physical effort is also evident in Thanawi's insistence on the importance of repeated good action that shapes an attitude. Knowledge is not true knowledge unless it is acted on; and when one acts, one's inner self is affected. Outer behavior is understood as both the cause of, and then reciprocally the fruit of, one's inner self. Knowing, doing, and being are inescapably one. The emphasis on creating a habit, *malika,* is one known in classical Muslim thought, where moral actions create a trace that ultimately makes habits of virtues. Adherence to ritual action is particularly transformative. Fulfilling the obligation of *zakat,* for example, purifies one's wealth and one's attitude toward money. But, more subtly, all divinely revealed ritual actions, in all their detail, act on people in ways beyond human comprehension—exactly, notes al-Ghazali, as do magic charts and the position of the stars.[3] It is not by chance that a fixed number of prostrations are prescribed for each prayer, for all is part of a divine transformative order. Thanawi emphasizes this classical theme, both in this section on physical cause and elsewhere, with an almost poetic sense of moral process and punishments that fit the sins.

Similitude can also create verity; even feigned emotions serve a legitimate end. Maulana Thanawi quotes the Prophetic *hadis* that in order to cultivate the appropriate emotion, one should pretend to weep if one does not do so naturally. If you check your tongue, "in a few days you will develop a real hatred of saying things you shouldn't say." If you learn to curb your anger, you curb the malice that is its root. If you force yourself to publicly praise someone you envy, "bit by bit [this behavior] will become easy, [and] your envy will disappear." In Book One, Maulana Thanawi explained that, as in medicine, the cure of each thing is its opposite. That is also true here. The miserly must give. The worldly must part with what they love. Those prey to false pride must humble themselves and sell stale bread and greet those beneath them in status. Thanawi thus teaches that correct external behavior is the first step toward creating inner virtues. This is a materialist theory, in which moral habits are learned like physical skills.

The importance of correct knowledge is evident. Again, Maulana Thanawi wants to make clear the grievousness of sins that may appear minor. Envy, for example, carries with it the thought that a certain person does not deserve the blessing granted by God; this is, in fact, to oppose God. Love of worldly things can drive a person to rail against God at the time of death and thus die an infidel; such love also leads to many other sins, as one attempts to secure endless wealth. Meditation on one's humble human nature, in contrast to God's glory and power, both checks vice and encourages good. This knowledge is not abstract but an element in creating habits of mind and of feeling.

Throughout, the disciple is learning a role as a "good Muslim," in contrast to those around her. She watches others (though she is warned not to judge them), she watches herself, and she thinks of herself as being watched. Among the *hadis* presented here is the reminder that an angel writes everything down. In this section, the instruction for "cultivating heartfelt reading of the Qur'an" is to imagine that God himself had asked to see the person read (making concrete by example the *hadis* that although you may not see God, God always sees you). Similarly, although Maulana Thanawi denies the popular belief that a *pir* knows his disciple's every act, the internalized image of the *pir* is expected to deter wrongdoing. Good friends, as Thanawi explains, check each other from wrongdoing. But, most important, the good

Muslim learns to watch herself, to become an observer of her own actions and thoughts, to recognize her true motives, personifying (as the *nafs*) all rebellious inclinations. The sample conversations with the *nafs* are a vivid document of self-observation. Reformist religion is thus not only self-conscious in the sense of making deliberate, systematic choices instead of practicing the received tradition uncritically; it is also self-conscious at the level of the individual person, in whom are inculcated principles of correct belief and habits of self-examination.

The relationship of master and disciple is also discussed in this section on amendment of the heart. It is followed by a list of forty points showing "the way in which every disciple—indeed, every Muslim— should live." They are a summary, yet again, of the book and of the entire work. This list is now available in Urdu book shops, printed separately on inexpensive scrolls, to be displayed as a reminder of the importance of following these teachings.

A concern with this kind of self-consciousness is implicit throughout in Thanawi's emphasis on recognizing the true motives behind one's ostensible or self-proclaimed intentions. The first *hadis* of the one hundred one included in Book Seven makes clear the importance of pure intention, of acting from righteousness and not, for example, for the sake of public acclaim. Next are *hadis* of praise for the person who dares to be different from others, who in a time of corruption will return to the truth; the praise is reinforced by a reminder of the reward due the brave and the punishment set for the feckless. Knowledge, granted by God's grace, is identified as the key to knowing how to act, and the importance of sharing this knowledge is underlined.

The *hadis* then list many points of correct behavior in ablution, prayer, Qur'anic reading, financial interactions, fair dealings, steadfastness in adversity, modesty, responsibilities to family and fellow Muslims, and virtues and ethics overall. The final *hadis* quoted speaks of the joys of heaven and the horrors of hell, a transition to an extended description, summarized vividly from the *hadis,* of the signs of Judgment, the final days, and the Day of Judgment itself.

The power of this description and the role it was intended to play in affecting the disposition of the heart toward righteousness are clear. The signs of the Day of Judgment are reversals of the properly ordered world. To see the *shari'at* completely turned on end is to realize the ultimate implications of one's own deviation. This is a world where *zakat* is spurned, trusts exploited, family ties ignored, worldly gain exalted, tyrants in control, corruption rampant, and the sainted dead mocked. The calamities that follow confirm what already is: humans have acted like the pigs and dogs they now actually become.

Great battles ensue, primarily with the Christians, called "Naza-renes," who, from a Muslim perspective, claim to follow Jesus but in fact have corrupted his teachings. Jesus himself, in Muslim tradition, comes again as a blessed presence to aid against the Nazarenes and other enemies. These *hadis* carried special power in the nineteenth and early twentieth centuries when the "Nazarenes," as colonial powers, were seen as enemies, as the Byzantine Christians had been in the early centuries of Islam. Also evident in the battle is the descendent of the Prophet's old enemy, Abu Sufyan.

There are wondrous signs of providence in the battles: the descent of the Imam Mahdi and of Jesus with his destructive breath; the power of the sacred soil of the Haramain, making an enemy army disappear into the ground and protecting the cities of Mecca and Medina with angels; the magic of the words "Allahu akbar" causing the walls of Constantinople to fall. On the other side are the great horrors: one-eyed Dajjal, the barbarians Gog and Magog, the strange animal who marks the faithful and the infidel, the Abyssinians who destroy the Ka'ba—joined by natural calamities of earthquake, fog, endless night, the terrifying reversal of a sunrise in the west, and the balmy breeze that brings death to Muslims. In the end comes the trumpet that will grow so loud that all will die of terror, heaven and earth will be rent, and the world brought to an end.

The Day of Judgment follows, the dead brought forth from their graves to stand in the blazing heat of the great plain of judgment. This is the moment prefigured in each year's great standing of the *hajj* at 'Arafat, when Muslims of every nation, the men wrapped in the shroudlike *ihram,* stand forth all afternoon as the great climax of the pilgrimage itself. Now, at last, the truth of Islam is made clear. The good Muslim alone is protected from the heat; only the prophet of Islam is able to intercede so that Judgment can begin at last. The quality of each individual Muslim life is also made clear, as the great weighing of deeds and the test of the bridge takes place. The interces-sion of the pious and the mercy of God will save all but the truly unregenerate; heaven will be stratified so that merit can be appropri-ately rewarded. Death, in the shape of a ram, will be killed. The dwellers in heaven and hell will be forever in their places.

"There will be no end to the rejoicing of the inhabitants of heaven and no end to the anguish and grief of the inhabitants of hell." Heaven brings endless youth, luxury that meets every heart's desire, complete contentment, and the very vision of God. All of the passions, the uncertainties, the strains of the life we know on earth are ended forever. Heaven brings the culmination of the moral and spiritual perfection that one only seeks on earth. Hell, by contrast, brings suffering beyond comprehension, with snakes as big as camels, and scorpions the size of "mules with pack saddles," whose poisons and the paroxysms they cause last forty years.

The list of seventy-seven points of faith that follows this description could not be more compelling. Here is the key to securing reward and avoiding punishment too awful to describe. The final section of the book then turns specifically to the two chief obstacles to a moral life: one's own lower soul, and the influence of other people. Here, the treatment of the *nafs* revolves around regularly scheduled private conversations with one's self. The self is reminded that it is like a trader whose goods are life itself and whose "bottom line" is nothing less than eternal life. The self is instructed to keep thoughts of the hour of death ever constant, as a way of shaping every day's behavior. The self's clever answers—for example, that God is merciful—are checked. The self is a patient who must take bitter pills for the sake of the promised cure; the harm of self-indulgence and the blessing of bitter pills is clear: "forever and ever in the form of heaven and hell."

The final image of the self—as a traveler through the world, which is never to be seen as home—is particularly evocative. The world itself is a serai. If travelers on a journey stop struggling to reach home and settle at an inn, where they collect furnishings and pretend it is home, they will never reach their real home. Such travelers are the symbol of a misspent life, absorbed in material things, in this world. The afterlife, not the present, is home. It is the self, the *nafs,* one's own evil tendencies that are distanced and alienated, that can mislead one from the homeward path.

There is no twentieth-century concern with introspection to uncover just why a person is defensive or insecure, let alone gluttonous or proud. The goal is not to possess oneself through this kind of knowledge but to identify sinful tendencies and to distance or split off from oneself another person, something less than the real person. The psychological bifurcation is made clear by pairing this discussion with a discussion of relationships to "ordinary people," as if the *nafs* were a person as well.

The key to many of these teachings, as discussed further in the introduction to Book Ten, is an ideal of a person of "minimal transactions," someone who engages in very limited relationships with other people, who limits her circle of acquaintances, who avoids conversation or dining with strangers, who eschews ceremonial gatherings. That principle is evident here. Only a few close friends of unimpeachable moral fiber are to be cherished. All trust and hope, all concern for approbation, are to be with God alone. With this, Book Seven ends.

The contrast with what the reformers opposed as false sufism could not be clearer. The unreformed cherished the descendents of the saints and the great saintly shrines as places of blessed power and mediation. They believed the saints able to intercede for them, indeed to manipulate powers on behalf of others. This was part of the "custom" so abhorred by the reformers. It challenged the focus on individual responsibility before God and absolute commitment to *tauhid* that were at the heart of reform. The Deobandis insisted that the real sufis, although they were men of spiritual power, were above all exemplars of moral character and piety. The whole point of sufism was greater adherence to the Prophet's model, to the *shari'at* in all its teachings of doctrine, actions, and dispositions. In a period of political fragmentation, non-Islamic rule, and geographic mobility, individual Muslims, committed to moral perfection, could embody Islam quite apart from the institutions of the larger society, much as Islam was carried on in earlier periods of challenge to the faith.

The goal of Book Seven is ethical, but one must not think of simple rules of right and wrong. The goal is the formation of a person—heart, mind, and body—living in the practice of the *shari'at*. The first step, as indicated in the section on eleven "virtues," is *tauba,* the turning away from sin and oblivion with which the sufis initiate the journey on the spiritual path. That journey has its fulfillment in wholehearted attentiveness to the *shari'at,* with ritual worship as its anchor and foundation. The instruction offered here may seem repressive and regimented to the reader. To the author and those like him, however, mastery of rules and self-imposed limitations were seen as a way of finding true freedom and of discovering one's essential and natural self. The person shaped by these methods ideally knew herself to be living well, was confident of the value of her actions, and enjoyed respect as a mature and cultivated person, happy in this world and expecting happiness in the world to come.

Righteous women are devoutly obedient and guard in their husbands'
absence what Allah would have them guard.

A pamphlet meant to instruct women and girls in the
way to act on this Qur'anic verse

Heavenly Ornaments

Book Seven

A discussion, by section, of everything that women need to
know about beliefs, legal points, ethics and social behavior,
child-rearing, and so on

Compiled by the Reverend Hazrat, Sun of the Scholars,
Crown of the Learned,
Maulana Hafiz Muhammad Ashraf 'Ali Sahib

Published at the direction of
Shaikh Hajji Zainu'd-Din Ahmad and
Muhammad Yamain, Book Dealers, Saharanpur

Printed at the Bilali Steam Press, Sadhaura, District Ambala

Contents of Book Seven

In the Name of God, the Compassionate, the Merciful

The Seventh Book
of the *Bihishti Zewar:*
On Comportment and Character,
Reward and Punishment

I. Amendment of Religious Duties (*'Ibadat*)*

On the Ablution and Purity

[There is in Islamic law and in this book great emphasis on matters of cleanliness and purity. The importance of the ablution is evident from the extended treatment it receives in Book One (in a section that is not translated here). Arrangements for the requisite ablution are an architectural feature of every mosque, because ritual purity is required for prayer. A well-known *hadis* calls the ablution "the half of faith and the key to prayer."]

1. Perform the ablution carefully, even on occasions when your lower soul (*nafs*) objects.

2. There is greater reward for a fresh ablution, even if it is not legally required.

3. When urinating or defecating, you should neither face the direction of prayer nor turn your back on it.

4. Avoid getting drops of urine on yourself. You will be punished in the grave for carelessness in this regard [because you are impure for prayer].

5. Do not urinate into a hole, for fear of disturbing a snake, scorpion, or other animal.

---

* From *Ta'limu'd-din* (Instruction in religion) and other works. [See Book Ten, "The Names of Several Worthwhile Books," item 20.]

6. Do not urinate in a place where people bathe.

7. Do not talk while urinating or defecating.

8. When you wake up, do not put your hands into water that will be used in food preparation or some other job until you have washed carefully.

9. Do not use water warmed in the sun. It may cause the illness of leprosy, in which white spots appear on the body.[1]

On the Canonical Prayer

[The prayer, called *namaz* or *salat,* is discussed at length in Book Two (not translated here). The required prayer is performed five times a day. It is always recited in Arabic, and one must follow carefully pre-scribed postures. The required prayers are pre-dawn (*fajr*), midday (*zuhr*), mid-afternoon (*'asr*), post-sunset (*maghrib*), and night (*'isha*). There are also three optional prayers; the most common is performed after midnight (*tahajjud*).]

1. Perform the prayer at the right time. Do the bow and prostra-tion properly. Pray with all your heart (*ji*).

2. You should insist that children seven years of age recite the prayer; you should beat children of ten years if they do not perform it.

3. It is not good to perform the prayer on a cloth or other covering that might divert your attention with its patterns of flowers and leaves.

4. There should be some screen in front of the place of prayer. At the least, place a stick or some other tall object in front of you, directly opposite the left or right eyebrow [that is, not directly opposite where you prostrate yourself].

5. It is best to move aside to perform supererogatory prayers (*nafl*) at the conclusion of the obligatory prayer (*farz*).

6. Do not look up or around during the prayer. Stifle yawns as much as possible.

7. If necessary, urinate or defecate before performing the prayer.

8. Undertake only as many supererogatory prayers and disciplines as can be regularly carried out.[2]

On Death and Affliction

1. If some past affliction comes to mind, recite: "***We belong to God, and to God we will return.***" You will receive the same reward as you did on the occasion of your original sorrow.

2. However minor your sorrow may be, recite: *"We belong to God, and to God we will return,"* and you will receive reward.

On *Zakat* and Charity

[Generosity to the needy and deserving is the basic ethical injunction of Islam; it is discussed in detail in Book Three (not translated here). *Zakat,* the tithe, is a fixed percentage of specific property that can be spent only in certain ways; some charity (*khairat*) is required (*wajib*), some is approved but not required (*mustahib*).]

1. As far as possible, you should give *zakat* only to people who do not beg but who simply remain at home, guarding their honor (*abru*).

2. Do not be ashamed of giving a small amount in charity. Give according to your means.

3. Do not think that you are excused from giving charity because you have given *zakat.* Always do your best to give in response to some need.

4. There is a double reward for giving charity to your relatives—the first, for charity; the second, for doing a favor for relatives. Always show concern for your poor neighbors.

5. Do not distribute so much charity from your husband's possessions that he becomes displeased.

On the Fast

[The fast referred to is primarily that of the month of Ramazan (discussed in Book Three, not translated here). During that month, believers allow no food or drink to touch their mouths from dawn to dusk. Fasts are kept on other occasions as well, for example, in fulfillment of a vow.]

1. It is wrong to talk foolishly or to quarrel during a fast. It is an even greater sin to talk about other people behind their backs.

2. Do not keep a supererogatory fast without your husband's permission, if he is at home.

3. Always increase your religious practices during the last ten days of noble Ramazan.

On Reading the Qur'an

1. Do not get upset and give up if you are having trouble reading the Noble Qur'an. Keep on reading. A person who does so is doubly rewarded.

2. You should keep rereading the Noble Qur'an once you have finished it, so that you do not forget it. To neglect this is a serious sin.

3. Recite the Noble Qur'an wholeheartedly, fearful of God.

On Supplication and *Zikr*

1. Keep the following points in mind when making your supplications (*du'a*) to God:[3] Pray fervently. Ask for nothing sinful. Do not become upset and give up if your petition is not immediately fulfilled, but trust that your prayer has been heard.

2. Do not in anger call down curses on your property, your children, or your own life. At that very moment, your prayer may be heard.

3. Continually recall God and the Messenger, *God's blessings and peace upon him,* in the midst of your everyday talk and occupations. If you do not, your daily occupations become a burden.

4. Continually repeat the prayer for pardon (*istighfar*). It makes anything that is difficult easy and gives blessing to your livelihood.

5. Repent immediately if you sin because of your lower soul. If you should sin again, immediately repent again. Do not think that such failure makes it useless to continue to repent.

6. Many prayers are made at specific times, including those listed below.[4]

When going to sleep, recite: *"O God, I die and live with your name."*

When you awaken, recite: *"O God, through you alone we have reached the morning, and through you alone we have passed the night, and through you alone we die, and we will rise to you."*

In the evening, recite: *"O God, through you we have passed the morning, and through you we have come to the evening. Through you alone we die, and we will rise to you."*

After both the morning prayer and the post-sunset prayer, recite this supplication seven times: *"O God, grant me refuge from the fire."* And repeat three times: *"In the name of God, with whose name nothing on earth can do harm without his hearing and his knowing."*

When sitting in a conveyance, recite: *"Praise be to him who has put this animal in our power, for we alone cannot put it under our control. We will return to our Provider."*

If you eat at someone's house, recite this after eating: *"O God, bless them in what you have provided for their sustenance; forgive them their shortcomings; and be merciful to them."*

Upon seeing the new moon, recite: *"O God, may the moon of the new month appear for us in peace, faith, well-being, and Islam. God is my sovereign and your sovereign."*

When you see someone afflicted, recite this prayer, and Almighty God will preserve you from misfortune: *"Praise be to God, who has saved me from that with which he has afflicted you, and who has given great preference to me over many of those whom he has created."*

When someone is taking leave of you, recite: *"I entrust to God your religion, your faithfulness, and the outcome of your deeds."*

In congratulating a bride or a groom upon marriage, recite: *"May God bless both of you, shower blessings upon both of you, and bring both of you together in well-being."*

In any trouble, repeat: *"O Ever Living One, O Eternal One, I seek help through your mercy."*

After the five prayers and when going to sleep, always repeat: *"I seek forgiveness from Almighty God. No one is worshipped other than him. It is he who is living and constant, and I turn to him."* (Three times.) And *"There is no other God but God alone. He has no partner. All praise be to him. He has power over everything."* (One time.) And *"Glory be to God."* (Thirty-three times.) And *"God is greatest."* (Thirty-four times.) And *"Say, I seek refuge in the Lord of the dawn"* [Sura 113]. *"Say, I seek refuge in the Lord of the people"* [Sura 114]. (Once.) And one time "The Throne Verse" [Sura 2].

In the morning, recite the chapter "Ya-sin" one time [Sura 36].

After sunset, recite the chapter "The Event" one time [Sura 56].

After nightfall, recite the chapter "Sovereignty" one time [Sura 67].

On Friday, recite the chapter "The Cave" one time and, when going to sleep, read from the words "the peace of the Messenger" to the end of the chapter [Sura 18].

Read the Pure Qur'an every day, as much as possible. Remember that to read these verses is a source of reward but failure to do so is not a sin.

On Oaths and Vows

1. Do not swear by anything other than God—not by your children, not by your health, not by your eyes. Such oaths cause sin. If you should, however, utter such an oath without thinking, immediately recite the attestation of faith.

2. Never swear by saying, "If I lie, may I turn apostate." It makes no difference if what you are saying is true.

3. You should break a sinful oath made in anger and offer restitution—for example, if you swore something such as, "I will not speak to my father and mother."

II. Amendment of Behavior (*Mu'amalat*)

On Dealings with Other People

1. Do not be so greedy that you fail to distinguish what is prohibited and what is permitted. Do not squander the money God gives you. Refrain from spending money unless there is a genuine necessity.

2. People who are forced to sell their goods in distress should be considered people in need. Do not take advantage of them. Do not force them to lower their price. Either help them or buy their things at a suitable price.

3. Do not harass poor debtors. Either give them extra time or remit part or all of the debt.

4. It is wrong to refuse a request to repay a debt if you have the means to pay.

5. As far as possible, do not borrow from anyone. If you must borrow, consider carefully how you will repay the loan. Do not be careless about this. If your creditor says something harsh to you, do not get angry and answer back.

6. It is wrong to take someone's belongings as a joke and hide them so that the person worries.

7. Do not underpay laborers for their services.

8. During a period of famine, some people will sell their own children or someone else's children. To use these children as slaves is forbidden.

9. A person who provides fire for cooking food or who gives even a small amount of salt for seasoning receives the same reward as if the whole meal had been provided.

10. It is a matter of great reward to give someone drinking water. Where water is amply available, it is as if you had freed a slave. Where it is scarce, it is as if you had given life to the dead.

11. Tell other people or keep a written record of your debts or of anything kept in trust for someone else. That way, if you die before you have settled these matters, your obligations can be met.[5]

On Marriage

1. In marrying off your children, take into account primarily whether the other person is religious. Do not give much consideration to whether the person brings riches and wealth. Nowadays, the very wealthy have begun to oppose Islam, because of studying English. Marriage with such people is not proper and would be, in fact, not marriage but fornication.

2. Women are often in the habit of describing the appearance of other women to their husbands. This is very unwise. If a husband's heart should incline to one of them, the wife will do nothing but weep.

3. You should not send a proposal on behalf of your own child to someone who is already giving favorable consideration to another proposal. Only if the other proposal is broken off or if one side refuses the offer is it proper for you to make an offer.

4. To discuss the private matters of husband and wife with women friends and companions is very displeasing in the sight of Almighty God. Often, bride and groom do not take proper account of this.

5. If asked, you must speak frankly if you know of some defect in a person who is being considered for marriage or if you are aware of some other problem in the arrangement. To speak ill of someone in these circumstances is not prohibited. Do not, however, slander a person for no good reason.

6. A wife may take money secretly if her husband is a person of means and does not provide resources adequate for her expenses. It is not right, however, to take from him for foolish expenditures or for carrying out worldly customs.[6]

On Causing Trouble to Others

1. No one other than a fully qualified *hakim* should give any medical treatment that might cause harm. Anyone who does so is sinful.[7]

2. Frightening someone with a sharp object, even in fun, is forbidden, for the object might slip from the hand.

3. Do not hand anyone an open knife. Either close it or put it down on a bed or somewhere else so that the other person can pick it up.

4. It is a great sin to confine a cat or a dog so that it suffers from hunger and thirst.

5. It is very harsh to taunt a sinner. There is, however, no harm in saying something by way of counsel.

6. It is not right to stare at someone who has done nothing wrong,

in order to frighten her. Remember that it is not right to stare at all, and thus it is clearly wrong to frighten someone by staring in jest.

7. If you are going to slaughter an animal, sharpen the knife carefully so that you do not cause unnecessary suffering.

8. Do not abuse animals while traveling. Do not load too many goods on them, and do not browbeat them. When you reach your destination, immediately make arrangements for their fodder.

III. Amendment of Habits (*'Adat*)

On Eating and Drinking

1. Say "*Bi'smi'llah*" (*"In the name of God"*) before eating.[8] Eat with your right hand. Eat from the side of the dish nearest you. If several kinds of things are served, such as several kinds of fruits or sweets, you may choose whatever you like and eat what your heart desires.

2. Lick your fingers and clean the vessel when the dish is finished.

3. If a morsel falls from your hands, pick it up, clean it, and eat it. Do not put on airs.

4. Take melon slices, dates, grapes, or sweets one at a time. Do not take two at a time.

5. When you eat something like raw onions or garlic, rinse out your mouth to get rid of the smell if you are going to sit in company.

6. Measure out flour and rice for the day's use before cooking. Do not just take out your supplies blindly.

7. Give thanks to Almighty God after eating and drinking.

8. Wash your hands before and after eating. Also rinse out your mouth.

9. Do not eat food that is burning hot.

10. Be considerate of a guest. If you in turn are a guest, do not stay so long that you begin to be a burden to your host.

11. Coming together for a meal brings blessing.

12. When you finish eating, have the tablecloth removed before you arise. To get up first is rude. If you finish eating before your companion does, keep her company by eating a little more, so that she does not get up hungry out of embarrassment. If for some reason it is necessary to get up first, ask her pardon.

13. It is obligatory to accompany a guest to the door.

14. Do not drink water in one gulp but in three. And when you take a breath, take the vessel away from your mouth. Before drinking, say

"*Bi'smi'llah,*" and after drinking, say "*Alhamdu'li'llah*" (*"Praise be to God"*).[9]

15. Do not put a vessel to your lips if you think the water may spill or if you think there may be something like an insect or a thorn inside.

16. Do not drink water standing up, except out of necessity.

17. If you want to pass the drinking water to someone else, give it first to the person on your right, who will pass it to the next person on the right. Anything to be shared, such as *pan,* perfume, or sweets, should be passed in this manner.

18. Do not drink water from a broken vessel.

19. Do not let children go outside after early evening. In the evening, say "*Bi'smi'llah*" and close the door. Then say "*Bi'smi'llah*" and cover the vessels. Before retiring, extinguish the lights and put out the fire or pack it down.

20. Cover all food and drink you send to someone.

On How to Dress

1. Do not walk around wearing only one shoe. Do not wrap a quilt or other covering around you in a way that makes it difficult to walk or to extend your hand quickly.

2. Begin getting dressed from the right side—for example, first the right sleeve, right leg, right shoe. Take off clothes from the left side.

3. Your sins will be forgiven if you repeat this supplication after dressing: *"Praise be to God who clothed me with this and favored me without any effort from me."*

4. Do not wear clothes that are revealing.

5. Do not associate often with rich women who wear expensive clothes and jewels, for fear that, without realizing it, you may grow fond of worldly things.

6. Do not consider it beneath your status to patch your clothes.

7. Wear neither very fancy clothes nor clothes that are dirty and unkempt. Strike a happy medium. Practice cleanliness.

8. Apply oil to your hair and comb it, but do not be busy with this every minute. Put henna on your hands.

9. Put three applicators of antimony in each eye.[10]

10. Keep your household clean.

On Illness and Its Treatment

1. Do not force a sick person to eat and drink.

2. Follow a careful regimen of eating when you are sick.

3. You must absolutely never make use of amulets or charms that are against the *shari'at*.[11]

4. Have someone suspected of casting an evil eye (*nazar*) wash her face, both arms up to the elbows, both feet, both knees, and her private parts. Collect the water and pour it over the head of the person afflicted, and, *Almighty God willing,* that person will be cured.

5. Those people sick with diseases that are hateful to others, such as mange or leprosy, should remain apart from others, so that no one is distressed.

On Dreams

1. If you have a frightening dream, spit three times to the left and repeat three times: *"I seek refuge in God from Satan, the Cursed."* Then turn over and mention the dream to no one. *Almighty God willing,* you will not be harmed.

2. If you have to tell your dream to someone, tell it to someone who is discriminating or who cares about you. Otherwise, you may get a bad interpretation.

3. To fabricate a dream is a very bad sin.

On Greetings

1. Always greet each other with *"As-salamu'alaikum"* (*"Peace be upon you"*). And answer with *"Wa'alaikum as-salam"* (*"And upon you, peace"*). All other greetings are nonsense.

2. When two people meet, whoever greets the other first receives the greater reward.

3. Answer whoever brings greetings from someone else with *"'Alaihim wa 'alaikum as-salam"* (*"Peace be upon him and upon you"*).

4. If one of a group of several people gives a greeting, it is as if all had given it; likewise, if one from the group answers, it is as if all had answered.[12]

On Sitting, Lying, and Walking

1. Do not strut proudly about, all decked out.

2. Do not lie on your stomach.

3. Do not sleep on a roof that has no railing, for fear that you might roll off.

4. Do not sit partly in the sun, partly in the shade.

5. If for some reason you have to go out, walk on the side of the street. It is immodest for a woman to walk in the middle.

On Sitting in Company

1. Do not move someone from her place in order to sit there.

2. No one should sit in the place of a person who gets up from a gathering to do something and is expected to return. That place is hers by right.

3. Do not sit between two women who are deliberately sitting together in a gathering. Of course, there is no harm if they invite you to join them.

4. If you see a woman coming to join you, move aside a little so that she will feel you value her.

5. Do not act as if you are in charge of a gathering. Sit down wherever there is a space, just as the poor would do.

6. If you have to sneeze, cover your mouth with a cloth or with your hand, and sneeze quietly.

7. Stifle a yawn as best you can. If you cannot, at least cover your mouth.

8. Do not laugh loudly.

9. Do not sit in a gathering with your nose turned up and your face flushed with pride. Sit humbly, like the poor. If you have something relevant to say, you may join in, but you must say nothing sinful.

10. In a gathering, do not extend your feet in anyone's direction.[13]

On Curbing Your Tongue

1. Do not say anything without thinking. You may speak only after you have thought something through and are certain that it is not at all sinful.

2. It is a sin to say that someone is irreligious or to say, "God curse him," or "God's anger fall on him," or "May he go to hell." It makes no difference whether you are speaking of an animal or a person—it is all sinful. If the person does not deserve the curses, they will all turn back on the speaker.

3. If someone says something improper to you, you may say the equivalent in return. You sin if you say the least thing more.

4. Do not engage in two-faced flattery, saying one thing to one person, another thing to a second.

5. Do not tell tales or listen to tale-telling.

6. Never tell a lie.

7. Never praise anyone to her face out of flattery, nor praise her excessively behind her back.

8. Never engage in backbiting. Backbiting is saying something behind someone's back that would make her unhappy if she heard. It makes no difference whether the comment is true. If it is false, it is slander and thus an even more serious sin.

9. Do not argue with anyone; do not insist that your point prevail.

10. Do not laugh too much, for such laughter takes the glow from the heart.

11. If you have slandered someone and have not secured her forgiveness, pray for her pardon. There is hope she will forgive you on the Day of Judgment.

12. Do not make false promises. Do not jest in a way that devalues someone else.

13. Do not boast about any of your possessions or skills.

14. Do not be preoccupied with poetry. There is no harm if you occasionally recite a verse of supplication or counsel in a soft voice, provided that the subject is not against the *shari'at.*

15. Do not pass on gossip. Often, what you hear is false.

On Miscellaneous Matters

1. Couch your point indirectly when you write a letter, in order to facilitate your purpose in writing.

2. Do not denounce the times as bad.

3. Do not mince your words or—the opposite—draw out your speech or exaggerate.

4. Do not lend your ear to anyone's singing.

5. Do not mimic anyone's bad appearance or bad speech.

6. If you see someone do something wrong, you should hide the fault. Do not sing it about.

7. Think about whatever you do. Consider its outcome, then do it calmly. A job is often spoiled by haste.

8. If someone seeks your advice, give the counsel you consider to be best.

9. Check your anger as far as possible.

10. Seek everyone's forgiveness for your disputes. Otherwise, on the Day of Judgment there will be great trouble.

11. Encourage others to do good works and always forbid bad ones. You may remain silent if there is no hope whatever of the others accepting your advice or if there is a likelihood that they will be an-

noyed. Still, know a bad thing to be bad in your heart, and do not meet refractory people except out of necessity.

IV. Amendment of the Heart (*Dil*)

[ON VICES]

The Evil of Excess Eating and Its Cure

Excess devotion to the stomach causes many sins. Keep the following points in mind: Do not insist on tasty food only. Avoid food that is legally prohibited. Do not stuff yourself beyond what you should eat, but keep yourself slightly hungry. This last point has many benefits.

First, your heart remains pure, inspiring recognition of God's blessings and enhancing your love for him.

Second, your heart remains soft and tender, so that you savor supplication and recollection of God.[14]

Third, pride and rebellion are extinguished in the lower soul.

Fourth, the lower soul feels discomfort and therefore remembers the wrath of God and avoids sin.

Fifth, the inclination to sin is less.

Sixth, your nature (*tabi'at*) remains light. You sleep little. There is no sloth in performing the supererogatory night prayer and other acts of worship.

Seventh, you pity the hungry and humble and feel tenderhearted toward everyone.

The Evil of Excess Talking and Its Cure

The lower soul enjoys excess talking. This ensnares it in hundreds of sins, including lies, backbiting, curses, accusations, self-exaltation, pointless disputation, flattery of the rich, and jesting that causes pain to others. Hold your tongue whenever possible in order to escape these banes. Here is what you must do: When you have something to say, do not blurt out whatever comes to mind, but first think carefully whether your point is sinful, worthy of reward, or just indifferent.

If it is sinful, to whatever degree, remain completely silent. If your lower soul protests from within, reason with it by explaining that it is easier to suppress the self here and now than to endure the torment of hell!

If your point is laudable, then say it. If it is indifferent, keep quiet unless your heart really insists. Speak briefly and then remain silent. If you continue to scrutinize every single word, in a few days you will develop a real hatred of saying things you shouldn't say.

Another strategy for guarding your tongue is to avoid meeting anyone unless necessary. In solitude, your tongue will remain quiet of itself.

The Evil of Anger and Its Cure

In anger, sense disappears. No one can think through an outcome. Your mouth speaks words that are out of place, and your hands commit acts that are violent. Anger must be firmly checked. To check it, immediately remove from your sight anyone with whom you are angry. If the person does not go away, you should leave. Then reflect that however much you may hold this person to blame, Almighty God holds you at fault even more. Just as you want God to forgive you, you must forgive this person. You should repeat several times: *"I seek God's protection . . ."* Drink some water, or perform the ablution. In this way, the anger will dissipate.

When your sense has returned, you may punish the offender if it seems appropriate. Do this, for example, for the sake of the person, as in the case of your children, who must be disciplined. You should also discipline a guilty person in order to give recompense to someone who has been unfairly treated. Weigh carefully how much punishment there should be for a certain fault, and exact punishment only to the extent that satisfaction can be obtained in accordance with the *shari'at.*

If you check your anger in this way for a few days, it will begin to come under control of its own accord. It will no longer be so intense. Anger, moreover, causes malice. When anger is controlled, malice will also disappear from the heart.

The Evil of Envy and Its Cure

When you feel envy, your heart burns with jealousy and you feel morose at seeing someone else flourishing, eating and drinking well, or living in respect and honor. You rejoice in the downfall of others. Envy is wrong and sinful. An envious person's whole life passes in bitterness. Both her worldly life and her religious life are without sweetness. You must make great effort to escape from this affliction. Its treatment is this: First, reflect that it is you yourself who is being hurt by this envy, whereas the other person is not harmed at all. The harm to you is that your good qualities are being destroyed. As the *hadis* says: "Envy eats up good qualities as a fire consumes wood." Implicit in envy is the thought that such and such a person does not deserve the blessings God has given. This, if you think about it—repent, repent!—is actually opposition to Almighty God. A very serious sin! The trouble it causes is clear, for someone consumed with envy is always lost in sorrow and grief, whereas the person envied suffers no harm at all. Envy does not make her good fortune disappear. Indeed, she *profits* because the good qualities of the envious woman come over to her!

When you finish thinking this over, force your heart to be kind to the other person and praise her in front of other people. Say, "Thanks be to Almighty God that she has such blessings. May Almighty God give her double!" If you have occasion to meet her, honor her and act with humility before her. At the beginning, this behavior will make the lower soul very uncomfortable, but bit by bit it will become easy. Your envy will disappear.

The Evil of Love of the World and of Wealth and Its Cure

Love of wealth is a very grievous sin, because it displaces the memory and love of Almighty God from the heart. It puts a person in the continual dilemma of figuring out how to get more money, choosing what kind of clothes and jewels she should have, and calculating how to get what she wants. She must have this many vessels ordered, this many items made, this kind of house built, a garden laid out, property bought. When day and night are spent in this, where is the chance to think of Almighty God? A particular evil is that when such love takes root in the heart, it makes dying and returning to God seem undesirable, because all this luxury will disappear. When such a woman is dying, she disdains to leave this world. When she concludes that it is Almighty God who is the cause of her leaving, then—repent, repent!— she rails against God and dies an infidel.

Here is a further evil. When a person throws herself into acquiring worldly things, she takes no account of what is permitted and what is prohibited. She no longer cares whether something belongs to her or to someone else. She indulges in lies and deceit. Her only remaining motive is to get whatever she can and stash it away. It says in the *hadis* that love of the world is the root of all sins.

Because this is such a serious matter, every Muslim must try to save herself from this evil and expunge such love of the world from her heart. One treatment is to reflect at length on death and on the fact that one day you must leave everything behind. What, then, is the profit in setting your heart on worldly goods? Indeed, the more you do so, the more grief there will be in leaving them. Second, do not increase your circle of acquaintances, but avoid associating with many people. Similarly, do not collect goods and chattels or buildings and property any more than necessary. Do not expand your dealings or livelihood excessively, but limit them to what is needed for comfort and necessity. In short, have little of everything. Third, do not make foolish expenditures, because they increase the greed for income that causes all ills. Fourth, make a habit of eating ordinary food and wearing ordinary clothes. Fifth, mix mostly with poor people and avoid the rich, because associating with rich people produces a yearning to have everything they have. Sixth, read and reread the tales and stories of those elders who abandoned the world. Seventh, give in charity or sell anything to which your heart is too much attached. *Almighty God willing,* with these strategies, love of the world will disappear from your heart, and all these excessive longings—such as collecting this, or buying that, or leaving such and such buildings and villages to the children—will bit by bit disappear as love of the world is no more.

The Evil of Miserliness and Its Cure

On account of miserliness, people neglect claims that are a duty and an obligation, among them *zakat,* the sacrifice, helping the needy, and looking after poor relatives. This causes sin and harm to your faith. It also causes worldly harm, for everyone regards a miserly person as worthless and contemptible. What greater evil is there than this? One treatment for miserliness is to expel love of wealth and the world from the heart. Once that love is gone, miserliness will never remain. A second treatment is to force yourself to give away whatever you do not need. Although there will be some discomfort to the lower soul, you must take courage and tolerate this discomfort. Keep this up until the last trace of miserliness is gone from the heart.

The Evil of Wanting Renown* and Its Cure

When a person's heart longs for fame, she burns with jealousy at the good reputation of anyone else. (You have already heard about this evil.) When she hears of someone else's faults or disgrace, she is happy. It is a grave sin to wish another ill. There is a further evil. Sometimes a person seeks a good reputation by illegitimate means—for example, by foolish expenditures and by squandering wealth on occasions such as weddings. Sometimes a person accepts bribes or takes loans with inter-

* In Arabic this is called *hubb jah.*

est. All this is for the sake of renown. The worldly harm is that a person who spends like this has many enemies who oppose and envy her. They want to defame and disgrace her and cause her harm and trouble.

One remedy is simply to remember that neither you nor those who will esteem you will long remain. After a few days, no one will even ask about you or them. It is sheer ignorance to be happy over something so fleeting. A second remedy is to do something that may not be illegitimate but is wrongly regarded by most people as low and contemptible. You can, for example, begin to sell stale, leftover bread to the poor cheaply. This will bring you fine disrepute!

The Evil of Pride and Its Cure

To be proud or put on airs (*ghurur, shaikhi, takabbur*) is to consider yourself superior to others and to hold others inferior, whether in knowledge, acts of worship, religiosity, pedigree, wealth and goods, respect and honor, intellect, or something else. This is a grave sin. A *hadis* says that anyone who has pride in his or her heart equal in size to a mustard seed will not go to heaven. In this world, moreover, people despise proud people and oppose them, even though they may treat them civilly (*a'o bhagat karna*) out of fear.

A proud person, moreover, does not accept anyone's good counsel and rejects what is in fact the truth. Indeed, she takes advice badly and wants to bring trouble to the person proffering it.

The remedy is to pay attention to your essential reality. "I am a creation of clay and impure water. All my good qualities are given by Almighty God. If he wishes, he can take everything away right now. Why should I put on airs?" At the same time, remember God's own greatness. That will dim any sense you have of your own superiority. Act with humility before anyone you consider contemptible, and always honor her. Haughtiness will disappear from your heart. If you can do nothing more, at least require yourself to greet people of low rank first. *Almighty God willing,* this will result in great humility in the lower soul.

The Evil of Acting with Arrogance and Its Cure

It is wrong for anyone to consider herself superior or to put on clothes and jewelry to show off, even if she does it without looking down on other people. The *hadis* says that this habit destroys faith. It is also a fact that such a person has no thought of improving herself.

Because she considers herself superior, she never sees her own faults. The remedy for this is to think about your faults continually and to recognize that what is good in you is the blessing of Almighty God and no perfection of your own. With this in mind, give thanks to God and pray that your blessings may remain.

The Evil of Doing Good Acts in Order to Be Seen and Its Cure

This kind of ostentation takes many forms. Sometimes people say outright that they have done something: "I have read such and such amount of the Qur'an"; or "I was up at night." Sometimes they mix a remark into other conversation. For example, there may be some mention of the Bedouin (the desert Arabs), and someone will say, "Oh, no, sir, all that is false; this is what happened to us." Although the conversation was about something else, everyone finds out that the speaker has performed the *hajj*. Sometimes people will do something like sitting with a rosary in front of everyone else, with the sole intention of being noticed. Sometimes they make a big fuss about doing something. For example, it may in fact be a certain woman's habit to read the Qur'an, but now she begins to make a big to-do about reading it in front of other women. Sometimes a person strikes a certain appearance or posture—sitting with bowed head and closed eyes, for example, to make observers think she is a devotee of God (*bari allah wali*), deep in meditation at every moment, awake at night so that her eyelids now droop from sleepiness.

This ostentation also takes many other forms. In whatever form, it is very bad. On the Day of Judgment, those good deeds that are done for the sake of show will receive the torment of hell instead of reward. The remedy for this is the same as that written above for undue seeking of renown, for ostentation is in fact exactly that.

An Important Clarification

There is no profit in acting on the remedies outlined above just a few times. These faults will not be removed so easily. For example, if you check your anger a couple of times, the root of the illness will not disappear. If once or twice you avoid getting angry, do not be deceived into thinking that your lower soul has now been tamed. Practice these treatments for many, many days; and if you forget, express your sorrow and regret, and try again. After a long time, *Almighty God willing,* the root of these evils will disappear.

A Further Important Point

An easy way to remedy faults of the lower soul and the sins of your hands and feet is to punish the lower soul whenever it commits some fault or sin. Two punishments are so easy that anyone can do them. One is to fix on yourself a fine of an *ana* or two or a rupee or two, according to your means. Whenever you err, distribute the fine to the poor. If you err again, distribute a fine again. The second punishment is to have no food at one or two meals. There is hope in God that by carrying out these punishments, **Almighty God willing,** you will be freed of your faults.

ON GOOD ACTS THAT RECTIFY THE HEART

[The English terms given below for these good acts, or virtues, must be taken as only approximations of what the terms convey in Urdu, as the statements themselves make clear. "Patience," for example, the conventional equivalent of *sabr,* must be understood as something like "self-restraint in fidelity to the religious law." "Gratitude" (*shukr*) is valid only as it leads directly to faithfulness in worship. "Truth" (*sidq*) is not an abstract concept but a true intention of fulfilling the *shari'at* for its own sake and not out of expedience. The point of *sidq* and other related virtues is to cultivate attentiveness and spiritual involvement in all acts of obedience.]

Repentance and the Way to Attain It

Repentance (*tauba*) is of great value because it brings forgiveness of sins. Anyone who pays attention to her own condition certainly knows that at every moment, in some way or another, she sins. Such a person will understand that repentance is continually necessary. The method of cultivating an attitude of repentance is to recollect and ponder the various torments for sins that are threatened in the Qur'an and *hadis*. This will cause the heart to sorrow at sin. At that point, you must repent verbally, and you must make up any canonically required prayer or fast you have missed. You must seek forgiveness or repay what is owed to anyone whose rights you have ignored. You must feel thorough repentance toward any sins you have committed, of whatever kind. Weep aloud and beseech forgiveness from Almighty God.

Fear (*Khauf, Dar*) of Almighty God and the Way
to Attain It

Almighty God declared: "Fear me, for dread is a most excellent
thing; through it, humanity avoids sin." The method is the same as for
repentance, that is, to dwell continually on the punishments of Almighty God.

Hope in Almighty God and the Way to Attain It

Almighty God declared: "Do not be without hope in the mercy of
Almighty God." Hope (*umid*) is of great value because it emboldens
the heart to do good deeds and gives one courage to repent. The way
to attain it is to ponder deeply the mercy of Almighty God.

Patience and the Way to Attain It

Patience (*sabr*) involves fixing the lower soul within the limits of
religion and forbidding it to do any act against religion. There are
many situations that call for patience. One is when a person lives in
comfort and peace, when Almighty God has given health, goods,
honor, servants, children, and a house and all accoutrements. At such
a time, patience means refraining from self-satisfaction, not being
oblivious of Almighty God, and not having contempt for the poor, with
whom one should always be gentle and kind.

A second opportunity for patience is in regard to acts of worship,
when, for example, the lower soul is lazy in getting up for the prayer or
is miserly at the time of giving *zakat* and charity. You must then display
three kinds of patience. First, you must fix a correct intention[15] and do
the act for the sake of God alone, free of any selfish motive. Second,
you should be resolute at the time of worship, offering properly whatever is owed in that act. Third, you should not mention the act of
worship in front of anyone else afterward.

The third opportunity for patience is when one is about to sin.
Patience at that time means checking the lower soul from sin.

The fourth opportunity for patience is when someone causes you
trouble or speaks ill of you. On such an occasion, patience means
refraining from revenge and remaining silent.

The fifth opportunity for patience is in a time of trouble, illness, loss
of wealth, or the death of someone near and dear. Patience then means
speaking no word against the *shari'at* and describing the event without
weeping.

To cultivate all these forms of patience, you should recall what your reward will be. You should remember that all that happens is for your own good. You should recognize that your fate will still not change if you act without patience—thus there is no point in unnecessarily jeopardizing your reward as well.

Gratitude and the Way to Attain It

The essence of gratitude (*shukr*) is to rejoice in the blessings of Almighty God, to love him in your heart, and, out of this love, to long to perform acts of worship and to consider disobedience to such a Benefactor a matter of deep shame. It is evident that every servant of God is, at any moment, blessed in thousands of ways. Any trouble there may be is for her own good and is also a blessing. When there is always blessing, then there should always be joy and love in the heart and nothing ever lacking in fulfilling the order of Almighty God. To achieve this state, you must always ponder deeply the blessings of Almighty God.

Trust in Almighty God and the Way to Attain It

Every Muslim knows that every profit gained and every loss sustained are by the will of Almighty God. Therefore, in whatever you do, you must not put your trust (*bharosa*) in your own plans, but put your sight on Almighty God, neither expecting too much of any creature nor fearing too much from any creature. Recognize that without God no one can do anything at all. This is called reliance (*tawakkul*) and trust. To attain this trust, you must ponder deeply the power and wisdom of Almighty God and the worthlessness of all creation.

Love of Almighty God and the Way to Attain It

Love (*mahabbat*) is to feel your heart drawn to Almighty God and to relish hearing his words and seeing his works. To attain this love, you must continually recite the name of God, always remember his virtues, and ponder the love that he has for his servant.

Contentment at the Order of Almighty God and the Way to Attain It

A Muslim should be content (*razi*) with all things and never be distressed or complain once she knows that whatever derives from

Almighty God is for the good of his servant and a source of reward. To attain contentment, you must think that whatever happens is for the best.

Truth (*Sidq*)—that is, True Intention— and the Way to Attain It

In performing any religious act, you should have no worldly motive such as ostentation or the satisfaction of your own comforts. For example, a person may decide to fast because her stomach feels heavy, thinking she will perform a fine fast and at the same time make her stomach feel better. Or, at the time of prayer, a person who has done her ablution earlier may decide to perform a fresh ablution, both to have a fresh ablution and to cool off her hands and feet on a warm day. Or someone may give to a beggar simply to escape his demands and be done with him. All these examples are the opposite of true intention (*sachchi niyat*). The method for gaining pure intention is to think very carefully before acting. Remove from your heart any worldly motive mixed into your action.

Contemplation (*Muraqaba*)—that is, Heartfelt Attentiveness to God—and the Way to Attain It

You should exercise attentiveness (*dhyan*)[16] at every moment, realizing that Almighty God knows everything about you, both outer and inner. God may punish any evil deed or thought in this world or the next. During worship, you should fix your attention on the thought that God sees your worship and that you therefore must perform it well. The key is to keep thinking this continually. In a few days, you will be fully attentive, and, **God willing,** you will do nothing against the wish of God.

A Method for Cultivating Heartfelt Reading of the Glorious Qur'an

As a rule, when someone is asked, "Let's see how well you read the Qur'an," that person reads with all possible care—diligently, beautifully, conscientiously. Now, you must always do as follows. If you intend to read the Qur'an, first think in your heart that it is as if Almighty God had asked to see how well you read. Remember that Almighty God is listening carefully. Consider that if you read with care at the request of an ordinary person, you should read especially well at

the request of Almighty God. Begin to read only after you have reflected on all this, and keep it in mind the whole time you are reading.
If you begin to err in your reading, or your heart is distracted here and
there, then stop reading for a little while to recollect these points and
then begin afresh. *Almighty God willing,* this method will help you read
clearly and correctly, and your heart will also grow attentive. If you
practice reading in this way, your heart will eventually come to be
readily involved.

A Method for Cultivating Heartfelt Prayer

Remember that in the prayer no act and no recitation should be
without intention, but should be performed deliberately and intention-
ally. For example, when you say, *"Allahu akbar"* (*"God is greatest"*)
when you are standing, at every word you should think: "I am reciting,
'Subhanaka'llahuma' (*'Glory to thee, O God'*)." Then think: "I am saying, *'Bihamdika'* (*'In praise of thee'*)." Then think: "Now I am saying,
'Wa tabaraka'smuka' (*'And blessed be thy Name'*)." Focus deliberately
on each separate word. Do this in reciting *al-hamd* and in the recitation
of a chapter of the Qur'an. Then, while performing the bow, repeat
with attention, *"Subhana rabbi'l'azim"* ("Glory to my Great Master").
In this way, direct your attention to each word. Adhere to this method
for the whole prayer. *Almighty God willing,* performing the prayer in
this way will keep you from distraction. Soon, your heart will readily
take pleasure and delight in prayer.

ON THE RELATION OF MASTER AND DISCIPLE (*PIRI-MURIDI*)

There are many advantages to becoming a disciple. One is that
faulty understanding can misguide you in carrying out the methods of
amending the heart that have been described above; a master, however, can explain the right path. A second advantage is that reading
something in a book is often not as effective as a master's explanation.
This is in part because of his blessed power (*baraka*). Moreover, a
disciple fears embarrassment before the master if she falls short in
some good work or does some evil deed. The third advantage is that,
because a disciple loves and believes in the master, her heart wants to
act as he teaches. The fourth advantage is that the disciple does not
take it amiss if the master is harsh or angry in giving her good counsel;
instead, she makes greater effort to do what he says. In discipleship
you will attain many other blessings filled with God's grace. It is only
when they are acquired that they are known.

If you intend to become a disciple, you should look for certain qualities in a master. Do not become a disciple of anyone who lacks them. First, the master should know the points of religion and be acquainted with the *shari'at*. Second, his beliefs should in no way oppose the *shari'at* but should be those you have studied in the first book of the *Bihishti Zewar*. He should follow the legal points and methods of amendment of the heart that you have already studied. Third, he should not practice *piri-muridi* for food and a living. Fourth, the prospective *pir* should himself be the disciple of someone who is regarded as venerable by good people. Fifth, good people should regard him as good, too. Sixth, his teaching should cause love and enthusiasm for religion to grow. This can be ascertained from seeing the state of his other disciples. If among ten disciples five or six are good, you can judge him to be a master with spiritual power; do not worry about one or two being bad. You have heard about the spiritual power (*tasir*) in elders. It is this. Do not look for other kinds of power—for example, the power to say something and make it happen; or to remove sickness by breathing on someone; or to make a wish come true by preparing an amulet; or to make someone feel agitated through direction of the *pir*'s attention (*tawajjuh*) toward that person. Never be deceived by these powers. The seventh important quality is that the master's religious counsel should not be swayed by his disciples' concerns but should stop them short in anything that is wrong.

When you meet such a master, ask permission of your parents, if you are an unmarried girl, or of your husband, if you are married. Then become a disciple with good intention, that is, purely with the intention of correcting your faith. Do not become a disciple if your family forbids it for some reason. After all, becoming a disciple is not a required obligation. Of course, it is an obligation to walk in the path of religion. Persevere even without being a disciple. Instruction on several points concerning the relationship follows:

1. Respect your master sincerely. Follow the method of reciting the name of God exactly as he tells you. Believe that you can benefit in reforming your heart through him more than through any other elder of this age.

2. If your heart is not yet set aright when the master dies, you should become the disciple of another perfect master who possesses all the qualities listed above.

3. Do not do anything on the basis of your own sense just because you have read something about daily practices (*wazifa*) or sufism (*faqiri*) in some book. Consult your master. Whenever anything new,

good or bad, comes into your heart or the intention of doing something new occurs to you, ask your master about it first.

4. Do not appear before the master unveiled. At the time of initiation as a disciple, do not give your hand into his hand. Discipleship is effected with a handkerchief or some other cloth or simply with words.

5. If in error you become a disciple of a master who acts against the *shari'at,* or if a person previously good goes astray, break off your discipleship and become the disciple of some good elder. If, however, the master commits some minor error, just remember that he is, after all, human; he is not an angel. His fault can be forgiven through repentance. Do not lose your faith in him over some minor matter. Should he remain fixed in error, you should, of course, break off your relationship.

6. It is a sin to believe that the master knows everything about you at every moment.

7. Never read books on sufism (*faqiri*) that on the surface speak against the *shari'at.* Nor should you ever read aloud poetic verses that are against the *shari'at.*

8. Many *faqir*s say that the path of the *shari'at* is one thing and the path of *faqiri* is another. Such a *faqir* has strayed and must be seen as deceitful.

9. You must not do anything against the *shari'at,* even if the master tells you to. If he insists that you do such a thing, break off your discipleship.

10. Do not tell anyone other than your master if, through the blessed power of reciting the name of God, you attain a good spiritual state in your heart, witness good dreams, or experience a voice or light in a waking state. Nor should you ever reveal to anyone else the nature of your daily practices and acts of worship, because that treasure disappears from exposure.

11. If the master has taught you some daily practice or recollection, do not let your heart feel constrained or lose belief in him if for some time there is no delight or effect on the heart. You should realize that the important effect of spiritual practices is simply to create in your heart the intention of reciting the name of God. This is in itself a source of grace. Never let your heart wish for such experiences as a vision of elders in a dream, knowledge of events about to happen, continuous weeping, or unconsciousness during worship that makes you unaware of all else. Sometimes these things happen; sometimes they don't. If they do, offer thanks to Almighty God; and if not, or if they lessen or disappear, do not sorrow. Certainly—God forbid—if you grow slack in

adhering to the *shari'at* or if you begin to sin, that indeed is a matter of grave concern. Quickly take courage, rectify your condition, inform your master, and act on what he tells you.

12. Never be disrespectful toward other elders or toward another sufi family, nor say to those who are disciples elsewhere that your master or your family is better than theirs.[17] Such foolish talk brings darkness to the heart.

13. Do not envy some other sister to whom the master shows greater kindness or who has greater profit in her daily recitations and recollections.

THE WAY IN WHICH EVERY DISCIPLE—INDEED, EVERY MUSLIM—SHOULD LIVE

1. Acquire what you are required to know about religion, either by reading books or by asking questions of religious scholars.

2. Avoid all sins.

3. Immediately repent if you sin.

4. Do not withhold anyone's due; cause no trouble to anyone by hand or by tongue; do evil to no one.

5. Do not love wealth, wish for fame, or think too much about good food and clothes.

6. Do not argue if someone calls some fault of yours into question; immediately admit it and repent.

7. Do not travel except out of great necessity. People are careless in travel. They neglect good works, omit their daily religious practices, and are invariably late.

8. Do not laugh and talk a great deal. You should especially avoid informal conversation with anyone of marriageable degree.

9. Do not argue or engage in disputes with anyone.

10. Keep the *shari'at* in mind at every moment.

11. Do not be slack in acts of worship.

12. Remain mostly alone.

13. If you must mix with others, act humbly with everyone; serve everyone; do not boast.

14. Associate little with the rich.

15. Stay far away from irreligious people.

16. Do not search out the faults of others. Do not suspect ill of others, but always look to your own faults and continually correct them.

17. Always keep the prayer firmly in mind—performed well and at the proper times.

18. Remain every moment in the recollection of God, whether with your heart or with your tongue. Never be heedless of God.

19. Offer thanks to Almighty God if recitation of his Name brings delight and joy to the heart.

20. Converse with gentleness.

21. Fix a time for every work, and carry out each work regularly.

22. Realize that any grief, sorrow, or loss is from Almighty God. Do not be distraught. Recognize that you will be rewarded for having suffered it.

23. Do not continually hold your worldly accounts and worldly work in your heart. Rather, keep the thought of God alone in your heart.

24. Benefit others as much as possible, whether in worldly things or in religious things.

25. Do not eat or drink so little that you become weak or sick. Nor should you indulge so much that you begin to be lazy in worship.

26. Do not hope for anything from anyone other than Almighty God. Do not turn your thoughts in anyone else's direction, expecting them to provide you with something or other.

27. Be restless in your search for God.

28. Offer thanks for any blessing, whether great or small. Do not let your heart grow bitter in poverty and hunger.

29. Overlook the errors and faults of those in your charge.

30. If you discover someone's fault, hide it, unless that person is about to cause harm to another.

31. Seek out occasions of service to guests, travelers, the poor, religious scholars, and *darwesh*.

32. Associate with good company.

33. Fear Almighty God at every moment.

34. Remember death.

35. Sit down at some point during each day and reflect on your acts of that day. Give thanks for any good deed that you remember; repent any sin.

36. Never speak any lie.

37. Never go to any gathering that is against the *shari'at*.

38. Live with a sense of shame, modesty, and forbearance.

39. Do not take pride in your fine qualities.

40. Always pray to Almighty God that he may keep you set on the good path.

V. On the Reward of Good Deeds and the Punishment of Bad Ones, from the *Hadis* of the Messenger of God[s]; To Encourage Affection for Good and Hatred of Evil

On Having Pure Intention

1. Once, a man called out, "O Messenger of God, *God's blessings and peace upon you,* what thing is faith?" He declared: "To have pure intention."

Moral: The meaning of this is that you should perform every act for the sake of God.

2. And the Messenger of God[s] declared: "The merit of all acts derives from their intention."

Moral: This means that if there is good intention, you will receive the reward of a good deed; otherwise you will not.

On Doing an Act for the Sake of Ostentation

3. The Messenger of God[s] declared: "If a person has performed good deeds in order to be well spoken of, Almighty God will have that person's faults spoken of on the Day of Judgment. If a person has done good deeds just for show, Almighty God will in return make a show of that person's faults on the Day of Judgment."

4. And the Messenger of God[s] declared: "Even a little ostentation is now a kind of *shirk,* joining partners to God."

On Acting on the Authority of Qur'an and *Hadis*

5. The Messenger of God[s] declared: "Whenever disorder in religion spreads among my people, any person who holds fast to my way will receive the reward of one hundred martyrs."

6. And the Messenger of God[s] declared: "I go, leaving among you things to which if you hold fast you will never go astray: one is the book of Almighty God, the Qur'an; and the other is the practice of the Prophet, the *hadis.*"

On Pointing Out the Path of a Good Work or Laying the Foundation of a Bad One

7. The Messenger of God[s] declared: "Any person who points out a good path, which other people then follow, will get credit for that

action and the actions of all those who followed. That person will gain merit equivalent to that earned by all those who followed, at the same time as there is no diminution of any person's individual reward. Any person who shows others a faulty path, which they then follow, will have both the sin of that one action and the sin of all those who followed. There will be no diminution of their sin."

Moral: If, for example, a person abandoned customary practices in the marriage celebration of offspring or if a widow remarried, and others took courage from seeing this example, whoever initiated the good act would continuously get merit.

On Searching Out Knowledge of Religion

8. The Messenger of God[s] declared: "Almighty God grants understanding of religion to anyone he wishes to favor."

Moral: That is, the person acquires greater enthusiasm for searching out the teachings of the *shari'at* (*masle masa'il*).

On Obscuring a Point of Religion

9. The Messenger of God[s] declared: "Whoever is asked about a point of religion and avoids a clear answer will be restrained with a bridle of fire on the Day of Judgment."

Moral: If you are asked about some point of religion that you know, do not be slow or refuse to answer, but explain it carefully.

On Knowing a Point and Not Acting on It

10. The Messenger of God[s] declared: "Knowledge is a burden unless the person who has it embodies it."

Moral: You must never act against the *shari'at* out of regard for the opinion of your kinfolk or as a result of following your lower soul.

On Being Careless While Urinating

11. The Messenger of God[s] declared: "Always be very careful about urinating, because the torment of the grave will result from carelessness in this matter."

On Washing with Careful Attention in the Ablution
and the Bath

12. The Messenger of God[s] declared: "Sins are washed away by performing the ablution carefully in situations when the lower soul feels reluctance."

Moral: A person may be reluctant to perform the ablution sometimes out of lateness, sometimes because it is cold.

On Using the Tooth-Stick

13. The Messenger of God[s] declared: "To perform a prayer of two bowings after using the tooth-stick (*miswak*)[18] is better than to do a prayer of seventy bowings without using it."

On Carelessness in the Ablution

14. The Messenger of God[s] declared: "I have seen many people whose heels remained dry even after they finished the ablution." And he declared: "There is severe punishment in hell on account of heels."

Moral: You should take care to wash under rings, bangles, and other jewelry. Soak your feet if they have become hardened in winter. Wash your face thoroughly, up to the ears, and not just in the front, as women often do. Keep all these points in mind.

On Women Going Out for Prayer

15. The Messenger of God[s] declared: "The best mosque for women is the inside of their houses."

Moral: It is clear that it is not good for women to go to mosques. You should weigh the fact that although nothing is the equal of the prayer, it is not considered good to go out even for that. Surely, then, to go out of the house for foolish gatherings or for carrying out customary practices must be very bad indeed.

On Fidelity to the Prayer

16. The Messenger of God[s] declared: "The analogy of the five prayers is bathing five times in a deep river that flows in front of one's door."

Moral: The meaning of this is that a person who regularly performs the five prayers washes away sins, just as a bath washes away dirt from the body.

17. And the Messenger of God⁵ declared: "On the Day of Judgment, first of all a reckoning of the prayer will be taken from each servant."

On Reciting the Prayer at the Earliest Permitted Time

18. The Messenger of God⁵ declared: "Almighty God delights in recitation of the prayer at the earliest time permissible."

Moral: O women, you do not need to go out to join a congregation. So why are you always late?

On Performing the Prayer Poorly

19. The Messenger of God⁵ declared: "If a person performs the prayer at the wrong time, does not do the ablution properly, does not pray wholeheartedly, or does the bowing and prostration carelessly, that person's prayer is black and lusterless. The prayer itself says, 'May God destroy you as you have destroyed me,' until it reaches its special place acceptable to God. Then, wrapped like an old cloth, it is struck against the face of the worshipper."

Moral: O women, you perform the prayer to attain reward. Then why recite it in such a way that instead you commit more sin?

On Gazing Here and There During the Prayer

20. The Messenger of God⁵ declared: "Do not look up during prayer, for fear that your sight may be snatched away."

21. And the Messenger of God⁵ declared: "Almighty God will turn back the prayer of anyone who stands up to pray and looks here and there."

Moral: In other words, he will not accept it.

On Walking in Front of Someone Performing the Prayer

22. The Messenger of God⁵ declared: "If the person passing in front of someone praying had only known the seriousness of the sin, that person would have preferred to remain standing for forty years instead."

Moral: It is all right to walk in front of someone praying if there is an object an arm's length or more raised in front of the person.

On Missing the Prayer Deliberately

23. The Messenger of God[s] declared: "God will be very angry with anyone who has omitted the prayer when that person comes before him."

On Giving a Loan

24. The Messenger of God[s] declared: "On the night of the ascension,[19] I saw written above the gate of paradise that the reward for charity is ten portions, but the reward for giving a loan is eighteen."

On Giving Respite to a Poor Debtor

25. The Messenger of God[s] declared: "If you give respite to a poor person up to the time set for repaying the loan, you will receive each day the reward of giving in charity an amount equal to the loan. And when the time of repayment comes, and you still give respite, you will receive each day the reward of giving in charity double the amount."

On Reading the Pure Qur'an

26. The Messenger of God[s] declared: "Whoever reads one letter of the Glorious Qur'an gets the reward of a good deed. And the rule is that for each good deed one gets ten portions. I do not consider, for example, *alif-lam-mim* to be one letter, but rather *alif* is one, *lam* is one, and *mim* is one."[20]
Moral: Thus, by this reckoning, for three letters one receives a reward equivalent to thirty good deeds.

On Cursing Your Life or Offspring

27. The Messenger of God[s] declared: "Do not curse yourself, your offspring, your servants, or your possessions, for fear that at that very moment Almighty God will accept your prayers and grant exactly what you have asked."

On Earning Forbidden Wealth and Spending It on Food and Clothes

28. The Messenger of God[s] declared: "Flesh and blood nourished on forbidden wealth will not go to paradise but merit hell."

29. And the Messenger of God^s declared: "Almighty God will not accept the prayer of a person who buys a garment for ten dirham, one of which was gained illegitimately, as long as that garment is being worn." (A dirham is worth a little more than four *anas*.)

On Deception

30. The Messenger of God^s declared: "Any person who deceives us is not one of us."

Moral: Deceit of any kind is wrong, whether in selling or in anything else.

On Borrowing

31. The Messenger of God^s declared: "Whoever dies owing a *dinar* or dirham will repay it with past good deeds in that place where there will be neither *dinar* nor dirham." (*Note:* A gold *dinar* was worth ten dirham.)

32. And the Messenger of God^s declared: "There are two kinds of loans. First, there is the debt of a person who dies intending to repay the loan. This debt is excused. Almighty God himself declares that he will help. Second, there is the debt of a person who dies with no such intention. That debt will be deducted from past good deeds, for on that day there will be no resort to dirham or *dinar*." (The meaning of "help" is discharging what is due.)

On Putting Off Someone's Due When One Has Means

33. The Messenger of God^s declared: "For a person of means to put someone off is tyranny (*zulm*)."

Moral: Many people are in the habit of making creditors or those who are waiting for wages run around in circles for no good reason. They make false promises, saying to come tomorrow or come the next day. They keep up their other expenditures but are careless in giving others their due.

On Dealing in Interest

34. The Messenger of God^s cursed both the person who takes and the person who gives interest.

On Usurping Someone's Land

35. The Messenger of God⁵ declared: "Whoever unjustly encroaches on one hand's width of land will be yoked around the neck with the seven divisions of earth."[21]

On Paying Wages Immediately

36. The Messenger of God⁵ declared: "Always pay wages before the sweat of the laborer has dried."
37. Almighty God declared: "I myself will exact a claim from three persons; one of them is the person who sets someone to work, exacts the full work, and then does not pay the wages due."

On the Death of Children

38. The Messenger of God⁵ declared: "Almighty God, out of his grace and mercy, will bring to paradise a husband and wife, if both are Muslim, who have lost three children." Several people then asked, "O Apostle of God, *on whom be the blessings and peace of God,* what if two die?" He declared: "There is the same reward for two." Then they asked about the death of only one. He declared the same reward for that loss as well. Then he declared: "I swear by that Pure Being in whose power is my life that the child who is miscarried will take the mother by the umbilical cord and pull her in the direction of paradise if the mother's object (*niyat*) has been to seek reward."
Moral: In other words, if she has been steadfast in the hope of reward.

On Women Wearing Perfume in Front of Unrelated Men

39. The Messenger of God⁵ declared: "If a woman applies perfume and passes near men not prohibited to her in marriage, she is that kind, that is, adulterous."
Moral: Do not apply perfume and then go to wherever your husband's brothers, your brothers-in-law, or your male cousins come and go.[22]

On Women Wearing Very Sheer Clothing

40. The Messenger of Gods declared: "Many women wear clothes in name but in fact are naked. Such women will not go to paradise, nor will they even catch a whiff of its perfume."

On Women Adopting the Appearance and Style of Men

41. The Messenger of Gods cursed any woman who dresses like a man.

Moral: In our country, the style of men is to wear high shoes (*khara juta*) and a long coat buttoned in front (*achkan*). It is forbidden for women to wear these things.

On Dressing in Order to Show Off

42. The Messenger of Gods declared: "Whoever in this world has dressed to get attention will, on the Day of Judgment, be dressed by Almighty God in garments of opprobrium and set on fire with the fire of hell."

Moral: This warning is intended for anyone who dresses up to get approval and to attract attention. Many women suffer from this disease.

On Oppressing Others

43. The Messenger of Gods asked those sitting near him, "Do you know the meaning of the word 'poor'?" They replied, "We call a person poor who has no wealth or property." He declared: "Among my people, the very poor person is the one who arrives on the Day of Judgment with the credit of the prayer, fast, and *zakat,* but brings as well the liability of slander, accusation of others, exploitation, murder, and beatings. Some of that person's good deeds will be assigned to one person, some to another. If all the good deeds are used up before meeting the outstanding claims, the remaining sins will be charged against the person, who will then be thrown in hell."

On Showing Kindness and Mercy

44. The Messenger of Gods declared: "Almighty God does not show mercy to those who do not show mercy to others."

On Explaining to Others What Is Good and Forbidding Them What Is Evil

45. The Messenger of God declared: "Any one of you who sees something against the *shari'at* should check it physically or, if that is impossible, should speak out against it; and if even that is too much, you should know in your heart that it is evil. Knowing in one's heart that something is evil is the least degree of faith."

Moral: O women, you have full power over your children and servants. Force them to perform the prayer. Immediately destroy any images drawn on paper or made of clay, sugar, or cloth, and discard any worthless book you may see. Do not give your dependents money for such things or for fireworks, kites, or the candy toys of Diwali.[23]

On Hiding the Faults of a Muslim

46. The Messenger of God declared: "On the Day of Judgment, Almighty God will hide the fault of anyone who has hidden the fault of a fellow Muslim. And he will expose the fault of anyone who has exposed the fault of a Muslim, even to the point of disgracing a person within one's very house."

On Rejoicing in Someone Else's Loss or Disgrace

47. The Messenger of God declared: "Do not express joy over the trouble of your fellow Muslim. God will show mercy on that person and will ensnare you in trouble."

On Taunting Someone About a Sin

48. The Messenger of God declared: "Whoever reproaches a fellow Muslim about a sin will not die before committing that very same sin."

Moral: It is very bad to make someone ashamed by bringing up a sin already repented of. If a person has not repented, then it is all right to say something by way of counsel. However, it is still very bad to speak of someone else's sin if you do so to bring on disgrace or to set yourself up as pure.

On Committing Minor Sins Without Concern

49. The Messenger of God declared: "O 'A'isha, avoid committing even minor sins, for there is someone sent from Almighty God to take their account."

Moral: That is, an angel writes them down.[24] On the Day of Judgment, there will be an accounting and the possibility of punishment.

On Keeping One's Mother and Father Happy

50. The Messenger of God[s] declared: "The happiness of Almighty God depends on the happiness of the mother and father; and the displeasure of Almighty God derives from their displeasure.

On Treating One's Relatives Badly

51. The Messenger of God[s] declared: "Every Thursday night,[25] the actions and worship of all people are presented in the divine court. Not a single good deed is accepted from people who treat their relatives badly."

On Nurturing Fatherless Children

52. The Messenger of God[s] declared: "Whoever takes responsibility for the support of an orphan[26] will be this close to me in paradise." And he indicated his index and middle finger, leaving only a small space between them.

53. And the Messenger of God[s] declared: "Whoever strokes the hair of an orphan for the sake of God alone will acquire the credit of as many good deeds as there are hairs under the palm of the hand that strokes the orphan's head. Those who do some kindness to an orphan girl or boy who lives with them will be as close to me in heaven as the index finger and the middle finger are close."

On Causing Trouble to One's Neighbor

54. The Messenger of God[s] declared: "Whoever gives trouble to a neighbor has given trouble to me; and whoever has given trouble to me has given trouble to Almighty God. Whoever has quarreled with a neighbor has quarreled with me; and whoever has quarreled with me has quarreled with Almighty God."

Moral: The point is that it is wrong to cause sorrow or raise an altercation without cause or over some very insignificant matter.

On Helping Out Another Muslim

55. The Messenger of God⁵ declared: "Almighty God will undertake a share of the work of anyone who shares in the work of a fellow Muslim."

On Modesty and Immodesty

56. The Messenger of God⁵ declared: "Modesty is intrinsic to faith, and faith brings one to paradise. Immodesty is intrinsic to bad character (*kho*), and bad character takes one to hell."[27]
Moral: You should never, however, be modest in regard to an act of religion. For example, women often do not perform the prayer during travel or during the days of a wedding. Such modesty is worse than immodesty.

On Good Comportment and Bad Comportment

57. The Messenger of God⁵ declared: "Good comportment (*khush khalqi*) dissolves sins just as water dissolves a block of salt. Bad comportment (*bad khalqi*) destroys acts of worship just as vinegar ruins honey."
58. And the Messenger of God⁵ declared: "Most beloved of all to me and closest of all to me in the afterlife is the person whose comportment is good. The person most distasteful to me and most distant from me in the afterlife is the one whose comportment is bad."

On Gentleness and Harshness

59. The Messenger of God⁵ declared: "Surely, Almighty God is kind and approving to those who show gentleness. He gives blessings for gentleness that he does not give for harshness."
60. And the Messenger of God⁵ declared: "Whoever is devoid of gentleness is devoid of all good qualities."

On Peeking into Someone's House

61. The Messenger of God⁵ declared: "Do not peek into someone's house until you have received permission to enter. If you peek, it is as if you had gone in."
Moral: Many women are in the disgraceful habit of peeking into the chamber of a bride and groom. This is a matter of great immodesty. In

fact, what difference is there between peeking and opening up the door panel and going in? This is a matter of grave sin.

On Eavesdropping on People in Conversation

62. The Messenger of God[s] declared: "Whoever sets an ear to hear someone else's conversation to that person's displeasure will have lead put into both ears on the Day of Judgment."

On Being Angry

63. A person requested the Messenger of God[s] to recount some act that would secure heaven. He declared: "Do not be angry. Then paradise is yours."

On Ostracizing Someone

64. The Messenger of God[s] declared: "It is not permitted that any Muslim should give up speaking to a fellow Muslim for more than three days. A person who does give up speaking for more than three days and dies in that condition will go to hell."

On Cursing or Calling Someone an Infidel

65. The Messenger of God[s] declared: "If anyone addresses a fellow Muslim as *kafir,* it is as great a sin as murder."

66. And the Messenger of God[s] declared: "To curse a Muslim is the same as murder."

67. And the Messenger of God[s] declared: "A curse directed at another person rises toward heaven, whose doors are closed. Then it descends to the earth, which is also closed. Then it wanders right and left and, when it finds a place nowhere, arrives at the person cursed. If that person deserves to be cursed, fine. If not, the curse falls upon the curser."

Moral: Many women have an ingrained habit of saying about everything, "May God curse her," or "May God strike them down." They call other people infidels. These are very bad habits, whether one is speaking of a person, an animal, or anything else.

On Frightening a Fellow Muslim

68. The Messenger of God[s] declared: "It is not permissible for a Muslim to frighten another Muslim."

69. And the Messenger of God[s] declared: "Anyone who has unfairly frightened a Muslim by looking in a certain way will in turn be frightened by Almighty God on the Day of Judgment."

Moral: If this was necessary because of some defect or shortcoming in the person, then it is all right.

On Accepting the Apology of a Fellow Muslim

70. The Messenger of God[s] declared: "A person who does not accept the apology of a fellow Muslim will not be able to come near me at the Pool of Kausar."[28]

Moral: That is, you must forgive anyone who offends you and then apologizes.

On Telling Tales

71. The Messenger of God[s] declared: "The tale bearer will not go to heaven."

On Backbiting

72. The Messenger of God[s] declared: "On the Day of Judgment, Almighty God will offer carrion to anyone who has eaten the flesh of a fellow Muslim in the world by backbiting. And he will say, 'Just as you ate the living, now you may eat the dead.' The person will eat the carrion with screams and a distorted face."

On Slander

73. The Messenger of God[s] declared: "Almighty God will send anyone who has spoken falsely of another Muslim to a dwelling place where the blood and pus of the inhabitants of hell have been gathered. The person will stay there until withdrawing the falsehood and repenting."

On Silence

74. The Messenger of God[s] declared: "The person who remains silent is saved from many calamities."

75. And the Messenger of God⁵ declared: "Do not say much beyond the repetition of God's name, because excess talk, other than the repetition of the name of Almighty God, makes the heart hard. Whoever's heart is hard is most far from Almighty God."

On a Sense of Inferiority

76. The Messenger of God⁵ declared: "Almighty God will exalt anyone who adopts humility for his sake. Almighty God will break the neck of anyone who shows pride."
Moral: That is, he will make that person contemptible.

On a Sense of Superiority

77. The Messenger of God⁵ declared: "Anyone whose heart holds pride, even equal in size to a mustard seed, will not enter heaven."

On Truth and Falsehood

78. The Messenger of God⁵ declared: "Be constant in telling the truth, because it leads you to the path of good. Truth and good works lead you to heaven. Avoid telling lies, because they lead you to the path of evil. Lies and evildoing lead you to hell."

On Duplicity

79. The Messenger of God⁵ declared: "On the Day of Judgment, a person who is two-faced will have two tongues—of fire."
Moral: The meaning of being two-faced is to talk one way in front of one person and another way in front of another.

On Swearing by Someone Other than God

80. The Messenger of God⁵ declared: "Whoever swears by someone other than God has committed an act of infidelity." Or, some believe, he called it "an act of polytheism."
Moral: Many people are in the habit of swearing "by your life," "by my eyes," or "by my children." All this is forbidden. It is written in a *hadis* that if ever you should utter such an oath, you should immediately recite the *kalima*.

On Swearing by Your Faith

81. The Messenger of God[s] declared: "A person who swears, 'If I lie, may I lose the faith,' will indeed lose the faith if lying. Even if that person is not lying, the faith will still have become flawed."

Moral: All oaths such as "May I be deprived of the *kalima*" or "May I be sent to hell" are forbidden. You must give up this habit.

On Clearing the Road of Something Troublesome to Passersby

82. The Messenger of God[s] declared: "A person who was going along a road found a thorny branch on the road and removed it. Almighty God valued this act greatly and pardoned that person's sins."

Moral: This shows that it is very bad to throw such things onto the road. Many foolish women will place a stool in the courtyard, then get up and leave the stool behind. Often, passersby trip and injure themselves. It is wrong to leave anything such as implements, beds, sticks, or grindstones in the way.

On Fulfilling a Promise or Trust

83. The Messenger of God[s] declared: "Whoever is unworthy of a trust is deficient in faith, and whoever does not fulfill an oath is imperfect in religion."

On Resorting to a Pandit, a Fortune-Teller, or a Palmist

84. The Messenger of God[s] declared: "Whoever goes to someone to ask about what is unknown and believes what is said will have no prayer accepted for forty days."

Moral: Many women ask questions of a *jinn* or a ghost who supposedly possesses someone. They ask when a husband will get a job, when a son will return, and so forth. This is all sinful.

On Keeping a Pet Dog or Images

85. The Messenger of God[s] declared: "The angels do not come into a house where there is a pet dog or an image."

Moral: That is, the angels of mercy do not come. Children's toys made as images are also forbidden.

On Lying on One's Stomach Unnecessarily

86. The Messenger of Gods passed someone who was lying face down. He pointed at the person with his foot and declared that lying like that was displeasing to Almighty God.

On Sitting or Lying Partly in the Sun
and Partly in the Shade

87. The Messenger of Gods forbade sitting partly in the sun and partly in the shade.

On Bad Omens and Charms

88. The Messenger of Gods declared that belief in bad omens is polytheistic.
89. And the Messenger of Gods declared that charms and spells are polytheistic.

On Not Coveting Worldly Things

90. The Messenger of Gods declared: "From not coveting worldly things the heart derives contentment and the body gets comfort."
91. And the Messenger of Gods declared: "There is not as much destruction from two ferocious wolves let loose among a large number of goats, who are thoroughly torn apart and eaten, as there is destruction to the religion of a person from coveting wealth and longing for fame."

On Remembering Death, Not Dwelling on the Future, and
Considering the Present an Occasion for Good Works

92. The Messenger of Gods declared: "Always keep firmly in mind that which will cut off all pleasures: namely, death."
93. And the Messenger of Gods declared: "When morning comes upon you, do not always think ahead to evening; and when evening comes upon you, do not always think ahead to morning. Before the coming of sickness, take advantage of your good health; and before dying, pluck some fruit from your life."
Moral: The meaning is to consider health and life a boon and to

apply yourself to good works, for in sickness and death nothing will be possible.

On Forbearance in Trouble and Calamity

94. The Messenger of God⁵ declared: "In all misfortune that happens to a Muslim—sorrow, trouble, grief, indeed, even minor distracting worries—in all, Almighty God pardons a Muslim's sin."

On Inquiring After the Sick

95. The Messenger of God⁵ declared: "Seventy thousand angels will pray until evening for a Muslim who asks in the morning about a Muslim who is ill. Seventy thousand angels will pray until morning for someone who makes an inquiry in the evening."

On Bathing the Dead, Providing a Shroud, and Comforting the Bereaved

96. The Messenger of God⁵ declared: "A person who bathes the dead becomes as pure as when born from a mother's womb. Whoever shrouds the dead will be dressed in the outfit of heaven by Almighty God. Whoever comforts the sorrowful will be dressed by Almighty God in the same clothing as a person who exercises self-control; and God will have mercy on that person's soul. Whoever comforts the afflicted will be dressed by Almighty God in two outfits from among the outfits of heaven, whose worth cannot be equaled in all the world."

On Lamenting and Weeping While Talking

97. The Messenger of God⁵ cursed a weeping woman and a woman who listened and joined in.
   Moral: O women, give up such behavior for the sake of God.

On Squandering the Wealth of an Orphan

98. The Messenger of God⁵ declared: "Many people will arise from the grave with flames of fire coming out of their mouths." Someone asked him, "O Messenger of God⁵, who will they be?" He answered: "Do you not know that Almighty God has declared in the Glorious Qur'an that those who unjustly eat up the wealth of orphans will have their stomachs filled with live coals?"

Moral: The meaning of "unjustly" is that these people have no legitimate right to use the wealth of orphans. O women, you must be wary. In Hindustan, it is common that the widow takes control of all the property when a husband dies leaving small children. She spends it on everything—the expenses of guests, oil for mosques, food for holy men. Although the orphans have a right to a share, the whole expense is treated jointly. Yet, as her heart wishes, the widow spends money on daily expenses and the wedding festivities of children. This is not lawful. To use property held jointly for such expenditures is a serious sin. Keep the children's share separate, and take from it only what is strictly necessary for their particular expenses. If you are to entertain guests or give charity, do so from your own share. Do not do it even then if the occasion is against the *shari'at.* Unless you act faithfully on this, at the time of death your eyes will open to what you have done.

The Reckoning on the Day of Judgment

99. The Messenger of God[s] declared: "On the Day of Judgment, no one will be able to move before answering four questions: first, how life ended; second, whether the *shari'at* was fulfilled to the extent known; third, how wealth was earned and disposed of; fourth, how the body was used up."

Moral: The final point is meant to ascertain whether the person acted on the *shari'at* or instead followed the lower soul.

100. And the Messenger of God[s] declared: "On the Day of Judgment, you will have to fulfill all outstanding obligations, to the point that recompense will be taken from the horned goat for the sake of the hornless."

Moral: That is, if the horned goat unjustly rammed the hornless one with his horns.

On Remembering Heaven and Hell

101. The Messenger of God[s] declared in a sermon: "Two things are very important; do not forget them. They are heaven and hell." After saying that, he wept greatly until his blessed beard was wet with tears. Then he declared: "I swear by that Being in whose power is my life that if you knew what I know about the afterlife, you would flee to the wilderness and place dust on your head."

MORAL

O women: Above are written one hundred and one *hadis,* and more are given elsewhere in this work. Our Hazrat Apostleˢ declared: "Whoever remembers forty *hadis* and tells them to my people will arise with the scholars on the Day of Judgment." Therefore now resolve to recount these *hadis* to others. *God willing,* you too will arise with the scholars on the Day of Judgment. How great a blessing to be attained so easily!

VI. A Brief Account of the Day of Judgment and Its Signs*

The Messenger of God, *God's blessings and peace be upon him,* described these initial portents of the Day of Judgment in the *hadis:*

As the Day of Judgment approaches, people will begin to think of the wealth owed to God as their own property; *zakat,* for example, will seem a burden, like a fine. They will regard trusts as their own wealth. A man will obey his wife and disobey his mother. He will consider his father a stranger but trust acquaintances as his own people. People will seek knowledge of religion only for the sake of worldly gain. Those in positions of leadership and governance will all be the most worthless of men: ill-born, greedy, and ill-natured. Whoever is unworthy of a job will be the very person entrusted with it. People will venerate tyrants and pay them regard in order to avoid trouble for themselves. They will begin to drink wine openly. It will be common to see women singing and dancing. There will be musical instruments—*dholak, sarangi,* and *tabla*—in abundance. People will begin to speak ill of the earliest elders of the community.

The Messenger of Godˢ declared: "At that time, be prepared for torment after torment. A red dust storm will come. People will sink into the earth. Stones will rain down from the sky. Appearances will change. People will be turned into pigs and dogs. Calamities will start to come quickly, one after another, like beads strung on a thread that breaks, with all starting to fall at once, pell-mell."

There will be other signs as well. People will have little knowledge

---

* From the *Qiyamat nama* (The Last Day) of Shah Rafiʻuʼd-Din Dihlawi, *on whom be the mercy of Almighty God.* [Shah Rafiʻuʼd-Din, who wrote in the early nineteenth century, was one of four sons of the great eighteenth-century scholar Shah Waliʼullah. He is known for his translation of the Qurʼan into Urdu and for his work in *hadis,* including the book noted here, which brings together scattered references to the Day of Judgment. See Book Ten, "The Names of Several Worthwhile Books," item 27.]

of religion. They will consider lying to be a desirable skill. Their hearts will lose any concern for fidelity in anything entrusted to them. They also will lose all modesty and shame. On every side, the infidels will have strength. Many false paths will appear.

When all these signs have appeared, the Nazarenes will hold sway over all countries.[29] At the same time, a descendent of [the evil] Abu Sufyan will be born in Syria and will set out to shed the blood of all *saiyid*s.[30] He will get control of Syria and Egypt.

Meanwhile, the Muslim emperor of Rum (the ancient Eastern Roman empire) will ally with one Nazarene faction in order to do battle with a different Nazarene faction. He will be defeated when the enemy faction attacks Constantinople. The king will flee to Syria, and there he will have his Nazarene allies join his army. After a major battle, the army of Islam, including the Nazarene allies, will be victorious over the enemy group.

Subsequently, one of the Nazarene allies will idly say in front of a Muslim, "We conquered through the blessing of the cross." In answer, the Muslim will say, "We conquered through the blessing of Islam." The issue will grow to the point that both men summon their fellow religionists and begin to fight. The emperor of Islam will be martyred.[31] Nazarene rule will now reach to Syria. The Nazarene factions will now unite. The surviving Muslims will go off together to Medina. Nazarene rule will extend to Khaibar.[32]

The Muslims at this point will decide that the time has come to search for [the ruler of the final days] Hazrat Imam Mahdi, *on whom be peace,* to deliver them from these troubles.[33] Hazrat Imam Mahdi[a] will then, in fact, be in Medina the Radiant; but out of fear that people will be after him to take up the government, he will leave for Mecca the Magnified.[34] All the saints and those holding the rank of *abdal* will join in the search for the Hazrat Imam.[35] Pretenders will begin to make false claims of being the Mahdi. Finally, as the Hazrat Imam is circumambulating the house of the Ka'ba and is between the black stone and the Station of Ibrahim,[36] many people will recognize him, forcibly surround him, and—swearing their allegiance by *bai'a*[37]—will claim him as their leader. While this is going on, a voice will come from heaven, heard by all those present. And the voice will say, "This is the deputy of Almighty God, the leader who is the Imam Mahdi."

With the appearance of the Hazrat Imam, the great signs of the Day of Judgment will appear. The Muslim armies that were in Medina will go to Mecca as soon as they hear of the oath. The saints and *abdal* of the countries of Syria, Iraq, and Yemen will all flock to his service.

Many armies of the Arabs will join him. As the news spreads among Muslims, a man from Khurasan will come at the head of a great army to offer his help. He will be named Mansur, and as he advances he will cleanse the way by destroying many of the corrupt. The descendent of Abu Sufyan, however, mentioned above as the enemy of the *saiyid*s, will send an army to fight the Hazrat Imam because he is a *saiyid*. That army will stop at the foot of a mountain in the wilderness between Mecca and Medina. Every last person in that army will disappear into the ground. Only two men will be saved. One will go to inform the Hazrat Imam, and the other will bring the news to that Sufyani.

The Nazarenes will gather armies from every side and prepare to fight the Muslims. The army on that day will have eighty standards, under each of which will be twelve thousand men—in sum, nine hundred sixty thousand men. The Hazrat Imam will go from Mecca to Medina to make a pilgrimage to the noble tomb of the Messenger of Gods. He will then set out for Syria and will succeed in reaching the city of Damascus. The Nazarene army will attack from the opposite direction. The Imam's army will split into three sections: one will flee, one will be martyred, and one will prevail. This is what will happen. The Imam will prepare his army to fight the Nazarenes. Many Muslims will swear to stand fast until victory. In fact, almost all of them will be martyred. The Imam will return with the remnant. On the next day, it will be the same: the Muslims will take an oath; most will be martyred; only a few will return. It will be the same on the third day. Finally, on the fourth day, through Almighty God, the few remaining men will fight and prevail. Only then, at last, will the infidels give up their ambition for rule.

The Hazrat Imam will begin to administer the country and will dispatch armies in all directions. After settling all necessary affairs, he will set off to conquer Constantinople. At the bank of its river, he will launch seventy thousand men of the tribe of Ishaq in boats and instruct them to conquer the city. When they are opposite the rampart of the city, they will shout, "*Allahu akbar, allahu akbar!*" in a loud voice. The wall in front of the city fortifications will fall down through the blessing of that Name. The Muslims will attack, penetrate the city, and slay the infidels. They will administer the country with justice and law. Six or seven years will pass between the time of the oath to the Hazrat Imam and the conquest.

Hazrat Imam Mahdi will devote himself to administering the city. A false rumor will spread that one-eyed Dajjal has come to Syria, fomenting rebellion and disorder within the Imam's own family.[38] At this news, the Imam will journey toward Syria, sending a few mounted men ahead to ascertain the situation. One of them will return with the news that the rumor was simply false. Satisfied with this, the Imam will then travel slowly and deliberately on to Syria, attending to the administration of the countries on the way.

Dajjal will appear a few days after the Imam arrives. He will be of the race of Jews. His first appearance will be in the area between Syria and Iraq. He will claim to be a prophet. He will travel to Isfahan, where he will be joined by seventy thousand Jews. He will claim to be divine. He will continue through many countries until he reaches the border of Yemen. Everywhere, he will be joined by men of false religion, until he approaches Mecca. There he will stop, unable to enter Mecca because of the angels protecting it. He will then resolve to go to Medina. There, too, a guard of angels will prevent him from entering. An earthquake will shake Medina three times.

Those people who are slothful and weak in religion will be afraid of the earthquake and will flee outside the city, where they will be entangled in Dajjal's snare. A great elder of the city will argue hotly with Dajjal. Dajjal will kill him in anger, revive him, and then challenge him again to accept that Dajjal is God. The elder will assert that now he knows even more clearly that this is Dajjal and not God. Dajjal will try to kill him again but will fail. The elder will be invincible.

Dajjal will then set out for Syria and draw near to Damascus. Meanwhile, the Imam will be in Damascus, preparing for war. Suddenly, at the call to afternoon prayer, Hazrat 'Isa [Jesus], *on whom be peace,* will be seen descending from the sky with his hands on the shoulders of two angels. He will come to rest on the minaret of the eastern side of the congregational mosque, place a staircase there, and descend. The Imam will want to entrust all the arrangements for the battle to him. Hazrat 'Isa[a] will insist that the Imam must manage the battle and that he has come only to kill Dajjal. After night passes and morning comes, Hazrat Imam will draw up his army, while Hazrat 'Isa[a] will take a horse and spear and set out after Dajjal. The people of Islam will attack the army of Dajjal and commence a fierce battle. At this time, there will be an effective power in the breath of Hazrat 'Isa[a] that can reach wherever he looks and immediately destroy any infidel on which it rests.[39] At the sight of Hazrat 'Isa[a], Dajjal will try to flee. Hazrat 'Isa[a], however, will follow him to the Gate of Ludd and finish him off with his spear. The Muslims will start killing the army of Dajjal. Hazrat Imam will travel from city to city in order to comfort those tormented by Dajjal. Through the grace of Almighty God, not a single infidel will remain.

Then Hazrat Imam will die, and Hazrat 'Isa[a] will take all arrangements in hand. The barbarous Yajuj and Majuj will appear from their dwelling place, seven provinces beyond where the populated part of the north ends.[40] This is the place where the sea is so frozen that no ship can move, because of the ice. Hazrat 'Isa[a], at the order of Almighty God, will lead the Muslims to the mountain of Tur.[41] Yajuj and Majuj will raise a great tumult until, at last, Almighty God will destroy them; and Hazrat 'Isa[a] will then descend from the mountain. After forty years, he will die and be buried in the tomb of our Apostle[s]. Jahjah [Jahjaj], resident of Yemen and of the tribe of the Qahtan, will sit on the throne. He will rule with great piety and justice.

Many kings will follow him, one after the other. Gradually, good deeds will be fewer and evil deeds common. A sort of fog will spread over the sky and rain on the earth. It will make the Muslims catch cold and will render the infidels unconscious. After forty days, the sky will clear.

It will then be near the month of Baqr 'Id.[42] Suddenly, after the tenth of the month, there will be a night so long that the hearts of travelers will be distraught. Children will weary of sleep. Animals will begin to howl and go into the wilderness. There will be no morning. Everyone will be in anguish, out of perplexity and fear. After the night has lasted the equivalent of three nights, the sun will begin to rise from the west, bringing with it a light as faint as that of an eclipse. No profession of faith or declaration of repentance will be accepted.[43] When the sun rises as high as the beginning of the second watch of the day, at God's order it will return to the west and will set. After that, it will always appear as usual, bright and luminous.

Shortly after this, Mount Safa, which is in Mecca, will be torn asunder by an earthquake. An animal, very strange in appearance and shape, will emerge and will converse with the people. It will travel over the earth at great speed. It will draw a radiant line with the rod of Hazrat Musa[a] on the forehead of all the faithful, making each face radiant. It will place a black seal on the nose or on the neck of the faithless with the ring of Hazrat Sulaiman[a], making each face dark. Then it will disappear.

A balmy breeze will blow from the south. It will produce a fatal growth in the armpits of believers. When the Muslims die, the rule of the infidels of Abyssinia will spread over the whole earth. They will destroy the House of the Ka'ba and end the pilgrimage. The Noble Qur'an will be effaced from all hearts and all paper. Fear before God and shame before humanity will vanish. No one will remain to repeat the name of God.

At this time in Syria, goods will be very cheap. People will head in that direction on camels and other mounts and on foot. A fire will break out that will drive all those who are left to Syria. (On the Day of Judgment, all creatures will be gathered in that land.) The fire will disappear, and there will be great progress in the world. After three or four years, on a Friday, the tenth of Muharram,[44] in the morning when all people are engaged in their respective work, a trumpet will suddenly be sounded. At first, it will be very, very soft. Then it will grow so much louder that all will die from terror. The heaven and earth will be rent. The world will be extinguished.

The period from the sun rising in the west until the sounding of the trumpet will be one hundred twenty years.[45] At this point begins the Day of Judgment.

THE DAY OF JUDGMENT

Forty years will pass in a state of desolation after the destruction of the world at the sound of the trumpet. Almighty God will then order the trumpet to be blown again. Heaven and earth will again be established. The dead will emerge, alive, from their graves and will be gathered on the Plain of Judgment. The sun will be very close, and people's very brains will begin to cook in its heat. People will sweat in proportion to their sins. Standing in this plain, hungry and thirsty, they will be distraught. For those who are good, however, the earth of this land will be like flour. They will assuage their hunger by eating it and will satisfy their thirst by going to the Pool of Kausar. When all are utterly distressed from standing on the Plain of Judgment, they will join together to beseech Hazrat Adam[a], and then the other prophets, to intercede on their behalf, so that the taking of accounts and subsequent judgment may be done quickly. All the apostles will give some reason for declining to intercede. The people will finally approach our Apostle[s]. At the order of Almighty God, he will accept the request and progress to Maqam-i Mahmud (the name of a place) to intercede. Almighty God will declare: "We have accepted your intercession. Now we shall display our Illumination on the earth and shall indeed take the account."

Angels in great number will descend from the heavens and surround everyone on every side. The throne of Almighty God, on which will be the Illumination of Almighty God, will descend. The accounting will begin, and the Books of Deeds will be opened. Of their own accord, the believers will come on the right hand and the unbelievers on the left. The scale for weighing deeds will be set up, and from it everyone's good and bad deeds will be known. Thereupon, everyone will be ordered to cross the Bridge of the Way. Anyone whose good deeds weigh more in the balance will cross the bridge and enter into paradise. Anyone whose sins weigh more, unless forgiven by God, will fall into hell. Anyone whose good and bad deeds are equal will remain in a place called A'raf, which is between heaven and hell. Our Apostle[s], the other prophets[a], learned men, saints and martyrs, those who have memorized the Qur'an, and all good servants will intercede for the pardon of the sinful people. Their intercession will be accepted. Those who have the tiniest manifestation of faith in their hearts will be taken out of hell and sent to paradise. Those in A'raf will, in the end, enter into heaven. Only those who are wholly infidel and polytheistic will remain in hell. They will never emerge from hell.

When all the inhabitants of heaven and hell are settled in their places, Almighty God will bring forth Death in the shape of a ram, in between heaven and hell. He will display Death to everyone and have it slaughtered. He will declare: "Now death will come neither to the dwellers in heaven nor to the dwellers in hell. All must dwell forever in their respective places." There will be no end to the rejoicing of the inhabitants of heaven and no end to the anguish and grief of the inhabitants of hell.

THE BLESSINGS OF PARADISE AND THE TORMENTS OF HELL

The Messenger of God[s] said, "Almighty God declared: 'I have prepared blessings for my good servants that no eye has ever seen, nor ear has heard, nor thought of which has come into the heart of any person.' "

The Messenger of God[s] declared: "In the construction of heaven, one brick is of silver and one brick is of gold. The mortar that joins the bricks is of pure musk. The pebbles of heaven are pearls and rubies; its earth is saffron. Whoever goes to heaven will dwell in joy and contentment and will feel no grief or sorrow. They will live there forever and ever, for they will never die. The clothes of those who dwell there never get dirty, and their youth never ends."

The Messenger of God[s] declared: "In heaven, there are two gardens whose vessels and furnishings are of silver. There are two gardens whose vessels and furnishings are of gold."

The Messenger of God[s] declared: "In heaven, there are one hundred levels, one on top of the other. The distance between one level and another is the same as that between earth and heaven, namely, five hundred years. The highest level of all is *firdaus*. From it flow the four rivers of heaven, those of milk, honey, the purifying nectar (*sharab-i tahur*), and water. Above it is the empyrean, *'arsh.*[46] When you pray to God, beseech him to grant you *firdaus.*" He also declared: "Each level of heaven is so big that it could easily accommodate the people of the whole world gathered there."

The Messenger of God[s] declared: "The trunks of all the trees in heaven are of gold."

The Messenger of God[s] declared: "The face of those who first enter heaven will be as radiant as the full moon. The faces of those who follow after them will be like the brightly shining stars. There will be no need of urination or defecation, of spit or mucus. Combs will be of gold. Sweat will be fragrant like musk." Someone asked, "Then where will food go?" The Messenger of God[s] declared: "There will be a belch with the fragrance of musk."

The Messenger of God[s] declared: "Almighty God will inquire of the person who is in the lowest level of heaven, 'If I give you a realm equal to that of an earthly king, will you be content?' The person will answer, 'O my Provider, I am now content.' God will then declare: 'Go, I have already given you five times that.' The person will answer, 'O God, I am made content.' Then God will declare: 'Go, I have given you this much and ten times more than this. Besides this, you will have whatever your heart desires and whatever your eye delights in.' " There is also a tradition that such a person will have the world and ten times its equal.

The Messenger of God[s] declared: "Almighty God will inquire of the inhabitants of heaven, 'Are you happy?' They will respond, 'Why should we not be happy? You have given us what until now has been given to no other creature.' He will declare: 'I will give you something even greater than all this.' They will reply, 'What could possibly be greater than all this?' Then God will declare: 'It is this: I will always be happy with you; I will never be angry.' "

The Messenger of God[s] declared: "When all the dwellers of heaven have entered, Almighty God will declare to them: 'Do you want anything else that I might give you?' They will respond, 'You have illuminated our faces; you have admitted us into heaven; you have given us salvation from hell. What more could we want?' At this time, Almighty God will lift his veil. No blessing will be lovelier than the delectation of the sight of Almighty God."

The Messenger of God[s] declared: "Hell was fanned for a thousand years, until its color was red. Then it was fanned another thousand years, until its color was white. Then it was fanned another thousand years, until it became black. Now it is completely black and dark."

The Messenger of God[s] declared: "The fire that you burn is seventy times less intense than the fire of hell; hell's fire is seventy times more intense than yours."

The Messenger of God[s] declared: "A great heavy rock placed on the edge of hell would have to roll continuously some seventy years until it reaches the bottom."

The Messenger of God[s] declared: "When hell is brought forth, it will have seventy thousand reins grasped by seventy thousand angels who will drag it along."

The Messenger of God[s] declared: "The lightest punishment in hell is wearing shoes of fire that cook a person's brain like a pot. That person believes that no one's torment is greater than this."

The Messenger of God[s] declared: "In hell, there are snakes as big as camels. If they bite a person, the poison will spread for forty years. Scorpions are as big as mules with pack saddles. If they bite, the paroxysms last for forty years."

Once, the Messenger of God[s], after performing the prayer, proceeded to the pulpit and declared: "Today during the prayer I saw heaven and hell as if they were before my eyes. Never before have I seen anything more wonderful than heaven or anything more terrible than hell."

VII. Seventy-Seven Points That Constitute Complete Faith

In the noble *hadis,* the Messenger of God, *God's blessings and peace upon him,* declared: "There are something over seventy matters related to the faith. The most important is the *kalima-i taiyiba* (the Most Excellent Saying): There is no god but God, and Muhammad is the prophet of God. The least important is that you remove any thorn, stick, or rock lying on the road that might inconvenience passersby. Shame and modesty are also important matters of faith." The complete Muslim, therefore, will clearly embody all the aspects of the faith. Anyone else is not fully Muslim. Everyone knows that it is necessary to be a complete Muslim, to keep these points in mind, and to strive to omit none. Here follows a list including each point, in all some seventy-seven.

THIRTY POINTS RELATED TO THE HEART

1. To believe in Almighty God.
2. To believe that, aside from God, all things were in the beginning nonexistent. They came into existence by God creating them.

3. To have certain faith that there are angels.

4. To have certain faith that all the books revealed by Almighty God to the prophets are true but that the authority of all but the Qur'an has ended.

5. To have certain faith that all the prophets were true but that now only the path of the Messenger of God[s] is correct.

6. To have certain faith that Almighty God knows all things from the beginning and that what happens is what is pleasing to him.

7. To have certain faith that the Day of Judgment is coming.

8. To believe in heaven.

9. To believe in hell.

10. To love Almighty God.

11. To love the Messenger of God[s].

12. If you love or hate anyone, to do so only for the sake of Almighty God.

13. To act in every undertaking only with religious intent.

14. To repent of all sins.

15. To fear Almighty God.

16. To have hope in the mercy of Almighty God.

17. To be modest.

18. To be grateful for blessings.

19. To fulfill agreements.

20. To show patience.

21. To consider yourself inferior to others.

22. To show mercy to other creatures.

23. To be content with whatever comes from God.

24. To trust in God.

25. Not to vaunt yourself on account of any good quality.

26. Not to be bitter or deceitful toward anyone.

27. Not to envy anyone.

28. Not to be angry.

29. Not to wish ill to anyone.

30. Not to have love for the world.

SEVEN MATTERS RELATED TO THE TONGUE

31. To recite the *kalima* orally.

32. To recite the Qur'an.

33. To acquire knowledge.

34. To impart knowledge.

35. To make supplication.

36. To recite the name of God.

37. To avoid all foolish and sinful conversations such as lies, backbiting, abuse, and singing songs contrary to the *shari'at*.

FORTY MATTERS RELATED TO THE WHOLE BODY

38. To perform the ablution, to bathe, and to keep your clothes clean.
39. To perform the prayer regularly.
40. To give *zakat,* charity, and the 'Id offering.
41. To keep the fast.
42. To perform the pilgrimage.
43. To keep seclusion (*i'tiqaf*) for prayer and meditation.
44. To leave any place where there may be harm to your faith.
45. To fulfill any vow made to God.
46. To fulfill an oath that is not made on anything sinful.
47. To cover the body, as obligatory.
48. To give recompense for any broken oath.
49. To make the sacrifice.
50. To shroud and bury the dead.
51. To repay any loan that may come due.
52. To avoid any matter against the *shari'at* in business dealing.
53. To hide no true evidence.
54. To marry if the lower soul demands.[47]
55. To fulfill your obligations to anyone in your charge.
56. To bring comfort to your mother and father.
57. To nurture your children.
58. Not to treat your relatives badly.
59. To obey your superior (*aqa*).
60. To do justice.
61. Not to follow any path apart from the community of Muslims.
62. To obey the ruler, but not in a matter that opposes the *shari'at*.
63. To reconcile those who fight.
64. To give help in a good work.
65. To point out the good path and to check evil.
66. To punish in accordance with the *shari'at* those for whom you are responsible.
67. To fight against enemies of the faith if the time should come.
68. To restore to the owner anything given to you in trust.
69. To advance loans to those in need.
70. To be hospitable toward your neighbors.
71. To take only untainted income.
72. To spend your wealth according to the *shari'at*.

73. To answer a greeting.

74. If someone sneezes and says *"Alhamdu'li'llah"* (**"Praise be to God"**), to respond with *"Yarhamuka'llah"* (**"God's mercy on you"**).

75. To cause no one trouble unnecessarily.

76. To avoid games and spectacles that are against the *shari'at*.

77. To remove clods of earth, rocks, thorns, and sticks from the road.

Look in the book *Furu'u'l-iman* (Ramifications of the faith) if you want to know the reward of each point separately.[48]

VIII. The Evil Influence of Your Own Lower Soul and of Ordinary People

There are two causes that disrupt one's ability to distinguish good from evil and to secure the reward described above. The first cause is your own lower soul, which at every moment is sitting right in your own lap. The lower soul suggests all sorts of things; it invents pretexts to oppose doing good; it rationalizes the necessity of doing evil. If you frighten it with the fear of torment, it reminds you that God is the Forgiver, the Merciful. On top of this, Satan lends it his support. The second cause of disruption involves those people with whom you have some relationship, whether relatives, acquaintances, or neighbors. Many sins are committed because of the company of these people and the influence of their bad deeds. Many sins are committed because of concern for not appearing inconsequential in their sight. Others are committed because someone has done you an ill turn, and you waste time in being miserable, engaging in backbiting, and thinking up revenge. This leads to all kinds of sins.

The entire problem stems from obeying the lower soul and from hoping for good from other people. You must realize that two things are necessary to avoid this trouble. First, you should suppress your lower soul, either by cajoling it or by threatening it, so that it keeps on the path of religion. Second, you should have no great attachment to anyone and take no account of whether others say something is good or bad. These two essential strategies will be discussed separately.

BEHAVIOR TOWARD THE LOWER SOUL

Regularly set aside a little time in the morning and a little time in the evening before going to sleep to sit alone, emptying your heart (*dil*) of all distracting thoughts as far as possible. Speak to your self (*ji*) as follows:

"O Self (*nafs*), you must recognize that in this world you are like a trader. Your stock-in-trade is your life. Its profit is to acquire well-being forever, that is, salvation in the afterlife. This is indeed a profit! If you waste your life and do not gain your salvation, you suffer losses that reach to your stock-in-trade. That stock-in-trade is so precious that each hour—indeed, each breath—is valuable beyond limit. No treasure, however great, can equal it. If other treasures disappear, you can always get more by expending some effort. But not one second of life can return, nor can you get another life. Moreover, with life you can earn the greatest wealth, namely, paradise forever and the joy and vision of God. No one can earn such wealth from any other treasure. This stock-in-trade is of very great worth and value indeed.

"O Self, recognize God's kindness that death has not yet come. Death ends your life. Almighty God has today provided you yet one more day of life. When you face death, you will entreat God with your whole heart and soul to grant you one more day of life in order to make a true and real repentance for all your sins and to promise him sincerely that you will never get entangled in sin again. You will pray to be able to pass that one day in remembering Almighty God and in obedience to him.

"If these will be your thoughts at the hour of death, it is surely better to act *now* in your heart as if the hour of death had in fact come and Almighty God had indeed answered your plea for one more day. You do not actually know if there will be another day after today or not. You must spend this day as if it were the last day of your life. Repent sincerely of all your sins; commit no act of disobedience, great or small; and spend the whole day in fear and contemplation of Almighty God, forsaking none of his commandments. When you have spent an entire day in this fashion, you should persevere on the next day, thinking, again, that this day may be the last.

"O Self, do not fall into the deception that Almighty God will surely forgive you. In the first place, how do you know that he will forgive you and not punish you? And if the punishment does begin, then what will you do? What regret you will feel! Even if, as we believe, there will be forgiveness of our sins, you will still not get the reward and rank given those people who have done good deeds. When you see with your own eyes others getting rewards and your self deprived, what sorrow and regret there will be!"

If at this the Self answers, "Then tell me what I should do and how I should make an effort," then you should answer, "Do this: Give up now what it is you forsake when you die, namely, the world and bad habits. From this time on, hold fast to what it is you will have to face and without which you cannot live, namely, Almighty God and all that makes him happy. Occupy yourself in remembering him and obeying him." Talk to the Self about bad habits and their cure, as well as about habits that please Almighty God and methods for learning them. All of this is written above. If you behave in accordance with these writings, evil will disappear from the heart and good will take root.

Say to your Self: "O Self, you are like a sick person. A sick person must follow a good regimen. Sinning is a bad regimen, and you must surely abstain from it. Almighty God has set a good regimen for your whole life. Just think a bit about what you would do if some ordinary *hakim* in this world told you, in the course of a severe illness, that if you ate a certain tasty thing it would greatly aggravate your illness and you would sink into great suffering. On the contrary, if you ate a certain bitter, ill-tasting medicine every day, you would keep well and your suffering would be eased. Because your life is dear, it is certain that you would act on the word of this *hakim*. However tasty this dish might be, you would give it up for your whole life. However ill-tasting and unpleasant the medicine, you would close your eyes and gulp it down day after day. We have learned that sin is very tasty and good deeds very unpleasant. Moreover, Almighty God has told us the harm of those tasty things and the blessing of distasteful acts—harm and blessing indeed, forever and ever in the form of heaven and hell! O Self, it is a sad and surprising thing that out of love for your life you believe the word of an ordinary *hakim* and adhere to it, yet out of love for your faith you do not fix your heart on the word of Almighty God and resolve to give up sins. You turn away your heart from doing good works. So what kind of Muslim are you—repent, repent!—that you do not consider the command of Almighty God the equal of the word of a petty *hakim*? How irrational not to value the everlasting comfort of heaven as much as the brief comfort of this world! And how foolish not to try to escape the harsh and long suffering of hell as readily as the brief suffering of the world!"

Say to the Self, "O Self, the world is a place of journeying, and on a journey complete comfort is never available. You must endure all kinds of trouble. Travelers put up with these troubles, because they know that when they reach home they will have all comfort. If, instead, they grow distressed by these troubles and settle at an inn, collecting all matter of furnishings and luxuries and making the inn their home, they will never return home their whole life long. In the same way, you must endure hard work and distress as long as you dwell in the world. There is work in acts of worship; there is distress in giving up sin; there are all kinds of other troubles. The afterlife is our home. When we arrive there, all trouble will be ended. Here, we must endure all work and troubles. If we seek comfort here, it will be difficult for us ever to reach our comforts at home. Just remember that you must never thirst for the pleasures and satisfactions of this world. For the sake of the afterlife, you must willingly bear trouble of every kind."

So saying these things to yourself, you must set yourself on the right path and reason in this way every day. Remember that if *you* do not strive in this way for your well-being and correction, there is no one else who will come along to do it for you. Now learn this—may you learn all that you must do.

BEHAVIOR WITH ORDINARY PEOPLE

There are three categories of ordinary people, namely, those with whom there is a relation of friendship, sisterhood, and companionship; those with whom there is only acquaintance; and strangers with whom there is not even acquaintance. There is a different manner of behavior with each group.

Strangers

Keep these points in mind concerning associating with strangers: Do not lend an ear to those who gossip about this and that. Make yourself completely deaf to those who indulge in disreputable talk. Do not meet with such people often. Do not have any expectations of them or make any request of them. If you see them doing something against the *shari'at,* explain the matter to them very gently, provided there is some hope that they will heed your counsel.

Friends

Keep in mind that you should not seek friendship and familiarity with everyone, because not everyone is worthy of friendship. However, there is no harm in close association with anyone who has the following five qualities:

1. She must be intelligent. A stupid person cannot sustain a friendship, and a foolish person might want to help you but might end up hurting you. For example, a person kept a bear. Once, this person fell asleep, and a fly kept landing on his face. The bear got angry and

picked up a big stone to kill the fly. He struck it right on his master's face. The fly flew away, but the poor fellow's head was smashed.

2. The second point is that her morals, habits, and disposition should be good. She should not make friends for her own ends; she should not lose her head in anger; she should not turn away her faithless eyes like a parrot over the least little thing.

3. The third thing is that she should be pious. A person who is not religious does not render what is owed to Almighty God; thus she will hardly be faithful to you. Second, when you see her sinning again and again, but as her friend treat her gently, you will stop hating sin. Third, you will be influenced by her bad company and begin to commit the same sins that she does.

4. The fourth thing is that she should not be greedy for worldly things. If she is, your own greed will increase from associating with her. When you see her every minute occupied with this and chatting about that, sometimes jewelry, sometimes clothes, sometimes household furnishings—how long can you keep from thinking about all this, too? If, on the contrary, you associate with someone who has no greed, whose clothes are ordinary, whose food is plain, who speaks of the transitory nature of the world, you yourself will lose whatever greed you may have in your heart.

5. The fifth point is that she should not have the habit of lying. You cannot rely on a liar. God knows who may believe her and be deceived.

Take these points into account before forming a friendship. When you see these five qualities in someone and establish a friendship, you must then fulfill your proper obligation to your friend. That obligation is to be of service to her in her need to the extent possible. If Almighty God gives you adequate means, help her. Do not tell her secrets to anyone. Do not tell anyone her faults. Do not tell her if anyone speaks ill of her. When she speaks to you, set your ear to listen carefully. If you see some fault in her, tell her privately, very gently, and as one who wishes her well. If she commits some fault, ignore it. Always pray to Almighty God for her welfare.

Acquaintances

With such people, great circumspection is necessary. Those who are your friends are concerned for your welfare. Those with whom there is no acquaintance may not be concerned with your welfare, but at least they don't wish you ill, either. Those who are in the middle, with whom there is neither friendship nor complete lack of acquaintance, are those who cause the greatest trouble and ill. With their tongues they profess friendship and good will, but deep within they dig up trouble, envy you, and every minute search for your faults and think about slandering you. To the extent possible, do not meet any of them; do not envy their worldly things; do not spoil your religion for them. If anyone is your enemy, do not be her enemy in return. That leads to her acting so badly toward you that it would be more than you could bear. You will be preoccupied with her, and you will find both your religion and your everyday life harmed. Ignoring her is better.

Do not be deceived into trusting someone who honors you and treats you well, praises you, and expresses love for you. Very few people are the same outside and inside. There is very little certainty that this behavior is done with a pure heart. Never hope for such good will from anyone.

If someone speaks ill of you behind your back, do not be angry at hearing it. Nor should you be surprised that a person could treat you badly, ignoring what she owes you in return for your kindness, forgetting your high status, and discounting your connections. If you are just, you will see that you yourself are not always the same in front of a person as you are behind that person's back. There is one kind of behavior in front of a person, another kind behind. If you yourself are susceptible to this evil, why be surprised at others?

In short, expect no benefit or respect from anyone. When you expect nothing from anyone, you will feel no sorrow at what anyone does. You yourself should always do well by others, as far as possible. If you think of something beneficial for someone else, tell her about it if you are sure she will accept it; otherwise remain silent. If someone does something of benefit to you, thank Almighty God and pray for the person. If someone harms you or causes you difficulty, consider it punishment for some sin, repent before Almighty God, and do not hold a grievance against this person. Do not look at the good or evil of any creature, but always keep your sight on Almighty God; deal always with him, obey only him, and absorb yourself in remembering him. May Almighty God grant you the ability to do so!

A Summary of Instructions for Teaching This Book

1. This book includes some sections on ethics and propriety.
2. Most of the book is related to reform of the heart, a subject called *tasawwuf* and *darweshi*. Its points are required, like other authoritative orders of the *shari'at*. One should follow them carefully.
3. If it is difficult for girls to understand the fourth or fifth books,

this book can be taught following the third. There is also the option of teaching the sixth book either before or after this one.

4. If the student does something or says something that is in opposition to the subject of this book, the teacher or a fellow student should immediately reproach her by reminding her that she is acting against what she just read. Such a reproach will stick.

5. Teachers themselves should follow the teachings of this book. That will have great influence.

6. If from the beginning the girls write the lesson on their slates or paper every day, they will develop a clear script and will plant the subject matter of the book in their minds. If in some circumstances it is considered imprudent to learn writing, do not teach the girl to write. Writing is not more dear than honor.

7. If you read this section aloud over and over to illiterate women, their hearts and habits will also be set right. You must also insist to the literate that they should review lessons they have learned so that their counsel will remain fresh.

8. It is appropriate to set a time for the students to read this book out loud to the people of their house. Such a reading is also beneficial for the illiterate.

4

Book Eight of the *Bihishti Zewar:*
Stories of Good Women

Translator's Introduction to Book Eight

Book Eight of the *Bihishti Zewar* brings to life the earlier abstract discussions of moral formation and personal development by providing brief biographies of one hundred women, supplemented by one other biography—that of the Prophet himself—bringing the total to an auspicious one hundred one. The stories of the women range from that of the first woman, Hazrat Hawwa—Eve—to tales of saintly women who lived in the early centuries of Islam. They are women who acknowledge their sins and humbly embrace correct action, abandon the false customs of their ancestors, and are faithful in prayer, grateful for God's blessings, steadfast in adversity, and devoted to the support of education. They love God and his prophets; they cultivate *'aql* and suppress *nafs*. The ideals set out in Book Seven and further developed in Book Ten are modeled here in specific lives made significant by fidelity and self-control.

This book is particularly important for what it tells us about Maulana Thanawi's implicit and explicit conceptions of gender. In this regard, nothing is more telling than the description of the Prophet Muhammad, the auspicious beginning of the accounts. In an essay on the virtues of good women, it is taken for granted that the apotheosis of virtue is in fact a good man. There is no specific model for women. The two prototypical women in Christianity, Eve and Mary, are included here: Eve as a model of true repentance, not temptation; Mary a model of obedience and piety, virtues not specific to women. Fatima, a more central figure in Muslim tradition, is also depicted as an embodiment of core values. The Prophet Muhammad's virtues turn out to be precisely those of good persons—women and men—taken to their ultimate human extreme. This is a telling indication of the extent to which women and men are regarded as essentially the same, however different their social places. This essential identity is further evoked in the love poetry of this culture, which celebrates at once human love and the soul's love for God; the beloved can be either female or male, as can the lover. (This is, one must note, a genre of poetry that Thanawi opposed, largely in vain.) Women and men may be complementary in social roles but not, in principle, in character or virtues. There are, one can argue, no virtues that are particularly feminine; only the context in which shared virtues find expression is different.

The sketch of the Prophet is perhaps the section of the *Bihishti Zewar* that will surprise the non-Muslim reader most. Far from the caricature of the Prophet known to Western tradition, Muhammad here appears as he is known through the *hadis* and as he has been cherished by Muslims: a man of kindness, gentleness, integrity, and humility. The first section of the biography recapitulates the historical events associated with his life, alluding to what are presumably well-known occurrences. It is elliptic and schematic. The night ascension, for example, is noted but not explained. His military career is covered by this sentence: "In his second year [in Medina], the Battle of Badr occurred, followed by other battles, altogether some thirty-five, both large and small." Some points are made in detail. Two Christian prophecies concerning the Prophet's greatness are described, for example, perhaps because of the importance of the ongoing confrontations with missionaries at the time the *Bihishti Zewar* was written. The names of Muhammad's wives and daughters are also meticulously recorded, as they figure prominently in the later text.

Thanawi's discussion of the events of the Prophet's life may be sketchy, but he waxes eloquent when discussing Muhammad's personal qualities in loving detail. This emphasis, of course, fits with the concern for moral character expressed in the *Bihishti Zewar* as a whole. The Prophet's disposition (*mizaj*) and his habits (*'adat*) are those urged upon women—indeed, they are those we may think of as particularly feminine: he is humble, gentle, given to few words, eager to serve others, always ready to work with his own hands, pious beyond measure. He keeps his gaze lowered—"What young girl would have been as modest as this?" In the well-known dyad that characterizes personalities in this culture, he is unfailingly tender (*narm*), not harsh (*sakht*).

For the readers of the original Urdu, the account makes the Prophet homey and familiar: in a house with a *takht* (platform) for sitting, a *kiwar* (door panel) to go in and out, and a *chapati* (unleavened Indian bread) to eat. The Prophet is not only a model for other men but, in his patterns of moral behavior, a pattern for women as well.

All we have learned about good behavior from the *Bihishti Zewar* is evident here, down to the fact that the Prophet ate little and was never concerned with the quality of the food. He was generous in all things, patient, attuned to measure, and so discriminate that he never exceeded proper bounds when it came to talking either too much or too little. "He always conducted himself according to rule." He treated all, even the most humble, with respect, so that each person believed himself or herself to be the best-loved. The task of Muhammad's follower is to cultivate the love such a leader draws forth, forging the bond with him through adherence to the *shari'at*, which makes a person's life as much like the Prophet's as possible.

The account of Muhammad's life not only is presented to be comprehended intellectually; it is also given as a *baraka*, a source of blessed power. It conveys an attachment to the Prophet's person, an attachment that is turned back into emulation precisely because it is to be realized only through faithful adherence to the *shari'at*. Women of the Prophet's day, it is explained in the first paragraph, were inspired by the power of his light, the *nur-i muhammadi* present from the beginning of time and embodied in him.[1] Now, however, all the blessings available to those who actually saw him can be attained only by adherence to his example. It is by emulating the Prophet's obedience to God's law that a woman can be like him, know him, and truly love him.

Besides being evident in the striking inclusion of the Prophet's life in a chapter on good women, the belief in the shared potential and achievements of women and men is further indicated by the nouns chosen to describe women. Even when, in some cases, feminine forms of the nouns are known, the accounts are characterized by the use of nouns typically associated with men: *badshah* (king); *ustad* (master, teacher); *'alim* (learned scholar); *wali* (saint); *sardar* (chieftain); *buzurg* (elder). It is unusual to hear a woman's name associated with nouns such as these.

The women described are divided into three groups defined by the time periods that, from a Muslim perspective, reflect the fundamental divisions of human history: before the time of Muhammad, during his lifetime, and during the time that follows. None of the women are from the subcontinent; most are well known or are associated with men who are well known, for these lives are considered most significant. Some of the accounts are universally moving, stories of women of piety and integrity. Some, though moving or even unforgettable, are emotionally remote for people outside the culture: there is, for example, a story of a woman who keeps from her husband the news that their baby has died, so that the husband's dinner, evening, and love-making will not be disturbed. Many of the accounts are interesting because of the different interpretation given to the lives of women whose stories are known from the Hebrew Bible and the Gospels. In Muslim tradition, Hawwa (Eve), for example, becomes the model of piety and repentance—as befits the first exemplar, for *tauba* is the first step in following a path of spiritual development. She is not the emblem of temptation and sin.[2]

Some of the accounts, however, especially from the earliest period, seem trivial. Almost all of the twenty-five stories in this section concern women related to men whom Muslims consider prophets in the line that culminated in Muhammad. Many of these women display remarkable behavior, but nearly half are relatives of famous men and are simply spoken of as virtuous. Because Lot and his family were warned to escape from destruction, and because that family included daughters, the daughters are listed as examples of women who must have been worthy of God's favor. Joseph's aunt (or perhaps his mother), whom he honored when his father and brothers brought her along to join him in Egypt, is counted as a worthy example because a prophet treated her with respect. Moses' sister-in-law, whose name is unknown, is described drawing water with her sister; thus she must have been hardworking and obedient to her father. When Hazrat Khizr kills a young boy, he explains that the boy would have been evil and that a virtuous daughter will be born in his place; we hear nothing of this daughter, but she is taken as an example because of this statement about her prospective goodness. Similarly, the boy's mother, unnamed, counts as yet another example of a good woman, for she was to benefit from this change. Solomon praises God for rewarding his parents; thus, the account concludes, his mother must have been worthy. Even given the expectation that part of women's role is to seek the approval of the men on whom they depend, these examples of models for emulation seem thin. One wonders about Maulana Thanawi's claim that he could have included many more stories but stopped in the interests of space. Is he hard-pressed to come up with a hundred stories of good women?

This is perhaps our first clue to the implicit belief that—whatever the theory—women are less able to achieve virtue than men are. Maulana Thanawi is committed to arguing in theory that a Muslim woman, albeit in her role of obedience to her husband and service to her children, has exactly the same endowment and opportunity as a man. But many assumptions—implicit here and explicit in Book Ten, where a separate list of women's shortcomings is given, and in Book Six, where the discussion of women's outings overflows with female foibles—undermine that theory. Even when women are celebrated, we find more than once a tone of astonishment that a woman could give good advice to a man (and a learned man, at that) or that a woman could show forbearance and patience under extraordinary duress. In calling on women to seek learning, moreover, Thanawi trivializes their ordinary domestic work: "It is easier for you to learn than it is for boys, because you do not have to go out to earn money. . . . As for sewing and similar skills, you can learn them in a few weeks. Why waste your whole life?"

At the conclusion of Book Eight, Maulana Thanawi includes verses from the Qur'an and *hadis* to encourage women. In these, the tension between the ideal of women's identity with men and their subservient social place is clear. In the *hadis,* for example, women are listed as possessions of men; they are dependent even for salvation on their husbands' happiness, and they are obliged to show obedience to them. As evident in the accounts of women during the third period of history (after the Prophet's lifetime), women's heroism is often defined as offering financial or moral support that permits accomplishments by men. A second list of *hadis* identifies women's particular flaws. Many are in hell for their ingratitude; others complain of illness or indulge in endless weeping over their sorrows; some mistreat animals, defy inheritance laws, or talk excessively; other women dress immodestly or wear gold. Some of these sins could be attributed equally to men (and indeed the *hadis* on inheritance speaks of women and men), but the implication is that women are especially likely to fall short.

As later editions of Book Eight were published, more material related to the issue of women's handicaps was included in two appendices. The first, however, *Risala kiswatu'n-niswa* (The dress of women), stressed positive examples. It included the second section of quotations from the Qur'an and *hadis* from the first edition, supplemented by a translation of Ibn Maja's (d. 273/886) *Kunzu'l-'amal,* a collection of *hadis.* The idea of including this pamphlet came to Thanawi during a visit to Dig in the state of Bharatpur during Ramazan of 1917. On that occasion, he had spoken in the *zanana* of his host and "out of necessity" focused on the shortcomings of women. After hearing his sermon, a woman sent him a message pointing out that she and the others had heard a good deal about the evils of women but needed to hear whether there were some good qualities common to women or whether women had any rights! Maulana Thanawi seized on this advice immediately and concluded that encouragement and good examples might be more efficacious than warnings and bad examples.

The second appendix, *Islahu'n-niswa* (The reform of women) strikes the latter note, however. Although not printed until later, the first section of it was actually written as part of the original Book Eight; it was left out, apparently, because of length. It is an account of twenty-five women, all drawn from the classical period and beginning with a near-contemporary of Adam and Eve. These are stories of evil women, but the final five strike a hopeful note, for the women all repent. The occasion for reviving this section came when a neighbor showed Maulana Thanawi an essay he had written out of bitter experience with women. Thanawi then conceived the idea of putting his stories together with the neighbor's document as a warning to those women who needed a stimulus to repentance. He was, however, quite concerned to make it clear that not all women were as this neighbor had described them and that, in fact, many men were rendered useless, "laid on the shelf, thanks to their oppressiveness, hard-heartedness, neglect of others' rights, and stupidity."

The neighbor's essay itself has also been printed in later editions. The anonymous author deplores the same characteristics Maulana Thanawi has warned against: above all, lack of proper discrimination of one's role (*be'aqli*) and distortions of hierarchic relations, particularly in women who seek to place themselves at the level of men. Women, the neighbor argues, have no concern for the dignity of men. They do not obey men or their own parents; they gossip about their high-handedness; they engage in dissension; they seek to set up separate households. The browbeaten husband seeks to be quiet to avoid public contention; the wife concludes that he is without discrimination and that he fears her, and "she shows the cloven hoof the more." The women of this age, the author writes, seek spells and amulets to ensnare all men as their *murids*—again a reversal of hierarchy. They secretly look to feed them owl's meat—a food many believed would render the eater stupid.

This unhappy author speaks at length of husbands who go away to take up service. This pattern was not uncommon in the social milieu for which the *Bihishti Zewar* was written and was perhaps part of the perceived necessity of writing such a work. The neighbor argues that some men are driven away because of their wives. Once the husband has left, the wife—the cause of his leaving—sits home and quarrels with the in-laws over being allowed to join her husband. She writes complaining letters, makes demands for money, keeps false accounts, takes loans, and accuses the husband of living lavishly when away. He has no knowledge of what goes on at home; and if he does come home, he regrets it. He works "like the oilman's ox," and that too away from home. She, at home, lies abed. Indeed—as the author commissioned by Thanawi to write Book Nine of the *Bihishti Zewar,* on medicine, also complains—women are often sick, and that sickness often feigned. Hundreds of rupees are spent on silver leaf, myrobalan syrup, and other strengthening medicines to give the wife an excuse to do nothing.

In many of the forty-one points of his argument, the anonymous author speaks of the women "of this age" or "of this new age." There is a sense that the changing times are responsible for women's degeneration. Two changes are noted. One is that women travel with men and grow bold on these journeys. The other is that women are educated—a proven source of corruption, pace Maulana Thanawi. They write letters to outside men; they read novels from the bazaar day and night. And of course the man himself is ruined. Not only is he kept from playing his role as a man, but he is also pushed to obtain illicit income and checked by his wife from paying his due to other people and to God in *zakat.*

Thanawi himself had made many of the same points, but he never suggested, as did his neighbor, that all women acted in such a fashion. To emphasize his unwillingness to generalize about either men or women, Maulana Thanawi approvingly quotes a Persian couplet both before and after the anonymous memo:

> Not every woman's a woman; not every man's a man;
> Nor did God make identical five fingers on a hand.[3]

This appendix aside, Book Eight primarily stresses the positive capacity of women, in their domestic role, to reach the high level of human realization made possible in Islam.

As in all writing of history, we learn from the accounts offered here a great deal about the present. We learn that the reformists believed ordinary Muslim women capable of aspiring to the qualities of the praiseworthy women described, women whose qualities are those of ideal behavior for both women and men: they are just, patient, grateful, humble, pious, modest, learned, free from love of wealth, and generous to the poor. We also learn of specific reformist practices that are exemplified in the stories. Asiya, Pharaoh's wife, is especially celebrated in Muslim literature for defying her tyrannical husband. In these accounts, both she and Bilqis are identified as women who rose above traditionally received custom—a goal the reformers encouraged above all else. The remarriage of widows, which custom was seen to have outrageously thwarted, is emphasized. Its acceptance by the Prophet himself, evident in account after account of the lives of the women he married, gives that reform its most compelling support. Ordinary women, Thanawi argues, can emulate such practices.

Similarly, as another note suggests, they can be inspired by the heroic women who found ways to educate nephews and sons by themselves contributing to the new religious schools that were increasingly a part of north Indian Muslim life—and by preferring religious education over education for colonial government jobs. A particular theme of the day, drawn in the moral to the story of Hazrat Halima Sa'diyya, a Companion of the Prophet, is the importance of each individual attaining moral qualities. Not even bonds to influential people—so important in family and social life in this society—can take the place of individual responsibility for what one is and what one does.

Book Eight fundamentally asserts the reformist theme of the trustworthiness and benign nature of a divine power working in history, whatever the appearance of events may seem to assert. This conviction affects both women and men. To illustrate this faith, Maulana Thanawi uses the historical stories because they are the most powerful and convincing. The first group of stories offers particularly compelling evidence of divine intervention: angels and suckling babies speak; fires do not burn; inspiration and revelation prove true; material objects are transformed; and a virgin gives birth to a son. The readers, like the models, must be faithful, whatever the appearance of evil and reversal of fortune they may face, in full confidence that their lives, in their day, can also have meaning. The stories are thus profoundly relevant to women, as they are to men, who are beset by the vicissitudes of everyday life and by the challenges of life in a colonized society undergoing political and social change.

Righteous women are devoutly obedient and guard in their husbands'
absence what Allah would have them guard.

A pamphlet meant to instruct women and girls in the
way to act on this Qur'anic verse

Heavenly Ornaments

Book Eight

A discussion, by section, of everything that women need to
know about beliefs, legal points, ethics and social behavior,
child-rearing, and so on

Compiled by the Reverend Hazrat, Sun of the Scholars,
Crown of the Learned,
Maulana Hafiz Muhammad Ashraf ʿAli Sahib

Published at the direction of
Maulana Maulawi Muhammad Yahya Sahib,
Dealer in Religious Books, Gangoh

Printed at the Bilali Steam Press, Sadhaura, District Ambala

Contents of Book Eight

In the Name of God, the Merciful, the Compassionate

The Eighth Book
of the *Bihishti Zewar:*
Stories of Good Women

I. An Account of the Prophet[s], to Inspire the Religious Resolve of the Readers*

Before beginning our account of good women, we turn first to a brief account of the Apostle of God, *God's blessings and peace upon him.* The reason for doing this is to gain the blessed power that is in his story, so that those who read it may learn about their Apostle[s] and about his habits and thus love and follow him. It goes without saying that all people gain the treasure of goodness in no other way but through the blessed power of the Prophet[s]. The women of the early community gained it through the presence of his light; the women of today's community gain it through the *shari'at.* First, we shall speak of him, and only then will we begin the stories of good women.

HIS BIRTH, LIFE, AND DEATH

The renowned and blessed name of the Prophet was Muhammad[s]. His father's name was 'Abdu'llah; 'Abdu'llah's father's name was 'Abdu'l-Muttalib; 'Abdu'l-Muttalib's father's name was Hashim; and Hashim's father's name was 'Abd Manaf. The mother of Muhammad[s] was named Amina; her father's name was Wahb; Wahb's father's name

* From the *Sirat ibn Hisham* and other works. [This is one of the historical works of the third and fourth centuries of the Muslim era that provide material on the Prophet. See W. Montgomery Watt, *Muhammad at Mecca* (Oxford: Clarendon Press, 1965), p. xi; Martin Lings, *Muhammad* (New York: Inner Traditions International, 1983), p. 349.]

was ʿAbd Manaf; and ʿAbd Manaf's father's name was Zuhra. (This is a second ʿAbd Manaf.)

Muhammadˢ was born on a Monday in the third lunar month of Rabiʿuʾl-awwal in the year that an infidel king tried to destroy the Kaʿba by attacking it with elephants.[1] He stayed for some time with a wet-nurse, who returned him to his mother when he was five years and two days old. When he was six years old, his mother took him to his paternal grandfather's maternal kin in Bani Najjar in Medina for a month's stay. She died on her way home, at a place called Abwa. Umm Aiman, *may God be pleased with her,* who was with her, then took the child to Mecca. Because the child's father had died before he was born, his paternal grandfather, ʿAbduʾl-Muttalib, looked after him. After the grandfather died, a paternal uncle, Abu Talib, took charge of the child, on one occasion taking him along to Syria, where Abu Talib was traveling for trade. On the road, Bahira, a Nazarene scholar and holy man, saw the child.[2] He directed the uncle to protect Muhammad because the child was a prophet. The uncle thereupon sent the child back to Mecca.

Later, Muhammadˢ himself set off for Syria with goods to trade on behalf of Hazrat Khadijaʳᶻ. On the road to Syria, Nastura, a second Nazarene scholar and holy man, also gave witness that Muhammadˢ was a prophet. When Muhammadˢ returned, he married Hazrat Khadijaʳᶻ. At this time he was twenty-five years of age, and Hazrat Khadijaʳᶻ was forty. At the age of forty years, he received the mantle of prophethood, and at the age of fifty-two or fifty-three, he undertook the night ascension. After receiving the prophethood, he remained in Mecca thirteen years, until Almighty God ordered him to go to Medina the Radiant because of the harassment of the infidels. In his second year there, the Battle of Badr occurred, followed by other battles, altogether some thirty-five, both large and small.

He married, as is well known, eleven women, of whom two died before him, namely, Hazrat Khadijaʳᶻ and Hazrat Zainabʳᶻ, who was the daughter of Khuzaima. He died leaving nine wives behind: Hazrat Saudaʳᶻ; Hazrat ʿAʾishaʳᶻ; Hazrat Hafsaʳᶻ; Hazrat Umm Salamaʳᶻ; Hazrat Zainabʳᶻ, the daughter of Jahsh; Hazrat Umm Habibaʳᶻ; Hazrat Juwairiyyaʳᶻ; Hazrat Maimunaʳᶻ; and Hazrat Safiyyaʳᶻ. His offspring included four girls: the eldest was Hazrat Zainabʳᶻ, followed by Hazrat Ruqaiyaʳᶻ, Hazrat Umm Kulsumʳᶻ, and Hazrat Fatimaʳᶻ. All were born of Hazrat Khadijaʳᶻ. There were also three, four, or five boys. Hazrat Qaʾimʳᶻ, Hazrat ʿAbduʾllahʳᶻ, Hazrat Taiyibʳᶻ, and Hazrat Tahirʳᶻ were born of Khadijaʳᶻ. Hazrat Ibrahimʳᶻ, who was born of the maidservant Mariyaʳᶻ, died in Medina while still a suckling. By this reckoning, there were five boys. Some say that 'Abdu'llah was another name for Taiyib and thus there were only four. Some say that Taiyib and Tahir were both other names of 'Abdu'llah and thus there were only three. Hazrat 'Abdu'llah[rz] was born after the prophecy began, and he died in Mecca. The other boys were born before the prophecy and died before it also.

The Prophet[s] himself lived in Medina ten years. He took ill on a Wednesday, two days before the end of the month of Safar. He died on the twelfth of Rabi'u'l-awwal, on a Monday at mid-morning, at the age of sixty-three. He was buried on Tuesday afternoon. Many say, however, that the Companions were so distracted by shock and sorrow and their minds so disturbed that a delay occurred, and the daylight hours of Tuesday passed and night came before the burial took place.

Among the daughters of Hazrat Apostle[s], Hazrat Zainab[rz] had one son, 'Ali[rz], and a daughter, Imama[rz], but their line died out. Hazrat Ruqaiya[rz] had 'Abdu'llah[rz], who died when he was six. Hazrat Umm Kulsum[rz] had no offspring. Hazrat Fatima[rz] bore Hasan[rz] and Husain[rz], whose progeny proliferated greatly.

HIS CHARACTER AND HABITS

Hazrat[s] was very generous of heart. He never said no to anyone who asked him for something. If he had something, he gave it to anyone who asked for it. If he didn't have it, he apologized gently and promised to give what was desired another time. He was very truthful in speech. His nature was very gentle. He was very considerate of everyone he associated with and employed such a gentle and easy manner that no one experienced any discomfort on his account. If he had to go outside at night, he would put on his shoes very softly, open the door panel very gingerly, and walk out very quietly. If he came home and the people of the house were sleeping, he would do everything very softly, so that no one's sleep would ever be disturbed.

He always kept his eyes lowered toward the ground. When he went out walking with others, he stayed at the rear. When someone approached, he was the first to give a greeting. When he sat in company, he did so with great humility. When he ate, he never ate his fill as the very poor would. Sometimes he did not eat the unleavened bread that was served. He never ate formally, on a saucer.

At every moment he was sober with the fear of Almighty God. At every moment he was sunk in thought of him. In this preoccupation, no amount of tossing and turning yielded rest. He remained silent most of the time. He uttered no speech unless it was necessary. When he did speak, however, he spoke so clearly that anyone could understand him easily. What he said was neither so long that it exceeded what was necessary nor so brief that the meaning could not be understood. There was not the least bit of harshness in his conversation, as there was not the slightest harshness in his behavior. He never deprecated or dishonored those who came to him. He never interrupted anyone. To be sure, if someone spoke against the *shari'at,* he stopped that person or simply walked away.

He considered God's bounty, no matter how small, to be very great. He never found fault with anything, never saying that it did not taste good or that it smelled bad. If his heart did not take to a certain thing, he neither ate it nor praised it nor found fault with it. He was never angry because of any worldly matter—for example, that someone had caused him some harm or had spoiled some undertaking of his. Hazrat Anas[rz] said, "I served him ten years. In these ten years, no matter what I did, he never said: 'Why did you do this?' If I failed to do something, he never asked, 'Why didn't you do this?' "

If some matter was against the teachings of the faith, however, then no one could bear his anger. But in his personal affairs, he was never angry. If he was displeased with someone, he simply turned his face away and never railed with his tongue. When he was happy, he lowered his gaze. What young girl would have been as modest as this? If others were laughing, he simply smiled and did not laugh aloud. He mixed with everyone, but he never made a display of himself to attract some-one away from other people. Sometimes, to make someone happy, he laughed and joked, but even in that he said only what was true.

He read so many supererogatory prayers that both his feet swelled from standing. When he read the Qur'an or heard it, he wept from fear and love of God. There was such humility in his disposition that he commanded his community not to glorify him.

If a poor maidservant came to him and said, "I have something to say to you privately," he replied, "Fine, let us sit somewhere on the street and talk." He sat wherever she did. If someone was sick, whether rich or poor, he inquired after that person. If there was a funeral procession, he honored it with his presence. If some slave or servant invited him to dine, he accepted. If someone invited him to a meal of barley bread and ill-tasting fat, he did not make some excuse for not accepting.

No useless word ever slipped from his tongue. He sought to know the wish of each person's heart. He never did anything to cause distress to another. He was prudent in defending himself against the mischief of oppressors and troublemakers, but he treated such people in turn with good cheer and good nature. If someone who usually came to be with him did not come, he always inquired after that person.

He always conducted himself according to rule, not sometimes one way and sometimes another. When he arose, he remembered God; when he sat, he remembered God.

When he joined in any gathering, he would sit to the side of the group and not leap over the others to put himself in the most important place. If it was time for discussion and there were several people present, he would face each in turn. He would not focus his attention in one direction, failing to look at others. He treated everyone in such a manner that each person thought, "He likes me most." If someone came and sat near him or began to speak with him, he remained seated and attended to that person. When that person arose, only then did he arise. His manner was informal with everyone.

When he went home, he would take a pillow and sit to rest. He undertook many household tasks with his own hands. Sometimes he milked goats; sometimes he washed his own clothes. He usually attended to his own personal needs. He met each person, however evil, with kindness, and he never hurt anyone's feelings.

In sum, he was the best-natured (*khush akhlaq*) of all people. If someone did something unpleasant, he never admonished that person face-to-face. There was no harshness in his personality, nor did he ever affect a severe expression the way some people do who put on an expression of feigned anger or speak angrily and threaten others. It was not his habit to shout. He did not requite evil with evil; rather, he forgave the offender and overlooked the deed. He never struck any slave, servant, or woman, or even any animal. Giving punishment at the command of the *shari'at* was another matter, although if someone committed some outrage against him personally, he did not seek revenge.

He was always cheerful. He never turned up his nose at anything; he never knit his brow. This does not mean that he was without sorrow, because, as we have said, he was always sober and lost in thought.

His disposition was very warm. There was neither harshness in his conversation nor harshness in his behavior. He was not an impetuous person who would curse and shout for what he wanted. He did not talk about other people's faults. He was not grudging in giving things away. He had not even a hint of boasting, argumentativeness, or involvement in any unproductive activities. He did no one ill. He never dug up other people's faults. He spoke only in ways that merit reward. He helped any strangers who asked questions, even if they did so without proper decorum. He refused to let anyone praise him.

Other excellent things about the Prophet[s] are written in the *hadis*. Those I have related here, however, are sufficient if you imitate them. Now listen to the stories of good women.

II. Stories of Women of Earlier Communities

Hazrat Hawwa, *on Whom Be Peace*

Hazrat Hawwa[a] was the wife of Hazrat Adam, *blessings and peace be upon him and upon our Prophet.*[3] She is the mother of all the people of the world. Almighty God created her with his perfect power from the left rib of Hazrat Adam[a] and married her to him. He gave them a place to live in heaven. There was a tree in heaven of which he forbade them to eat. At the urging of Satan, they wrongly ate of the tree. Almighty God expelled them from paradise to go into the world. When Hazrat Hawwa[a] came into the world, she wept over her fault. Almighty God forgave her. She was apart from Hazrat Adam[a] until Almighty God reunited them. From them, innumerable offspring were born.

Moral: O women, look how Hazrat Hawwa[a] acknowledged her fault and repented. Many women keep pretending that they have never done anything wrong and deny any suspicion directed at them. Then, too, there are many who simply sin and keep on sinning their entire lives. They are especially given to backbiting and to practicing false customs. O women, give up these habits! When you commit an error, renounce it immediately and repent.

The Mother of Hazrat Nuh, *on Whom Be Peace*

It is in the Noble Qur'an that Hazrat Nuh, *peace be upon him and upon our Prophet,* prayed for his mother as well as for himself. The commentaries say that his mother and father were Muslims.[4]

Moral: Consider the blessed power of faith, that even an apostle will pray for those who are faithful. O women, keep your faith firm!

Hazrat Sara, *on Whom Be Peace*

Hazrat Sara[a] was the wife of the apostle Ibrahim[a] and the mother of the apostle Ishaq[a]. The Qur'an recounts that she spoke with angels and that the angels said to her, "You are God's mercy and blessing upon all the members of the household."[5]

In the *hadis,* there is a story of her chastity and the granting of her prayers. When Hazrat Ibrahim[a] emigrated to Syria, she accompanied him on the journey. On the way, they reached the land of a tyrannical king. Someone went to this wretched king and incited him by saying that a beautiful woman had come into his realm. The king then summoned Hazrat Ibrahim[a] and asked about the woman with him. He answered that she was his sister in religion, not saying "wife," because he feared that the king would kill him if he knew that he was her husband. When Ibrahim[a] returned to Hazrat Sara[a], he told her not to deny his statement, because she was, in fact, his sister in religion.

The king then had Hazrat Sara[a] seized. When she learned that his intentions were evil, she performed the ablution, recited the prayer, and prayed: "O God, I am one who believes in your apostle and who guards my honor. Oh, do not let this infidel gain control over me!"

Then something came over the king; he began to thrash around in pain and to cajole her, saying: "Pray to God that I may become well.* I pledge a firm vow that I will say nothing to disturb you."

She was afraid that if he died people would say she must have killed him, and thus she prayed for him to get well. He did so immediately. But then he again decided on evil. She prayed against him. Again, he cajoled her to pray for him. This happened three times. Finally, he was enraged. He said to his servants, "What devil have you brought me?" and told them to take her away.

He entrusted Hazrat Hajira[a] to her as a servant. She was a Copt by race, whom he had unjustly made a slave. God had also preserved her honor. *As God wills!* Hazrat Sara[a] returned to Hazrat Ibrahim[a] with her honor (*'izzat, abru*).

Moral: O women, look at the blessed power of chastity and see how Almighty God guards a chaste person. Also remember that the canonical prayer averts trouble and lets our supplications be heard. When you are worried, apply yourself to prayers (*namaz*) of supererogation and make continuous supplications (*du'a*).

Hazrat Hajira, *on Whom Be Peace*

The tyrannical king whose story has just been told kept Hazrat Hajira[a] as a slave before giving her to Hazrat Sara[a], who in turn gave her to her husband, Hazrat Ibrahim[a]. She bore Hazrat Isma'il, *on whom be peace*.[6]

---

* From Bukhari Sharif [one of the *sahih* (sound) collections of *hadis,* recognized as having great authority, compiled by Muhammad al-Bukhari (d. 256/870)].

Hazrat Isma'il[a] was a mere suckling when Almighty God decided to settle the noble city of Mecca with his progeny. The place was then a wilderness, and the Ka'ba had not even been built. Almighty God ordered Hazrat Ibrahim[a] to leave Hazrat Isma'il[a] and his mother Hajira[a] in the wilderness. He promised to be their guardian. Following God's order, Hazrat Ibrahim[a] took both the mother and the child to the wilderness where Mecca stands today and left them with a small leather bag of water and a sack of dates. As he was leaving, Hazrat Hajira[a] came after him and asked if he was leaving them there alone. Hazrat Ibrahim[a] gave no answer. Then she asked if God had ordered him to leave them there. Hazrat Ibrahim[a] answered that he had. She replied, "There is then no cause for sorrow. He will look after us."

She went to her place and sat down. She ate the dates, drank the water, and nursed Hazrat Isma'il[a]. When the water in the bag was finished, mother and son were overcome by thirst. The child soon began to writhe in discomfort. The mother could not bear to see her child in this state. She set out to climb Mount Safa to look for water, and she searched hopefully in all directions. She found nothing. She came down from the hill and went toward Mount Marwah to climb it. In the middle of the intervening plain, there was a piece of land like a hollow. As long as she remained on level ground, she could turn to look at her baby, but she could not see him from the hollow. So she ran through the hollow until she came again to level ground. She reached Mount Marwah and climbed it. Again she found nothing. She came down from the hill, distraught, and went toward Mount Safa again. She made seven circuits of both hills, each time running through the hollow. Almighty God was so pleased by her behavior that he later ordered pilgrims, forever and ever, to make seven circuits between the two hills and to run through the place that was once a hollow. Finally, on the last circuit, as she stood on Mount Marwah, she heard a voice. She turned toward the sound and stood still. The voice came again. There was no one in sight making the noise. She called out, "I hear a voice. If someone can help me, please come and help!"

An angel suddenly appeared where the well of Zamzan is now. He struck the ground with his arm, and water began to flow. Hazrat Hajira[a] surrounded the place on four sides with a boundary wall of clay and filled a bag with the water. She herself drank and gave some water to the child to drink. The angel said: "Do not fear. This place is the house of God, that is, the Ka'ba. This boy, in company with his father, will build the house, and the place will be settled."

In a few days, all these things became manifest. A caravan passed through, saw the water, halted, and settled down. Later, Hazrat Is-

ma'il[a] was married. Hazrat Ibrahim[a] arrived at the order of Almighty
God. Father and son together built the House of the Ka'ba. At that
time, the water of Zamzam came out from the ground, but later a well
was built.

Moral: Look what trust Hazrat Hajira[a] had in Almighty God! When
she learned that she was to stay in the wilderness on his order, she
became calm. What blessings appeared from this trust! O women, you
too must trust God. **Almighty God willing,** all will work out well. Look
at how well she acted when she ran in search of water. Her behavior
was so dear to God that he made her actions an act of worship for
pilgrims. God prizes the behavior of his favored servants. O women,
try to obey God so that you too may be favored. Then your everyday
acts will be made part of religion!

The Second Wife of Hazrat Isma'il, *on Whom Be Peace*

Before he built the Ka'ba, Hazrat Ibrahim[a] came again to Mecca
twice; but neither time did he find Hazrat Isma'il[a] at home. He did not
wait for him on either occasion, for God had not commanded him to do
so. The first time he came, he met only a wife at the house of Hazrat
Isma'il[a], and he inquired of her how she was managing. She answered,
"With great difficulty."

He replied, "When your husband comes home, give him my greetings and say that he should change the threshold of his door." When
Hazrat Isma'il[a] came home he heard all this and realized that the visitor
had been his father and that the message meant he should leave his
wife. He divorced her and married another woman.

When Hazarat Ibrahim[a] came the next time, he found the new wife
at home. She welcomed him solicitously. He inquired of her concerning
their situation, and she replied, "Thanks be to Almighty God, we are
very comfortable."

He blessed her and declared, "When your husband comes home,
give him my greetings and say that he should retain the threshold of his
door." When Hazrat Isma'il[a] came home and learned this, he explained
to his wife that the visitor had been his father, who wanted him to keep
her at his side.

Moral: Look at the fruit of the ingratitude of the first wife. One
prophet was displeased with her; another left her. Look at the fruit of
the gratitude and patience of the second wife. She was blessed by one
prophet; she was permitted to live in the service of a second. Women,
never be ungrateful! Live under any conditions with gratitude and
patience.

The Daughter of Namrud, the Infidel King

Namrud was the tyrannical king who threw Hazrat Ibrahim[a] into the fire.[7] A daughter of his, named Ra'za, stood above the fire, looking down, and saw that the fire had no effect on Hazrat Ibrahim[a]. She called down, "What is happening?"

He answered, "Almighty God has saved me through the blessing of faith."

She called out, "I want to come into the fire, too."

He answered, "Come, repeating, *'There is no God but God, and Ibrahim is the friend of God.'* "

She entered the fire fearlessly, reciting this profession of faith. The fire had no effect on her whatsoever. When she came out, she denounced her father, who then treated her very harshly. She, however, remained firm in her faith.

*Moral: **Praise God*** for such a courageous woman, who even when grievously harassed did not abandon her faith. O women, you too must keep your courage firm if you are harassed and must do nothing that is even a tiny bit against your religion.

The Daughters of Hazrat Lut, *on Whom Be Peace*

Almighty God sent angels to Lut[a] to inform him that all of Lut's people (*qaum*) who had not believed in God would be destroyed.[8] Almighty God also sent word that Lut[a] should take his Muslim family away from the city in the depth of night. His daughters were part of this Muslim family. They too were saved from destruction.

Moral: Consider the blessed power of faith, which can even deliver us from the wrathful judgment of God when it falls upon the world. O women, keep your faith strong. It grows strong when you adhere to all God's commandments and avoid all sins.

The Wife of Hazrat Ayyub, *on Whom Be Peace*

The wife of Hazrat Ayyub[a] was named Rahmat.

When Hazrat Ayyub[a] was afflicted with sores over his whole body, everyone except his wife ceased visiting him. This wife alone devoted herself to his service and suffered all kinds of misery. Once, she was late in coming to him. Hazrat Ayyub[a] in anger took an oath that he would beat her one hundred strokes with a stick when he was better. When his health was restored, he resolved to fulfill his oath. Almighty

God, in his mercy, tempered this intention by commanding Ayyub[a] to take a broom made of a hundred straws and strike with it only once.[9]

Moral: What a patient wife she was to continue to serve her husband under circumstances such as these! The story of the oath taken when he was ill shows that he had become very bad-tempered. She bore that also. The blessed power of such patience and service was that our Lord and Master saved her from the beating, tempering the judgment on her because she was so dear. (If anyone else should swear this kind of oath, it could not be fulfilled by using a broom. If one were to break this oath, one would have to make expiation.) O women, obey your husbands and patiently endure their bad temper. You then will be as dear as Rahmat was.

Hazrat Liya, the Maternal Aunt of Hazrat Yusuf, *on Whom Be Peace*

Hazrat Liya is mentioned in the Glorious Qur'an. When Hazrat Yusuf[a] became king of Egypt, there was a great famine. All of his brothers came to him to buy grain. Hazrat Yusuf[a] revealed himself to them and gave them his coat to place on the eyes of his father, Ya'qub[a], telling them to return with the entire family.

Hazrat Ya'qub[a] recovered his sight, then left his homeland to journey to Egypt to meet Hazrat Yusuf[a]. Yusuf[a] placed his father and his aunt on the royal throne to honor them. Both they and all the brothers prostrated themselves before Hazrat Yusuf[a]. (At that time, it was correct to perform a prostration in place of a greeting; now it is not correct.) Almighty God declared this aunt to be Yusuf's mother, for his own mother had died. Ya'qub[a] then married her. Some have said that this story is actually about Yusuf's own mother, whose name was Hazrat Rahil.[10]

Hazrat Yusuf[a] declared of the episode above, "This provides an interpretation of a dream of my childhood, when I saw the sun and moon and eleven stars bow to me."

Moral: Look how esteemed the aunt must have been, to have been so honored by a prophet.

The Mother of Hazrat Musa, *on Whom Be Peace*

The mother of Hazrat Musa[a] was Yukhand.[11]

The priests (*pandit*) frightened Pharaoh by saying that a boy who would destroy his kingdom would be born among the Bani Isra'il.

Pharaoh therefore ordered any boy born among them to be killed. Thousands of children were slaughtered.

Hazrat Musa[a] was born in this troubled time. Almighty God put the thought into the heart of his mother—this is called inspiration, or *ilham*—to nurse him without fear and to place him in a box in the river whenever there was danger of detection. Then, God declared, "I will restore him to you as I please." The mother did as commanded with no hesitation. Almighty God fulfilled all his promises.

Moral: Look what trust and confidence she had in Almighty God and what blessed power was made manifest because of this trust.

The Sister of Hazrat Musa, *on Whom Be Peace*

This sister's name has been reported by some as Maryam, by others as Kulsum.

When the mother of Hazrat Musa[a] placed the child in the box in the river, she told the sister to keep track of the box. The box was carried by the river to the palace of Pharaoh, where it was taken out of the water and a beautiful baby revealed. Pharaoh wanted to kill the child. His wife, however, who was a good and God-fearing woman, persuaded him to spare the child's life. Both husband and wife took the boy as their own and tried to feed him. But Musa[a] would not take the milk of any nurse they could find. All were distraught, not knowing what to do. Then this girl, the sister of Hazrat Musa[a], arrived on her quest and said, "I can tell you of a nurse who is devoted and kind and has fine milk." She told them of the mother of Hazrat Musa[a], who was then summoned and Musa[a] entrusted to her. The promise made by Almighty God to return the child to her was thus fulfilled.

Moral: Consider the importance of intelligence. It helped the sister to find her brother and then, at the risk of her own life, to act with such loyalty and obedience to her mother that the enemy had no idea who she was. O women, obedience to your parents, joined to sense and discrimination, is a great blessing.

The Wife of Hazrat Musa, *on Whom Be Peace*

The wife of Hazrat Musa[a] was Safura. She was the elder daughter of Hazrat Shu'aib, *on whom be peace.*

Hazrat Musa[a] accidentally killed an infidel in a city in Egypt. When Pharaoh heard of this, he ordered his chiefs to find him and kill him. Musa[a], therefore, when he learned of this, secretly left for the city of Madyan. As he approached the boundary of the city, he saw many herdsmen drawing water from the well for watering goats. There were two girls nearby, keeping their goats apart from the water. One of these girls would later be his wife, the other his sister-in-law. He approached them and asked what they were doing. They replied, "There is no man in our house able to work, and we must work ourselves. Because we are women, we wait for the men to leave. After all of them are gone, we water our goats."

He took pity on their state, drew water himself, and gave it to their goats. They told this story to their venerable father, who sent his elder daughter to fetch this excellent person. She went modestly and gave the message to Musaᵃ. He accompanied her and met Hazrat Shu'aibᵃ.

Shu'aibᵃ provided him with every comfort and declared: "I should like to give you one of my daughters in marriage, but on the condition that you graze my goats for eight or ten years." Musaᵃ accepted this offer and was married to the elder daughter.

When returning with her to his homeland, they needed fire because of the cold. They saw fire visible on Mount Tur. When they reached the mountain, they saw the light of God. And there Musaᵃ attained prophethood.

Moral: Look with what industry these women did the work of their house. How modest they were when they had to speak to strange men! O women, do not be lazy or seek your own ease in housework. Remember as well the need to be shy and modest at all times.

The Sister-in-Law of Hazrat Musa, *on Whom Be Peace*

The sister-in-law of Hazrat Musaᵃ has just been mentioned above. Her name was Safira. In company with her sister, she did the work of the household with great industry and served and obeyed her father.

Moral: O women, you should also serve your mother and father and do the work of the household diligently and industriously. Do not look down on the work done by the poor. Consider this: Is your rank (*rutba*) greater than that of the daughters of an apostle?[12]

Hazrat Asiya, *on Whom Be Peace*

Hazrat Asiyaᵃ was the wife of Pharaoh, the king of Egypt who claimed divinity. *God's power!* The husband was Satan; the wife, a saint who is praised in the Qur'an. Our Apostleˢ declared her greatness, saying: "Among men, many were perfect; but none among women reached the rank of perfection except Hazrat Maryamᵃ and Hazrat Asiyaᵃ." Asiyaᵃ saved the life of the child Musaᵃ from the tyrant Pharaoh, as described in the account above. It was written in this woman's fate to believe in Hazrat Musa[a], whom she loved with her heart from his earliest childhood. When Hazrat Musa[a] attained prophethood, Pharaoh had no faith—but she did. When Pharaoh learned of her belief, he was very harsh and caused her all kinds of difficulties. But she did not abandon her faith. She died in a state of belief.[13]

Moral: Look how strong her faith was. Her husband, who was corrupt in religion, was a king and tried everything; yet she did not support him. Nowadays, at the least trouble, women begin to speak words of infidelity. O women! Faith is a great treasure. Whatever trouble may happen to you, do nothing against the faith. If your husband acts against the faith, never support him. In that day, marriages with unbelieving men were permitted, but in our *shari'at* there is now the injunction that marriage with an unbelieving husband is improper. If the husband later becomes an unbeliever, the marriage is abrogated.

An Attendant of a Daughter of Pharaoh

In the book called *Rauzatu's-safa,* it is written that a daughter of Pharaoh had a maidservant who acted as her agent and hairdresser.[14] She believed in Hazrat Musa[a], but, for fear of Pharaoh, she did not reveal her belief. Once, she was combing the princess's hair when the comb slipped from her hand and she said, "*Bi'smi'llah!*" while picking it up. The princess asked, "What did you say? Whose name is that?" The attendant answered, "It is the name of him who created your father and gave him his kingdom."

The princess was very surprised that someone was greater than her father, and she ran to Pharaoh to recount the whole story. Pharaoh, in great anger, summoned the attendant and tried to frighten her. She replied clearly that he could do whatever he liked, but she would not abandon her faith. First, he stuck nails into her hands and feet and threw hot coals and embers on her. When this had no effect, he took the son from her lap and threw him in the fire. The child cried out from the fire: "Stand firm, O Mother! Do not abandon your faith!"

She stood firm in her faith. Then Pharaoh seized the hapless woman and threw her into the burning oven too. In Sura Buruj, section 'Am, which is the story of the diggers of the trench, there is the story of a similar woman and her child.

Moral: Look how strong her faith was. O women! Faith is a great blessing. Never ruin your faith to indulge your lower soul or to escape some difficulty or sorrow. Never do any deed against God and his Messenger, *God's blessings and peace upon him.*

An Old Woman in the Encampment of Hazrat Musa, *on Whom Be Peace*

When Pharaoh began to oppress the people of Isra'il in Egypt, he extracted all kinds of forced labor from them. He beat them and caused them manifold sorrows. Almighty God ordered Hazrat Musa[a] to lead his people out from Egypt in the depth of night to save their lives from Pharaoh's oppression. When they arrived at the River Nile, they lost their way, and no one recognized the road. Musa[a] was dumbfounded at this and called out, "Let anyone who can explain what is happening come forward and tell us."

At that point, an old woman came forward and declared, "When Hazrat Yusuf[a] was approaching death, he declared as a final injunction to his brothers and nephews that if they should ever leave Egypt they should take along the coffin containing his corpse. If they failed to do so, they would lose their way."

Hazrat Musa[a] inquired where the coffin was buried. Again, it turned out that only this old woman knew. She declared: "I will not tell you where it is until you grant me one thing."

He asked what she wished. She said she wished to die in faith and to find a place in heaven at the same level as Musa[a] himself. Musa[a] beseeched Almighty God to grant her wish, for such a matter was not in his power. He was instructed to grant it, and he assured her that God would indeed fulfill her wish. She then told him that the coffin was buried in the middle of the river. They had to pull out the coffin in order to find the road. Once this was done, they found the road immediately.

Moral: Look what a worthy person this old lady was. She asked for no worldly wealth but only sought to set her afterlife aright. O women, you must not long for worldly things, for you will get whatever is in your portion (*qismat*). You must seek to improve your religious life.

The Sister of Haisur

It is told in the Noble Qur'an, in the story of Hazrat Musa[a] and Hazrat Khizr[a], that Hazrat Khizr[a], on the order of Almighty God, killed a young boy.[15] Hazrat Musa[a] was distressed and asked what evil this boy had done to deserve death. Hazrat Khizr[a] answered: "If this boy had grown to manhood, he would have been an infidel. Moreover, his parents were faithful, and, out of love for him, they too might have strayed. It was expedient to kill him for this reason. Almighty God will bestow a daughter in his place. She will be free from evil and will bring well-being to her parents."

In other books, it is written that such a daughter was in fact born and was later married to a prophet. Among her offspring were seventy prophets. The name of the boy was Haisur, and the girl was his sister.

Moral: If Almighty God says someone is free of all evil and a source of well-being for her parents, she must indeed be very good. Look at how wonderful it is to live free of sin and to give joy to one's parents. Such a person gains such high rank that she is praised by Almighty God himself. O women, always exert yourselves to live this way.

The Mother of Haisur

The parents of Haisur, that child mentioned above, were declared to be faithful in the Glorious Qur'an. Whomever Almighty God declares to be faithful would not be halfway but fully and wholly faithful. From this, it is clear that the mother of Haisur was a very worthy person.

Moral: Firmness in faith is such a great treasure that it is praised by Almighty God. O women! Be strong in your faith. It is strong when you carefully fulfill the requirements of the *shari'at* and avoid all evil acts.

The Mother of Hazrat Sulaiman, *on Whom Be Peace*

It is in the Noble Qur'an that Sulaiman[a] said in a prayer, "O God, you have rewarded my parents." This makes it clear that his mother was worthy, because the great reward is faith and religion.[16]

Moral: Just consider how important faith is. The names of the faithful come readily to the tongues of prophets. O women, give luster to your faith!

Hazrat Bilqis

Hazrat Bilqis was the monarch of the country of Saba.[17] A hoopoe informed Hazrat Sulaiman[a] that he had seen a queen who worshiped the sun. Hazrat Sulaiman[a] then wrote a letter for the hoopoe to deliver to the queen. In the letter, he told her to become a Muslim and to come to him. Bilqis read the letter and sought counsel from her nobles and ministers. After much discussion, she herself decided to send him some rare gifts. If he took them, she would judge him to be a worldly monarch; if not, a prophet. When the gifts arrived, Hazrat Sulaiman[a] sent them all back along with a message: "If you do not become a Muslim, I will bring my army for battle."

When Bilqis heard this message, she was certain that Sulaiman[a] was a prophet, and she set out from her city in order to become a Muslim. Hazrat Sulaiman[a] miraculously summoned her enormous and valuable royal throne to his court so that Bilqis might witness a miracle. He extracted the pearls and jewels from the throne and had them put back in a different pattern. When Bilqis arrived, she was asked, at his order, if this was her throne. This was meant to test her sense. She looked at the throne attentively and said, "It is like mine." She thus implied that its appearance had slightly changed. From this answer, it was clear that she was a woman of great intelligence.

Sulaiman[a] wanted to show Bilqis that the royalty given by his God was greater than her worldly royalty. He ordered a pool to be filled with water and a floor of clear glass to be built over it in such a way that it was invisible. Sulaiman[a] sat so that the pool would be in the path of anyone who wanted to reach him. He ordered Bilqis to attend him. When she arrived, she did not see the glass. She assumed that she would have to cross the water and began to pull up her trousers. She was then told about the glass and instructed to walk on it.

When Bilqis saw the miracle of the summoning and reworking of the throne, she understood that Sulaiman[a] had more royal power than she did. She therefore recited the profession of faith and became a Muslim. Some scholars say that Hazrat Sulaiman[a] married her himself, and some say that he had her married to the king of Yemen. God alone knows what happened.

Moral: Look at her lack of self-will (*be-nafs*). In spite of her wealth and status, she accepted religious truth when she saw it. She put on no airs when it came to accepting the truth. She did not cling to the customs of her forebears. O women, you must be like her. If you are informed on some point of true religion, do not resist it out of modesty or the customs of the family. None of these are of use. Religion alone will stand by you.

A Slave Girl of the People of Isra'il*

There is a story in the *hadis* that a woman of the people of Isra'il was nursing her baby when a horseman passed before her in great splendor and pomp. The mother prayed: "O God, make my son just like him!" The baby let go of his mother's breast and said: "O God, do not make me just like him!"

He began to nurse again. Some people then passed in front of them

* From Bukhari Sharif.

who had seized a slave girl and were taking her away in dishonor and distress. The mother prayed: "O God, do not let my child be like her."

The child spoke again: "O God, let me be like her." The mother was dumbfounded.

The child said: "The horseman was a tyrant. The people accused the slave girl of being a thief and immoral, but the poor girl was in fact innocent."

Moral: The point is that the horseman's worth existed only in popular opinion, not in God's opinion. The slave girl was worthless in popular opinion, but worthy in the opinion of God. To be worthy in the sight of God is what is necessary, no matter what people may think. If you are unworthy before God, of what use is popular esteem? Reflect on this slave girl's miracle, that a nursing baby began to speak in order to show her purity. O women! Many women are in the habit of dismissing the poor as contemptible. They accuse them, moreover, of thievery and evil on the least suspicion. This is very bad. Perhaps in the sight of God they are better than you.

An Intelligent and Religious Woman of the People of Isra'il

Muhammad bin Ka'b recounted that there was an elder among the people of Isra'il, very learned and very pious, who loved his wife very dearly. By chance she died, and he was so burdened with sorrow that he closed himself behind his door and gave up meeting with anyone. Among the people of Isra'il there was a woman who heard this story and came to him. She said to those coming in and out of the house that she had to consult him about a problem and could ask about it only in person. She sat there, glued to the door. Finally, he learned of her and gave her permission to enter.

She entered and said, "I have a problem to ask about."

He said, "Speak."

She said, "I asked for some jewelry from my neighbor, and I wore it for some time. Then she sent someone to ask for its return. Must I return the jewelry?"

The scholar said, "Of course you must return it."

The woman said, "But I have kept it a very long time. How can I return it?"

The scholar said, "You must return it with even more pleasure, because she did not ask for it for a long time. That was a kindness on her part."

The woman said, "May God show you kindness. Why are you sad?

Almighty God loaned you something; then, when he wanted to, he took it back. It was his."

When the scholar heard this, it was as if his eyes had opened. He profited greatly from her words.

Moral: Just look at what a woman she was, who gave reasoned advice to a man, and to such a learned man at that. O women, you too must understand the logic of her argument in times of trouble and explain it to others as well.

The Mother of Hazrat Maryam, *on Whom Be Peace*

The name of the mother of Hazrat Maryam[a] was Hanna, and Hanna's husband, who was the father of Maryam[a], was named 'Imran.[18]

When Hanna was expecting a child, she made a vow to our Lord and Master that she would offer the child in her womb for service to the mosque—in other words, the child would be exempt from worldly work. She expected a son to be born, because only a boy could do service for the mosque. At that time, such a vow was legitimate. When the child was born, it was a girl.

In sorrow, Hanna prayed to God, asking that the girl would somehow be even better than a boy.

God accepted this prayer. Hanna named the girl Maryam[a]. She prayed that the child and her offspring might be saved from Satan. Indeed, our Hazrat[s] declared that Satan touches all children at the time of birth, but he could not touch Hazrat Maryam[a] and her son, Hazrat 'Isa[a].

Moral: Look what blessed power came from Hanna's purity of will. God granted her a pure child and accepted her prayer. It is clear that Almighty God greatly favored her. O women! Such blessed power comes from purity of will. You must seek such purity of will. Whatever good work you do, do for God's sake alone. You too will be valued in the court of our Lord and Master.

Hazrat Maryam, *on Whom Be Peace*

The story of the birth of Hazrat Maryam[a] has just been recounted.

When she was born, her mother, in accordance with her vow, took her to the mosque of the Baitu'l-muqaddas and said to the elders who lived there, "Take this child born of my vow."[19]

Everyone wanted to take the child and rear her, because she was of a venerable family. Hazrat Zakariya[a], the maternal uncle of Hazrat

Maryam[a], had the greatest right.[20] Other people made claims, but he prevailed in the final decision, to which, in the end, all agreed. He took Maryam[a] and began to care for her.

She grew far more quickly than other children, and in a short time she seemed grown-up. From her very childhood, she was innately a saint (*buzurg, wali*), as born to her mother. Almighty God declared her a saint in the Qur'an and described her miraculous power.

Fruits came to her out of season from the unknown. Hazrat Zakariya[a] asked, "Where have these come from?"

She answered, "From our Lord and Master."

All her deeds were wondrous to the point that when she was mature, she became pregnant by the power of Almighty God, without a man. She bore the prophet 'Isa[a]. The Jews, seeing the birth of a fatherless child, began to abuse her. Almighty God, however, gave Hazrat 'Isa[a] the power of speech from the very time of his birth. He said such excellent things that all just people knew that his birth was a manifestation of the power of God. They realized, without any doubt, that he had been born without a father and that his mother was wholly pure.

Our Prophet[s] said of her greatness that among women only two were perfect: one was Hazrat Maryam[a], and the other was Hazrat Asiya[a]. (This point was discussed in the account of Hazrat Asiya[a] above.)

Moral: Consider how her mother dedicated her to God. How worthy she was! She set herself to that obedience to God that makes a person into a saint. Through her blessed power, God saved her from great blame. O women! Obey God and you will be saved from all calamity. Keep your offspring steadfast in religion. Do not let them be slaves of the world.

The Wife of Hazrat Zakariya, *on Whom Be Peace*

The wife of Hazrat Zakariya[a] was named Isha'.[21] She was the sister of Hazrat Hanna and the maternal aunt of Hazrat Maryam[a]. About her, Almighty God said, "We have set aright the wife of Zakariya." Many scholars have understood the meaning of this to be that her habits were amended. Hazrat Yahya[a], the prophet, was born in her old age.

Hazrat 'Isa[a] was the grandson of the maternal aunt of Hazrat Yahya[a]. The grandson holds the same place as a son. Our Prophet[s] therefore referred to each of them as the son of the other's aunt.

Moral: Good habits are so excellent a thing that Almighty God himself praised them. O women, improve your habits in every way. We have set forth a method for this in Book Seven.

*   *   *

These twenty-five stories have dealt with the good women of the earlier communities (*ummat*). Now listen to some stories of the good women of this community.

III. Stories of Women Who Lived at the Time of the Prophet[s]

THE WIVES AND DAUGHTERS OF THE PROPHET[S]

Hazrat Khadija, *May God Be Pleased with Her**

Hazrat Khadija, *may God be pleased with her,* was the first wife of the Messenger of God, *God's blessings and peace upon him.* She was esteemed for many fine qualities. Once, the Apostle[s] declared to her that Hazrat Jibra'il[a] had brought her a greeting from Almighty God. He also declared that among the women of the whole world, four were the very best: first, Hazrat Maryam[a]; second, Hazrat Asiya[a], the wife of Pharaoh; third, Hazrat Khadija[rz]; and fourth, Hazrat Fatima[rz]. The Apostle[s] always told her his worries that arose from the behavior of the infidels. She always said something so comforting that his worries disappeared. He held her in such regard that, even after her death, he always sent some meat to her various friends whenever he slaughtered a sheep or other animal.

She had been married previously. The name of her first husband was Abu Hala Tamimi.[22]

Moral: In the opinion of Almighty God and the Messenger[s], her greatness was derived from her faith and obedience. O women, you must seek these qualities. It is evident how excellent it is to fathom the heart of a worried husband and comfort him. Nowadays, many women do the opposite and drive a good heart to worry, sometimes with demands, sometimes with talking back. Give up such habits!

---

* This entire section on the wives and daughters taken from *Isti'ab* [presumably, Abu 'Umar Yusuf b. 'Abdallah al-Qurtubi (d. 436/1071), *Kitab al-isti'ab fi ma'rifat al-ashab* (The book of comprehension of the knowledge of the Companions)] and from other works. [See Carl Brockelmann, *Geschichte der Arabischen Litteratur* (Weimar: Verlag von Emil Felber, 1898), vol. 1, p. 658.]

Hazrat Sauda, *May God Be Pleased with Her*

Hazrat Sauda[rz] was also a wife of our Prophet, *God's blessings and peace upon him.* She gave her turn with him to Hazrat 'A'isha[rz]. Hazrat 'A'isha[rz] said, "I never saw any woman I wanted to be like, except Hazrat Sauda[rz]. I saw her and longed to be just like her."

The name of her first husband was Sakran ibn 'Amr.

Moral: Look at the good resolve of Hazrat Sauda[rz] in giving her turn to her co-wife. Nowadays, wives fight and envy one another for no reason. Look at the fairness of Hazrat 'A'isha[rz], who praised her co-wife. Nowadays, wives knowingly impute blame to one another unjustly! O women! You must adopt resolve and fairness like hers.

Hazrat 'A'isha Sadiqa, *May God Be Pleased with Her*

Hazrat 'A'isha[rz] was the much beloved wife of our Hazrat[s]. She was married to him from her maidenhood. She was such a fine scholar that the great Companions would consult her on points of the *shari'at.*

Once, a Companion asked our Hazrat[s], "Whom do you love most?"

He declared, "'A'isha[rz]."

Then the Companion asked, "And whom among men?"

Hazrat[s] declared, "Her father, that is, Hazrat Abu Bakr[rz]."

She had many excellent qualities.

Moral: Just consider that there was once a woman whom great scholars consulted on problems of religion; now there are today's women, who do not even wish to *consult* scholars or read books! O women, seek knowledge of religion diligently.

Hazrat Hafsa, *May God Be Pleased with Her*

Hazrat Hafsa[rz] was also a wife of our Apostle[s] and the daughter of Hazrat 'Umar[rz]. Hazrat[s] divorced her for some reason, but, at the word of Jibra'il[a], he returned to her. Hazrat Jibra'il[a] declared: "Return to Hafsa[rz], because she often fasts in the day and arises at night to worship. In heaven she will be your wife."

She made a will for her brother, 'Abdu'llah ibn 'Umar[rz], to distribute an amount of wealth as charity. She also bequeathed some land as a pious endowment and made a bequest for its management.

The name of her first husband was Khunais b. Huzafa.

Moral: You have seen the blessed power of piety that produced intervention from the seat of our Lord and Master. At the hand of an angel, the Prophet[s] was commanded to respect Hafsa[rz] by revoking his divorce. And note her generosity, how she made arrangements for charity in the way of God and gave land as an endowment as well. O women, be pious and expel all love of wealth and all greed from your hearts.

The Daughter of Khuzaima, Hazrat Zainab, *May God Be Pleased with Her*

Hazrat Zainab[rz] was also a wife of our Apostle[s] and was so generous that she was known by the name of Mother of the Poor.

The name of her first husband was 'Abdu'llah ibn Jahsh.

Moral: Look what greatness there is in service to the poor.

Hazrat Umm Salama, *May God Be Pleased with Her*

Hazrat Umm Salama[rz] was also a wife of our Apostle[s]. Another wife recounted a story that happened once when she was with Hazrat Umm Salama[rz]: "A great many poor people once approached us, including both men and women. They settled down around us and began pestering us. I said, 'Go away! Make yourselves scarce.'

"But Hazrat Umm Salama[rz] said, 'We have no commandment to act like this. Come, girl, let us give each of these people something, even if only a dried date.' "

The name of her first husband was Abu Salama[rh.]

Moral: Consider that she did not become annoyed with the persistence of those in need. Nowadays, women not only drive away the poor in a moment but also start to curse and call them names. O women, never do this!

The Daughter of Jahsh, Hazrat Zainab, *May God Be Pleased with Her*

Hazrat Zainab[rz] was also a wife of our Apostle[s].

Hazrat Zaid[rz] was a Companion whom our Hazrat[s] made his son. (In those days, it was correct according to the *shari'at* to adopt a son as he did.) When Hazrat Zaid[rz] became a young man, Hazrat[s] was concerned with arranging his marriage. He asked the brother of Zainab[rz] about her availability. Neither the brother nor the sister considered Hazrat Zaid[rz] an equal in terms of descent, however. At first they hesitated, but Almighty God sent a verse that there should not be any objection by a Muslim to any suggestion of the Apostle[s]. So both agreed, and the marriage took place.

But the husband and wife did not get along, and it came to the point that Hazrat Zaid[rz] decided to divorce her. He came to Hazrat[s] for consultation. Hazrat[s] counseled him to refrain but finally concluded that there was no alternative to divorce.

He then reflected on the fact that at first the heart of neither brother nor sister had been reconciled to the marriage but that they had relented only because of what he had said. If there were a divorce, the situations of both brother and sister would be even worse than now. Their hearts would be broken. What strategy might be devised to comfort them? At last, after long thought, he realized that the tears of Zainab[rz] would be dried if he were to marry her himself. Other than that, he could think of nothing. There remained the problem of people's opinion. Those without faith would certainly taunt him, saying that he had taken his son's wife to his own house, even though, in the *shari'at,* a son in name only is not a real son. But who can make the populace hold their tongues, especially those without faith for whom the least matter is more than enough for taunts?

While Hazrat[s] was mulling this over, Hazrat Zaid[rz] carried out the divorce. After the legal waiting period had passed, Hazrat[s] decided that it was necessary to send a message offering marriage. He sent the message.

Zainab[rz] said, "I declare to my Provider that I do nothing on the basis of my own reason. He will arrange whatever is acceptable to him." Zainab[rz] then performed the ablution, approached her prayer rug, and was absorbed in prayer. After the prayer, she made supplication to Almighty God.

Then God revealed a verse to his Apostle[s] that he had married him to Zainab[rz]. Hazrat[s] went to Zainab[rz] and recited the verse. Zainab[rz] took pride in the fact that the marriage of the other wives had been performed by their parents, but hers had been performed by God.[23] The very first time that seclusion (*parda*) was ordered was at their wedding.

This woman was very generous and very skilled at handicrafts. She always gave charity from the income of her handicrafts. It is recounted that once all the women gathered and asked our Hazrat[s] which wife would go first from the earth to join him after he was gone. He declared it would be the one whose hands were longest. In Arabic, they say "a long-handed person" to mean someone who is generous; but the women did not understand this. They thought it meant length by measure, and all set to measuring their hands with a stick. The longest hand was that of Hazrat Sauda[rz]. The first to die, however, was Hazrat Zainab[rz]. Only then did the women understand what the expression had meant. Her generosity was valued by God and the Messenger[s].

Hazrat 'A'isha[rz] said, "I have never seen a better woman than Hazrat Zainab[rz]. She was perfect in religion and always feared God. She was very true in speech. She was very kind to her relatives. She gave charity generously, and she was very hardworking in her handicrafts, which were done for the sake of charity."

Our Apostle[s] said about her, "She was one who bore great humility in her heart. She was one who humbly beseeched God."

Moral: O women, you have heard a description of the excellence of generosity, the value of handicrafts, and the need of turning to God in every work. You must never consider working with your hands to be degrading. Never think of any skill or profession as a disgrace.

Hazrat Umm Habiba, *May God Be Pleased with Her*

Hazrat Umm Habiba[rz] was also a wife of our Hazrat[s].

Many Muslims went off to the country of Abyssinia before the migration to Medina, in order to escape the torments of the Meccan unbelievers. The king of Abyssinia, whom they called the negus, was of the Nazarene religion. He became a Muslim after the arrival of the Muslims. Among those who went to Abyssinia was Hazrat Umm Habiba[rz], who was widowed there. The negus sent a messenger named Abraha to her, to convey an offer of marriage to the Messenger[s]. She agreed to the offer and as a reward gave Abraha two silver bracelets and some rings.

The name of her first husband was 'Ubaidu'llah ibn Jahsh.

Moral: What a pious woman she was to leave home and become homeless to protect her religion! What satisfaction and what status God gave her in return for her effort! She married Hazrat[s], and a king arranged it. O women, when your faith is at stake, never set your sights on worldly comforts, your reputation, your heart, or your home. All things are to be sacrificed for your faith.

Hazrat Juwairiyya, *May God Be Pleased with Her*

Hazrat Juwairiyya[rz] was also a wife of our Hazrat[s].

She came as a prisoner from the city of the unbelievers, in a battle known as the Battle of the Bani Mustaliq. She was apportioned to a Companion, either Sabit ibn Qais or some cousin of his through his paternal uncle. She asked her master to free her from slavery in return for a certain amount of money. He agreed, and she came to Hazrat[s] to ask his assistance in getting the money. He took pity on her piety and poverty and declared, "If you ask me to, I will pay the entire amount you need—and I will marry you."

She accepted his offer with her heart and soul, and the marriage took place. When people learned of the marriage, they emancipated the many prisoners of her family and tribe who were in the hands of various Muslims. They were now in the relationship of in-laws to Hazrat[s], and making them slaves would be against propriety.

Hazrat 'A'isha[rz] said, "We did not know many women like her who brought such great profit to a people."

The name of her first husband was Musafi' ibn Safwan.

Moral: Piety is a wondrous blessing, for, through it, she became the wife of Hazrat[s], though she had been a slave. O women, no one is more worthy of respect (*'izzat*) than Hazrat[s], yet he did not consider it a fault to take a slave as his wife. If someone, for some reason, marries into a low family (*ghatiya jagah*) or brings someone into the family from outside, do not consider the wife contemptible.[24] To do so is a sickness and a sin. Look at the courtesy (*adab*) of the Companions[rz], who respected this wife so much that they would not tolerate the abasement of her kinfolk. Nowadays, there is such ignorance that women do not show even the wife herself respect, no matter how religious she may be. There is precious little hope that they will respect her kin.

Hazrat Maimuna, *May God Be Pleased with Her*

Hazrat Maimuna[rz] was also a wife of our Apostle[s].

A great scholar who knows *hadis* has said that her marriage to Hazrat[s] came about this way. She declared that she was dedicating her life to him. This implies that she agreed to come into the marriage without a marriage portion and that he accepted.[25] This kind of marriage was especially fitting for our Apostle[s]. A great scholar who knows the commentaries on the Qur'an says that the verse permitting such a marriage was first revealed for this wife.

The name of her first husband was Huwaitib.

Moral: Look at how these women loved religion! They understood service to Hazrat[s] to be an act of worship, and they cared nothing for the marriage portion. At that time, moreover, the portion was always given in cash, unlike our own time, when it is merely a credit until death or the Day of Judgment.

O women! Consider religion alone to be real wealth! Do not love the world so much that you waste your time and energy over it. If you are preoccupied with worldly things night and day, you will rejoice over acquisitions whether they are praiseworthy or sinful. If you fail to get something, you will sink under sorrow. You complain; you envy the prosperous; your good intentions begin to waver.

Hazrat Safiyya, *May God Be Pleased with Her*

Hazrat Safiyya[rz] was also a wife of our Messenger[s].

The Muslims battled with the Jews in a settlement called Khaibar. This woman was imprisoned in the battle and was apportioned to one of the Companions[rz]. Hazrat Apostle[s] bought her, set her free, and married her. She was among the descendents of Hazrat Harun[a], the apostle. She was a very forbearing and rational woman, filled with fine qualities.

Her forbearance is known from a story recounting how one of her slave girls slandered her falsely on two matters before Hazrat 'Umar[rz]. First, this girl said that Safiyya[rz] continued to love Saturday, the day greatly respected by the Jews. The point of this was to imply that although she had become a Muslim, she was still influenced by Judaism—that is, she was not a complete Muslim. Second, the slave girl charged that she continued to have extensive dealings with Jews. Hazrat 'Umar[rz] asked Hazrat Safiyya[rz] to explain.

She answered, "The first point is completely false. Since I have become a Muslim, for whom Almighty God has given the day of Friday, I have no inclination at all in my heart toward Saturday. As for the second point—it is true. The reason for it is that those people are my relatives, and to treat one's relatives well is not against the *shari'at.*"

Then she asked this slave, "Who told you to slander me falsely?"

The girl replied, "Satan."

She answered, "Go, I have freed you from slavery."

The name of her first husband was Kinana ibn Abu'l-Haqiq.

Moral: O women, this is called forbearance. You must likewise forgive the transgressions and shortcomings of all your servants. It is low-minded to take revenge for every matter. See, too, how truthful she was, for she clearly declared what was fact. She did not invent excuses, as is the habit of many nowadays who never accept any blame at all. They go to all lengths to save themselves from blame. It is wrong to invent excuses.

Hazrat Zainab, *May God Be Pleased with Her*

Hazrat Zainab[rz] was a daughter of our Hazrat Apostle[s], who loved her very much.

She married Hazrat Abu'l-'As ibnu'r-Rabi', who refused to become a Muslim when she did. She therefore left him and emigrated to Medina. A few days later, her husband became a Muslim and came to Medina. Hazrat^s then married her to him again. And her husband also loved her very much.

Another story recounts that as she was going to Medina, she met two unbelievers on the road, one of whom pushed her so hard that she fell on a rock. She was pregnant, and she miscarried because of the fall. She was ill until the moment she died, finally passing away as a result of the fall.

Moral: See her courage and piety. For the sake of her religion, she abandoned her homeland and her husband, and she suffered at the hands of unbelievers, to the point of death. Still she remained firm in her religion. O women, you must abandon all else before religion. If trouble befalls you, you must endure it. If your husband is irreligious, do not support him.

Hazrat Ruqaiya, *May God Be Pleased with Her*

Hazrat Ruqaiya^rz was also a daughter of our Hazrat Apostle^s.

Her first marriage was with 'Utba, the son of the unbeliever Abu Lahab, whose evil is recounted in the Qur'anic Sura Tabbat [111]. Neither father nor son became a Muslim. When 'Utba left Ruqaiya^rz at his father's order, Hazrat^s married her to Hazrat 'Usman^rz. When our Hazrat^s departed for the Battle of Badr, he left Hazrat 'Usman^rz in Medina to watch over her because she was sick. He told him that he would receive a reward equal to that of those who had undertaken holy war. Hazrat 'Usman^rz was given a share of the spoils along with those who fought.

Hazrat Ruqaiya^rz passed away on the very day that the war was won and the Muslims returned to Medina.

Moral: Consider her stature, in that the reward set for serving her was the same as the reward for undertaking holy war. Her greatness was a result of her piety.

O women, always be steadfast in your religion. Avoid all sin, for that weakens religion.

Hazrat Umm Kulsum, *May God Be Pleased with Her*

Hazrat Umm Kulsum^rz was also a daughter of our Apostle^s.

She first married 'Utaiba, the second son of that unbeliever Abu Lahab. She had not even departed to her husband's home when apostlehood came to our Hazrat$. Neither the father, Abu Lahab, nor the son became a Muslim. The son, at the word of his father, abandoned his wife. She married Hazrat 'Usman^{rz} after her sister Hazrat Ruqaiya^{rz} passed away.

At the same time that Hazrat Ruqaiya^{rz} passed away, Hazrat Hafsa^{rz} also became a widow. The father of Hafsa^{rz}, Hazrat 'Umar^{rz}, wanted her to marry Hazrat 'Usman^{rz}. Hazrat 'Usman^{rz} himself had no opinion.

The Apostle^s heard all this and declared: "I will announce a better husband for Hafsa^{rz} than 'Usman^{rz} and a better wife for 'Usman^{rz} than Hafsa^{rz}." He married Hazrat Hafsa^{rz} himself and married Hazrat Umm Kulsum^{rz} to Hazrat 'Usman^{rz}.

Moral: The Apostle^s called her good; and if an apostle calls someone good, it is because of her faith. O women, perfect your religion and faith.

Hazrat Fatima Zahra, *May God Be Pleased with Her*

Hazrat Fatima Zahra^{rz} is the youngest sister in age and the greatest in rank.

She was the most beloved daughter of our Apostle^s. Hazrat^s declared her a very piece of his life and the chief of all the women of the world. He said, "Whatever causes sorrow to Fatima causes sorrow to me also."

He hid the sickness from which he died from everyone, except her alone. He gave her the news of his approaching death. When she began to cry, he whispered, "Do not sorrow. For one thing, you will be first to come to me; and second, in heaven you will be the chief of all women."

When she heard this, she laughed. No matter how much the wives of Hazrat^s asked why, she told his secret only after his death. She married Hazrat 'Ali^{rz}. The *hadis* recount much more concerning her greatness.

First Moral: All the love and attachment of Hazrat^s came about because she was so religious, patient, and grateful. O women, cultivate religion, patience, and gratitude so that you will also become beloved of God and the Messenger, *God's blessings and peace upon him.*

Second Moral: Remember that at the very beginning of this section, where there is an account of the Apostle^s, there is a list of all the names of his wives and daughters.

Third Moral: O women, you must consider one more matter. You have read the stories of the eleven wives and four daughters of Hazrat^s. These describe how all the wives except Hazrat 'A'isha^{rz} had been married previously and how two daughters (other than Hazrat Zainab^{rz} and Hazrat Fatima^{rz}) also remarried (both to Hazrat 'Usman^{rz}). These twelve women are greater than all other women in the world in honor and rank. Is a second marriage a transgression, meaning that these wives—repent, repent!—committed some transgression? It is most unfortunate that people of little understanding judge remarriage to be a transgression. Where is your faith when an act performed by a member of the household of Hazrat[s] is judged to be a disgrace? What kind of Muslim considers the acts of Hazrat[s] a transgression and the acts of unbelievers deserving of respect? The seclusion of widowed women is peculiar to the unbelievers of Hindustan.

Furthermore, there is also a great difference between widows of earlier times and widows today. Those unfortunate ones may have been ignorant, but they guarded their honor (*abru*), they suppressed their lower souls, and they avoided any improper act (*unch nich*). Nowadays, widows adorn themselves more than married women. Things happen that should not be repeated. Nowadays, widows should not be kept secluded at home, for they lack the shame and modesty of an earlier time and men lack the earlier sense of honor (*ghairat*). Women do not think to simply pass their widowhood quietly; nor are others concerned about providing food and clothes. You should not even inadvertently just keep them at home! May Almighty God grant understanding and grace.

[THE WOMEN COMPANIONS OF THE PROPHET[s]]

This book began with an account of the women of the earliest communities. That was followed by an account of the eleven wives and four daughters of Hazrat[s]—fifteen women in all. Below is a description of other women who lived at the time of Hazrat[s], including many who had a special connection with him.

Hazrat Halima Sa'diyya, *May God Be Pleased with Her**

Hazrat Halima Sa'diyya[rz] nursed our Apostle[s]. When he later waged war on the city of Ta'if, this woman came with her husband and son to be in attendance. He praised her greatly and spread out his shawl for her to sit upon. All her family became Muslims.

Moral: Despite her deep connection with Hazrat[s], she knew that

---

* From *'Aja'ibu'l-qisas* (The most wondrous of stories). [These are stories of the prophets by 'Abd al Wahid ibn Muhammad Mugani, translated from Persian to Urdu by Muhammad Fakhr al-Din Husain (Delhi, 1849), cited in J. F. Blumhardt, *Catalogue of Hindustani Printed Books in the Library of the British Museum* (London: British Museum, 1889), p. 15.]

without faith and practice she would have no reward on the basis of her connection alone. Therefore she came to him and accepted the faith. O women, do not rest content with being one of the offspring of a holy man or with being the mother or grandmother of a scholar or a *hafiz;* do not assume that they will effect your pardon. Remember that unless you yourself have faith, these people cannot speak on your behalf to our Lord and Master. If you lack faith, such connections will be of no use to you whatsoever.

Hazrat Umm Aiman, *May God Be Pleased with Her**

Hazrat Umm Aiman[rz] looked after our Apostle[s] in his childhood. He would occasionally visit her. Once when Hazrat[s] honored her with his presence, she gave him something to drink. Hazrat[s] did not want it. God knows whether he simply did not want it or whether he was fasting, but he demurred. Because she took pride in her nurturing, she grew stubborn, got up, and said without any shyness at all, "No, you must drink it."

Hazrat[s] always used to say, "After my real mother, Umm Aiman[rz] is my mother."

After the death of Hazrat[s], Hazrat Abu Bakr[rz] and Hazrat 'Umar[rz] went to visit her from time to time. Whenever she saw them, she would remember Hazrat[s] and begin to weep, whereupon these two gentlemen would begin to weep, too.

Moral: See how worthy she was, that Hazrat[s] himself and such great Companions[rz] would visit her. Her worth was a result of her service to the Messenger of God[s] and a result of her perfection in religion. O women! Nowadays, service to Hazrat[s] is to influence other women properly, to instruct them in religion, to give your offspring instruction in what is good, and to remain strong in religion yourself. *If Almighty God wills,* you too will have the reward that is due to those of great worth.

Do not, by the way, think that "visiting" means that she would have been unveiled before all those visitors. "To visit" can mean to go to someone in order to sit with the person and converse on good matters, even with a curtain in between.

---

* From Muslim [Muslim b. al-Hajjaj (d. 261/875), compiler of one of the *sahih* (sound) *hadis* collections] and Nawawi [Abu Zakariyya Yahya b. Sharaf al-Nawawi (d. 676/1278), author of a famous commentary on Muslim] and from other books.

Hazrat Umm Sulaim, *May God Be Pleased with Her**

Hazrat Umm Sulaim[rz] was a Companion of the Messenger of God[s] and the wife of a Companion, Abu Talha[rz]. She was also the mother of a Companion, Hazrat Anas[rz], who was a special servant of Hazrat[s]. She was a distant maternal aunt of our Hazrat[s]. Her brother was a Companion who was in battle with Hazrat[s] and was martyred. For all these reasons, our Hazrat[s] regarded her very highly. From time to time, he would honor her with his presence at her house. Our Hazrat[s] also saw her in heaven.

There is a wondrous story about her, that she had a child who became sick and died. It was night. Now, look at her steadfastness:

She thought, "If I tell my husband, he will be agitated the whole night; he will not eat a bite of food."

So she sat, silent. Her husband came in and asked, "How is the child?"

She answered, "He is comfortable."

In saying this, she did not lie. For a Muslim, what comfort is greater than to go to one's real home? Her husband did not understand. She brought food before him and set it down, and he ate. Then he wished to lie with her, and this slave of God did not object to this either. When all was finished, she asked her husband, "If someone gave someone else a loan and then asked for it back, would there be any right to refuse?"

He said, "No."

Then she said, "Be patient about the baby."

He was very angry and said, "Why didn't you tell me right away?"

He told this whole story to Hazrat[s], who prayed on his behalf. Through the power of God, Umm Sulaim[rz] became pregnant that very night, and a child was born who was given the name ʿAbdu'llah. ʿAbdu'llah became a scholar, and there were many scholars among his offspring.

Moral: O women, learn steadfastness from her. Learn a lesson from her concerning bringing comfort to your husband. What a true and good point she made in the example of a borrowed thing. If a person understands that, she will not waver. Look at the blessed power gained by her patience: how quickly our Lord and Master gave a substitute for this child, and how blessed the substitute, in whose lineage were learned men.

---

* From the books of *hadis* and their commentaries.

Hazrat Umm Haram, *May God Be Pleased with Her**

Umm Haram^rz was also a Companion, the sister of Hazrat Umm Sulaim^rz, whose story has just been told. She was also a distant maternal aunt of our Hazrat^s, and he often honored her with his presence at her house. Once, he ate at her house; then, feeling drowsy, he slept. He awoke laughing. She asked the reason.

He declared, "I saw the people of my community on their way to a holy war, riding in a ship. From their belongings, they appeared to be kings and nobles."

She besought him, "O Messenger of God, pray that Almighty God may place me among them."

He prayed. Then he slept and awoke again, laughing in the same way, and recounted the same kind of dream. In this dream, there appeared more people like the earlier ones.

She besought him again, "O Messenger of God, pray that Almighty God may place me among them."

He answered, "May you be among the first."

When her husband, whose name was 'Ibada, started off for holy war by crossing a river, she went along. After crossing the river, she started to mount an animal who then balked, and she fell, entrusting her soul to God.

Moral: The prayer of Hazrat^s was granted, because a person is on a voyage of holy war from the time she leaves until she returns home. She gets the reward of martyrdom, no matter how she dies. Look how pious she was, that in her desire for reward she did not even love her life. She asked for a prayer to receive the reward for holy war. O women, cling to the conviction that suffering is no cause for worry in any holy work. You too, in the end, will have your reward.

Hazrat Umm 'Abd, *May God Be Pleased with Her*

Hazrat Umm 'Abd^rz was the mother of a very great Companion, Hazrat 'Abdu'llah ibn Mas'ud^rz. She herself also was a Companion. She had so much say in the affairs of the house of our Hazrat^s that onlookers thought she was one of the household.

Moral: This degree of preference in the house of the Apostle^s was accorded her only because of her religion. O women, if you reform your faith, you too will be granted nearness to Hazrat^s on the Day of Judgment.

* From Muslim and its commentaries.

The Mother of Hazrat Abu Zarr Ghifari, *May God Be Pleased with Him*

The mother of Hazrat Abu Zarr Ghifari[rz] was a Companion. At the time when the news of the apostleship of Hazrat[s] became known and the unbelievers denied it, Abu Zarr[rz] came to Mecca from his homeland to ascertain the matter. He no sooner arrived than he became a Muslim. When he returned home, his mother heard the whole story and said, "I have no objection to your religion. I too am a Muslim."

Moral: To accept the truth as soon as you know it, without taking into account the ways of your forebears, shows purity of nature. O women, whenever you come to know the truth of some point in the *shari'at,* do not oppose it in the name of your family customs. Happily accept the teachings of religion and act on them.

The Mother of Hazrat Abu Huraira, *May God Be Pleased with Him*

Abu Huraira[rz] was a Companion who reasoned with his mother to accept the faith. Once, his mother said something about religion and faith that was such a blow to him that he went weeping to Hazrat[s] and begged him to pray for his mother so that God might guide her. Hazrat[s] prayed to God to guide the mother. Then Abu Huraira[rz] returned home happy. He saw the door of the house closed and heard the noise of falling water as if someone were bathing. His mother heard the footsteps of his approach and called out for him to wait there.

After she had bathed, she opened the panel of the door and said, *"I testify that there is no divinity other than God, and I testify that Muhammad is the Messenger of God."*

Because of his happiness, such a state came over him that he began to weep uncontrollably. In this state, he went and recounted the whole story to Hazrat[s], who thanked Almighty God. Abu Huraira[rz] said, "O Messenger of God, pray to our Lord and Master that we, mother and son, may love Muslims and that Muslims may love both of us."

He so prayed.

Moral: Look at the benefits good children bring you. O women, teach your children knowledge of religion, for your faith will be set right through them.

Hazrat Asma bint 'Umais, *May God Be Pleased with Her*

Hazrat Asma bint 'Umais[rz] was a Companion. When the Muslims in Mecca were tormented by the unbelievers, many went to the country of Abyssinia. She was among them. When Hazrat Apostle[s] shifted to Medina, all the Muslims went there. Again, she was among them. Hazrat[s] gave her the good news that because she had undertaken two migrations for the sake of the faith, she would have great reward.

Moral: Look how she left her home to become homeless for the sake of religion and then reaped reward. O women, do not chafe if you must endure some hardship for the sake of religion.

The Mother of Hazrat Huzaifa, *May God Be Pleased with Him*

Hazrat Huzaifa[rz] was a Companion. He recounted that his mother once asked him how many days it had been since he had visited Hazrat[s]. He told her how many days had passed, and she denounced him. He said he would go and recite the post-sunset prayer with Hazrat[s] and would beseech him to pray for forgiveness for himself and for her. He went and recited both the sunset and the night prayers. As he left, he joined Hazrat[s], who, hearing his voice, asked, "Is it Huzaifa?"

He answered that it was.

Hazrat[s] declared, "What do you want? May God forgive you and your mother."

Moral: Look what a good woman she was. She took into account whether her children had visited Hazrat[s]. O women, you must likewise insist that your children sit with venerable people. They should learn about religion from them and derive blessed power from good company.

Hazrat Fatima bint Khattab, *May God Be Pleased with Her*

Hazrat Fatima bint Khattab[rz] was the sister of Hazrat 'Umar[rz] and became a Muslim before her brother did. Her husband, Sa'id ibn Zaid[rz], also became a Muslim. Still Hazrat 'Umar[rz] did not. The sister and her husband kept their Islam hidden, out of fear of Hazrat 'Umar[rz]. Once, Hazrat 'Umar[rz] heard them reading the Qur'an, and he was very harsh with both of them. The brother-in-law—well, he was a man; but it was this woman who took courage and clearly said, "Indeed we are Muslims, and we were reading the Qur'an. If you wish, beat us; if you wish, let us be."

Hazrat 'Umar[rz] said, "Show me the Qur'an." He needed only to look at the Qur'an and hear it, and suddenly the light of faith entered into his heart. He came into the presence of Hazrat[s] and became a Muslim.

Moral: O women, you must also be steadfast in matters of the *shari'at* and religion. You should not act against the *shari'at* for the sake of money, nor should you carry out customs that are against the *shari'at* out of thoughts for your family and people. Never favor any position at all that is against the *shari'at*.

An Ansari Woman*

There is a tradition of Ibn Ishaq that the husband, father, and brother of an Ansari woman were all present with Hazrat[s] at the Battle of Uhud and that all of them were martyred.[26] When the woman heard this news, her first question was, "How is Hazrat[s]?"

People answered, "He is safe and sound."

She said, "If he is safe and sound, then no one need sorrow."

Moral: Praise be to God! What love for Hazrat[s]! If you have resolved to love him, then follow his *shari'at* fully and completely. From this, love will come to you and will bring you the rank of being close to him in paradise.

Hazrat Umm Fazl Lubaba bint Haris, *May God Be Pleased with Her*

Hazrat Umm Fazl Lubaba bint Haris[rz] was the paternal aunt of our Hazrat Apostle[s], the wife of Hazrat 'Abbas[rz], and the mother of 'Abdu'l-lah ibn 'Abbas[rz].

It says in the Qur'an that any Muslims who cannot worship God because they live among infidels must leave that country and settle elsewhere. If they do not do this, it is a great sin. Women and children who do not know how to travel to another place and who are less courageous are excused, however.

Hazrat ibn 'Abbas[rz] declared, "My mother and I were among those of less courage. She was a woman and I was a child."

Moral: See the value of her resolve. In her heart, she did not like to live among infidels, but she was helpless. Therefore our Lord and Master had mercy on her and forgave her sin. O women, you must make a heartfelt resolve to act on your faith. If you do so, your helplessness may be forgiven. But anyone who does not even wish to fulfill the *shari'at* in her heart will not be saved from sin.

Hazrat Umm Salit, *May God Be Pleased with Her*

Once, Hazrat 'Umar[rz] was distributing shawls to the women of Medina. He had one extra and asked the people to whom he should give

---

* From the books of biography (*sira*).

it. They replied, "To the daughter of Hazrat ʿAli, Umm Kulsum, your wife. Give it to her."

He replied, "No, instead it is the right due Umm Salit." This woman was one of the Ansar who had pledged allegiance to Hazratˢ.

Hazrat ʿUmarʳᶻ said, "In the Battle of Uhud, she circulated among the Muslims, carrying a water bag to bring them food and drink. She was like another woman, Khawla, who took up a sword to do battle in the fight."

Moral: See the courage of these women in the work of God, that Hazrat ʿUmarʳᶻ valued them so highly. Nowadays, those of little courage do not even recite the five prayers correctly.

Hazrat Hala bint Khuwailid, *May God Be Pleased with Her*

Hazrat Hala bint Khuwailidʳᶻ was the sister-in-law of our Apostleˢ and the sister of Hazrat Khadijaʳᶻ.

Once, she came into the presence of Hazratˢ and, from outside the door, asked permission to enter. Because her voice was like that of her sister, he thought it was Hazrat Khadijaʳᶻ and was startled and said, "O God, may it be Hala."

Moral: From this prayer it is clear that he loved her. Of course, she was his sister-in-law, but the main reason for his love was her righteousness. O women, be righteous, and both God and the Messengerˢ will love you.

Hazrat Hind bint ʿUtba, *May God Be Pleased with Her*

Hazrat Hind bint ʿUtbaʳᶻ was the mother of Hazrat Muʿawiyaʳᶻ, who was the brother-in-law of our Hazratˢ.

Once, the mother said to our Hazrat Apostleˢ: "Before becoming a Muslim, I wanted no one to be disgraced more than you; now, in contrast, I want no one to be more respected than you."

He said, "I feel the same about you."

Moral: From this exchange it is clear, first, that she was truthful, and, second, that she loved Hazratˢ and that Hazratˢ loved her. O women, always speak the truth, love Hazratˢ, and do deeds that will cause Hazratˢ to love you.

Hazrat Umm Khalid, *May Almighty God Be Pleased with Her*

Hazrat Umm Khalidʳᶻ was among those who undertook to emigrate to Abyssinia. At that time she was a child. When the Muslims returned, they came to Medina. Once, her father came into the presence of Hazrat[s], and she came too, wearing a yellow blouse.

Hazrat[s] had a small flowered shawl, and he draped it on her and said, "That is very fine, that is very fine."

Then he prayed that the shawl might one day be old and worn out. The meaning of this prayer was that he wished she might reach a great age. People recounted that they had never heard of a woman of as great an age as hers.

When she was of a very advanced age, people used to gossip that she had once been just a child who used to play with the signet ring of prophecy belonging to Hazrat[s].[27] Her father had scolded her, but Hazrat[s] said: "Leave her alone; what harm is there?"

Moral: She was very fortunate. O women, the shawl of the Prophet[s] is a symbol of the shawl of religion, just as in the Qur'an moderation is spoken of as clothing. If you want such a reward, adopt religion and moderation.

Hazrat Safiyya, *May Almighty God Be Pleased with Her*

Hazrat Safiyya[rz] was the paternal aunt of our Apostle[s]. When her husband, Hamza[rz], was martyred in the Battle of Uhud, Hazrat[s] declared: "I am thinking of the blow to Safiyya[rz], and that is why I have buried Hamza[rz]. Otherwise, the animals would have eaten him, and on the Day of Judgment he would have been gathered from the stomachs of the animals."

Moral: This tells us that Hazrat[s] thought so highly of her that he took action on her behalf. O women, this happened because of her righteousness. You must also be righteous so that you may be worthy of the approval of the Apostle of God[s].

The Wife of Hazrat Abu'l-Husaim, *May Almighty God Be Pleased with Him*

Hazrat Abu'l-Husaim[rz] was a Companion. Our Hazrat[s] felt such friendship for him that once, when he had no food and grew very hungry, he honored the house of Abu'l-Husaim[rz] with his presence without any ceremony. The husband was not at home; he had gone to fetch fresh water. The wife treated Hazrat[s] with great respect. When the husband came, he rejoiced and arranged a feast.

Moral: If Hazrat[s] had not been satisfied with the purity of this woman, he would have left when he found that her husband was not at home. It is clear that he knew that the husband would be very happy to have him there. For someone to be happy with the Apostleˢ and for the Apostleˢ to consider someone good is no small greatness. O women, Hazratˢ at that time was a guest. Always rejoice at the coming of guests. Do not close your heart.

Hazrat Asma bint Abu Bakr, *May Almighty God Be Pleased with Her*

Hazrat Asma bint Abu Bakrʳᶻ was the sister-in-law of our Apostleˢ and the sister of Hazrat 'A'ishaʳᶻ. When Hazratˢ was about to emigrate to Medina, he needed something to tie up his bag of food. She immediately tore her sash in half and used one piece for her waist and the other to tie up the bag.

Moral: Only a very righteous person has such love that she would ruin such a useful thing for the comfort of Hazratˢ. O women, you must have such love of religion that you gladly give up worldly things to foster it.

Hazrat Umm Ruman, *May Almighty God Be Pleased with Her*

Hazrat Umm Ruman was the mother-in-law of our Hazratˢ and the mother of Hazrat 'A'ishaʳᶻ. A hypocrite made an allegation against 'A'ishaʳᶻ—repent, repent!—convincing many good and straightforward Muslims of the charge. Even Hazratˢ himself became somewhat silent with her. Then Almighty God revealed the purity of Hazrat 'A'ishaʳᶻ in the Glorious Qur'an. Hazratˢ recited these verses about her and propounded them within the house.

At that time, Hazrat Umm Ruman told Hazrat 'A'ishaʳᶻ simply to arise and thank Hazratˢ. Even before this, although she felt this blow about her daughter very deeply, there was not a chance that she would say the least thing that might hint at a complaint about Hazratˢ.

Moral: Among women such restraint and control are surprising things. Especially in a situation like this, most women would let something or other slip out of their mouth. For example, someone might have said, "Alas, they have dragged down my daughter for no reason." Or, even more, when her purity had been proven, at that point there surely would have been anger and sorrow that there had been suspicions about someone so pure. But Umm Ruman, on the contrary, restrained her daughter and sided with Hazratˢ. O women, on the occasion of sorrow and dispute, you should not encourage your daughter or side with her in a fight with her in-laws.

Another woman is mentioned in this story. Her son, through his own simplemindedness, supported the accusers. On one occasion, the woman cursed her own son and sided with Hazrat 'A'isha^{rz}. She was called Umm Mastah. See how her love of the truth is evident in her refusal to support her own son and her decision to side with the truth. She denounced her own son.

Hazrat Umm 'Atiyya, *May Almighty God Be Pleased with Her*

Hazrat Umm 'Atiyya^{rz} was a Companion and accompanied Hazrat^s in six battles. She treated the ill and bound up the wounded. She so loved Hazrat^s that whenever she took his name, she always added, "May my father be sacrificed for him."

Moral: O women, exert yourselves in works of religion and show love like hers for Hazrat Messenger^s.

Hazrat Buraira, *May Almighty God Be Pleased with Her*

Hazrat Buraira^{rz} was a slave until Hazrat 'A'isha^{rz} bought her and set her free. She lived at the house of Hazrat 'A'isha^{rz} and served both her and our Hazrat^s. Once, someone gave her some meat, but our Hazrat^s himself asked for it and ate it.

Moral: What good fortune to serve Hazrat^s! Hazrat^s had full confidence in her love when he ate her food and knew that she would be happy to have him do so. O women, nowadays the service of Hazrat^s is service to the faith. This is love for Hazrat^s.

Fatima bint Abu Hubaish, Hamna bint Abu Jahsh, and Zainab, the Wife of Hazrat 'Abdu'llah ibn Mas'ud, *May Almighty God Be Pleased with Him*

Fatima bint Abu Hubaish, Hamna bint Abu Jahsh, and Zainab are described in the *hadis* as having come from their homes to ask Hazrat^s about certain problems. For this reason we have written the three names together, because their stories are similar. The first woman asked about irregular menstrual flow. The second, the sister-in-law of Hazrat^s and the sister of Hazrat Zainab^{rz}, asked about the same matter. The third woman asked about giving charity. She was the wife of 'Abdu'llah ibn Mas'ud^{rz}, a very great Companion.

Moral: O women, enthusiasm for religion is shown in consulting pious scholars about anything you do not know. If the issue deals with something embarrassing, you should ask the wives of these scholars to inquire for you.

IV. Stories of Women Who Lived After the Time of the Prophet[s]

The preceding description of twenty-five women who were contemporaries of Hazrat, *God's blessings and peace upon him,* has followed the account of his daughters and wives. The stories of many more such women are recorded, but we have included only a selection so that the book would not be too long. A description of some women who lived after the time of Hazrat[s] follows now.

LATER WOMEN WHO LOVED KNOWLEDGE

The Women Teachers of Imam Hafiz ibn ʿAsakir*

This *imam* was a very great scholar of *hadis.* More than eighty of the teachers from whom he acquired knowledge were women.

Moral: Alas, in our day women do not study enough even to be pupils!

Hafid ibn Zahra Tabib's Sister and Her Daughter

Hafid ibn Zahra Tabib was a famous doctor. His sister and his niece had a good knowledge of *hikmat.*[28] There was a king, Khalifa Mansur, who entrusted treatment of his queens to them.

Moral: This knowledge has completely disappeared among women. It merits great reward and benefits others as long as it meets three conditions: it must be practiced with good intent and not with greed or deceit; it must not use any prohibited medicine; and it must not distract you from your religious obligations. Ignorant midwives bring ruin to women. If they had been educated, would this have happened? Those women whose fathers, brothers, or husbands are doctors should resolve to learn from them, for it is a very easy matter for them to acquire this knowledge.

---

* The section from here to the end of the description of the sister of the *qazizada* taken from the pamphlet *ʿUlama-yi salaf* (The scholars of former times).

The Slave Girl of Imam Yazid ibn Harun, *May God Have Mercy upon Him*

Imam Yazid, *may God have mercy upon him*, was a great *imam* of *hadis*. In his final years, his sight became very weak, and he could not see a book. This slave girl helped him by looking at the book herself, memorizing the *hadis,* and then telling them to him.

Moral: Praise be to God! In those days slave girls and bond maids were scholars. Now even ladies are often ignorant! Blot out this stain for the sake of God.

The Slave Girl of Ibn Sammak Kufi

Ibn Sammak Kufi was a scholar of his time. Once, he asked his slave girl her opinions about his teaching.

She said, "Your teaching is fine, but you have the fault of repeating a single matter many times."

He said, "I say one thing many times so that people of little understanding may understand."

She said, "By the time those of little understanding understand, those of understanding are fed up."

Moral: Only a scholar could understand such a profound point in the discourse of another scholar. It is clear that the slave girl was herself a scholar. O women, do not be less able than slave girls. Make a real effort to obtain knowledge. Resolve even to study Arabic if there is some man in the house who is a scholar. It gives a real taste for knowledge. It is easier for you to learn than it is for boys, because you do not have to go out to earn money. Set yourself to it resolutely. As for sewing and similar skills, you can learn them in a few weeks. Why waste your whole life?

The Paternal Aunt of Ibn Jauzi, *May God Have Mercy upon Him*

The elder Ibn Jauzi[rh] was a great scholar. When he was a child, his aunt would take him to hear scholars teach. Because knowledge had fallen on his ears when he was so young—*as God wills!*—he himself began to give sermons like a scholar at the age of ten.

Moral: Look at the excellence of teaching religious knowledge to younger family members. The aunt must have been very old, yet she herself took the child to hear scholars. You can do at least this much:

until your children have studied religious subjects, do not ensnare them in English. Stop them from keeping bad company, and warn them of its dangers. Insist that they go to religious schools.[29] Nowadays, there is no enthusiasm for education; and, if there is, it is for English: "My son will be a *tahsildar* (a subcollector of revenue)," "Mine a deputy." No matter whether on the Day of Judgment he goes to hell and takes his mother and father with him! Remember that knowledge of religion takes precedence over every other thing. If that is lacking, there is nothing.

The Mother of Imam Rab'iyyatu'r-Ra'i

Imam Rab'iyyatu'r-Ra'i was also a great scholar. Imam Malik[rh] [d. 795] and Hasan Basri[rh] [d. 728], who are more famous than the sun, were both his pupils. His father's name was Farukh. At the time of the reign of the Bani Umayya, the father served in the army and was sent on many campaigns at royal order. Imam Rab'iyyatu'r-Ra'i was in his mother's womb at the time that his father set out for travels that would take twenty-seven years. When the father returned, his son had been born and had become a great scholar.

At the time of his departure, the father had given his wife thirty thousand *ashrafi*s. This high-minded woman spent them all on her son's instruction. When the father returned after twenty-seven years, he asked his wife about the *ashrafi*s.

She said, "I have put them away safely."

Meanwhile, Hazrat Rab'iyyat had gone to the mosque and was busy expounding *hadis*. Farukh, who saw this sight with his own eyes, said, "My son is becoming a leader of the world." He could not contain himself for joy.

When he returned to the house, his wife asked, "Tell me, which is better, thirty thousand *ashrafi*s or this blessing?"

He said, "The *ashrafi*s are worthless!"

When she told him that she had spent the *ashrafi*s to secure this blessing of their son's learning, he declared with great joy, "I swear by God you did not waste the *ashrafi*s!"

Moral: You have seen what these women were like and how they valued knowledge of religion. She spent thirty thousand *ashrafi*s to secure knowledge for her son. O women, like her, you should not care about any expense made to secure religious knowledge for your offspring.

The Mother and Sister of Imam Bukhari

There has been no scholar of *hadis* the equal of Imam Bukhari. He was fourteen years old when he undertook a journey in quest of knowledge. His mother and sister were responsible for his expenses.

Moral: It is not surprising that a mother would pay these expenses, but what was the motive of a sister, who does not have this responsibility for a brother? Clearly, at that time women were ready to sacrifice their wealth and goods if someone even mentioned religious knowledge to them. O women, you should be like them.

The Sister of the Qazizada of Rum

The Qazizada of Rum was a very famous learned man.[30] After acquiring learning from the teachers of Rum, he wanted to gain further knowledge from distant scholars. He quietly began to prepare his belongings for a journey. When his sister learned of this, she silently placed a large amount of her jewelry in his baggage and did not even tell him.

Moral: What good women they were! They had no desire for fame. They simply wanted knowledge, somehow or other, to stand firm. O women, giving help in support of knowledge is a source of great reward. Keep in mind how easy it is, for example, to support religious schools.

* * *

This has been an account of the stories of ten women who lived after the time of Hazrat[s], all of whom longed for knowledge. Here follows an account of several women whose hearts inclined toward the inner life (*faqiri*).

LATER WOMEN WHO WERE *DARWESH*

Hazrat Ma'aza 'Adawiyya, *May God Have Mercy upon Her**

The state of Hazrat Ma'aza 'Adawiyya[rh] was so wondrous that when morning came, she would say, "Perhaps this will be the day on which I die."

Then she would not sleep until evening, lest she die oblivious of the memory of God at the time of death. In the same way, when night

---

* The section from here to the end of the account of Hazrat Nafisa taken from the translation of *Tabaqat-i shi'rani*.

came, she would repeat this same sentence and not sleep until morning. If she felt overcome by tiredness, she would walk around the house and say to her lower soul: "The time for sleep comes later."

She meant that she would sleep after death until the Day of Judgment. She recited six hundred supererogatory prayers each day. She never looked up toward the sky. From the time that her husband died, she never lay on her bed. She met Hazrat 'A'isha, *may God be pleased with her,* and heard *hadis* from her.

Moral: O women, this indeed is love and remembrance of God. Only open your eyes!

Hazrat Rabi'a 'Adawiyya, *May God Have Mercy upon Her*

Hazrat Rabi'a 'Adawiyya[rh] wept continually and would swoon at the mention of hell. If someone gave her something, she would return it, saying, "You should not give me anything."

At the age of eighty, she could no longer walk without seeming to fall. She always kept a shroud before her. Her place of prostration at prayer was always wet with tears. Her strange and wondrous sayings are famous, and she is also known as Rabi'a Basriyya.

Moral: O women, you must create in your heart something of this fear of God and the remembrance of death. After all, she too was a woman.

Hazrat Majida Qurashiyya, *May God Have Mercy upon Her*

Hazrat Majida Qurashiyya[rh] used to say, "After every step I take, I think that death comes next."

She would say, "The news of decamping has been given to the inhabitants of the world, yet they are as oblivious as if they had not heard and expect to remain here."

She also said, "No blessing of heaven or God's pleasure is attained without work."

Moral: O women, what useful counsels! Plant them in your heart and reflect on them.

Hazrat 'A'isha bint Ja'far Sadiq, *May God Have Mercy upon Her*

The rank of Hazrat 'A'isha bint Ja'far Sadiq[rh] was one marked by pride (*naz*). She used to say, "If they throw me into hell, I shall say to everyone, 'I believed that God was One, and then they punished me.' " In A.H. 145 she passed away; her tomb is at the gate of Qarafah in Egypt.

Moral: O women, her high rank is not granted to everyone. Those who attain it do so as a result of the blessed power of complete obedience. Adopt this obedience, and remember that to fully believe God is One means that you should neither worship anyone, nor expect anything from anyone, nor fear anyone, nor think of making anyone happy, nor care about anyone's being angry. If someone says, "Good," you are not to be happy; if they say, "Bad," you are not to be sad. If someone torments you, do not give her a glance. Think only, "This was pleasing to God. I am a slave. I must remain content in whatever condition I am." Why did a person, who believed as she did that God is One, talk about hell? She intended this as a way of describing the greatness and blessed power of believing God to be One.

The Wife of Rabah Qaisi, *May God Have Mercy upon Him*

The wife of Rabah Qaisi[rh] would engage in acts of worship the whole night. When one segment of the night had passed, she would ask her husband to arise. If he did not, she would soon awaken him again. Then, near dawn, she would say, "O Rabah, arise, the night is passing and you are asleep."

Sometimes she would pick a blade of grass from the ground and say, "I swear by God I consider the world to be of less worth than this."

After reading the night prayer, she would put on beautiful clothes and ask her husband if he felt any desire for her. If he did not, she would place these clothes aside and be absorbed in supererogatory prayers until morning.

Moral: O women, you have seen how she worshipped Almighty God and yet how she offered her husband his rights. She also drew her husband toward religion. All this is required of you.

Hazrat Fatima Nishapuri, *May God Have Mercy upon Her*

There was an elder, a very accomplished person, Zu'nun Misri, who said he had received grace from Hazrat Fatima Nishapuri[rh].

She used to say, "Those who do not continually meditate on Almighty God fall into every kind of sin and babble anything that comes into their mouths. But whoever meditates continually on Almighty God falls silent at foolishness and feels shame and modesty before him."

Hazrat Abu Yazid[rh] said, "I never saw any woman the equal of Fatima[rh]. She knew the news of any place even before it was given to her."

She passed away in Mecca while undertaking the lesser pilgrimage in A.H. 223.[31]

Moral: Look how she praised meditation—grasp hold of it and be saved from all sins. It is clear that this woman received revelations (*kashf*). This is not an indication of a high rank, but it is certainly desirable if it happens to a good person.

Hazrat Ra'i'a (or Rabi'a) Shamiyya bint Isma'il, *May God Have Mercy upon Her*

Hazrat Ra'i'a[rh] would worship through the whole night and always kept the fast.

She would declare, "When I hear the call to prayer, I remember the angel who calls to the Day of Judgment. When I feel heat, I recall the heat of the Day of Judgment."

Her husband, Ahmad ibn Abi'l Hawari[rh], was also a very great person. He used to say to her that he loved her like a brother, by which he meant that his lower soul felt no desire for her.

She used to say, "When you engage in worship, Almighty God informs you of your faults. When people know their own faults, they do not see the faults of others."

And she used to say, "I see the *jinn* coming and going, and the houris appear before me."

Moral: O women, this is worship. You, who at every moment are occupied with the faults of others, should look at her excellent cure for this. She has told you to look at your own faults so that you will not even see the faults of others. It is evident that she received revelations (whose significance is described in the story of Hazrat Fatima Nishapuri[rh]).

Hazrat Umm Harun, *May God Have Mercy upon Her*

The fear of God greatly dominated Hazrat Umm Harun[rh]. She worshipped a great deal and ate nothing but dry bread. She would say, "At the coming of night, my heart is happy; and when it is day, I am sad."

She would stay awake the whole night. For thirty years she did not oil her hair, yet when she let down her hair it was clean and sleek.

One time, she went out and someone happened to call out to someone else, God knows who, "Seize it!" She thought of the Day of Judgment, lost consciousness, and fell down.

Once, in the jungle, a tiger approached her. She declared, "If I am meant to be your food, then eat me." He turned his back and went off.

Moral: Praise be to God! How steeped in the recollection of God she was, and how greatly she feared God! The matter of the tiger shows her miraculous power (*karamat*). (Such power has the same significance as revelations, as explained above.) O women, you too must foster recollection and fear of God in your heart. After all, the Day of Judgment is coming. Put aside some provisions for it.

Habib 'Ajami's Wife, Hazrat Umara, *May God Have Mercy upon Her*

Hazrat Umara[rh] would worship the whole night. When the night was over, she would say to her husband, "The caravan [of those communing with God] has gone ahead, and you have remained behind sleeping."

Once, her eyes began to hurt, and someone asked her why. She answered, "The pain of my heart is greater still."

Moral: O women, let love of God cause you such pain that all other pain becomes light before it.

Hazrat Amatu'l-Jalil, *May God Have Mercy upon Her*

Hazrat Amatu'l-Jalil[rh] was very obedient and abstemious. Once, there was a conversation among several elders over what a saint was like. Everyone said, "Come, let us go ask Amatu'l-Jalil[rh]."

When they asked her, she declared: "There is no hour when a saint is occupied with anything other than God. Anyone lies who ascribes any other occupation to a saint."

Moral: What a woman of eminence she was! Great men asked her opinion on a saint's qualities, and she provided a good key to recognition. O women, you should also long to be occupied with the recollection of God as the greatest of all your occupations.

Hazrat 'Ubaida bint Kilab, *May God Have Mercy upon Her*

Malik ibn Dinar was a very accomplished elder. Hazrat 'Ubaida bint Kilab[rh] came and went in his presence. Many elders said that her rank was greater than that of Rabi'a Basriyya.

She heard someone say that a person is wholly pious who feels that going to God is dearer than all else. As she heard this, she swooned and fell.

Moral: What desire she felt for going to God, that she swooned at the very mention of it! Nowadays, people do not like even the mention of death. The reason is simply love of the world. Remove worldly desire from your heart, and you will want to go to God.

Hazrat ʿAfira ʿAbida, *May God Have Mercy upon Her*

One day, a great many pious people came to Hazrat ʿAfira ʿAbida[rh] and said, "Pray for us."

She declared: "I am so sinful that if the punishment of sin was to be mute, I would indeed be mute. But to pray is right, and therefore I will pray." Then she prayed for everyone.

Moral: See how, despite her great piety and obedience, she thought herself sinful and lowly. Nowadays, a person who recites a few rosaries considers herself an elder. Almighty God dislikes pride. In every case, consider yourself inferior to everyone else, for this is in fact true. There are hundreds of faults in every act. If you look at these faults and not only at your acts of obedience, you will have no thought of pride.

Hazrat Shaʿwana, *May God Have Mercy upon Her*

Hazrat Shaʿwana[rh] wept a great deal. She said, "I want to cry so much that no tears remain; then I will weep so much blood that no blood will remain."

Her maidservant said, "Since being with her, I have received such grace that I have never desired the world and I have thought no Muslim to be contemptible."

Hazrat Fazil ibn ʿAyyaz[rh], a very famous elder, used to go to her to ask her to pray for him.

Moral: To weep out of love or fear of God is a very great treasure. If weeping does not come naturally, then act as if you are crying.[32] Our Lord and Master will have pity on your humility. Look at what grace derives from being with the great, as her maidservant described. You too should seek out good company and avoid bad people.

Hazrat Amina Ramliyya, *May God Have Mercy upon Her*

There was an elder, Bishr ibn Haris[rh], who would come to visit Hazrat Amina Ramliyya[rh]. Once, he fell sick and she went to inquire about him. Ahmad ibn Hanbal[rh], who was a very great *imam,* had also gone to inquire after him. He learned that this woman was Amina who came from Ramla. Imam Ahmad[rh] said to Bishr[rh], "Have her say a prayer for us."

Bishr[rh] spoke to her about the prayer, and she prayed, "O God, Bishr[rh] and Ahmad[rh] want refuge from hell; grant that refuge to both of them."

Imam Ahmad[rh] says that that night a paper descended from above. On it, after *bi'smi'llah,* was written: "We have agreed, and there are more blessings yet where we are."

*Moral: **Praise be to God*** at how her prayer was accepted. O women, the blessed power of obedience is all. Almighty God grants fully the request of whoever does the command of God fully. Only try to accept his commands.

Hazrat Manfusa bint Zaid Abu'l-Fawaris, *May God Have Mercy upon Her*

When the child of Hazrat Manfusa[rh] died, she held his head in her lap and said, "Your going before me is better than if you had remained after me. You will go ahead and obtain my pardon. You are a child and will be forgiven, whereas if you had remained alive after my death, you would have committed hundreds of sins. God knows if you would have been deserving of pardon or not."

And she used to say, "It is better to be patient than to be anxious."

And she said, "Although there is the sorrow of separation, the joy of reward is greater."

Moral: O women, if upon a death you console yourself with her words, *God willing,* that will be sufficient.

Hazrat Saiyida Nafisa[rz], bint Hasan ibn Zaid ibn Hasan ibn 'Ali, *May Almighty God Have Mercy upon Them*

Hazrat Saiyida Nafisa[rz] was of the family of our Hazrat[s], because she was the granddaughter of Zaid[rz], who was the grandson of Hazrat 'Ali[rz]. She was born in Mecca in A.H. 145. She was preeminent in worship.

Imam Shafi'i[rh], a very great *imam,* used to come to see her when he came to Egypt.

Moral: O women, knowledge and greatness are such that even a great *imam* came to her. You too must attain knowledge of religion and act on it, so that you may attain greatness.

Hazrat Maimuna Sauda, *May God Have Mercy upon Her*

There was an elder, 'Abdu'l-Wahid[rh] ibn Zaid, who said, "I prayed to God to grant me the sight of the person who would be my companion in paradise.

"God declared: 'Your companion in paradise is Maimuna Sauda.'

"I asked, 'Where is she?'

"The answer came: 'She is in Kufa in such and such a tribe.'

"I went there and asked for her. People said she was a crazy woman who tended goats. When I reached the wasteland, I saw her standing to recite the canonical prayer. Wolves and goats were wandering about, mixed together, in one place.

"When she concluded her prayer, she declared: 'O 'Abdu'l-Wahid, you must go; our promised meeting is to be in heaven.'

"I was stunned. 'How did you know my name?'

"She said, 'You do not know that those souls which have already become acquainted in heaven are familiar with each other.'

"I said, 'I see wolves and goats in one place. Why is this?'

"She said, 'Go away and do your own work! I have set my affairs aright with the Almighty. Almighty God has set aright the affairs of my goats with the wolves.' "

Moral: Both the revelations and the miracles of this woman are clear from this account. All is blessed power gained from rendering complete obedience. O women, prepare yourselves for obedience to God!

Hazrat Raihana Majnuna, *May God Have Mercy upon Her*

Abu'r Rabi' was a great elder who said, "Muhammad ibn Munkadir and Sabit Banani (these two were also elders) and I were at one time all guests at the house of Raihana[rh].

"Before midnight, she arose and said, 'The lover goes toward her beloved, and the state of her heart is such that it goes out from her with joy.'

"When midnight was over, she said, 'No one should be absorbed in things that separate one from the remembrance of God. Everyone should spend the night in worship and in that way become a friend of God.'

"When the night had passed, she cried, 'Alas, I am lost!'

"I said, 'What happened?'

"She answered, 'The night, when the self is sunk in God, has passed.' "

Moral: Look at what value the night had for her! Whoever wants to savor worship will value the night. O women, you should fix a small part of the night for worship. She described what an evil it is to absorb yourself in anything other than God. You should not be absorbed in anything else—not wealth, goods, clothes, jewelry, offspring, property, or house and household goods.

The Disciple of Hazrat Sari Saqati, *May God Have Mercy upon Him*

A disciple of Hazrat Sari Saqati[rh] [d. ca. 867] recounted this story: "Our *pir* had a woman disciple whose son studied at the religious elementary school. One day, the teacher sent him on some errand. He fell into the water and drowned. The teacher learned the news and went to Hazrat Sari[rh] to inform him. He arose and went to the house of his disciple to counsel her to be patient.

"She said, 'Sir, why are you counseling patience?'

"He answered, 'Because your son has drowned.'

"She was stunned and asked, 'My son?'

"He said, 'Yes, your son.'

"She said, 'My son never drowned.'

"Saying that, she arose and went to the spot where he had fallen in the water and called him by name: 'O Zar!'

"He answered, 'What, Mama?' and emerged alive from the water and came forward.

"Hazrat Sari[rh] asked Hazrat Junaid[rh] [d. 910] what was happening.

"He declared, 'This woman has such a special place (*maqam*) and rank that she is told in advance of any trouble that is going to happen to her.[33] Because there had been no prior warning of the drowning, she knew that it had never happened.' "

Moral: Each saint has a different rank. No one should think that her rank is greater than that of a saint who does not have prior knowledge of what will happen. Almighty God has the power to grant a person what he will. Hers was indeed a great miracle. All this blessed power derives from obeying God and the Messenger[s]. You must strive to do the same. Then, *God willing,* he may grant you an equal rank or an even higher one.

Hazrat Tuhfa, *May God Have Mercy upon Her*

This story is written in the account of Hazrat Sari Saqati[rh], who said: "I once went to a hospital where I saw a young girl who was bound in chains, weeping and reciting verses of love.

"I inquired about her with the superintendent, who said, 'She is crazy.'

"Hearing that, the girl wept the more and said, 'I am not crazy; I am in love.'

"I asked, 'Whom do you love?'

"She said, 'I love him who gave us blessings and who is with us at every moment—Almighty God.'

"Meanwhile, her owner came and asked the superintendent where Tuhfa^rh was.

"He said, 'She is inside, and Hazrat Sari^rh is with her.'

"He paid his respects to me, but I said, 'This girl is more worthy of respect than I am. Why have you put her in here?'

"He said, 'I sank all my wealth into buying her. I bought her for twenty thousand rupees and expected to sell her for a good profit. But she won't eat or drink and just cries day and night.'

"I said, 'Sell her to me.'

"He said, 'You are a *faqir*. Where will you get the money?'

"I went home and pleaded with Almighty God. A person rapped at the door. I went and saw a person standing there, carrying many bags of thousands of rupees.

"I said, 'Who are you?'

"He said, 'I am Ahmad ibnu'l-Musanna. I was commanded in a dream to bring money to you.'

"I rejoiced and went to the hospital in the morning. Meanwhile, the owner arrived weeping.

"I said, 'Do not sorrow, I have brought the money. If you only ask me, I will give you as much as double your profit.'

"He said, 'If I got the whole world, I would not sell her. I am freeing her for the sake of God.'

"I asked what had happened.

"He said, 'I saw a dream in which anger was directed at me. As you are my witness, I have given up all my wealth in the path of God.'

"Then what did I see but Ahmad ibnu'l-Musanna, also weeping.

"I asked what had happened to him.

"He said, 'I too have given all my wealth as charity in the path of God.'

"I said: *'Praise be to God!* What blessed power on the part of Bibi Tuhfa^rh, who brought guidance to so many people!'

"Tuhfa^rh then arose and went off weeping. We all went with her a short distance. God knows where she went. Then we all went to Mecca. Ahmad ibnu'l-Musanna passed away on the road. The owner and I reached Mecca. We were performing the circumambulation when we heard a piteous voice. Approaching, we asked who it was.

"The person answered, *'Praise be to God!* You have forgotten; I am Tuhfa.'

"I said, 'Tell us what you received.'

"She replied, 'God tied my heart (*ji*) to himself and turned it away from others.'

"I said, 'Ahmad ibnu'l-Musanna has passed away.'

"She replied, 'He has attained many high ranks.'

"I said, 'Your owner has also come.'

"She said something that I could not hear. When I looked closely, she was already dead. When the owner saw this, he lost control of himself and fell down. When I shook him, he too was dead. I gave each a shroud and buried them."

*Moral: **Praise be to God!*** How much she loved God! O women, desire to have such love yourselves. Our *pir* Imdadu'llah Sahib, the emigrant to Mecca, has written this story with more detail in his book *Tuhfatu'l-'ushshaq* (A gift to lovers).[34]

Hazrat Juwaira, *May God Have Mercy upon Her*

Hazrat Juwaira[rh] was the slave girl of a king who freed her. An elder, Abu 'Abdu'llah Turabi, saw her acts of piety and married her. She was always engaged in worship. One time, she dreamed of some very large, very fine tents and asked whose they were. It seemed they were for those who read the Qur'an during the night devotions. After that, she gave up sleeping at night and would awaken her husband and say, "The caravan has passed on."

Moral: O women, you yourselves must worship and instruct your husbands to do so also.

Hazrat Shah ibn Shuja' Kirmani's Daughter, *May God Have Mercy upon Her*

Hazrat Shah ibn Shuja' gave up his kingship and became a *faqir.*

He had one daughter. A king sent a message offering marriage to her, but she did not accept it. Instead, she married a poor but good boy whom she saw performing the canonical prayer conscientiously. When she arrived at her husband's home, she saw a piece of dry bread covering a water jar and asked what it was.

The boy said, "I saved it from last night for breaking the fast."

Hearing that, she turned right around and started to leave.

The boy said, "I knew before that the daughter of a king could not be content with my poverty."

She spoke: "The daughter of the king is not angry because of your poverty. She is angry that you do not have confidence in God. I am surprised at my father, because he told me you were abstemious. If a person does not have confidence in God, how can he be abstemious?"

The boy began to make excuses.

She said, "I do not know excuses. Either I leave this house or the bread does."

The boy immediately gave away the bread as charity, and then she agreed to stay in the house.

Moral: O women, she too was a woman. Learn steadfastness from her and yearn less for wealth and goods.

The Little Girl of Hazrat Hatim Asamm, *May God Have Mercy upon Him*

Hazrat Hatim Asamm[rh] [d. 851] was a great elder. A rich man who was traveling by felt thirsty and stopped at his house to ask for water. After drinking the water, he threw down some change and left. All there lived with no resources other than trust (*tawakkul*) in whatever God sent, so all were happy. There was, however, a small girl in the house who began to cry. The people of the house asked why.

She said, "An ordinary person saw our state, and we felt free from want. Almighty God sees us at every moment, and yet, alas, we do not keep our heart free from want [through trust in him]."

Moral: What understanding that child had! Alas, even venerable women do not have that degree of intelligence now. They do not fix their sights on God but on creation, hoping there will be a profit from so and so and help from such and such. Set your heart aright for God.

Hazrat Sittu'l-Muluk, *May God Have Mercy upon Her*

Hazrat Sittu'l-Muluk[rh] was a dweller in the Arab country. All the saints and scholars of her time paid her respect. Once, she came to visit the Baitu'l-muqaddas at Jerusalem.

At that time, there was an elder there, ʿAli ibn ʿAlbas Yamani, who recounted that he had once been in that mosque and seen a thread of light stretched from heaven to the dome of the mosque. He went and saw that beneath this dome there was a woman performing the canonical prayer and the thread was joined to her.

Moral: This is the light of abstemiousness. It is created in the hearts of all those who are abstemious. At times, Almighty God shows it visibly, but the real place of this light is in the heart. O women, cultivate abstemiousness. Be attached to good works. Avoid those things that are forbidden.

The Slave Girl of Abu 'Amir, the Preacher

Abu 'Amir said, "I saw a slave girl being sold at a very bad price. Her color had become yellow, her stomach and back were one, her hair was matted from dirt. I felt pity for her and bought her.

"I said, 'Go to the market and buy goods for Ramazan.'

"She said, 'Thanks be to God. For me, the twelve months are equal. I fast in the day and worship in the night.'

"Then when 'Id came, I intended to buy goods for it.

"She said, 'You are so entangled in the world.'

"Then she prayed. She recited a verse in which there was mention of hell. She screamed, fell down, and died."

Moral: Look, for this is truly fear of God. Such a state is beyond your control, but it is necessary to stop yourself from sin, whatever kind of sin it may be, whether of the hands and feet, of the heart, or of the tongue.

*   *   *

Moral: In this section we have described a full one hundred stories of good women: twenty-five women of the early communities; fifteen wives and daughters of Hazrat⁵; twenty-five other women from the time of Hazrat⁵; ten learned women of the period after him; and twenty-five *darwesh*. Altogether there are one hundred. There are many more stories available in books, but for those who accept good counsel, this has been sufficient and finishes here.

V. A Selection from the Qur'an and *Hadis*

IN PRAISE OF GOOD WOMEN, THEIR CHARACTER AND HIGH RANK,
AS FOUND IN THE QUR'AN AND *HADIS*

You have now read one hundred stories written about good women. Because the real purpose in telling these stories has been to set forth the good qualities of these women, it now seems appropriate to translate a summary of a few of those Qur'anic verses and *hadis* in which God and the Messenger⁵ have praised women and particularly described their characteristics and rank. When women hear that God and the Messenger^s have spoken about them in particular, their hearts will swell and they will long to have these good qualities themselves. Then the difficult will indeed be made easy.

A Selection of Qur'anic Verses

Almighty God declared: "Those women who do the work of Islam are those who adhere to the prayer and the fast and are attentive to what merits punishment and what merits reward. They keep their faith sound, not fixing their heart on any matter that is against the *hadis* or the Qur'an. They are obedient, putting on no airs. They give charity and alms. They keep the fast. They guard their honor, not appearing before other people, or calling out to them, or wearing clothes forbidden by the *shari'at,* or laughing and talking with anyone unnecessarily. They abstain as well from all other kinds of shamelessness. They remember God continuously, meditating on him both with their heart and with constant repetition of his name. For such women, Almighty God has prepared his gifts and his great reward."

Almighty God declared: "Certain qualities characterize good women, namely, that they are obedient and protect their honor, even if their husbands are not at home."

Almighty God declared: "Those women are good who adhere to the works of the *shari'at,* hold correct beliefs, and are obedient. Whenever they do any deed against the *shari'at,* they immediately repent. They set themselves to the worship of Almighty God, and they keep the fast."

A Selection of *Hadis*

1. The Messenger of God^s declared: "May the mercy of Almighty God descend on that woman who arises at night to read the supererogatory prayer and who awakens her husband so that he may read the prayer, too."

2. The Messenger of God^s declared: "Whoever dies in a state of virginity, during pregnancy, at the time of childbirth, or in the period of forty days thereafter will have the rank of martyrdom."

3. The Messenger of God^s declared: "Any woman who has lost three children and accepts that as her lot, with patience, will enter paradise."

A woman spoke up: "O Messenger of God⁵, and if two of her children have died?"

He said, "There is the same reward for two."

According to another tradition, a Companion also asked about the death of one child and was told that there would be great reward for that, too.

4. The Messenger of God⁵, in fact, declared: "A child who dies in the womb will pull the mother into paradise if she understands this loss as her lot and bears it with patience."

5. The Messenger of God⁵ declared: "The greatest treasure is a good woman in whom a husband rejoices. When he asks her to do some task, she carries out his order. When he is not at home, she keeps guard over her honor."

6. The Messenger of God⁵ declared: "Among Arab women, the Quraish are best in two matters: first, they are very solicitous of their children; and second, they guard the wealth of their husbands."

Moral: This *hadis* makes it clear that women should cultivate these qualities. Nowadays, women squander their husbands' wealth mercilessly. And as for children, there may be solicitude for their food and drink, but there should be much more solicitude for improving their habits—otherwise, it is but solicitude half-done.

7. The Messenger of God⁵ declared: "Marry virgin girls because they converse gently with their husbands out of modesty. They are not disrespectful or abusive. They are happy, even if you give them modest sums."

Moral: This *hadis* makes clear the value of modesty, respect, and contentment. It does not mean that you should not marry widows; it is simply in praise of virgins. In many *hadis,* our Hazrat⁵ has said a prayer for a Companion who was marrying a widowed woman.

8. The Messenger of God⁵ declared: "When a woman continually reads the five prayers, keeps the fast of Ramazan, guards her honor, and obeys her husband, she will surely enter paradise through whichever door she chooses."

Moral: The point is that if she fulfills the basic religious duties, she has no need of undertaking acts that require great effort. The rank a man attains by extraordinary acts is attained by a woman through obeying her husband, looking after her children, and managing the house.

9. The Messenger of God⁵ declared: "Any woman who dies whose husband is happy with her will surely go to paradise."

10. The Messenger of God⁵ declared: "Any person whose lot is

these four things has the wealth of both this world and the next: first, a heart that renders thanks for blessings; second, a tongue that takes the name of God; third, a body that is patient in calamity and distress; fourth, a wife who does not play false with either her honor or her husband's wealth."

Moral: She should neither lose her honor nor, without approval, spend her husband's wealth.

11. The Messenger of Gods declared: "A woman who becomes a widow and who, although wealthy and wellborn, wears herself out taking care of her children until they grow up and move away or die will be as close to me in paradise as is the index finger to the middle finger."

Moral: The point of this *hadis* is not that there is greater recompense for a widow who stays home quietly. Rather, it emphasizes the high rank given a widow who feels that her children would be desolate if she remarried and who herself feels no desire for adornment or gratification of the lower soul.

12. A man submitted this issue to the Messenger of Gods: "O Messenger of God, a certain woman performs supererogatory prayers and fasts and distributes charity, but she also gives her neighbors endless trouble with her tongue."

He declared: "She will go to hell."

Then the questioner continued: "A certain woman does not perform many extra prayers or fasts, nor does she distribute much charity—she may just give out some pieces of cheese—but she does not give trouble to her neighbors with her tongue."

He replied, "She will go to paradise."

13. A woman was in the presence of the Messengers, and with her were two children, one in her lap and one held by the finger.

Seeing her, he proclaimed, "These women first keep babies in their womb, then they give birth to them, then they shower them with love and kindness. If their behavior with their husbands is not evil, then any who adhere to the prayer will indeed go to paradise."

THE COUNSEL OF THE QUR'AN AND *HADIS* ON THE FAULTS OF WOMEN

It seems appropriate to follow the section on the good qualities of women with a summary of the faults that blemish their goodness. God and the Messengers have singled out women in particular in relation to these faults. We include this section to encourage women to taste the hatred of these faults, avoid them, and make their own virtue full and firm.

A Selection of Qur'anic Verses

1. Almighty God declared: "First give counsel to those women whom you know from various signs to be disobedient. If they still do not obey, give up sitting and sleeping with them. If they still do not obey, beat them. If after that they are obedient, do not seek pretexts to give them further trouble."

Moral: This shows that disobeying the word of one's husband is a very bad thing.

2. Almighty God declared: "Do not place your foot on the ground heavily as you walk so that strange men hear the sound of your jewelry and so forth."

Moral: It is not at all correct to wear jingling jewelry. One piece may not jingle by itself, but it strikes against another. This verse warns against that. Consider how much close oversight there should be of the sound of the woman's voice or the sight of her body if there is this much concern simply about the sound of her feet.

A Selection of *Hadis*

1. The Messenger of God^s declared: "O women, I have seen many of you in hell."

The women asked the reason for this.

He declared: "You always disparage everything. You are often ungrateful to your husbands and turn up your noses at what they give you."

2. A lady spoke ill of fever before the Messenger of God^s. He declared: "Do not speak ill of a fever, for it brings forgiveness of sins."[35]

3. The Messenger of God^s declared: "If a weeping woman will not repent, then on the Day of Judgment she will stand with oil spread on her body like a shirt. Fire will quickly spread over it, and there will be mange over her whole body, just like a shirt. She will, in short, have two miseries: she will claw her whole body because of the mange and will also burn with the fire of hell."

4. The Messenger of God^s declared: "O Muslim women, no woman should ever think of anything sent to her by a neighbor as insignificant or contemptible, even if it is only the hoof of a goat."

Moral: Many women have the habit of turning up their noses at anything that comes from someone else's house, and they never fail to deride it.

5. The Messenger of God^s declared: "A woman earned punishment because of a cat. She caught it, tied it up, and neither fed it nor let it go. It strained and struggled until it died."

Moral: Keeping an animal without concern for its food and water deserves punishment.

6. The Messenger of God^s declared: "Many men and women worship God for sixty years and then, at the time of death, they make a will against the *shari'at* and thus merit hell."

Moral: For example, it is common to die saying: "Look, give my things to my daughters—do not give to my brother"; or "Give more of such and such a thing to this daughter and not to the other." All this is prohibited. Ask a scholar about wills and inheritance, and act in accordance with his word, never against him.

7. The Messenger of God^s declared: "No woman should meet with another woman and then describe her to her own husband so that it is as if he were seeing her."

8. Once, the two daughters of the Messenger of God^s were sitting with him. A blind Companion came, and he ordered them to veil themselves.

Both were surprised and said, "But he is blind."

He answered: "You are not blind; you see him."

9. The Messenger of God^s declared: "When a woman causes troubles to her husband in this world, the houri who will meet him in paradise says, 'May God devastate you! He is your guest and will soon leave you to come to us.' "

10. The Messenger of God^s declared: "I have not seen women like this who deserve hell, but after my time there will be born women who will be wearing clothing and yet be naked. There will be clothes in name on their bodies, but the cloth will be so thin that the whole body will show. They will strut and make a display of their bodies. They will put ribbons or cloth in their hair and do it up with coils so that it appears to be as thick as the hump of a camel. Such women will not go to paradise, nor will they even get a whiff of its perfume."

Moral: When pious women go to paradise, those other women will not be allowed to go with them. Perhaps after enduring punishment, with the blessed power of faith, they may ultimately go.

11. The Messenger of God^s declared: "Any woman who wears gold jewelry for show will be punished for doing so."

12. The Messenger of God^s set out on a journey. He heard a voice as if someone were cursing someone. He asked who it was.

People replied that it was a certain woman cursing her she-camel, perhaps because it was not walking properly or was being disobedient. "She was probably calling out, 'May God curse you!' as women often do."

The Messenger of God[s] gave the people an order: "Take this woman and her belongings down from the camel. In her opinion, the camel is worth nothing but curses, so why does she put it to work?"

Moral: He punished well.

*   *   *

In the two sections above—namely, that of praise and that of advice—there are five verses from the Qur'an and twenty-five *hadis*. Moreover, at the beginning of this book, many of the blessed habits of our Apostle[s] were described. These are necessary models for every single act you undertake. Preceding this, seven books gave detailed examples of every good virtue and counsel. Meditate on all this and act on it. *If Almighty God wills,* on the Day of Judgment you will find very high rank. Otherwise, may God preserve you in his care! The condition of wretched women will be wretched. If, at some time, you are able to understand the Qur'an yourself, you will become acquainted with stories of women of faulty religion, faulty breeding, faulty belief, and faulty behavior.

May God make our life and yours be spent in good deeds; make our ending in good deeds; and in good deeds summon the final gathering. *Amin.*

5

Book Ten of the *Bihishti Zewar*

Translator's Introduction to Book Ten

The final book of Thanawi's work presents what any reader might well regard as a hodgepodge. In part, one feels, the author is using a last opportunity to fit in whatever he has not had a chance to cover before. Book Ten starts with the by-now familiar lists of good advice, here under five different rubrics—in all, some two hundred-odd points on everything from keeping house and raising children to observing everyday courtesy and ethical injunctions. The lists are followed by a celebration of manual work, made practical by suggestions of thirty-eight ways women can earn money at home and a wide variety of "methods" or recipes for household work and products.

Next, women are instructed in how to write weights, measures, and amounts of money using the cryptic shorthand called *raqam*. Lessons in bookkeeping follow. A short section is tucked in concerning the names of months, seasons, and directions of the compass, along with a list of frequently mispronounced Urdu words. Detailed instructions on how to use the post office are followed by advice—practical and moral—on how to write letters.

The book concludes with three "essays." The first sets out guidelines for readers who wish to continue studying beyond the introductory level of this work, offering a list of current books approved and an index of those condemned. The second essay gives advice for teaching Book Ten, a feature common to several of the books. Finally, Thanawi offers a reprise of the poem "The True Jewelry of Humanity," which he so fancies and with which he began his work.

The interest Book Ten holds for the social historian is evident. The atmosphere of a comfortable north Indian household during this period becomes almost tangible. The house is busy, with maids and relatives moving through courtyards and verandas that all look inward. Women are at the center of the household economy, responsible for supervising finances and overseeing the storage and preparation of household goods, for managing children and fostering family harmony. The recipes supplied here are not only for goodies; imagine preparing several months' supply of soap, with the quantities of natron and lime measured in eighty-pound units.

What also emerges is a picture of a society in change. Why is household lore not simply passed on from mother to daughter? In part, as we have already seen, *new* lore is being passed on. This is certainly true of religious orientation, for the *Bihishti Zewar* springs from a self-conscious reformist movement—in religion, mothers themselves were expected to change. But the everyday practical world was changing as well. In many of the families for whom this work was intended, women were taking on new responsibilities, as men were posted far from home in government jobs or trade; and these women needed new skills.

New institutions—the post office and the railroad, for example—and new products were becoming part of everyday experience. Many of the recipes in Book Ten introduce women to newly fashionable foods, such as European leavened bread ("double" *roti*) and biscuits, and to unfamiliar ingredients. The many English loan words found in the original are a clue to this novelty: biscuit, soda, twill, turpentine, and varnish, as well as many of the post office terms such as postcard, register, book post, and parcel. (Some of these words are set off by quotation marks in the translation, as examples.) The increasingly important Urdu publishing industry also had to be addressed—hence the lists and guides to direct the newly literate woman through the recent proliferation of titles. The *Bihishti Zewar* itself is an important example of this new literature, and Book Ten in particular is in part a response to this development, as an attempt to preempt the appeal of missionary or modernist publications that also offered moral and material advice to women.

Maulana Thanawi, no doubt recognizing that recipes for mango pickle were hardly characteristic of the writing of the weighty *'ulama,* opens Book Ten with a defense of the disparate subjects included. His argument is simple and straightforward, namely, that the religion of the Prophet allows—indeed requires—all Muslims to seek the comfort of both others and themselves. No one should deliberately seek to be uncomfortable; no one should miss an occasion to protect another from emotional or physical distress. "These matters may appear worldly," he writes, but they have, in principle, the approval of the Prophet. Islam, we are thus reminded, is a religion that eschews asceticism, although, as the teachings in this work make clear, it also rejects the opposite extreme of luxurious living and self-indulgence.

Despite the variety of its contents, Book Ten reflects a striking coherence—however implicit—in its vision and concerns. It is, I think, a profoundly appropriate finale to this work, summing up a great deal about the kind of person who masters—or should master—the hundreds of pages on ritual and social law, on custom, on spiritual development, and on the moral exemplars who have come before.

Book Ten presents, above all, a picture of the well-formed person whose creation is central to the *Bihishti Zewar* and to reformist teaching. The key to that person, as we have seen, is control, and this is a book about control—about self-control and control of any situation in which a woman may find herself. Behind the detailed injunctions in the sixty-point list exhorting discrimination and promising well-being, a distinctive personality is evident, one associated with sustained formation and discipline. The woman Thanawi envisions is quiet and guarded, doing nothing without reflection, speaking little and weighing the impact of every word on other people's feelings and on their evaluation of her. She is cheerful, orderly, clean, systematic. She is not spontaneous, unpredictable, a lively conversationalist, creative, or artistic—any of the characteristics another culture might consider desirable.

She is, one might say, a person of "minimal transactions," to use a concept developed for Indic cultures by the anthropologist McKim Marriott.[1] For some groups in some societies, the ideal is the opposite: maximal exchanges that build up relationships and networks, creating clients and patrons, offering and receiving food, gifts, money, one's very substance. Here, however, everything that comes and goes must be guarded and measured. This is the theme of the Qur'anic verse on the title page of each installment of the *Bihishti Zewar*. A woman must guard her honor, her self, from all males except her husband. She must restrict social interaction. She must measure her words, in quantity and audience. She must measure and count every item that comes to hand. She must confine her prayers and worship to God alone. She should eat little, and certainly nothing from a stranger's hand. She should pay what is owed everyone, and pay it unfailingly; but she should not dispense largesse casually or without just cause. No wonder Thanawi shuddered at the customary wedding celebration, with its easy mingling, abundant food, obligatory gifts, and scattering of coins! His is a puritan world of cleanliness, order, regularity, and self-control, with a person at the center who relies only on God and on herself. It was in a society of such persons that the reformists placed their hopes.

The themes of moderation and self-control are implicit in the opening lists. The first sixty points deal with everyday opportunities to exercise control and good common sense. In substance, if not style, some could be Dear Abby's answers to letters: "Every time my sister-in-law comes and we sit down to chat . . ."; "Little did I think that when I told my husband how beautiful my cousin was . . ." A sprinkling could be Heloise's household tips: "Remember you can always add more salt, but you can't take it away . . ."; "Nothing works like sunshine in freshening up your clothes and linen . . ."; "Here's a simple tip for putting peppers into recipes. . . ." Still others might intrigue Miss Manners. The subjects are, of course, far from resembling those in the advice columns of today's American newspapers, especially in the importance given to propriety and modesty. The emphasis of the section is on avoiding any reproach to oneself and acting with genuine courtesy and thoughtfulness to others, with self-reliance, and with self-restraint.

The second list, of defects particularly characteristic of women, best exemplifies the central focus on discrimination and control. In Book Seven, Maulana Thanawi insists that all humans, men and women both, must strive to discipline the willful lower soul, the *nafs,* by exercising sense, *'aql,* that leads one to live in harmony with the natural order that is Islam. Elsewhere, however (for example, in Book Six's condemnation of women's excursions and in his statement later in Book Ten that "Almighty God has endowed men with more sense"), Thanawi reiterates the widespread cultural understanding that women are deficient in *'aql* and thus handicapped in that quest; they must therefore make special efforts at self-discipline. That attitude is even more evident in the twenty-nine points of this list. More than half these points suggest that the failure of *'aql* is the failure to control one's discrimination and one's subsequent behavior—that is, women exceed proper limits. The faults here are mostly of excess: women dawdle too long, talk too loud, spend too much, take too much time, and take along too much luggage. They rush in too quickly, they do too much at once, they give too much food, they cry too readily. They are careless with valuables and with time. Thanawi clearly states his opinion that women must learn to be sober and reflective in order to show the discrimination, *tamiz,* of a person controlled by good sense and capable of self-control.

Many of the fifty-nine points in the third list, "practical and useful warnings," rehearse specific strategies for controlling one's environment. They warn of actions that may seem innocuous but are likely to produce harm. Many urge caution in dealing with outsiders, who should not be let into the house or entrusted with goods or information. One must control one's possessions by carefully securing them and by listing in order whatever items—dirty clothes, grain to be milled—are sent out. Medicine should be labeled, mail carefully addressed and provided with a return address, animals confined, children taught their proper names in case they get lost. One should try to control the uncontrollable: fruit trees should not be planted in courtyards where fruit may unexpectedly fall; insane people should be avoided, because what they say is unpredictable; kerosene and fire should be used with caution. The reader must even try to control other people's tongues by avoiding occasions of gossip, such as a double wedding or talking in front of outsiders.

The fourth list is concerned with those in one's life who are potentially the most uncontrollable, namely, children. These twenty-four points suggest that children will be raised in sobriety and decorum: no excess swinging, no spoiling, no attachment to a particular person, no association with uncouth playmates. They must be instructed from the earliest age in *adab* and *qa'ida* (good habits and decorum). Children should be kept clean and safe, their food controlled, and their activities supervised.

The fifth and final list reiterates in its forty-two points many of the concerns above, but it focuses particularly on kind and prudent behavior toward others, on courtesy, forbearance, helpfulness, honesty, fair dealing, gratitude, thoughtfulness, respect, sobriety. And, of course, the reader is reminded yet again of the need to cultivate quiet simplicity and modesty and to apply her time to useful pursuits.

The next topic covers handicrafts and skills useful to women. Thanawi introduces this section by discussing the dilemma faced by widows, a subject that reappears frequently throughout the work. By Brahmanical custom, a widow did not remarry but was regarded as an embodiment of misfortune, implicated in her husband's untimely death, her moral corruption made manifest by her unhappy fate. If she was of childbearing age, she represented sexuality uncontrolled by marriage. With shaven head and mourning garments, a widow was expected to live on scraps and serve others. Wellborn Muslims emulated this custom. Thanawi makes no reference to the Indic concepts that surrounded what he deemed objectionable treatment of widows, except to identify the custom as characteristic of Hindustan and to attribute it to ignorance. For him, it was a violation of religious law and ran counter to the direct example of the Prophet.

In his discussion of the fate of widows, Thanawi's concern, interestingly, is not with controlling them; rather, he emphasizes their own control of their environment. He displays a humane concern for the worries and troubles of widows, with their dependence on others who are often unable or unwilling to look after them. He encourages them to adopt one of two active strategies: either remarry or learn skills to earn a living. He reproaches his readers for having contempt for manual labor and reminds them of the humble activities of every one of the prophets.

Bibi Ashraf's autobiography describes a personal case of the remarriage of a widow that suggests the depth of the attitudes the reformers were attempting to change. Her childhood teacher had been married at eleven and widowed at fifteen, then hired out as a teacher for a dozen years while she lived "with extreme modesty and propriety." When the teacher's parents subsequently arranged a remarriage, Bibi Ashraf wrote:

> My grandfather was terribly shocked when he heard the news. Out of his sense of shame, he did not stir out of the house for a whole month. Everyone reasoned with him: "Why must you feel so bad about it? She was only a hired teacher in your household; she was not, God forbid, a kin."

Bibi Ashraf herself, also left a widow sometime around 1870, supported herself and her children for a time by sewing clothes and making lace, just as Maulana Thanawi recommends.[2]

Thanawi lists a wide range of activities suitable for women, including activities associated with low-status groups, as well as some associated with men. They often overlap those proposed in the subcontinent today as "income-generating activities" for women who must work in their homes. About a third of the thirty-eight activities listed involve sewing; some describe decorative fine work, some the basic production of clothes and bedding. Thanawi notes the existence of the sewing machine. He encourages "agro-based" products, selling or processing foods, fabric, tobacco, and so forth. He lists craft projects such as woodworking, bookbinding, and soap making. There are suggestions that women should involve themselves in trade, selling their products or buying and selling produce as the price increases. And, of course, women are reminded that they can teach in their homes.[3]

There follow several pages of recipes and instructions suitable for making household items or saleable products or for carrying out household work: making soap, ink, paint for wood, and a wide range of dyes of various subtle shades for block printing and other uses; tinning and soldering; curing tobacco; preparing leaven, pickles, chutney, and pre-serves. Current editions of the book often add new instructions. (The translation of this section has been abridged.)

In this translation, metric equivalents for the traditional measures are added. I have attempted to use round units (e.g., 250 grams instead of 226.8 grams for a *pa'o*) while keeping the correct ratio: *chhatank: pa'o:ser:man* = 1:4:16:640 = 60 grams (approximately):250 grams:1 kilogram:40 kilograms. I have calculated metric equivalents for *masha* and *tola* (used for items measured in small amounts) in a ratio of 1:12. An appendix at the end of Book Ten, not part of the original work, gives a chart of weights, currency, and measures used in this book.

The section that follows the recipes deals with measures in detail. It is largely of historical interest, for metric measurements and decimal coinage have now been introduced in the subcontinent. Nevertheless, some items today are still measured by the old system, especially in rural areas (e.g., silver by the *tola,* meat by the *ser,* firewood by the *man*), and older people still use it, of course. Like the recipes, the measures continue to be included in new editions of the *Bihishti Zewar.*

The next section teaches the *raqam* system of numerical writing (largely based on the initial letter of the Arabic name of the numbers), which provides a kind of shorthand for keeping accounts. This system is no longer widely used and is not included in detail here.[4] But the ability to read and write numbers and keep accounts and the rationale for keeping a daily ledger are important examples of the kind of control that is the implicit organizing principle of Book Ten as a whole.

A brief section next lists terms "in constant use" that a woman should know, presumably to enhance her competence and her control of situations. The names of the months are given in both Arabic and Urdu. The Urdu folk names, presented without comment, are criti-cized in Book Six for reflecting the emphasis on resorting to holy persons and custom that the reformers so deplored. The list of incor-rectly pronounced words recalls how the author, in Book One, urged women to learn correct vocabulary and diction in order to ensure that they themselves and their families are accorded proper respect.

The section on the post office is the only part of the book that has been continually updated in later editions (if it is included), although the basic format and points continue unchanged. Behind the practical advice, Thanawi is concerned that women effectively control their ac-tivities, avoiding inconvenience and embarrassment to themselves and others. Careful instructions for postage, insurance, registration, and even wrapping are offered. The postal system itself also brings into question the control and self-control at stake in women's seclusion; the mail must in no way jeopardize that, as the directions for writing letters make clear.

In his final essays, Thanawi takes up the question of further education for those who have completed the *Bihishti Zewar*. Maulana Thanawi, of course, played a part in some fundamental changes in the very basis of education, in who was educated and how they were taught, and in the content of that education. One key to these changes was the new wealth of printed materials that took education out of the privileged relationship between master and selected pupil and into a public domain where learning was widely available.

This change carried with it an emphasis on active, not rote, learning. Thanawi intersperses directions for such learning throughout the *Bihishti Zewar*, including the list in his second essay here. Pedagogically, the list calls for the student to internalize the lessons, to know them in her own words, to be taught at the right level, to have what we would call group discussions with other students. She was, above all, to act on what she learned.

In these concluding essays, Thanawi restates his fundamental belief, namely, that girls can and should pursue religious knowledge with the same range and the same goals as boys. He insists that Arabic is crucial for anyone who is serious about religious knowledge, and he makes specific suggestions about learning it, envisioning girls who will be *maulawi*s, able to give guidance exactly as learned men do. But his main emphasis is on the knowledge now available in Urdu—clearly a mixed blessing, to his mind, for he fears that the books available may ruin a girl's habits rather than enhancing her true knowledge and skill. To guide the reader through the thicket of available works, he presents two fascinating lists of books: seventy-one are listed as acceptable; twenty-eight titles (or categories) are disapproved.

The subjects of the approved books are evident from many of the titles. (About half are identified in the British Library catalogue, as indicated in notes.) They cover topics such as Qur'anic texts and commentaries, prayer, funeral customs, the *'aqiqa* ceremony of infancy, civil law, the Last Judgment, the Prophet, the remarriage of widows, and sufism (including two works by Thanawi's own preceptor Hajji Imdadu'llah, who had settled in Mecca). These books would have, at least in part, deplored local customary practices such as elaborate ceremonials, reciprocal exchange of gifts, and feasts. Some titles are given limited approval—for example, three books on the Prophet that mistakenly approve of celebrating the Prophet's birthday (an increasingly popular event, disapproved of by *'ulama* like Thanawi, as discussed in Book Six).

Also included as an approved book is an Urdu translation of Shah Rafi'u'd-Din's *Qiyamat nama,* a collection of *hadis* on the Last Judgment, prepared by one of the great sons of Shah Waliu'llah a hundred years earlier and used extensively by Thanawi in the *Bihishti Zewar* to underline the seriousness of all he had to say. Another is an Urdu version of a work by Shah Waliu'llah himself (item 62), described elsewhere as "providing directions for leading a holy life." Yet another (item 50) is an abridged translation of al-Ghazali's great classic the *Ihya 'ulum al-din.* Overall, these are books that teach the details of the *shari'at,* the example of the Prophet and other holy persons, and the way to moral perfection.

At least five books on Thanawi's list offer advice specifically to women, making it clear that Thanawi's work was only one of many. The best known is the *Tahzibu'n-niswan wa tarbiyatu'l-insan* (The cultivation of women and the instruction of humanity). It was written by the ruling princess of the state of Bhopal, a woman deeply influenced by the reformist group that opposed the Deobandis, a group that discounted the medieval classical schools of law in favor of consulting Qur'an and *hadis.* Thanawi writes, "This is a very good book, but its legal points are not in accord with the law school of our Imam. Therefore, act on those points with the *Bihishti Zewar* as a guide." Again, the reader can direct herself, as long as she has the proper books as guides.

Beyond religion narrowly defined, the approved list includes two works on Greco-Arabic medicine, newly revived in this period (and taught in brief in Book Nine of the *Bihishti Zewar*). There is a book on composition, another on the shorthand script called *shikasta,* and a book on arithmetic, all of use to the girl who was learning to be competent and to control herself and her affairs. These are works that cover more or less the same ground as the *Bihishti Zewar* and that, overall, share Maulana Thanawi's reformist views.

Thanawi disapproved of girls reading any novels—these volumes are "worse than poison"—but one novel crept into the list of approved books: Deputy Nazir Ahmad's *Taubatu'n-nasuh,* widely regarded as among the first and best Urdu novels.[5] The story clearly posits religion as the necessary source of values, a view Thanawi shared. The hero, Nasuh, on his sickbed, experiences a vision of the Day of Judgment and returns to health to reform both himself and his family. His wife, daughters, and two younger sons eventually share in the reform. One boy joins the education department; the other becomes a *hakim*. Only the youngest son, Kalim, adheres to unreconstructed *sharif* culture: poetry, chess and cards, pigeons and kites. The colonial state, it should be noted, provides the context for reform; Kalim leaves for a princely state where, in the end, he becomes a soldier and dies. It is he who is the "traditionalist"; Nasuh, Nazir Ahmad, and Maulana Thanawi represent what is new. Nasuh, in what C. M. Naim suggests "must be one of the most horrifying scenes in Urdu novels," burns Kalim's library of the books that from Nasuh's and Thanawi's perspective were central to his ruin.

That fictitious library would have held many of the books on Thanawi's second list, his index of proscribed reading. Thanawi gives no general explanation for his choices. In his earlier discussions of custom, we saw that although the origin of a custom was not the basis of judgment, certain fault lines did in fact emerge, separating what was local or regional from what was normative—for example, in life-cycle rituals. In literary culture, the fault line separates around the cosmopolitan, whether Persianate or European. Most of the disapproved works listed here represent the Persianate, urban culture of the cognoscenti and the court. To critics, they epitomize a *nawabi,* or princely, lifestyle of dancing girls, extravagance, and all-night poetry recitations. At their worst, these books encourage values other than the puritan virtues of sobriety, righteousness, and godliness that inspire the reformers' work; at best, they provide a self-indulgent distraction from the duties that should come first. The list may seem short, but its first item is in fact a genre—nothing less than all *diwan*s and books of *ghazal*s. These collections of poetry were the pride of Urdu literature, beloved of Urdu speakers in that day as well as our own. Thanawi had no use for poetry, even if its themes stressed the passion for the worldly beloved as analogue of the soul's passion for God. Nazir Ahmad, like the writer and critic Hali (associated with the modernists of Aligarh), also sought to encourage morally uplifting, utilitarian poetry and prose.[6] On the need for such literature, Nazir Ahmad, Hali, and Maulana Thanawi were in agreement.

Hali's celebrated poem on decline and resurgence, known as the *Musaddas* (1879), had long since condemned most Urdu poetry; his prose *Muqaddama* (1893), a sustained attack on that poetry, invoked Western theorists from Plato to Bentham and has been influential to the present. Hali saw a love of "immoral" poetry as part of the explanation for Indian "backwardness" in relation to the British. Maulana Thanawi, though not wanting to emulate British values, may have been influenced by Hali's critique. Certainly the logic of his own concerns with printed literature would have brought him to the same conclusion. We recall his enthusiasm for what can only be called the doggerel of "The True Jewelry of Humanity," reproduced in both Books One and Ten.[7]

Thanawi's list of unacceptable books included other works that are regarded as masterpieces of Urdu literature.[8] Not only lovers of Urdu literature but also the British of Thanawi's day might have been disappointed by the list. Many titles are the Urdu editions of classic fabulous tales and adventures prepared for use at Fort William College (1800), a training school for British administrators. Under the leadership of John Gilchrist, the goal of these translations at the college was twofold: to help shape the vernacular into a popular and usable language for Indians; and to make accessible those works deemed necessary for the British to understand the "native culture." Of these books, Thanawi's list includes the *Qissa-yi badr-i munir;* the *Qissa-yi shah-i yaman;* the *Dastan-i amir hamza;* the *Gul-i bakawali;* the *Alif laila,* known, of course, as *The Thousand and One Nights;* the *Ara'ish-i mahfil,* a translation of the Persian story of Hatim Ta'i; and the *Jang nama-yi muhammad hanif.* Also included was that product of what Thanawi no doubt regarded as the decadent—even polytheistic—court of Lucknow: the *Indar sabha,* usually identified as the first drama written in Urdu.

Most of these proscribed works are quest stories whose noble heroes undergo marvelous adventures. It is not hard to see why Thanawi would dislike these stories, despite the moral character of the heroes and the invocations of God. They are above all stories of the fabulous and unpredictable, of a dream logic beyond human control; they are stories of disproportion—for example, of obsessive love. Toward the end of the nineteenth century, as mass publishing continued to develop, these works were ever more available, and some continue to be popular today.[9] The popularity of these tales and the other proscribed books is suggested by the fact that all but a half dozen of the disapproved works are among the items listed by Blumhardt in the library of the British Museum in its collection of early Urdu literature. Those few not listed by Blumhardt tend to reflect the customary religion the reformers deplored, discussing omens, miracles, and inappropriate veneration of the Prophet.

The final four proscribed books were Nazir Ahmad's four novels that deal with women. Perhaps Thanawi put these four at the end of his list because he was reluctant to put them here at all. He had, after all, approved the *Taubatu'n-nasuh.* He admits that much of the material in these four books is conducive to the discernment (*tamiz*) and proficiency (*saliqa*) he espouses, but, on balance, he concludes that these works are of the sort that "weaken faith." His ambivalence is not surprising. Two of the novels, *Mir'atu'l-'arus* and *Banatu'n-na'sh*, deal with the benefits of proper training for girls; the third, *Ayama*, concerns the need for widows to remarry—his own persistent themes. But the fourth, *Muhsinat*, takes up the problems caused for women by multiple marriages, a subject Thanawi would not have found congenial either abstractly or personally (he himself, being childless, had taken a second wife). Moreover, in these novels, books from both Thanawi's approved and disapproved lists are read, and women go beyond the bounds of being competent and responsible to become more independent than their received domestic role comfortably allows. We can assume that, as lines were drawn, these novels went too far in the direction of the cosmopolitan, at the risk of what was seen as the normative cultural core.

The most popularly beloved of the books Thanawi condemns is Nazir Ahmad's *Mir'atu'l-'arus* (1869), a story that seems in many ways a fictional account of the girl the *Bihishti Zewar* was meant to produce.[10] It is the story of two sisters, the elder a mean-tempered, uneducated failure and the younger, Asghari, a literate, competent, and pious source of blessing to everyone she encounters. Asghari brings order to household accounts and to people's lives—and is able to correspond with her wise father, who is posted away from home. Patient and sober, she controls her self and her environment. In *Banatu'n-na'sh*, Nazir Ahmad continues the story of Asghari, focusing on the school for local girls that she establishes in her home. There, the girls read the Qur'an and other books and learn to cook, sew, and manage household budgets. Their handicrafts are sold to support the costs of the school. Asghari is concerned with moral development, and her charges learn the humility, selflessness, and good habits that Thanawi also enjoins.

It is clear that Nazir Ahmad has a somewhat more cosmopolitan orientation toward literature and culture than does Thanawi.[11] The girls in the school learn geography and history, are given a favorable impression of Englishwomen, and even read Urdu newspapers. They play with dolls as a technique for learning certain skills. Perhaps, as C. M. Naim suggests, in the end Maulana Thanawi is uncomfortable with women who are "competent, stronger, and more effective than almost all the male characters." Women must, in Thanawi's view, develop their intellectual and moral skills exactly as men do, but they must never deviate from their prescribed position in the familial hierarchy.

Yet we will not be far off the mark if we look at Asghari as Maulana Thanawi's ideal. She has been nurtured to develop excellent habits and educated to a suitable standard under the tutelage of her aptly named father, Durandesh Khan ("The Far-Sighted"). She is wholly self-controlled, clear in her reasoned assessments, unfailingly respectful and tactful as she seeks to guide even those who are her superiors. There are deep satisfactions but no frivolities in her life. She fosters the moral and material well-being of her family and those around her. Her economies permit her to dispense largesse that becomes legendary and that would delight a Deobandi's heart: improvements to a mosque, food to wayfarers at a mosque, a serai for travelers, the distribution of five hundred copies of the Qur'an in a day and a thousand blankets to the poor every winter. These achievements, and her moral development as a whole, all take place within the received structure of family and society, as important to Nazir Ahmad as it was to Maulana Thanawi.

Maulana Thanawi never questioned the underlying structure of society or women's role in it. But, within that structure, he insisted on the value of individual moral achievement, whatever one's place by gender or by birth. The key to that achievement was self-control, honed by adherence to the religious law, which alone directs people to their true and essential selves. Thanawi's vision was to perfect women so that they could be nothing less than "*maulawi*s, like men." These teachings, like those of many others in this century who have sought to "manage" women, have had complex implications not only for women's lives but also for the societies of which these women are a part.

Righteous women are devoutly obedient and guard in their husbands'
absence what Allah would have them guard.

A pamphlet meant to instruct women and girls in the
way to act on this Qur'anic verse

Heavenly Ornaments

Book Ten

A discussion, by section, of everything that women need to
know about beliefs, legal points, ethics and social behavior,
child-rearing, and so on

Compiled by the Reverend Hazrat, Sun of the Scholars,
Crown of the Learned,
Maulana Hafiz Muhammad Ashraf 'Ali Sahib

Published at the direction of
Shaikh Hajji Zainu'd-Din Ahmad and
Muhammad Yamain, Book Dealers, Saharanpur

Printed at the Bilali Steam Press, Sadhaura, District Ambala

Contents of Book Ten

The Tenth Book of the
Bihishti Zewar

Most of the points discussed in this book are meant to make your everyday life more satisfying and your relations with other people inoffensive. These matters may appear worldly, but the Apostle, *God's blessings and peace upon him,* declared, "The complete Muslim is one whose hand and tongue cause trouble to no one." He also said, "It is not appropriate for Muslims to debase themselves by getting entangled in any severe trouble."* The Apostle[s], it is said, was of the opinion that the audience of a sermon should not be bored; nor should guests distress the master of the house by staying too long. These examples make it clear that unnecessary discomfort, harm to others, and behavior that produces irritation and distress are all, in fact, against the teachings of religion. For this reason, this book takes up not only specific religious teachings but also a number of subjects conducive to your comfort as well as the comfort of others.

I. [Five Useful Lists]

[LIST ONE:] PRACTICAL WAYS TO SHOW GOOD SENSE
AND CREATE COMFORT

1. At night, before locking up the house, look around carefully to be sure no dog or cat is left inside. During the night, an animal could

---

* Recorded in *Kanzu'l-'amal* (A treasure of deeds).

either hurt someone or damage something. If nothing more, the animal's clattering around all night is enough to keep a person awake.

2. Put your clothes and books out in the sun from time to time.

3. Keep your house clean, and keep each thing in its own place.

4. If you want to be healthy, do not always seek your own ease. Do some physical work with your own hands. The best work for women is grinding, pounding, and spinning. Doing this keeps the body healthy.

5. If you go visiting, do not overstay your welcome; do not talk so much that the hosts get upset or that you interfere with something they are doing.

6. All the people of the house should make a habit of keeping each thing in its own place. Anyone who takes an item out to use should put it back in the same place, so that no one has to ask around and look all over to find it. If you keep moving things, no one will find them! Everyone is inconvenienced. Fix a spot for any item that you use frequently, so that when you need it, you can lay your hands on it instantly.

7. Do not leave anything such as cots, stools, vessels, bricks, stones, or grindstones in the way. It can easily happen that in the dark, or even during the day, someone will come dashing along without paying any attention—as they do every day—and trip and fall and hurt themselves some place or other.

8. When someone tells you to do something, be sure to say yes or no out loud as soon as you hear her. That way, she knows for sure that you have heard. Otherwise, she may think that you have heard when in fact you haven't. If she thinks that you will do a certain task and you have not agreed to do it, she is falsely misled to expect something.

9. Use salt sparingly. There can be a remedy for too little salt, but not for too much.

10. Do not put chopped peppers in lentils or greens unless you have ground them up first. With chopped peppers, the seeds stay in the pieces, and they set on fire the entire mouth of a person who gets one.

11. If you want a drink of water at night, check the water carefully, if there is a light. Otherwise, you should always put a cloth over the jug or other vessel so that you do not accidentally drink any foreign matter.

12. Do not toss children up in the air as a joke or dangle them out of windows. God forbid that they slip from your hands and your laughter choke in your throat. Do not make a game of chasing them, because they may fall and be hurt.

13. When a vessel is empty, always wash it and turn it over. When you want to use it again, wash it again.

14. If you want to serve food out of containers that have been on the

ground, do not put them just as they are on the tray or cloth. First, check the bottoms and wipe them off.

15. If you are a guest at someone's house, do not make any special requests. Frequently, the item is of no consequence, but it is a matter of time. The host may be unable to fulfill the request on short notice and be unfairly embarrassed.

16. Do not sit down and spit where other people are sitting. Do not clean your nose in public. If necessary, go off to one side and then return.

17. When eating, do not talk about things that will turn the stomachs of the other people. Those of delicate constitutions will be very upset.

18. Do not say anything in front of a sick person or the relatives that gives the impression of concern for that person's life. You should not break someone's heart unnecessarily. Speak comforting words such as, "**Almighty God willing,** everything will be all right."

19. If you have to say something privately about someone who is present, do not signal in her direction with your eye or hand, for she will be unnecessarily suspicious. This assumes that what you are saying is acceptable according to the *shari'at*. If what you are discussing is illegitimate, it is a sin even to talk about it.

20. Do not wave your hands a lot while you are talking.

21. Do not wipe your nose with the hem of a skirt, the border of a veil, or a sleeve.

22. Do not clean yourself on the footstep of a privy. Set aside a separate footrest for washing after elimination.*

23. Always shake out a shoe before wearing it, for some noxious animal could be inside. Do likewise with clothes and bedding.

24. If someone has eruptions on a covered part of the body, do not ask her where they are. She will be unfairly embarrassed.

25. Do not sit in a passageway. Both you and others will be inconvenienced.

26. Do not let your body or clothes get smelly. If your clothes have not come back from the washerman's house, then wash the very clothes on your body and bathe.

27. Do not have a place swept where other people are sitting.

---

* Men should not take water inside the privy at all, but only a lump of dirt; they should cleanse themselves in the bathroom. [The "footstep" is, as Platts puts it, "one step of the (brick) compartments in a necessary" (John T. Platts, *A Dictionary of Urdu, Classical Hindi, and English*, 5th ed. [London: Oxford University Press, 1930; reprint 1960], p. 789).]

28. Do not throw peelings and pits from a place where someone may be sitting or passing below.

29. Do not play with knives, scissors, needles, or other sharp things, because you may accidentally get cut.

30. As soon as a guest arrives, point out the privy. Immediately arrange for stationing the conveyance and for grass and fodder for the bullock or horse. Do not take so much trouble with the meals that the guest does not eat on time. Cook the food on time, even if it is simple and modest in amount. When the guest is ready to leave, prepare breakfast early in the morning. In short, do everything to ensure a guest's comfort and welfare.

31. Do not come out of the privy or bathroom tying your belt, but tie it carefully before coming out.

32. When someone asks you a question about something, answer it before getting involved in another job.

33. Whatever you say, or whatever answer you give, open your mouth and speak clearly so that the other person understands exactly what you are saying.

34. If you have to give something to someone, do not throw it from a distance. The person may not catch it, and the thing will be damaged. Go up close and hand the item to the other person.

35. If two people are reading or talking, you should not come between them to shout or talk to someone.

36. If someone is busy with some task or conversation, do not go up and begin your own conversation. Wait until she pays attention to you.

37. If you have to give something to someone who, for whatever reason, cannot take the item properly at the moment, just wait. If you let go of it, the item may drop between the two of you and be damaged.

38. If you are supposed to fan someone, be careful not to touch the head or anywhere else on the body or the clothes. Do not fan so vigorously that it disturbs the person.

39. While eating, pile any bones in one place, likewise any peelings and so forth. Do not spread them out in all directions. Throw out the whole collection at the appropriate time.

40. Do not run along with your head in the air, for you may fall.

41. Close books with great care and attention. Frequently the first and last pages get creased from carelessness.

42. You should not praise any unrelated man in front of your husband. This is annoying to many men.

43. Likewise, do not praise unknown women to your husband. He may start to feel attracted to one of them and withdraw from you.

44. When you meet people with whom you are not on intimate

terms, you should not ask them about their family, belongings, wealth, ornaments, or clothes.

45. Set aside three or four days each month for cleaning the house thoroughly. Clean out the cobwebs. Take up the carpets and sweep. Put everything in order.

46. You should not pick up and look at a paper or book that someone else is reading. If the paper is handwritten, it may be something private. If it is printed, something handwritten may be kept with it.

47. Take great care going up and down stairs. It is best to put both feet on each stair. Putting one foot on one step and the next foot on the next step is completely inappropriate for girls and women. You should also forbid boys to do this when they are children.

48. You should not shake out a cloth or book or anything else in a place where the dust will fall on someone sitting below. You should not even dust with a cloth or blow away dust until the other person has left.

49. If you hear news of some grief, hardship, sorrow, or sickness, do not mention it to anyone and especially do not speak to the person's relatives until it is definitely confirmed. If it is a mistake, then you have worried another person unnecessarily. People will reproach you, saying, "Why did you say something so unlucky?"

50. Similarly, do not write to relatives in a distant place about ordinary illnesses and troubles.

51. Do not spit on walls or spit betel nut juice on them. Likewise, do not wipe greasy hands on walls or doors; wash your hands instead. Do not say that oil left over from cooking is unclean, as many ignorant women do.

52. If you need to set out more of some dish on the cloth spread for eating, do not take away a dish already in front of a guest; instead, bring the additional food in another dish.

53. Do not bump into a cot or platform where someone is lying or sitting. If you do go near it, be careful not to stumble against it. If you have to put something on the platform or take something off, put it down or pick it up very gently.

54. Do not keep any food or drink uncovered. You should even cover things placed on the cloth that are to be eaten later or at the end of the meal.

55. When guests are no longer hungry, they should leave a little meat or bread on the table, so that the people of the house will not worry that the food was insufficient and therefore feel embarrassed.

56. Any completely empty vessel that is to be kept in a cupboard or on a shelf or other place should be stored upside down.

57. When walking, pick each foot up completely and move forward.

Do not shuffle your feet. If you do, your shoes will wear out quickly. It also looks very bad.

58. Pay attention that the hem of your shawl or veil does not drag on the ground.

59. If someone asks for some salt or something else to eat or drink, bring it in a container. Do not bring it in your hand.

60. Do not talk about private matters in front of girls, or their sense of shame will disappear.

[LIST TWO:] FAULTS AND ANNOYANCES FOUND AMONG WOMEN

1. Women do not give appropriate answers that satisfy the questioner. They mix in foolish comments here and there and do not make the main point clear. You must remember to pay attention and try to understand the meaning of whatever is asked. Then answer as necessary.

2. Women hear a request to do something, but they say nothing. The speaker is then left in doubt—"God knows whether she heard or not"—and often mistakenly thinks the other must have heard. If in fact she has not heard, the job does not get done, because of this contrary impression. Then, when she is asked about the task, she answers abashedly, "I didn't hear"—in short, the job is left undone. Or the opposite may happen: the speaker mistakenly thinks that the other person has not heard and asks again, only to be torn to shreds—"I heard, I heard! Why do you torment me?" In short, there is grief between them. If only the person addressed had said, "All right," in the first place, the other would have known.

3. Women will shout from far off to tell the maidservant to do some job or to tell something to someone else. There are two evils in this. One is the shamelessness (*behaya'i*) and immodesty (*bepardagi*) of a woman's voice reaching not just to the door but even to the street. The other is that some things are understood from a distance, but some are not. Whatever is not understood is not done. Now the mistress becomes angry: "Why have you not done this?" The servant answers, "Well, I did not hear." In short, they start arguing. So much for the job. When the maidservants bring some news from outside, they are also likely to come in the door shouting. Once again, something of what they say may be understood, but not all. It shows good sense either to go up to anyone you have to talk to or to call the person over to you. Explain carefully and deliberately whatever you have to say; listen and understand carefully whatever is said to you.

4. Women take a sudden liking to something, whether it is neces-

sary or not. They don't even care if they have to borrow money. Loans aside, is it prudent to squander your money uselessly? Extravagance is, after all, also a sin. Whenever you are about to spend something, first think carefully whether there is some religious value or worldly need that will be gained by the expenditure. If, after thinking carefully, there seems to be need and value, then go ahead. Otherwise, do not squander the money. As far as possible, never take loans, even if this causes you a little trouble.

5. When women have to go somewhere, whether within the city or on a trip, they stall and procrastinate so much that the time grows tight. If they make a trip, they arrive at their destination very late. If night falls when they are on the road, they risk their lives and goods. If it is the hot season, they themselves will burn in the sun and the children will be uncomfortable. If it is the rainy season, they face even more delay, first, from the likelihood of rain, and second, from the difficulty of moving the cart in deep mud. If they go at dawn, there is every sort of profit. If you are going to a village, the palanquin bearers are distressed because they are standing around waiting to go. Then they have to return late, because of the delay in getting started. Your own work is also disturbed. There will be delay in arranging for meals. Here, the food is ruined from haste; there, a husband is making demands; somewhere else, the children are crying. If everyone had left early, these troubles would not have happened.

6. On a trip, women pack and take along many unnecessary goods that give a great deal of trouble to the animals and crowd the available space. The greatest trouble is caused for the men who go along. They have to manage the goods and load them up from place to place. They must pay the porters. In short, these poor wretches have all the worry on their minds. Meanwhile, the ladies are sitting just fine, without a care, in their carriages. Always take very few goods along on a trip. That makes for great convenience. This is especially important on a rail journey, for even more trouble is caused by taking too many goods on a train.

7. When women are getting into their carriages or whatever conveyance, the women say to the men, "Cover your face!" "Hide in a corner!" When they are properly settled, however, they fail to tell the men that there is no longer any need of cover. There are two problems in this. Sometimes the poor man sits there covering his face and is distressed for nothing. And sometimes he guesses that the women are back in seclusion, and he uncovers his face or comes forward, only to find that the women are there unveiled. These transgressions come

from not speaking a second time. If you did, everyone would know that there is a habit of calling out a second time and would wait for it and not come forward otherwise.

8. Another problem is that, although the women are not ready to go, seclusion is set a half an hour early and the road is blocked off. For no good reason, God's creatures are inconvenienced while the women are cooking up amusements in the house.

9. After dismounting from the carriage or palanquin, women rush into the house where they have arrived. Often, a woman will come face-to-face with some man of the house who is inside. You should not get out of the carriage or palanquin until you first send some maidservant into the house to have a look and give news of your arrival. If some man is there, he will go away. When you hear that there is no man in the house, only then should you get out and go inside.

10. When two women are talking among themselves, one often begins talking before the other has finished. Indeed, many times, both speak at the same time. This one is saying her thing, and that one bawling hers, and neither in fact hears the other. Well! What is the use of such a conversation? Always remember that when one speaker is finished, only then should the other speak.

11. Women keep jewelry and sometimes even money carelessly, sometimes under pillows or openly on a shelf. Out of laziness, even though there are locks and keys, they do not keep things safely. Then, when something disappears, they go around blaming everyone.

12. If you send women off to do one job, they get involved in another. When they are finished with both, they return. This causes trouble and confusion to the person who sent them, because she has calculated only the time needed for one job and begins to worry when that time has passed. These geniuses say, "As long as we are here, we may as well do the other task, too." Do not act this way. Do the first job as requested. Then do the other job calmly on your own.

13. Women are lazy, and they put off a job scheduled for one time to another time. This often causes harm and disruption.

14. Women by nature (*mizaj*) have no sense of getting to the point. They do not see the necessity of recognizing that on some occasions time is short and a job should be limited to what is essential. It never occurs to them to do anything except carry out every last detail. In all this fuss, the essential job is often spoiled or the chance to do it at all is lost.

15. If something is lost, women lay the blame without investigation. If a woman knows that someone has stolen something previously, she just says, "All right, it is her doing!" Why does it have to be the same

person who commits every misdeed? In other situations like this, women also jump to conclusions on such "absolute certainty."

16. Women spend so much money on *pan* and tobacco that, if they are poor, they exceed their means and, if they are rich, they lose the chance to provide for four or five needy people. Women should reduce these expenses. The problem is that women start to use these things for no good reason and then become addicted to these vices.

17. If a woman hears two people talking about something, she will, without being asked, intrude and start to give advice, whether they like it or not. Until someone asks your advice, just sit there, deaf and dumb.

18. After coming back from a gathering, women describe the appearance, clothing, and jewelry of the other women to their husbands. What a disaster for you if your husband's heart inclines toward one of them, and he starts thinking about her!

19. If women have something to say to someone, no matter what the other person may be doing, they will never wait to talk until her job or conversation is over. They just butt right into the middle. This is a very bad habit. You should wait until the person can pay attention to you.

20. Women never complete a conversation or give a complete message. If what they say is misunderstood, a job will be done wrong, and there will be trouble between the two people.

21. Women do not listen to a conversation with their full attention; instead, they keep working or talking to someone else. The speaker's heart is not satisfied, nor can she expect her concerns to be met. How can she, when the other has not listened?

22. Women will never admit their errors and mistakes. They invariably try to feign innocence, whether successfully or not.

23. Women turn up their noses at any small thing they receive as a share from some festivity or as a little gift. They will ridicule it. "What was the necessity of sending such a thing? She should have been ashamed to send it!" This is very bad. At least the giver caused you no harm. Women have the same habit with their husbands and hardly ever accept an item happily. They first spurn the item and find fault with it— and only then accept it.

24. If you ask women to do something, they have to rant and rave before doing the task. When the work has to be done anyway, why indulge in this nonsense? You wrong the other's heart unfairly.

25. Women sew clothes while wearing them and, not surprisingly, get pricked. Why look for unnecessary trouble?

26. Women always cry at arrivals as well as at departures. Even if

tears do not come naturally, they cry for fear that someone will reproach them for lack of love.

27. Women often stick a needle in a pillow or lay it down somewhere, then get up and go off. Someone comes along, sits down, and gets pricked.

28. Women do not protect children from cold or heat, with the result that the children often get sick. The women then arrange for amulets (*ta'wiz*) and charmed cords (*gande*).[1] They fail to give the children proper treatment or to take care in the future.

29. Women feed children when they are not hungry and similarly insist on giving food to guests. The children and the guests are the ones who have to suffer by eating when they are not hungry!

[LIST THREE:] PRACTICAL AND USEFUL WARNINGS

1. If at all possible, do not celebrate the marriages of your two sons or two daughters at the same time. There is sure to be a difference in the daughters-in-law. There is sure to be a difference in the bridegrooms. There is even certain to be a difference in the appearance, the style of clothing, the good nature, and the modesty and deportment of your own sons and daughters. There will, in fact, be other differences as well. People will certainly talk, denigrating one and praising the other. This unnecessarily hurts the feelings of the one who is criticized.

2. Do not trust everyone. In particular, do not entrust your house to anyone. You must not rely on another person until she has been tested in every possible way. Especially in cities, women go around gaining entrance to houses by pretending to have made the pilgrimage to Mecca and brought back a piece of the covering of the Ka'ba. They put on some kind of show, making amulets and charms, performing exorcisms, taking omens. Do not even let them into the house. Stop them right at the door. Such women have cleaned out many a house.

3. Do not get up and leave open the small boxes or *pan* containers in which you keep money, trinkets, and jewelry. Padlock them, or pick them up and take them with you.

4. As far as possible, do not buy anything on credit. If you are absolutely compelled to do so, ask the price and write it down with the date. Pay back the amount as soon as you have the money.

5. Always write down a list of the clothes given to the washerman's wife[2] and a list of grain given to the miller's wife, along with the grinding price. Do not depend on remembering what was said.

6. As far as possible, disburse your household expenses with great thrift and order. You should, in fact, save something out of whatever expense money you get.

7. Do not say anything in front of women who come into the house from outside—that is, anything you do not want known elsewhere. Such women go to ten different houses and recount each household's chitchat.

8. Do not cook flour or rice by guesswork. Calculate your amounts needed for both meals, measure and weigh everything, and then use it. Just ignore anyone who may tease you.

9. You should not let girls who go outside wear any jewelry at all. This is a danger to both life and property.

10. If some man comes to the door and claims to be an acquaintance or friend of your husband, father, or brothers, do not ever invite him into the house. Even if you keep yourself secluded, still do not invite him in. Nor should you let him handle any expensive item. Send him food or whatever as if he had no relationship with you at all. Do not be very affectionate or friendly. Do not use anything he gives you until some man of the household has acknowledged him. If he feels insulted, do not fret about it.

11. Similarly, if some unknown woman arrives in a palanquin or whatever and says, "I have been sent from such and such a house to invite you to come over," you must not get into the palanquin at her word. In short, do nothing at the request of people you do not know. Do not give them anything from your house, whether they are men or women, or whether they make a request in their own name or in the name of someone else.

12. Do not let any tree grow inside the house in a courtyard where the fruit could fall and hurt someone. The wood apple is an example of a fruit that can be dangerous.

13. Wear a little more clothing during the cold season. Often, women wear insufficient clothing and come down with a cold or a fever.

14. Children should be made to remember the names of their mother and father, even their grandfather. Ask them from time to time, so that they remember. The advantage is that if, God forbid, the child gets lost and someone asks, "Whose child are you? Who are your mother and father?" then the child will remember a name and say it. Someone or another will recognize the name. If the child does not remember and simply says in reply, "I am mama's, I am daddy's," there is no knowing which mama or which daddy.

15. A woman left her child somewhere and went off to do something. A cat came and scratched him so badly that he died. Two things are clear from this. First, you should never leave a child alone; and, second, there is no trusting cats, dogs, or other animals. Many women commit the folly of letting cats sleep with them. Why trust a cat? If at night it paws and bites or scratches or grabs your throat, then what will you do?

16. Always show medicine to a *hakim* before using it, and be sure that it is clean. Sometimes a blockhead druggist will give an altogether different medicine from what is intended. Sometimes something is mixed in whose effect is not good. If medicine is left over, put it in a carefully labeled bottle or packet. Otherwise, you may forget what it is and be forced to throw out what might have been an expensive medicine. Or someone may remember wrongly and mistakenly use the medicine in a different illness and cause harm.

17. Do not take loans heedlessly, nor should you lend out much. Lend out only as much as will not seem burdensome on you if it is not collected.

18. Before undertaking any new or important job, first seek the advice of some sensible, pious person who wishes you well.

19. Keep your money, property, and goods hidden. Mention them to no one.

20. When you write someone a letter, write your address completely and clearly. Even if you have written to the same person previously, do not think that because you wrote your address on the earlier letter, it is now not necessary. God knows if the first letter is still at hand. If it is not, you will cause the other person a great deal of trouble. Perhaps the person does not remember your address exactly. Or perhaps the person is illiterate and cannot tell the scribe but must show him.

21. If you have to make a journey by railway, keep your ticket with great care or leave it with your menfolk. Do not be heedless in the carriage and sleep too much. Do not tell your heart's secrets to another traveler, and do not discuss your belongings or jewelry. Do not eat anything anyone gives you, whether *pan,* sweets, cooked food—whatever. Do not sit on a train wearing jewelry; take it off and keep it in a box. When you arrive at your destination or at home, then you can wear whatever you want.

22. Be sure to carry enough money on a trip.

23. Do not tease insane people or even talk to them. Because they have no sense, God knows what they might say or do, and then you might be unfairly embarrassed or grieved.

24. Do not place your bare foot anywhere in the dark. Do not reach out in the dark. First, take the light of a lamp; then reach out your hand.

25. Do not tell everyone your secrets. Many people tell base people their secrets and then forbid them to tell anyone. This makes these people want to tell the secrets even more.

26. Always keep necessary medicines in your house.

27. Think of the outcome of every undertaking before beginning it.

28. Do not buy china and glass vessels and so forth unnecessarily, for it wastes a good deal of money.

29. If women are traveling on a train and the men with them are sitting in another car, the women should not get off the train as soon as they arrive at their destination, even if they hear the name or see it written on a board. Many cities have two or three stations. Perhaps the men with them will get off at another station, and, if the women should hurriedly get off now, then both will be in a predicament. Or the men may be dozing and not get off at all. If the women do get off, then again there will be trouble. They should get off only when the men of the household come.

30. On a trip, literate women should keep these things with them: a book of legal religious points, pencil and paper, some postcards, and a vessel for ablutions.

31. To the extent possible, do not ask any favors of people who are going on a trip, such as buying something for you or delivering some item or letter to someone. Such requests often inconvenience the other person. Moreover, you may be hurt by relying on someone who proves forgetful. You can send a letter anywhere you want for two *paisa*s—no, one *paisa*. You can order and send things by rail. If the thing is available here, you can buy it, even if it is at greater expense. It is not good to worry others in order to save yourself a little money. Often, something is of no consequence, but arranging to get it is a great bother. If you feel you have no choice, give the cost of the thing when you make the request, and, if the person is going by rail, give an additional sum, for all the luggage will have to be weighed.

32. On a train, or during any kind of journey, do not ever eat anything given to you by a stranger. Many evil people will feed someone poison or a drug and flee with their goods and luggage.

33. In the hurry of travel by train, remember not to sit in a class whose ticket is more expensive than the one you have. It is easy to be sure, because the ticket will be the same color that is painted on the car of that class. For example, the cheapest fare is third class. Its car is

yellow, and so is its ticket. You look at both colors and match them. The rule is the same for all classes.[3]

34. If a needle gets stuck in the fabric while you are sewing, do not pull at it with your teeth. You may break a tooth, or the needle may slip and prick your tongue or the roof of your mouth.

35. Always be sure to have a clipper for your fingernails. If from time to time the barber's wife is delayed, you can easily clip the nails yourself.

36. Never use a ready-made medicine without first showing the whole mixture to an experienced and intelligent *hakim* and getting his permission. You must be especially careful about any medicine put into the eyes.

37. Do not entrust any work you are not sure about to someone else, or there will be trouble and regret.

38. Do not interfere or give advice for someone else's good, unless the person is in your charge or explicitly asks for help. Then there is no harm.

39. Do not insist overmuch on someone's eating or staying longer, for it often causes trouble and distress to another. What good is love that produces annoyance and reproach?

40. Do not lift anything that is difficult to pick up. I have seen many people who suffered their whole lives long because in childhood they lifted an object that caused something to go wrong. Girls and women must be especially careful. The joints, veins, and muscles of their bodies are weaker and softer.

41. Do not get up and leave behind a needle, large or small, or anything of that sort. Someone may sit on it by mistake and get pricked.

42. Do not pass to anyone anything heavy or dangerous, or anything to eat or drink, over another person. It may slip from the hand.

43. If you have to punish someone else's children, do not beat them with a heavy stick or kick them or hit them with your fist. God save you if some delicate place is injured—you will have to take punishment instead of giving it. Do not strike the head or face.

44. If you go somewhere as a guest, as soon as you arrive you must inform the people of the house if you have already eaten. Out of politeness, they themselves will not ask. Everyone will sit quietly worrying, whether it is mealtime or not. They will go to the trouble of cooking food. When it arrives, you say that you have eaten. Then how they will regret it! Why not say something at the beginning? If someone invites you for a meal or a visit, get permission from the people of your

house. If it is arranged so that you have a choice, pick a time when the hostess will not have to prepare a meal.

45. It is not appropriate to conduct business dealings with people with whom there is great formality. Matters cannot be straightforward, nor can demands be made. One person thinks one thing in his or her heart; the other thinks something else. The result is not good.

46. Do not pick your teeth with a penknife or any such thing.

47. A child who is studying should always be fed something to strengthen the brain.

48. As far as possible, do not remain alone in the house at night. God knows what might happen. Necessity is, of course, another matter. But people staying alone have died, and no one knew it for days.

49. Do not let small children climb up on wells. In fact, if there is a well in the house, have a board put over it and always keep it locked. Never give children a vessel and send them for water. They may go themselves and start pulling the bucket from the well.

50. Scorpions and similar animals are often found under stones, grindstones, and bricks that are left undisturbed for many days. Do not pick these things up suddenly, but take a good, careful look, and then pick them up cautiously.

51. When you go to lie down on your bed, first brush the bedding off with a piece of cloth in case some creature has climbed in.

52. Put *nim* leaves and camphor in layers of silk and woolen cloth to prevent pests from getting in.

53. If you hide some money in the house, tell one or two people of the house on whom you can rely completely. One time, a woman hid five hundred rupees of her husband's earnings, and then she died. No one knew exactly where she had hidden the money. So they dug up the whole house, with no sign of it. The husband was a poor man. Think what a blow this must have been.

54. Many people padlock things but leave the keys lying around. This is a very bad mistake.

55. Kerosene does a lot of harm. Do not burn it. Make the lamp wick with your own hands, neither too thin nor too thick. Many maid-servants with no sense make very thick wicks that waste double or triple the oil for no reason. Pull the wick up carefully with a stick or wire made of iron or brass; otherwise, you will dirty your fingers. Take care when snuffing out the lamp. Do not wave your hand with such force that the lamp itself falls over. A fan or cloth is appropriate. Blow it out only if you have to.

56. If, at nighttime, you have to count money and so on, do it softly so that no one hears. There are thousands of enemies in this case.

57. Do not go out and leave a burning light in an empty house. Likewise, do not throw away a lighted match. Either extinguish it and throw it out, or throw it down and step on it so that not a spark remains.

58. Never let children play with matches, fire, or fireworks. In our neighborhood, a boy was striking matches. The fire caught, and it burned his entire chest. One time, a boy blew off his hand with fireworks.

59. If you take a lamp into the privy with you, be very careful that it does not catch your clothes on fire. Many people have been burned this way. Kerosene is an even greater bane.

[LIST FOUR:] PRECAUTIONS CONCERNING CHILDREN

1. Clean a child's hands, face, neck, ears, groin, and so on very thoroughly with a damp cloth every day. If dirt collects, the flesh becomes irritated and sores develop.

2. When a child urinates or defecates, immediately clean the area with water; do not just wipe it with a rag, which causes a rash and chafing on the child's body. If the weather is cold, make the water lukewarm.

3. Put the child to sleep alone, and, for safety, put two cots touching either side of the bedstead or put pillows on either side so that there is no danger of the child falling out of bed. If you put children to sleep near you in bed, you risk crushing them in their sleep when you turn over. Children's limbs are very delicate, and it is not surprising that they may be hurt easily. In one place, a baby was crushed in this way. In the morning they found her dead.

4. Do not get the child into the habit of too much swinging in a hanging cradle, because cradles are not found everywhere. Nor should you hold a child in your lap too much, for fear of weakness developing.

5. Teach a small child to turn to different people. It will cause the child trouble to be too much the pet of one person, for that person may die or be dismissed from service.

6. If the baby is to have a wet nurse, choose carefully one whose milk is good and who is young. Her milk should be fresh; that is, her own baby should not be more than seven months old. She should be good-natured and pious, not stupid, immodest, ill-behaved, miserly, or greedy.

7. When the baby begins to eat solid food, do not leave the feeding to a nurse. Have the feeding take place in front of you or in front of some other sensible and trustworthy person, to avoid having the child become sick from immoderate eating. If the child is sick, have the medicine prepared in your presence and given in your presence.

8. When old enough, the child should be taught to eat independently, with the hands washed first. Teach the habit of eating with the right hand and of eating little, so that the child will be saved from illness and greed.

9. The parents and anyone in charge of the baby should keep in mind that the child should always be clean. Be sure to have dirty hands and face washed immediately.

10. If possible, a maidservant or someone else should always be with the child and should watch to prevent too much running and jumping during play. She should not take the child onto a high building to play. She should encourage playing with the children of gentlefolk and forbid playing with the children of menials. She should not permit playing with too many children or allow playing in streets and alleys. She should not take the child with her to the bazaar and other such places. She should watch the child every minute and carefully teach the manners (*adab*) and rules (*qa'ida*) appropriate to the occasion. She should stop the child from doing anything inappropriate.

11. Insist that the nurse not let the child eat outside the house. If any food or drink is offered to the child, she should bring it back to the house and show it to the parents rather than just letting the child eat it.

12. Get the child into the habit of not asking for anything from anyone except family elders and the habit of not taking anything from anyone without permission.

13. Do not show too much affection, or a child will be spoiled.

14. Do not dress a child in very tight clothes or put too much trimming on the borders of the clothes. There is no objection to doing so on 'Id or Baqr 'Id, however.

15. Get the child into the habit of using a dentrifice and tooth-stick.

16. Teach children to become accustomed to all the rules concerning eating and drinking, conversation, meeting people, and mixing in company that are written in Book Seven. Do not trust that the children will learn these rules independently when they are grown up or think that you will get around to teaching them later. Remember, no one will do this teaching except you. A person can spend a whole lifetime in studying but still not develop good habits. As long as a person, however well educated, does not have good habits, that person will do things that are

rude and worthless and will sorrow the heart. Keep in mind also the points that are written about children near the conclusions of Book Five and Book Nine.

17. Do not heap too much study on the child. Start with one hour for studying, then two hours, then three hours. Schedule the work according to the child's strength and capacity. Do not teach for the entire day. For one thing, the child will begin to lose heart from tiredness; for another, the heart and brain are spoiled from too much work, and the mind and memory grow languid. The child begins to act slowly, like a sick person, and will not put any effort into studying.

18. Do not give holidays, except ordinary ones, unless there is some great necessity. Too many holidays make a person feel indifferent to work.

19. As far as possible, have each subject taught by someone who is very learned and advanced in it. Many people hire inexpensive teachers to teach. The children then learn incorrectly, and correction is difficult.

20. Always teach an easy lesson in the afternoon and a hard lesson in the morning, because later in the day a person tires and is distressed at a difficult lesson.

21. Be sure to teach children, especially girls, how to cook and sew.

22. A great difference in the age of bride and groom in marriage is a cause of many evils.

23. Do not marry off your children at a very early age; this too causes great harm.

24. Teach boys that they should not dry themselves with clods of earth in public after going to the toilet. This is especially forbidden in front of girls and women.

[LIST FIVE:] GOOD COUNSEL ON GOOD ACTS

1. It is wrong to reproach someone about some old offense. When something new happens, women have the bad habit of insisting on bringing up old grievances that were already cleared up and pardoned. This is a sin and increases grief and vexation in the heart once again.

2. Do not complain about your in-laws when you go to your parents' home. Many a complaint is a sin and a form of impatience. Often, it causes grief to grow on both sides. In the same way, do not praise and boast of your own parents' home to your in-laws. Often, this is the sin of pride and boasting. Your in-laws will feel that the daughter-in-law does not value them—and they will begin to devalue her.

3. Do not get in the habit of chattering away. When you talk a great deal, you will certainly come out with something inappropriate, and the outcome will be grief in this world and sin in the next.

4. As far as possible, have no one else do your work; do your work with your own hands. In fact, you should do the work of others. This will bring you reward and make you dear to everyone's heart.

5. Never be familiar with women who come to the house to talk about this and that; do not lend them your ear at all. Even listening to them is a sin, and sometimes there is further wickedness.

6. If you hear some complaint about your mother-in-law, sister-in-law, the wife of your husband's older or younger brother, or any relative close or far, do not keep it in your heart. Either decide it is a lie and expunge it, or, if you lack resolve for this, confront the person who told you face-to-face and clear it up. Then wickedness will not grow.

7. Do not always be strict and harsh with your servants. Watch your children, and stop them from tormenting the servants or their children. These people, out of respect, will say nothing, but they will curse you in their hearts. And even if they do not, you have surely committed the sin of oppression.

8. Do not waste your time in foolishness. Set aside a good block of time for teaching girls the Qur'an and books of religion. At least, after the Qur'an, be sure to have them read this book, BIHISHTI ZEWAR, from start to finish. Whether the girls are yours or someone else's, be sure they learn some skills. Until they have finished the Qur'an, however, do not have them do any other work. When they have finished the Qur'an and done it well, have them read in the morning, then take a break and have their meal, then practice writing. In the remainder of the day, teach them cooking and sewing.

9. Do not have the girls who come to you to study do the housework in your house or look after your children. Treat them like your own offspring.

10. Never take on any worry or burden for the sake of appearances. It leads to nothing but sin or misfortune.

11. Do not make a rule of needlessly changing your outfit and bedecking yourself with jewelry when you go out. The only motive in doing this is to make onlookers think that you are important. Thus the intention itself is a sin. Dressing up, moreover, makes you late, and that causes all kinds of harm. Keep yourself humble and simple. Sometimes, you should simply go out in the clothes you were wearing; sometimes, if the clothes are too dirty or if there is some occasion, you should change as quickly and easily as possible, and let that be enough.

12. When getting back at someone, do not air the faults of that person's family or deceased loved ones. This is a sin and causes unnecessary grief to others.

13. When you have finished using someone else's belongings, or when a vessel is empty, return it immediately. If by chance no one is able to take it back, do not mix it up with your things that are in use, but keep it separately so that it is not damaged. It is a sin, moreover, to use someone else's belongings without permission.

14. Do not cultivate the habit of fine food and drink. The times do not always remain the same, and at some point everyone has to suffer.

15. Do not forget anyone's favor, however small. If anyone wishes a favor of you, however great it may be, do not boast of your kindness.

16. At any time when there is no work, the best occupation is reading books. The names of a number of books are given at the end of this book. Look over the list. Never read books whose influence is not good.

17. Never shout when you talk. How shameful if your voice should reach outside!

18. If you get up at night and the people of the house are sleeping, do not go banging and clattering about. You had to wake up—fine; but why wake up others? Do what you do quietly. Open the door panel quietly, get water quietly, spit quietly, walk about quietly, cover the jug quietly.

19. Do not laugh and jest with elders. To do so is, in fact, a form of disrespect. Do not be informal with people of low status. Either they will become disrespectful, and you will dislike that, or they will debase you elsewhere by being disrespectful.

20. Do not praise your children or the people of your house in front of anyone.

21. If everyone stands up in a gathering (when it is no sin), you should not stay seated, for others may see pride in your doing so.[4]

22. If there is a grievance between two people, do not say anything to them that would be a cause for embarrassment if they become reconciled.

23. As long as money or kindness will solve a problem, do not resort to harshness or risk any danger.

24. Do not be angry at anyone in front of a guest. The guest's heart will not be as open as it was before.

25. Behave with courtesy, even toward an enemy, so that enmity does not increase.

26. Do not let pieces of bread lie around. Whenever you see them, pick them up, clean them, and eat them. If you cannot eat them, give

them to some animal. Do not brush crumbs off a cloth onto an area where people may walk.

27. When you have finished eating, do not get up and leave, for that would be impolite. First, have the vessels removed; then get up.

28. Insist that girls not play with boys, because that spoils the habits of both. The girls should withdraw when unrelated boys come to the house, even if the boys are young.

29. Never tickle anyone. People are often sorry they have done so when someone gets hurt. Do not laugh out loud so much that other people get upset and begin to quarrel. It is especially stupid to joke with guests, as people often do with a wedding party.

30. Do not sit at the head of a bed on which your elders are sitting. If, for some reason, they should insist that you sit there, then it is a courtesy to do what they say.

31. If you borrow something from someone, first of all treat it with great care, and then, when the container is empty, send it back immediately. Do not wait for them to ask for it. In the first place, they do not know that it is now empty. Second, they may not ask, out of politeness. They may not remember where it is and may be worried when they need it. Similarly, if you owe a loan, keep it in mind, and when you have any means at all, pay back as much as you can.

32. If ever out of some necessity you have occasion to go somewhere by foot, whether night or day, take your anklets and other ornaments from your feet and carry them in your hand. Do not go along the road letting them jingle.

33. Do not open the door suddenly to go into a place where someone is completely alone. God knows if the person may be naked, partly undressed, or sleeping, and thus unfairly disturbed. First, call out very softly and ask permission to come in. If permitted, go in; otherwise, be silent and come another time. Of course, if there is something urgent, call out and awaken the person, but until that person speaks, you should still not go in.

34. Never speak ill of a city or a people (*qaum*) in front of someone you do not know, because that person may belong to that city or people. Then you will certainly be embarrassed.

35. In the same way, do not say, "What idiot did this?" or anything of the sort if you do not know who did it. Perhaps someone you respect did it. When you find out, you will certainly be embarrassed.

36. Never take the side of a child who wrongs someone, especially not in the child's presence. To do so will spoil the child's behavior.

37. In the marriage of girls, look most to see whether the groom's temperament is God-fearing and pious. Such a person always keeps his

wife in comfort. If a person has considerable wealth and no religion, he will not recognize his wife's rights, nor will he be faithful. Indeed, he will not even give her money; or if he does give her some, he will squander more.

38. It is the habit of many women to call someone from seclusion by standing behind something and throwing a clod of dirt to summon her. Sometimes the clod hits someone. Do not do anything where there is a chance of causing trouble to someone. Sit somewhere and bang a brick or something else to make a noise.

39. Sew some mark, flower, or other sign on your clothes so that they do not get mixed up at the washerman's house. Otherwise, you will mistakenly use someone else's clothes and they will use yours. You will unintentionally commit a sin and have material harm, too.

40. When the Arabs want something from an elder as a relic, they customarily take something along and ask him to use it for a few days and then give it back to them. This causes the elder no anxiety. Otherwise, if twenty people each ask for a piece of cloth, he will not have even an old rag left in his bag. In our Hindustan, people just out-and-out ask. They should consider the desirability of adopting the custom of the Arabs.

41. If you want to give a suitable answer to someone's argument, you should speak for yourself. Do not refer to someone else, saying, "You say this, but so and so disagrees." If the person repeats your assertion, the person you quote will be unhappy.

42. Do not make an accusation on the basis of guesses and suspicion without investigation. This causes great heartache.

II. [Household Work]

ON HANDICRAFTS AND OCCUPATIONS

Many poor women who are widowed with no resources have no way to provide for their food and clothing. They are so worn down with worry and troubles that God is their only refuge. There are two solutions to their problems: one is to remarry; a second is to earn a pittance by the skill of their hands. The ignorant people of Hindustan, however, condemn both remarriage and manual work. Yet at the same time no one has the means to take on the expenses of these poor women. Just how are these unfortunate widows supposed to manage?

Women! Even if you cannot control other people, Almighty God has given you power over your own heart and hands and feet. Do not let your heart speak ill of anyone who remarries or earns her own living. A woman of marriageable age should marry. An older woman or one who demurs—not because she considers marriage a sin but because she just does not wish it or is upset at the disruption it would bring—should have a chance to manage by some respectable skill. Simply ignore anyone who looks down on such a woman or laughs at her. Remarriage has been discussed in Book Six; a discussion of respectable occupations follows here.

Women! Would the prophets have engaged in manual labor if it were dishonorable (*be'izzat*)? Who is more deserving of respect? It is in the *hadis* that the Apostle of God, *God's blessings and peace upon him,* herded goats. In fact, he declared that there was no prophet who did not graze goats. He also declared that the best livelihood is that of one's own hands. Hazrat Da'ud, *on whom be peace,* earned a living by the skill of his hands. Our Apostle^s declared all these things. A description of many of these activities of the prophets is given in the Noble Qur'an, and many are described in books written about the prophets. A few examples follow, based on these descriptions.

MANUAL LABOR PERFORMED BY PROPHETS AND ELDERS

Hazrat Adam^a worked the land, ground flour, and baked bread. Hazrat Idris^a worked both as a scribe and as a tailor. Hazrat Nuh^a carved the ark from wood, thus doing the work of a carpenter. Hazrat Hud^a engaged in commerce, as did Hazrat Salih^a. Hazrat Zu'l-qarnain, a great king who was even called a prophet by some, would weave *zanbil*s (which are something like the baskets we have here). Hazrat Ibrahim^a plowed the land and did construction; he built the house of the Ka'ba. Hazrat Lut^a worked the land. Hazrat Isma'il^a made arrows and practiced archery. Hazrat Ishaq^a, Hazrat Ya'qub^a, and their sons grazed goats and marketed the young goats. Hazrat Yusuf^a sold wheat at a time of famine. Hazrat Ayyub^a reared goats and camels and worked the land. Hazrat Shu'aib^a grazed goats. Hazrat Musa^a for many years grazed goats (which were in fact part of the bride-price he paid for his wife). Hazrat Harun^a engaged in commerce. Hazrat Alyasa'^a worked the land. Hazrat Da'ud^a forged armor, thus doing the work of an ironsmith. Hazrat Luqman^a, a scholar of great wisdom, who was even called a prophet by some, grazed goats. Hazrat Sulaiman^a wove *zanbil*s. Hazrat Zakariya^a worked as a carpenter. Hazrat 'Isa^a dyed cloth for a shopkeeper. Our Prophet^s—in fact all the prophets, as mentioned above—tended goats.

These activities were not the main occupations of these prophets, but they did these jobs and did not feel ashamed of them. Of the many great saints and scholars whose books are authoritative, one wove cloth, one worked with leather, one cobbled shoes, one made sweets. Then who is—repent, repent!—more respected or of greater dignity than all of these?

EASY WAYS OF EARNING A LIVING

1. Making soap.
2. Making gold and silver lace edgings.
3. Doing *chikan* embroidery.
4. Making lace.
5. Making sashes.
6. Making buttons out of cotton cloth.
7. Knitting woolen and cotton socks.
8. Making neckwear.
9. Sewing and selling caps, vests, bodices, or shirts.
10. Making ink.
11. Dyeing cloth.
12. Doing gold-thread embroidery.
13. Embroidering caps like those sold in Meerut.
14. Sewing. (If a sewing machine can be procured, the work will go faster, and there will be great profit. Nowadays, machines have become quite cheap.)
15. Selling chicken eggs and chicks.
16. Painting boxes and bookstands.
17. Teaching girls.
18. Buying cotton, separating the seeds from the cotton, and selling both.
19. Spinning thread on a spinning wheel, or weaving cloth strips for cots (*nawar*) or cloth for sale.
20. Buying rice and selling it after separating out the chaff.
21. Binding books.
22. Making pickles and relishes.
23. Stringing and knotting string cots.
24. Making rope.
25. Making *nawar*.
26. Making and selling *churan* tablets or Solomon's salt.[5]
27. Making mats or fans out of date leaves.

28. Making and selling pomegranate and jujube fruit *sharbat*s or vinegar.
29. Trading in gold and silver edgings.
30. Tinning utensils.
31. Preparing tooth powder.
32. Printing cloth, such as turban cloths, prayer carpets, handkerchiefs, sheets, single sheets and quilts, and so on.
33. Storing mustard at harvest time and selling it when it becomes expensive after the harvest.
34. Grinding antimony to a fine powder or mixing some useful medicine in it, making it up into small packets, and selling it.
35. Curing and selling tobacco for smoking.
36. Making and selling biscuits or loaves of bread.
37. Weaving cords out of thread.
38. Making calx out of pewter or coral.

Opportunity presents many such light and easy jobs. Some of these cannot be mastered without a demonstration; you must learn them from a teacher. Any sensible person can learn the others by reading, for the method of doing them is written down clearly. Many of these jobs are useful for your own daily household routine. In Book Nine, we have included the recipes for making *churan,* Solomon's salt, pewter, and calx.

[RECIPES FOR HOUSEHOLD PRODUCTS AND FOOD]

A Method for Making Soap

Natron (*sajji*)	1 *man* [40 kg]
Lime	1 *man* [40 kg]
Castor oil (*tel rendi* or *gulu*)	9 *ser* [9 kg]
Fat	17 *ser* [17 kg][6]
Water	

The names and descriptions of all necessary utensils:[7]

1. One perforated ladle, either iron or wood, long-handled, of the sort used for cooking pilaf. It is used for stirring.
2. A vessel similar to the copper pot used for getting water in mosques, with a handle, able to hold 3 *ser* [3 liters] of water, made of "tin." It is for pouring the extract or liquid.

3. A utensil for removing the soap from the pot—for example, the kind of ladle used for serving pilaf or stew. This is for removing the soap from the pot and putting it into the tank.

First, place the natron in a clean place, such as a brick or masonry terrace or platform, so that dirt does not get mixed in. Break up the lumps of natron with a stone or rock, then pour in the lime. If the lime is lumpy, sprinkle water on it so that the lumps dissolve and can be mixed in. Mix the lime and natron together very thoroughly. Prepare a brick or masonry vat by putting boards around a platform, as in the diagram below, and place four bricks at the four corners.

[The diagram shows a square vat with an outlet through the wall on one side. A brick is placed diagonally in each corner.]

Place an iron screen, like a strainer, on the four bricks. The mesh should be large. Over the screen, place burlap large enough to extend over the sides of the vat. This provides a filter. Pour the mixture of lime and natron from above, and it will drip through the burlap and the screen into the vat below. The bricks keep the screen elevated. If no screen is available, you can attach a mat of bamboo or wood, and put the burlap over that.

(If you are making only a little soap, you do not need to use a vat. You can use a string cot placed over a container, as women do when they stretch cloth over a cot to drip safflower color [*kusum*, used for red dye].)[8]

Place a pot below the mouth of a conduit attached to the vat. After the lime and natron have been poured, fill the vat with water, but do not stir it. The liquid from the vat will drip through the conduit into the pot. When the pot is full, remove it, and replace it with an empty one. Add more water to the tank to replace what drips out. When you have finished, or almost finished, stir the vat and remove the first batch of water. You can identify the first water by its red color; the second water is a lighter red. The third water is whitish. Thus three grades of water can be separated, although this is in fact not completely necessary. There is no harm if you do not separate all the grades, but you should reserve a small pot of the third or final batch of water.

When all the water has dripped through, pour a small pot of clean water into the first pot you have filled, then add the fat and the oil. Bring to a boil. Pour in a little of the last batch of water that you have already separated out, adding more as the mixture thickens. As the water boils off, continue to add a little of the water reserved in the other pots. ("A little" equals the amount in a little spouted vessel for drinking.) Finish adding water in this way, and cook thoroughly.

When the mixture is very thick, remove some with a perforated ladle, cool it, and shape it into a ball with your hands. If it is sticky, it needs to be cooked more. When it is no longer sticky, make a ball. If it hardens immediately into soap, the mixture is at the right consistency. Lower the heat—in fact, remove all the wood and fire from below. After a short while, collect the mixture in a second vat made either of bricks or of four boards surrounded on four sides by bricks to keep the boards from falling.

[The diagram illustrates a square vat.]

Place an old thick cotton cloth without holes or patches inside the vat; the cloth should reach over the sides. Pour the mixture from the pot into the tank, using a ladle. Stir it with a perforated ladle, so that the mixture dries out quickly, then pour in some more and stir. Continue adding more in this manner until the pot is empty. When the mixture cools, remove the boards that have formed the improvised container, spread out the soap, and cut it into small pieces with a wire.

The hearth on which the pot is placed for boiling should be round like the pot.

[A drawing shows the hearth in the shape of a horseshoe, allowing firewood to be added through the opening.]

The opening of the hearth where wood is placed is called a *bhatti*. The pot should be placed on it in such a way that the fire reaches all sides equally.[9]

A Method for Printing Cloth

Yellow color

Good Nagauri gum	¼ *ser* [¼ kg]
Water	1 *ser* [1 liter]
Wheat flour	6 *masha* [8 gm]
Ghee	6 *masha* [8 gm]
Green vitriol (*kasis*)	¼ *ser* [¼ kg]
Red "twill"	3 heaping *masha* [5 gm]

Steep the gum in water. When the gum and water become a paste, thoroughly mix in the wheat flour and the ghee. Then mix in the green vitriol and red "twill" (which is sold in the bazaar), and dissolve thoroughly in the paste. Filter the mixture through a cloth, and let it harden. It can now be used for printing cloth. Hold the dye in a piece of cloth, and press a block on it to stamp the cloth you want to print. Blocks made with wooden flowers and vines are sold in Lucknow, or you can have them made locally by a carpenter.

[Thanawi next offers directions for preparing a black dye used in block printing; for making ink; for making "English (-style) ink"; for painting and varnishing wood; for tinning vessels (e.g., copper vessels); and for soldering. Later editions provide a recipe for making "fountain pen ink that can surpass Swan Ink!" Also in later editions store-bought brushes replace the squirrels' tails, bird feathers, and cloth-mesh sticks originally recommended for use in these processes.]

A Method of Curing Smoking Tobacco

Tobacco
Syrup or molasses

Select tobacco of a type agreeable to your constitution. Pound it well; then add syrup or molasses. In summer, add an amount somewhat more than the tobacco itself; in the rainy season, somewhat less; and in winter, an equal amount. Mix and pound again. Pounding tobacco is difficult, so it is best to hire a conscientious and respectable shopkeeper or laborer.

[The recipe above is a reminder of the holism characteristic of this culture: temperament, weather, and food all interact and, ideally, create a balance. Different personalities use different tobacco, prepared differently in different seasons. In the original, a recipe follows for "fragrant smoking tobacco"; then a section on bread begins.]

A Recipe for Making Bread Loaves, "Biscuits,"
and So Forth

Leaven
Flour

Add leaven to semolina or white flour, and knead it well. Pound it on a board and place it in a mold. Make the oven very hot; then reduce the heat by removing all flames and ashes. Place the mold(s) inside and close the opening of the oven. When the bread is done, take it out. Detailed instructions follow.

A Recipe for Leaven for Bread

Cloves

Small cardamom

Nutmeg

Mace

Seed of *indar-jau* [*Nerium anti-dysentricum*, or sparrow's tongue]

Samandar-phen [*Sepia officie-nalis*, or dorsal scale or bone of the cuttlefish]

Samandar-sokh [*Convolvus argenteus* or *speciosus*]

Tal makhana [*Barleria/Aster-canthce longifolia* or seed of *Solanum indicum*]

Flower of the water lily (*Phul makhana*)

Lotus seeds

Root of *munga* [*Hyperanthera moringa*]

Rose flower

Indian rose-chestnut [*Messua ferrea*]

Cinnamon

Seed of the *kanghi* tree [*Sida populifolia* or *indica*]

Caltrop [*Ruellia longifolia* or *Tribulus lanciginosus*]

China root [*Smilax china*]

Cubebs [*Piper cubeba*]

Saffron

Yoghurt

Wheat flour

Grind and strain 6 *masha* [7–8 gm] of saffron and 3 *masha* [4–5 gm] each of all the ingredients above except the last three. Keep the mixture tightly sealed in a corked bottle. The measure of each ingredient can be as little as 1½ *masha* [1–2 gm], but not less than that. Whenever needed, take 1½ *masha* of powder from the bottle; stir it with 1¼ *tola* [19 gm] of yoghurt, and beat it with two fingers for one minute. Then add enough wheat flour to make a consistency that is not too stiff. The mixture should stay as soft as your earlobes. This is the clue.

Shape the mixture into a ball with the palms of your hands. Tie the ball loosely into a cloth. Hang it on a peg, and leave it for three days. On the fourth day, examine it to see if the leaven has risen. If so, remove the crust that has formed on the outside of the ball and extract the sticky leaven. Add 1 *chhatank* [60 gm] of yoghurt to flour as above—that is, so that the consistency is as soft as your earlobes—and mix in the leaven extracted from the ball, using your hands just as you do to crush tobacco. Form a new ball, wrap it in the cloth, and hang it up for six hours. Remove the dry crust and extract the leaven. Again add flour, this time to 2 *chhatank* [120 gm] of yoghurt, and mix in the leaven. Put this in a cloth and hang it up for another six hours.

Repeat the procedure: take out the leaven, mix flour into 2 *chhatank* of yoghurt, mix and hang up the ball. After six hours, take it down and, for the fourth time, extract the leaven. This time, you do not need to remove the dry crust on the ball. Add flour to 2 *chhatank* of yoghurt just as before, and mix in the leaven thoroughly by hand. When this is mixed, keep it carefully in a basket or some container.

Remove it from the container after four hours. Add flour to ½ *chhatank* [30 gm] of yoghurt, and mix the ½ *chhatank* of leaven into it and hang it up.

After six hours, take it down again, just as you have done before. Keep on adding flour, just as before, and the leaven will keep on increasing. Remove ½ *chhatank* of leaven and use the remainder to make "double" *roti,* that is, bread loaves. The next time you need leaven for bread loaves, again reserve ½ *chhatank* and use the rest for your bread. In this way, you can keep making leaven indefinitely.

[Recipes are then given for bread loaves, "double" *roti;* sweet bread (*nan*); sweet "biscuits"; and salty "biscuits." Recipes for preserving vegetables and fruits follow: mango pickle; sweet-and-sour pickle; salt-water pickle; a long-lasting turnip pickle; nine-jewel chutney; preserves of gourd, apple, myrobalan, or mango; saltwater mango; and lemon pickle. The recipe for nine-jewel chutney is given here as an example.]

A Recipe for Nine-Jewel Chutney

Mango pulp	1 *ser* [1 kg]
Vinegar or essence of mint	1¼ *ser* [1¼ kg]
Garlic	½ *chhatank* [30 gm]
Red pepper	½ *chhatank* [30 gm]
Kalaunji	2 *tola* [30 gm]
Anise seed	2 *tola* [30 gm]
Dry mint	2 *tola* [30 gm]
Cloves	4 *masha* [5 gm]
Nutmeg	4 *masha* [5 gm]
Ginger	1 *chhatank* [60 gm]

Salt	1 *chhatank* [60 gm]
Sugar or raw sugar	1 *pa'o* [250 gm]

Mash the mango pulp in vinegar. Then grind all the spices in vinegar and mix them into the mango. Boil the sugar, mango pulp, and spices in the remaining vinegar. When syrupy, the mixture is ready to use. If you want to give the chutney some color, add 2 *tola* [30 gm] of turmeric, roasted over hot ashes, then ground.[10]

[This section ends with directions for preparing dyes in an array of shades, not just puritan browns and greys. They include black, yellow, orange (two variations), emerald (two variations), brown or purple, a reddish brown or purple (colorfast), grey, green, pale green, almond, blue-grey (colorfast), red (colorfast), pistachio (two variations), and sky blue. There is also a recipe for mordant, should it not be available in the market. The ingredients include ochre earth, fruits and vegetables and their rind, milk, rice and flour starch, henna, indigo, spices, bark, gall nuts, sugar, flowers, and minerals.]

III. [Weights and Measures]

[WRITING NUMBERS BY *RAQAM*]

[This section begins by introducing the *raqam* system of writing numbers, which was widely used until recent years for keeping accounts. The combinations of symbols, based on letters, are taught by explaining their logic, as the following excerpt suggests.]

To write "three *chhatank*," think, "What are three *chhatank*?" You know this is half a *pa'o* plus one *chhatank*, so join the symbols for *chhatank* and for half a *pa'o*. . . . Similarly, to write "one *ser*, less one *chhatank*," think of what you have just said—"one *chhatank* less than a *ser*"—and it is obvious that this is one-half *ser* plus one-quarter *ser* plus one-half *pa'o* plus one *chhatank*. Just write all of the symbols for each one of these items, one after another. . . . Think first of the component parts of whatever it is you have to write. Write the symbols for each component, and, at the end, make the [terminal] symbol. . . . Remember, when writing several symbols together, to write the symbol for the largest item first and then the symbols for the smaller ones.

[The next section teaches the *raqam* system for money, followed by instructions for lengths (*gaz, girih*) and apothecary weights (*masha, tola*). Instructions for doing addition follow.]

ADDITION OF SMALL AND LARGE NUMBERS

You must learn this skill thoroughly. If you buy several things, you have to add all the prices together to see what the total is. Some of the prices, however, will be in rupees, some in *ana*s, and some in *paisa*s. Or perhaps you have grain sent to the house on various occasions, and some arrives in *man,* some in *ser,* and some in half-*ser* or quarter-*ser* amounts. Or perhaps a goldsmith makes several things of gold, some in *tola,* some in *masha,* and some in *ratti.* How do you know the total amount of gold? You need the accounting skill of addition.

The rule is first to write all the amounts in rupees and *ana*s, or all the weights in *ser* and *chhatank* or in *tola* and *masha.* Now, go through them to see which is the smallest amount or the smallest weight. Then look for the next larger amount or weight, and keep adding them in your head. As you do so, see if the total is or is not divisible by the next higher denomination or measure. If the division is even, add the quotient to the total of the next higher denomination or measure. If the division is not even, write the remainder in the column for the smallest denomination or measure, and carry over the quotient to the total of the next higher column. If it is a multiple of the next higher amount or weight, add it after dividing to the next higher denomination or measure. If it is not a multiple, then divide as before, and write the remainder with the previous one, adding the quotient to the higher denomination or measure. Finish the addition in this manner to the end. The final result is called the sum total. [Thanawi provides a detailed example for adding the cost of five sewing items.]

RECORDING DAILY INCOME AND EXPENDITURE

This is called account-keeping. It is most useful, for one may forget a mental note, or a husband may not believe what you tell him. Sometimes, for no good reason, doubt arises when a person first hesitates before speaking. Sometimes, if you forget, you have to either tell a lie or be embarrassed by saying nothing. Account-keeping also gives you control over the servants. If they take something, they cannot deny it. You will know that ghee was purchased on a certain day and that one *chhatank* is used daily. One *ser* of ghee, therefore, lasts sixteen days.

How did it get used up in eight days? The cook cannot say, "Madam, you forget. It was purchased sixteen days ago."

You should consider it incumbent upon yourself to write down the income (the amount you receive) as well as the expenditures (the amount you spend). Morever, do not depend on making your entries later, for they are often forgotten by then. An important advantage in writing things down is that you will not wrongly suspect anyone of ill-doing. For example, if you had ten rupees and spent six, but remembered spending only five, there would be four rupees left—but, according to your memory, there should be five. You spent one somewhere, but you forgot, and now you blame everyone for stealing it. "So and so must have taken it!" Do not let anything go by without writing it down. If you send out clothes, write it down. If you give pots to the tinsmith, write it down. If you pay laborers, write it down. If you order something, write it down; and write it down again when the order arrives. We will now review the rules for recording income and expenditure. Whether you want to keep the account by the week or by the month is up to you.

[A sample account for the month of Ramazan is given, arranged as a table. (An original footnote explains the ditto marks used in the account; borrowed from English, they were presumably an unfamiliar sign.) A list of income is kept, by date: the example shows a balance carried forward (Rs. 10), with additional payments from a clerk, a grain sale, and a sister-in-law's repayment (totaling Rs. 24/7, that is, 24 rupees, 7 *ana*s). A second list shows expenditures: rice, ghee, sugar, milk, spices, oil for the mosque, and food for students before and after the fast. These last two items of charity cost a little more than half the cost of the foodstuffs: Rs. 7/4, in contrast to Rs. 13/4. The example suggests both piety and good management, with figures carefully checked.]

Here is another useful check. Add the amount written as the balance to the expenses. If this amount is equal to the total assets, then the account is correct. If not, the balance is wrong. If it is wrong, go back and figure out how much cash is left after your expenses, and write it down. Then calculate again the sum of the balance and the amount of the expenses. Check to see if it is or is not equal to the total assets. . . . Remember all this carefully. If there is a deficit, subtract that amount from the expenses and see if that amount equals the total assets. If not, figure it out again.

SHORTCUTS IN CALCULATIONS

There are some little rules that make it easy to do mental calculations. A few, which are the most useful, are written here.

1. If a *man* of something costs a certain number of rupees, 2½ *ser* will cost that same number of *ana*s. For example, if a *man* of rice costs 8 rupees, 2½ *ser* of rice will cost 8 *ana*s.

2. If a certain number of *ser* of something cost 1 rupee, that same number of *man* will cost 40 rupees. For example, if you get 1½ *ser* of ghee for 1 rupee, you will get 1½ *man* for 40 rupees.

3. If a certain number of *ser* of something cost 1 rupee, a *chhatank* of that item will cost 1 *ana*. For example, if 20 *ser* of wheat cost 1 rupee, 20 *chhatank* will cost 1 *ana*. (This amount equals 1¼ *ser*.)

4. If 5 *ser* (also called *dhari* or *panseri*) of something cost 1 rupee, a *man* will cost 8 rupees. For example, if you get 4 five-*ser* measures of wheat for 1 rupee, you will get 4 *man* for 8 rupees.

5. If you get a certain number of yards of cloth for 1 rupee, you will get 1 *girah* for 1 *ana*. For example, if 4 yards of coarse long-cloth (*latha*) cost 1 rupee, 4 *girah* will cost 4 *ana*s.

These few rules for quick calculation are quite sufficient for women. If you need to know more, ask someone for help, because these rules are hard to understand from simply reading them.[11]

IV. Useful Vocabulary and Correction of Mispronounced Words

THE ARABIC AND URDU NAMES OF MONTHS

Arabic	*Urdu*
Muharram	Daha[12]
Safar	Tera tezi[13]
Rabi'u'l-awwal	Bara wafat[14]
Rabi'u's-sani	Miranji[15]
Jumada'l-awwal	Shah Madar[16]
Jumada'l-akhir	Khwajaji[17]
Rajab	Maryam roza[18]

Sha'ban	Shab-i Barat[19]
Ramazan	Ramazan
Shawwal	'Id[20]
Zi-qa'd	Khali[21]
Zi'l-hij	Baqr 'Id[22]

HINDI MONTHS AND SEASONS

The four months of Phagan, Chet, Baisakh, and Jith are called summer.

The four months of Cisarh, Sawan, Bhadun, and Kanwar (also called Asoj) are the rainy season.

The four months of Katak, Aghan (also called Mangsir), Pus (or Puh), and Magh (also called Mah) are winter. The rain during these months is called Mahawat.

Remember that every third year the intercalary month called Laund comes twice. Also keep in mind that these months do not begin from the new moon but from the full moon, that is, from the fourteenth night of the moon.

The season in which wheat and chick-peas are produced is called the spring season, Rabi' or Sarhi. The season in which rice and small grains are produced is called the winter season, Kharif or Sawani.

THE NAMES OF THE DIRECTIONS

The direction in which the sun rises is called *mashriq;* it is also called *purab.* Where the sun sets is called *maghrib;* it is also called *pacchim* or *pachan.* If you turn your face toward the east, the direction of your right hand is called *janub* or *dakkhin,* and the direction of the left hand is called *shimal, uttar,* or *pahar.* The Pole Star is visible in this direction. [For each direction, the Sanskrit-based word is given second.]

THE CORRECTION OF SEVERAL FREQUENTLY MISPRONOUNCED WORDS

Below is a list of incorrect words in parentheses, with the correct form of the word next to them. Keep the correct forms in mind when speaking, for incorrect speech is a defect. [A list of twenty-two words is given.]

V. [The Post Office and Letter Writing]

These regulations are useful for literate people who use the mail.[23]

POST OFFICE REGULATIONS

Rules for Letters

1. In sending a one-*paisa* postcard, write on the address side the name and address of the person to whom it is going. You can also write your own name, address, and the date, but do not write anything else. If, as people often do, you write something like "answer required," the card becomes postage-due and the person to whom the card is addressed will have to pay two *paisa*s.

2. In using a two-*paisa* envelope, it is permitted to write on the envelope. But do not scribble all over it, in case the postman has to write something on the envelope in English.

3. You can make a postcard by putting a one-*paisa* stamp on a piece of good thick paper the same size as a postcard. If you do not put on a stamp, the card will arrive with two *paisa*s' postage due. This kind of card is called a "private postcard." On these cards, you can write the message on the address side as well as on the reverse. Keep in mind, however, that you should leave space for the address, the stamp, and the post office cancellation. If you put a two-*paisa* stamp on a blank envelope, that becomes a two-*paisa* envelope; if you do not put on a stamp, it will arrive with postage due. If on some occasion you do not have a stamp, you can cut out the picture from a government postcard for a one-*paisa* stamp or the picture from a government envelope for a two-*paisa* stamp. Previously, this was not allowed, but it now is, as a convenience.

4. Do not erase the writing on a card or envelope in such a way that the stamp gets dirty. Do not use a tattered stamp that appears suspect. Do not write your own name on the stamp or draw any line on it. Keep the stamp completely clean. Otherwise, the stamp will be useless and the letter regarded as postage-due.

5. Many people sew one card to another and send both. These cards will have postage due. If you want to send a card for an answer, ask for an attached card that costs two *paisa*s.

6. Put the letter in an envelope and weigh it on a little pair of scales called a *nazazi*. On one side, put a one-and-one-half-*paisa* coin,* and

---

* In fact, the calculation is by *tola* and *masha,* but a *paisa* is suggested for convenience because it is the same weight as six *masha,* just as either one rupee or two *paisa*s are the same weight as one *tola.*

weigh it. If the letter weighs less than the one-and-one-half *paisa* coin, it can be mailed with a half-*ana* stamp. If it weighs more, but less than three *paisa*s, it can be mailed with a one-*ana* stamp. For an even heavier letter, reckon by its equivalence to coins: two half-*ana* stamps for the weight of a three-*paisa* coin. If you send a letter without a stamp, it will arrive with postage due, and the person addressed will have to pay double the amount of stamps required by weight.

7. Do not write several letters and put them in one envelope, expecting the person who gets the letter to go about distributing them. This is against post office regulations and is also forbidden in religious law. Of course, there is no harm if you just write two or three lines to someone in a letter sent to someone else.

8. If you send bank notes and so forth in a letter, you should have insurance, for safety. Insurance is discussed below in relation to parcels.

9. If you put fewer stamps than needed on letters or other post, the person addressed will have to pay double whatever is deficient.

Rules for Book Post

If you wrap any book, newspaper, notice, or paper (other than a letter) in such a way that both ends are left open, it can be sent book post. Weigh it against ten rupees (or twenty *paisa* coins); if the parcel weighs less, it can be mailed with a half-*ana* stamp. If it weighs more than ten rupees but less than twenty (or less than forty *paisa*s), use a one-*ana* stamp. For any weight greater than this, use a two-*ana* stamp for every ten rupees' worth of weight, or else it will be postage-due. Increase the number of stamps accordingly. If you do not, the person addressed will have to pay twice as much as the stamps required according to weight. If the addressee refuses the parcel, the sender will have to pay the double amount. It is forbidden to place a letter inside something sent book post, unless a stamp is placed on the letter.

Rules for Parcels

1. A parcel is any item—jewelry, money, medicine, perfume, and so on—that can be closed up in a container or box, wrapped in a covering cloth, and tied on all four sides. Weigh a parcel against twenty rupees or forty *paisa*s. If the parcel weighs less than this, put on a two-*ana* stamp. If it is heavier, but less than forty rupees' worth of weight, put on a four-*ana* stamp. For every forty rupees' worth of weight, add an additional two-*ana* stamp.

2. You are permitted to put one letter inside a parcel.

3. Put hot sealing wax on top of every seam of the parcel, and stamp it with a seal in several places. This protects the parcel.

4. Do not make the parcel so small that there is no place for the post office seal.

5. If the things being sent are valuable, insurance is necessary. Give the post office person a list of the goods and their value. If the value is not more than fifty rupees, one *ana* of insurance will be charged; from fifty rupees to one hundred, the charge is two *ana*s. The cost of insurance increases by two *ana*s for each hundred rupees. You must get a voucher from the post office for the insurance. Keep it carefully.

6. Parcels cannot be sent postage-due.

General Rules

1. If you especially want to protect your letters, book post, or parcels, have them registered. To do this, put on two *ana*s' worth of extra stamps. Either add the stamps yourself or send cash for this to the post office with a servant who will ask the post office clerk to register it. He will get a receipt. Keep it carefully. Registration is required if you want to send money. It is safest to send money by sending half a note in an envelope. When its receipt is confirmed, then send the other half.

2. If you want a receipt from the person to whom you are writing, so no one can deny that the letter or parcel arrived, tell the postal clerk that you want a "registered answer." This costs one additional *ana*. You will get an ordinary receipt from the clerk, and, when the item arrives, the postman will have the recipient sign a piece of paper that will also be sent to you.

3. Have your address and name and the address and name of the recipient written fully and clearly on everything sent, so that all will arrive expeditiously. If the mail does not arrive, or if it is refused, then there will be no delay in returning the items to you. Otherwise, the mail is sent to the office of unclaimed letters. There, it is opened to see if there is a clear return address inside. If so, it will be sent to you, but only after a delay.

Rules for Money Orders

1. To send money from one place to another by means of a money order, request a printed form in Urdu from the post office. Fill out the name and address of the person to whom you are sending the order,

your name and address, and the amount of rupees and *ana*s as indicated. Send the paper and the money to the post office along with the fee (as explained below). You will get a receipt. Keep it carefully. When the money arrives, the postman will get the signature of the person on a piece of paper that will be sent to you from the post office. At that point, it is no longer necessary to save the original receipt.

2. Fees for money orders are as follows: for up to five rupees, the charge is one *ana,* even if you are sending only one or two *ana*s; up to ten rupees, the charge is two *ana*s; up to fifteen rupees, three *ana*s; up to twenty-five rupees, four *ana*s. You can keep going by this reckoning: for example, the fee for one hundred rupees is one rupee.

3. There is a bit of blank space on the form. In this space, you are permitted to write a note to the person to whom the money order is being sent. Write whatever you like.

Written above are some of the rules that are most useful. If you need to know more, inquire at the post office. These rules do change; but when they change, the information will be made available.

RULES FOR WRITING AND READING LETTERS

In Book One, you studied the way to write letters to people who are older and younger than you, as well as the way to address envelopes. Here are some additional useful and essential points for letter writing.

1. Learn to make a pen.

2. When you are first learning to write, use a slate with a thick pen. When your hand grows steady, and your teacher permits, write with a somewhat finer pen on heavy paper. Only after you have learned to write well should you use a fine pen on good paper.

3. Do not write quickly. Settle yourself carefully, and write the letters methodically. As far as possible, make the letters exactly like those of the book you are copying or like the letters made by the teacher. When your writing becomes skillful, you will be able to write more quickly.

4. Do not write your whole life long leaving tracks, blotted-out words, and spots.

5. If some phrase is written incorrectly or if what was written seems inappropriate, do not rub it out with spit or water. Most good writers regard this as a fault. Instead, strike out the error with a line drawn through the phrase, as follows: ~~Bring a mat for me~~. Cover with ink anything that you want to hide completely. Or simply start over.

6. Do not write tiny letters, nor should you write above or below the line.

7. Study all kinds of writing styles, so that reading letters will come easily.

8. Unless there is an urgent need, never write a letter to a man from whom the *shari'at* prescribes seclusion.

9. Do not write about anything shameless or comical in a letter to anyone.

10. Always show your husband any letter you write. Those who are unmarried should be sure to show their letters to some man of the household, to either a father or a brother. This is beneficial because Almighty God has endowed men with more sense. You may have written something inappropriate that you do not recognize as such. They will see your error and either correct it or strike it out. A second advantage is that they will have no suspicions of any kind about you. Remember: for suspicion to fall on a woman is as good as being dead. So why do something to make someone suspicious of you? Similarly, you should always show your menfolk any letters you may receive. Of course, there is no harm in not showing anyone a letter you have written to your own husband or that he has written to you. Even then, however, you should show the envelopes of all letters received or sent.

11. As far as possible, have the men in your family get the envelope addressed, for it sometimes happens that one has to go to the government offices to ask about it. This is completely inappropriate for a woman to do.

12. If a card or two-*paisa* envelope is a bit spoiled near the address, never wash it, for fear that the place where the stamp is may be ruined. The postman may become suspicious and may even initiate a case against you. In one place, this has already happened. When the government people asked, this woman got an upset stomach [from nerves]. The tale was settled with great difficulty. Do not even use a dirty stamp.

13. Never place your own signature on a paper that is to be presented in a government office unless there is great necessity.

14. Do not keep writing letters to the whole world for mere enjoyment or with the idea that writing will bring reward. If it is necessary, fine. For example, if some poor person is inconvenienced in some important matter and there is no one else available to write for him or her, you have no choice. Otherwise, say, "Friend,[24] I am no *munshi*. It would be immodest for my letters to circulate before the eyes of strange men. If I have to, I can manage to draw a few squiggles. Better to have someone else write it." The point is that in a number of situa-

tions such dealings have influenced bad people for the worse. God save us from such bad times!

15. When you finish answering a letter, burn it in the fire. This will not be disrespect to the paper; rather, the paper will not be floating around. Besides, there may be a thousand things in the letter; God knows who will see it. Is it necessary for news of your home to find its way somewhere else? Of course, it is another matter if it is necessary to keep some letter for a few days for some special reason. But if you keep it, keep it carefully in a box. It should not be floating around.

16. If you have to write something confidential, do not write on a postcard.

17. Be sure to write the date, month, and year on a letter. The date is the day of the month in which you are writing. For example, if it is the month of Jumada'l-akhir, and today is the eighteenth day of the month, then the date is the eighteenth day. To write this, write the number of the date and after that the name of the month. For example, write the eighteenth of Jumada'l-akhir this way: 18 Jumada'l-akhir. The year, *sanah,* means *baras* [in everyday Hindi]. As Muslims, we count the years from when the Apostle of God, *God's blessings and peace upon him,* performed the *hijra* (migration) from Mecca to Medina. Thirteen hundred twenty-two years have now passed [1904–1905]. This is called the *hijri* year, because it is reckoned by the *hijra.* Thirteen hundred twenty-two is written by first writing *sanah,* drawn out; then the number over it; and the "two-eyed h" [the first letter of *hijra*] after it.

The year changes with the month of Muharram. For example, with the coming Muharram, the year 1323 will begin. You will let the number 13 stay in its place, and you will write 23 in place of 22.

In this way, this figure will keep changing with every Muharram. With the next Muharram, you will write 24 in place of 23; with the third Muharram, you will write 25 in place of 24. The number 13 will be written in its place until seventy-seven more years have passed, and a full fourteen hundred years have been completed. Then the number 13 will change. Those who will be around at that time will ask one another how to write it.

There is great advantage in writing the date and year. For one thing, it is clear how many days it took to get the letter. With the date, moreover, you avoid confusion if you have written about something in the past. Also, if you have written more than one letter without a date, the recipient will not know which of two letters is first, which last, and which thing she should do and which she should not do. If there is a date and year, she will know that one letter is later and that she should act on that letter. There are other advantages, too.

18. Write the address very clearly, both the address to which the letter is being sent and the address from where it is sent. Write the letters in full, making sure all the points and dots of each letter are clearly written. Otherwise, there can be great difficulty. Sometimes the letter never arrives; sometimes the address cannot be read at the time of sending an answer, and therefore an answer cannot be sent. Always write your full address on every letter; perhaps the other person does not remember it, and no earlier letter has been kept.

19. Do not write with paper or ink that makes the letters spread or stains the other side so that it is difficult to read. Do not use heavy paper, or the unnecessary additional weight will increase the postage.

20. Do not write all over the page so that the reader cannot tell which phrase follows which. Start writing from one direction, completely straight, and keep writing properly so that the reader can keep reading right along.

21. When you have completed writing a page, dry it thoroughly with clay or blotting paper, and then begin the next page. Otherwise, the letters will be effaced and illegible.

22. Many people have the habit of putting too much ink in the pen and getting rid of the excess by shaking it on the mat or floor or wall. This shows lack of good sense. Put the ink in carefully from the beginning. If there is too much, shake it inside the inkpot.

VI. The End of the Work: Three Essays

FIRST ESSAY: [ON ACQUIRING FURTHER KNOWLEDGE (AND THE NAMES OF WORTHWHILE AND HARMFUL BOOKS)]

With the help of Almighty God, I have now written down, after careful reflection, a summary of the important issues concerning religion and everyday life that are of greatest use. There are three alternate methods to follow if you wish to know more. One method is to study some Persian and then begin to study Arabic, as men do. Arabic contains much great and good knowledge. The truth is that a real taste for religious knowledge and a full mastery of it are simply not accessible without Arabic. If you resolve to do this, then, when you finish this book, take the name of God and turn to the *Taisir al mubtadi* (The facilitator for beginners),* written by a *maulawi sahib* friend of mine. I

* This book is available in Thanah Bhawan from Maulawi 'Abdu'llah Sahib, teacher at the Imdadu'l-'ulum, for the price of three and one-half *ana*s.

have had it printed myself, with great enthusiasm. I like it very much. I have had children under my care study it, and they have gained great skill from it. You should order this book and begin to read it, being careful to understand everything as you read. You will find that the first pages provide a guide for what you read later. Continue to study by this method. In a short time, *God willing,* you will master the skill of reading Arabic.

The short and quickly mastered method of studying Arabic, actually devised by me and given in the first pages of this book, will permit you, *Almighty God willing,* to become a *maulawi*—that is, a scholar of Arabic—within three years. You will achieve the rank of a learned person, and you will be able to give judicial opinions, as learned men do. You will begin to teach Arabic to girls, just as learned men do. Then, as are learned men, you will be granted the reward equal to that bestowed on each person to whom you have given guidance with your preaching and opinions, teaching and books. You will then, moreover, be rewarded for the guidance given by each one of them in turn right up to the Day of Judgment. The reward granted the whole succession will be written in your Book of Deeds. Just look how much great wealth is obtained with just a little effort! This is the best method of acquiring knowledge of religion.

A second method is this. If there is a scholar in your household, question him about all points of religion. If there is no such one in your household, inquire of someone in your town or village, using your menfolk or sensible boys as intermediaries. Be sure to consult a fully learned and pious person, not someone mediocre or unconcerned with what is lawful or unlawful because of his love of the world. Such a person's opinion does not deserve confidence.

The third method is this. Read Urdu books on religion, and reflect on them carefully so that you understand them well. Whenever you are uncertain, do not figure out the problem on your own, but inquire of some scholar. If there is an opportunity, it is better to read these books like lessons with someone who is well informed. Now, you must realize that in these times there are many so-called religious books, including some that are faulty and some that include outright mistakes. The influence of these books is not good. These books, which are not about religion at all, have spread great harm. Women and girls, however, do not see this at all. They buy and start to read any book they want. Instead of profit, there is harm. Habits are ruined. Thought is sullied. Indiscretion, shamelessness, and Satanic matters are encouraged. Learning unjustly gets a bad name: "Sir, teaching women to read is not a good thing." Learning about religion is in every respect a good thing.

You cannot blame proper learning about religion if the learning is about something else, or if it is not obtained methodically, or if it is not acted on.

To avoid all this, first show to a scholar any book being bought or read. If he says it is useful, then read it. If he says it is harmful, do not look at it or even keep it in the house. If children of yours should look at it secretly, take it away from them. In short, do not read any book without consulting a scholar. In fact, without a scholar, do nothing at all. Even if you become a scholar yourself, continue to consult scholars who are more learned than you. Do not be proud of your own knowledge.

At this point, it seems appropriate to indicate, as examples, the names of books that are popular nowadays—both those that are worthwhile and those that are harmful.[25] As for other books, if their subject matter is the same as that of worthwhile books, consider them to be worthwhile; otherwise, consider them harmful. The easiest thing, of course, is to show each book to a scholar.

The Names of Several Worthwhile Books

1. *Tafsir-i qadiri,* the translation of *Tafsir-i husaini* (The Qur'anic commentary of Qadir).[26]

2. The translation of *Mashariqu'l-anwar* (The splendid eastern places).

3. *Saliqa* (Nature), a translation of *Adabu'l-mufrad* (The singular code).

4. *Salatu'r-rahman* (Prayer to the Merciful).

5. *Rah-i najat* (The path of salvation).[27]

6. *Nasihatu'l-muslimin* (Advice to Muslims).[28]

7. *Miftahu'l-jannat* (The key to heaven).

8. *Bihisht ka darwaza* (The door to paradise).

9. *Haqiqatu's-salat* with *Risala-yi benamazan* (The truth of prayer, with a pamphlet on those who neglect prayer).[29]

10. *Risala-yi 'aqiqa* (Ceremony of shaving the head of an infant on the sixth day).

11. *Risala-yi tajhiz o takfin* (Preparing and shrouding the body).[30]

12. *Kashfu'l-hajat* (The unveiling of the needful).

13. The translation of *Mala bad manah.*[31]

14. *Safa'i-yi mu'amalat* (Purity in transactions).[32]

15. *Tamizu'l-kalam* (Discrimination of speech).

16. *Mahasinu'l-'amal* (The beauties of action).

17. *Sa'adat-i darain* (Happiness in both worlds).

18. *Subh ka sitara* (Star of the morning).[33] Its sources (*riwayat*) are not very sound, however.

19. *Tuhfatu'z-zaujain* (A gift for the spouses).[34]

20. *Ta'limu'd-din* (Instruction in religion).[35]

21. *Furu'u'l-iman* (Ramifications of the faith).[36]

22. *Jaza'u'l-'amal* (Rewards of deeds).[37]

23. *Zamanu'l-firdaus* (The guarantees of paradise).[38]

24. *Randon ki shadi* (The marriage of widows).[39]

25. *Zawajir* (Exhortations), in Hindi.

26. *Mambahat* (Warnings), a translation of *Zilzalutu's-sa'at* (The earthquake of the time).

27. The translation of the *Qiyamat nama* (The Last Day), by Shah Rafi'u'd-Din.[40]

28. *Nisabu'l-ihtisab* (The base of reckoning), in Urdu.

29. *Islahu'r-rusum* (The reform of customs).[41]

30. *Shari'at ka lath* (The rod of the law).[42]

31. *Tanbihu'l-ghafilin* (Warning to the heedless).[43]

32. *Asar-i mahshar* (Signs of Mahshar, the place of congregation on the Day of Judgment).[44]

33. *Zajaru'sh-shubban wa shaibah* (A warning to young men and old).

34. *'Umdatu'n-nasa'ih* (The best advice).

35. *Bihisht namah, dozakh namah* (On heaven, on hell).[45]

36. *Zinatu'l-iman* (The ornament of faith).

37. *Tanbihu'n-nisa* (A warning to women).[46]

38. *Ta'limu'n-nisa* with *Dulhan namah* (The education of women, with a book for brides).

39. *Hidayatu'n-niswan* (Guidance for women).[47]

40. *Mir'atu'n-nisa* (A mirror for women).[48]

41. *Taubatu'n-nasuh* (The repentance of Nasuh).[49]

42. *Tahzibu'n-niswan wa tarbiyatu'l-insan* (The cultivation of women and the instruction of humanity). This is written by Begam Shahjahan of Bhopal. This is a very good book, but its legal points are not in accord with the law school of our Imam. Therefore, act on those points with the *Bihishti Zewar* as a guide. Similarly, in matters of medical treatment, you should not undertake a cure by looking at the book above without asking a *hakim*. Other points written here are all ones that encourage a good disposition, offer good counsel, and are conducive to comfort. All these are worth acting on.[50]

43. *Firdaus-i asiya* (The paradise of Asiya).[51]

44. *Rahatu'l-qulub* (Satisfaction of hearts).

45. *Khuda ki rahmat* (God's mercy).[52]

46. *Tawarikh-i habib allah* (The chronicle of the beloved of Allah).[53]

The three books just mentioned all concern Hazrat Apostle, *God's blessings and peace upon him*, but here and there they discuss joining the celebration of his birthday and the custom of standing during it, points that have been discussed in Book Six of this work. Do not act against these points.[54]

47. *Qisasu'l-anbiya* (Tales of the prophets).[55]

48. *Al Kalamu'l-mubin fi ayat-i rahmatu'l-'alamain* (The clarifying word in the verses dealing with the mercy of the two worlds).

49. *Sirru'sh-shahadatain* (Secret of the two martyrdoms).[56]

50. *Iksir-i hidayat* (The elixir of guidance).[57]

51. *Hikayatu's-salihin* (Stories of the virtuous).

52. *Maqasidu's-salihin* (Purposes of the virtuous).[58]

53. *Munajat-i maqbul* (Acceptable supplication).

54. *Ghiza-yi ruh* (Food for the soul).[59]

55. *Jihad-i akbar* (The greater jihad).

56. *Tuhfatu'l-'ushshaq* (A gift to lovers).[60]

57. *Chashma-yi rahmat* (The fountain of mercy).

58. *Gulzar-i ibrahim* (The garden of Ibrahim).[61]

59. *Nasihat nama* (On advice).[62]

60. *Banjara nama* (On banjaras [gypsy traders]).[63]

61. *A'mal-i qur'ani* (Qur'anic deeds).

62. *Shifa'l-'alil* (Cure of the sick).[64]

63. *Khairu'l-matin* (A solid good), a translation of *Hisn hasin* (An impregnable fortress).

64. *Irshad-i murshid* (Guidance from the guide).[65] Do not perform the devotional disciplines of *zikr*, repetition of the name of God, or *shaghl*, meditation, that are written in this book without a *pir*'s permission. You may, however, use the *wazifa*, the set prayers fixed for repetition.

65. *Tibb-i ihsani* (Ihsani's medicine).[66]

66. *Makhzanu'l-mufradat* (A treasury of simples [uncompounded medicines]).

67. *Insha-yi khirad afroz* (A writing style to illuminate comprehension).[67]

68. *Kaghazat-i karrawa'i bi khat-i shikasata* (Business documents in the *shikasta* script).[68]

69. *Mabadi'l-hisab* (Principles of arithmetic).[69]

70. *Muraqqa'-i nigarin* (An embellished album).

71. *Tahzibu's-salikin* (Polishing of the pious).

The Names of Several Harmful Books

1. Books of poetry.[70]
2. *Indar sabha* (The court of Indra).[71]
3. *Qissa-yi badr-i munir* (The story of Badr-i Munir).[72]
4. *Qissa-yi shah-i yaman* (The story of the shah of Yemen).[73]
5. *Dastan-i amir hamza* (The tale of Amir Hamza).[74]
6. *Gul-i bakawali* (The flower of Bakawali).[75]
7. *Alif laila* (The thousand and one nights).[76]
8. *Naqsh-i sulaimani* (Solomon's seal).[77]
9. *Fal nama* (Book of omens).[78]
10. *Qissa-yi mah-i ramazan* (The story of the month of Ramazan).[79]
11. *Mu'jiza-yi 'al-i nabi* (The miracle of the family of the Prophet).[80]
12. *Chahal risala* (Forty pamphlets), in which most are simply lies.[81]
13. *Wafat nama* (On death), in which many traditions are completely without authenticity.[82]
14. *Ara'ish-i mahfil* (The adornment of the gathering).[83]
15. *Jang nama-yi hazrat 'ali* (On the war of Hazrat 'Ali).
16. *Jang nama-yi muhammad hanif* (On the war of Muhammad Hanif).[84]
17. *Tafsir-i surat-i yusuf* (Commentary on the Sura Yusuf).[85]
18. *Hazar mas'ala* (A thousand issues).[86]
19. *Hairatu'l fiqh* (Consternation in *fiqh*).[87]
20. *Guldasta-yi mi'raj* (A bouquet on the ascension).
21. *Na't hi na't* (Only praise).
22. *Diwan-i lutf* (Diwan of Lutf).[88]

The preceding three books are of the sort that praise Hazrat Messenger[s] in name but in fact include many subjects that are against the *shari'at*.

23. *Du'a-yi ganju'l-'arsh* (On the supplication "Treasury of the Heavenly Throne").
24. *'Ahd nama* (On covenants).

The two books above, and many like them, include prayers that are fine, but these prayers are given false attribution, and for their recitation one is promised enormous reward in the name of Hazrat Messenger[s]. This is all fabricated.

25. *Mir'atu'l-'arus* (The bride's mirror).[89]
26. *Banatu'n-na'sh* (Daughters of the bier).[90]
27. *Muhsinat* (Chaste women).[91]
28. *Ayama* (Widows).[92]

These four books are of the sort that include some points encouraging discernment and decorum but elsewhere have sections that weaken faith. The effect of novels of all kinds, in fact, is so bad that it is worse than poison. As for the newspapers of the various cities, they are often without any value at all, and some of their articles are even harmful.

SECOND ESSAY: [HOW TO STUDY THIS WORK]

Here is advice for studying all the sections of this work, summarized in a list of points to be kept firmly in mind. Whether you are a woman or a man teaching women, you should begin by reviewing this section. If you follow the method given here, your students will profit greatly.

1. In teaching Book One, you should acquaint your students thoroughly with the letters of the alphabet, and you should drill them in reading connected letters [for the shape of the letter changes according to its position]. From then on, as far as possible, you should elicit the lesson from the children themselves.

2. From the beginning, tell the children to write the daily lesson on their slates. Continue this practice to the end of the work; thus the whole work will be written out. This will develop good writing.

3. The children should memorize the numerals (written in Book One) and be able to write them without even looking.

4. Explain the beliefs and legal points carefully, and instill them thoroughly. Have the student say them in her own words, so that it is clear she understands.

5. You should have the children memorize and recite all the supplications given in this work.

6. At the beginning, when you are teaching a child to recite the canonical prayer, you should let her repeat it seated, simply speaking out all the Qur'anic chapters and prayers. When she has memorized the prayer thoroughly, then have her pray according to the proper form.

7. If something is embarrassing because the teacher is a man, or if some matter is too much for the child's understanding, leave it and make a little mark with some color or a pencil. These points can be explained at a later occasion. A male teacher can have embarrassing matters explained through his wife.

8. In Books Four and Five, there are some complicated matters. If the child cannot grasp them, then first teach Book Six, Seven, Eight, or Ten; even in these, teach first only whatever you consider appropriate.

9. Insist that the student always study the lesson carefully and figure out the meaning by her own power—as much as she can figure out. Have her recite the lesson several times after studying it, and do it

on her own. This gives her the ability to explain things. Listen from time to time to the parts already studied, and have the student read daily some of what has been learned before, so that she remembers it. If two or three girls are studying together, have them ask each other questions.

10. If a student does anything contrary to what she is studying in this book, restrain her immediately. Likewise, whenever someone else does something in opposition to these teachings and causes harm, you should alert the students to consider how the person acted and what the results were. By this method, the benefit of good actions and the harm of bad actions are firmly planted in the heart.

THIRD ESSAY: [A FINAL WORD]

[For his final word, Thanawi again turns to the poem "The True Jewelry of Humanity," translated in Book One but not reproduced here.]

Here, once again, are the verses in praise of the ornaments of virtues that were given in the beginning of this work. These virtues are the heavenly ornaments. The verses describe the subject matter and provide the title of this work. They inspire the flourishing of love of virtue in the heart and cause the greed for false ornaments to grow less. This greed has caused the true jewelry to be forgotten. If you have not seen these verses before, you can read them here. If you have already seen them, then you should read them again, and cleave even more to the idea of correct action. With these verses, the book ends.

May Almighty God keep us all on the right path and bring us to a good end.

The tenth book of the *Bihishti Zewar* is ended.

[Appendix:
Table of Weights,
Currency, and Measures]

WEIGHTS

chhatank	$\frac{1}{16}$ *ser* (60 gm)
pa'o	$\frac{1}{4}$ *ser* ($\frac{1}{4}$ kg)
ser	$\frac{1}{40}$ *man* (1 kg)
man	(40 kg)
ratti	*Abrus precatorius* seed, equal to 8 barleycorns (85 mg)
masha	8 or 10 *ratti* (1.1 gm)
tola	12 or 16 *masha,* the weight of the Sicca rupee (15 gm)

CURRENCY

chhadam	6 *dam* (copper coin, rarely used now), 16 cowries, $\frac{1}{4}$ *paisa*
dhela	$\frac{1}{2}$ *paisa*
pa'o ana	$\frac{1}{4}$ *ana,* 1 *paisa*
ana	$\frac{1}{16}$ rupee, 4 *paisa*s
rupee	16 *ana*s, 48 *paisa*s

MEASURES

girih	$\frac{1}{16}$ of a *gaz*
gaz	a short yard (33 inches)

Notes

A Note on Translation

1. Thanawi often consulted his father's elder brother's wife (his *ta'i*), known as Bi Amman, who was also the maternal aunt (*khala*) of his senior wife. This information comes from a conversation with one of Maulana Thanawi's grandsons (his adopted daughter's son), Qari Ahmad Miyan Thanawi, in Lahore, December 1977.

2. The famous contemporary scholar and writer Saiyid Sulaiman Nadwi judged Thanawi's twelve-volume Qur'anic commentary, the *Tafsir bayanu'l-qur'an,* and his collection of judicial opinions, *Fatawa-yi imdadiyya,* as the "most important" of his estimated one thousand works; but Nadwi claimed that the *Bihishti Zewar* was the most famous. See Ashraf 'Ali Thanawi, *'Aksi bihishti zewar mukammal mudallal muhashsha* (Delhi: New Taj Office, n.d.), p. 20.

3. This opinion was expressed by the Delhi essayist and critic Shamsur Rahman Faruqi in a private communication. The comment about parallel constructions is a tentative opinion offered by Bruce Pray.

4. Based on Muhammad Abd-al-Rahman Barker, *A Course in Urdu* (Montreal: Institute of Islamic Studies, 1967), vol. 1, pp. 358–359.

5. Seyyid Hossein Nasr, *Ideals and Realities of Islam* (Boston: Beacon Press, 1975), p. 61. Some of the quotations that follow are based on Nasr's interpretations, supplemented by observations from C. M. Naim.

An Introduction to the *Bihishti Zewar*

1. The term "scripturalist," used here interchangeably with "reformist," is taken from Clifford Geertz, *Islam Observed* (Chicago: University of Chicago Press, 1968).

2. Feminist critics who argue that the *Bihishti Zewar* prevented women from reading poetry and novels miss a centrally important point: the restrictions and ideals held out were precisely the same for women and men. See, for example, Ariel, "*Bihishti Zewar*'s Do's and Don'ts for Women," *Dawn Overseas Weekly*, 14 April 1983.

3. On the Deobandi movement in general, see Barbara Metcalf, *Islamic Revival in British India: Deoband, 1860–1900* (Princeton, N.J.: Princeton University Press, 1982).

4. Personal communication from C. M. Naim.

5. For example, a journal of the scholarly *'ulama* family of Farangi Mahal, more concerned with elite scholarship and literature than with Muslim reform, devoted no fewer than seventeen weekly articles in 1916–1917 to criticizing the *Bihishti Zewar* for its humble diction, its inclusion of indecorous topics, and its opposition to customary religious practices (held in fact even by the Deobandis to be acceptable for the sophisticated but dangerous to the masses). See Francis Robinson, "An-Nizāmiyya: A Group of Lucknow Intellectuals in the Early Twentieth Century" (1988, typescript).

6. Maulana Ashraf 'Ali Thanawi, *Bihishti Zewar: Heavenly Ornaments, Complete Twelve Parts,* 3d ed., trans. M. Masroor Khan Saroha, enlarged by Hazrat Qutbe-Alam Mohammad Abdullah (Delhi: Dini Book Depot, 1982), p. ix.

7. Reported in a conversation with Maulana Thanawi's grandson Qari Ahmad Miyan Thanawi in Lahore, December 1977.

8. I am grateful to Muhammad Ishaq Shor Sahib (now of Lahore but a native of Thana Bhawan), who, over a friendship of many years, has shared his childhood memories of Maulana Thanawi. See also the entry "Ashraf 'Ali," in the *Encyclopedia of Islam,* new ed. (Leiden: E. J. Brill, 1960–), vol. 1, pp. 701–702; Muhammad 'Abdu'l-hayy 'Arifi, *Masir-i hakimu'l-ummat* (Karachi: Daru'l-kutub imdadiyya, 1971); 'Azizu'l-hasan and 'Abdu'l-haqq, *Ashrafu's-sawanih* (Lahore: Muhammad Sana'u'lla and Sons, 1935–1936; reprint 1960).

9. Robin Horton discusses the emphasis on religious universals and abstract principles in the context of a larger-scale and more integrated social structure ("African Conversion," *Africa* 41, no. 2 [April 1971]: 85–108). In the Indian context, see Mattison Mines, "Islamization and Muslim Ethnicity in South India," in *Ritual and Religion Among Muslims in India,* ed. Imtiaz Ahmad (New Delhi: Manohar, 1981), pp. 65–89.

10. Scholars, following Weber, have also speculated on the relationship of normative Islam to capitalist economic development, particularly given the puritanlike teachings of certain Islamic positions, especially those of reformers. For discussion of these issues, see the bibliography and the various contributions in *Webers Sicht des Islam: Interpretation und Kritik,* ed. Wolfgang

Schluchter (Frankfurt am Main: Suhrkamp Verlag, 1987) (including Barbara Metcalf, "Islamische Reformbewegungen," pp. 242–255).

11. On scholarly neglect of the proponents of this kind of reform movement, the classically educated, see Dale F. Eickelman, *Knowledge and Power in Morocco: The Education of a Twentieth-Century Notable* (Princeton, N.J.: Princeton University Press, 1985), pp. 12–13.

12. The term "neo-sufi" is a contribution of Fazlur Rahman in *Islam,* 2d ed. (Chicago: University of Chicago Press, 1979).

13. Nepalese banglemakers, for example, brought home the *Bihishti Zewar* and other reformist works after working in Indian cities following World War I. Contrary to expectations, it was such artisans, not the educated or dominant, who favored an end to the worship of saints. See Marc Gaborieau, "The Transmission of Islamic Reformist Teachings to Rural South Asia" (1988, typescript).

14. For the background of the Tablighi Jama'at movement, see Anwarul Haq, *The Faith Movement of Muhammad Ilyas* (London: Allen & Unwin, 1972); for the Tabligh in France, see Gilles Kepel, *Les Banlieues de l'islam* (Paris: Editions du Seuil, 1987).

15. Thanawi, *Bahishti Zewar: Heavenly Ornaments,* trans. Saroha, enl. Abdullah, p. x.

16. This argument, sketchily delineated here, has recently stimulated great self-consciousness among scholars of Muslim societies, largely thanks to the work of Edward Said (*Orientalism* [London: Routledge and Kegan Paul, 1978]). See also David Waines, "Through a Veil Darkly: The Study of Women in Muslim Societies," *Comparative Studies in Society and History* 24, no. 1 (October 1982): 642–659.

17. Talal Asad, *The Idea of an Anthropology of Islam,* Occasional Papers Series (Washington, D.C.: Georgetown University, Center for Contemporary Arab Studies, 1986).

18. Concerning the stake of women in upholding these codes in a different Muslim context, see, for example, Lila Abu-Lughod, *Veiled Sentiments: Honor and Poetry in a Bedouin Society* (Berkeley and Los Angeles: University of California Press, 1986). Several essays documenting sexual norms and attitudes toward women are collected in Afaf Lutfi al-Sayyid Marsot, ed., *Society and the Sexes in Medieval Islam* (Malibu, Calif.: Undena Publications, 1979).

19. Waines, "Through a Veil Darkly," p. 647.

20. See Janet Abu-Lughod, "The Islamic City—Historic Myth, Islamic Essence, and Contemporary Relevance," *International Journal of Middle Eastern Studies* 19, no. 2 (1987): 155–176. She criticizes the study of Islamic cities by Western orientalists and proposes a new model, of which a central element is the segregation of the sexes, expressed in urban spatial organization.

21. This argument about the *shari'at* discourse on women follows the suggestive essay of Faisal Fatehali Devji, "An Introduction to the Sexual History of Islamic Reform in India" (1988, typescript).

22. Brinckley Messick, "Kissing Hands and Knees: Hegemony and Hierarchy in Shari'a Discourse," *Law and Society* 22, no. 4 (1988): 637–660.

23. See David S. Lelyveld, *Aligarh's First Generation: Muslim Solidarity in British India* (Princeton, N.J.: Princeton University Press, 1978), chap. 1.

24. For a discussion of this "idiom" of British colonial rule, see Peter Hardy, *The Muslims of British India* (Cambridge: Cambridge University Press, 1972).

25. Faisal Devji, "Introduction to the Sexual History of Islamic Reform in India," pp. 23–24.

26. Hannah Papanek, "Afterword," in Rokeya Sakhawat Hossain, *Sultana's Dream and Selections from The Secluded Ones,* trans. and ed. Roushan Jahan (New York: Feminist Press, 1988), p. 61. Although I disagree with the particular comment quoted in the text, the afterword and the book as a whole are important contributions.

27. I am grateful to Dr. Marc Gaborieau for sharing with me Maulana Karamat 'Ali Jaunpuri's *Miftahu'l-jannat* (Lucknow: Munshi Tej Kumar, 1954). Karamat 'Ali, as he himself writes in this work, was a follower of Saiyid Ahmad Shahid, who led a movement to purify Islam in the 1820s and was killed on the frontier trying to carve out a kingdom of his own against the Sikhs in 1831. Karamat 'Ali wrote this book, according to the colophon, in 1243/1827–1828, addressing its call for reform to both women and men. He urged readers to educate women in both families and neighborhoods; if education was impossible, he recommended at least reading aloud to women. He was particularly concerned that women did not know the rules of pollution concerning menstruation (pp. 6–7). The edition cited above is an augmented one (noted with the date in the volume), but the author implies that the changes were minor. This call for women's education in the 1820s is the earliest I am aware of in Urdu literature. Being associated with eastern India, Karamat 'Ali may have been influenced by the lively debate on women's status among Bengali intellectuals, stimulated by the British presence during these years; the Delhi *'ulama* presumably would have been less influenced, even indirectly, by such debate.

28. See, for example, Mubarak Ali, "*Bahishti Zewar* and the Image of Muslim Women," *South Asia Bulletin* 8 (1988): 59–63.

29. See, for example, William J. Bouwsma, *John Calvin: A Sixteenth-Century Portrait* (New York: Oxford University Press, 1988); and Philip Greven, *The Protestant Temperament: Patterns of Child-Rearing, Religious Experience, and the Self in Early America* (New York: Knopf, 1978). For these themes in contemporary Hindu reform, see Kenneth W. Jones, *Arya Dharm: Hindu Consciousness in Nineteenth-Century Punjab* (Berkeley and Los Angeles: University of California Press, 1976); and Dennis Hudson, "Armuga Navalar and the Hindu Renaissance Among the Tamils" (1988, typescript). The resonance of Muslim reform with sixteenth-century Protestant reform is suggested by the title of James Peacock's book on a Southeast Asian reform movement: *Muslim Puritans: Reformist Psychology in Southeast Asian Islam* (Berkeley and Los Angeles: University of California Press, 1978).

30. For a provocative essay on women's religion in Muslim societies, see Robert A. Fernea and Elizabeth W. Fernea, "Variation in Religious Observances Among Islamic Women," in *Scholars, Saints, and Sufis: Muslim Religious Institutions Since 1500,* ed. Nikki R. Keddie (Berkeley and Los Angeles:

University of California Press, 1972), pp. 385–401. See also Zekiye S. Eglar, *A Punjabi Village in Pakistan* (New York: Columbia University Press, 1960), for a study of women's role in reciprocal gift-giving. In India, there was even a tradition in some families of the women being Shi'a; there is a predominance of Shi'a women over men in the census returns. In Lucknow, for example, the reported Shi'a population had dropped from 23 percent in 1881 to 14 percent in 1904; of this 14 percent, two-thirds were women (statistics provided by Sandria Freitag from official gazetteers).

31. The organization and vitality of indigenous medicine are products of the colonial period. See Charles Leslie, ed., *Asian Medical Systems: A Comparative Study* (Berkeley and Los Angeles: University of California Press, 1976). On the reorganization of *tibb* in late nineteenth-century Delhi, see Barbara Metcalf, "Hakim Ajmal Khan: Ra'is of Delhi and Muslim 'Leader,' " in *Delhi Through the Ages,* ed. Robert Eric Frykenberg (Delhi: Oxford University Press, 1986), pp. 299–315.

32. Because of space constraints, the translation of that section is not included here. I hope to publish it on a future occasion. It has not been included in the other existing English translations I have seen.

33. Ashis Nandy, *The Intimate Enemy: Loss and Recovery of Self Under Colonialism* (Delhi: Oxford University Press, 1983).

34. Barbara Ehrenreich and Deirdre English, *For Her Own Good: One Hundred Fifty Years of the Experts' Advice to Women* (Garden City, N.Y.: Anchor/Doubleday, 1978), p. 114.

35. For a discussion of the "physiology of incommensurability," elaborated in the nineteenth century to define men as fundamentally different from women, see Thomas Laqueur, "Orgasm, Generation, and the Politics of Reproductive Biology," *Representations* 14 (Spring 1986): 1–41. Laqueur's argument is cited and discussed in contrast to the ancient model, which confined women to a lower place than that of men in shared hierarchy, in Peter Brown, *The Body and Society: Men, Women, and Sexual Renunciation in Early Christianity* (New York: Columbia University Press, 1988), p. 10.

36. Mubarak Ali (*"Bahishti Zewar* and the Image of Muslim Women") quotes an article that translates the title as "Ornament for Gaining Paradise" (*Dawn* [Karachi], 22 November 1987), suggesting the title's intent.

37. Quoted in Ehrenreich and English, *For Her Own Good,* pp. 17–18.

38. Partha Chatterjee, "Colonialism, Nationalism, and Colonised Women: The Contest in India" (Paper presented to Symposium no. 107 of the Wenner Gren Foundation for Anthropological Research, "Tensions of Empire: Colonial Control and Visions of Rule," 5–13 November 1988, Mijas, Spain), pp. 23–24. This summary of Bengali social reform is stimulated by the argument of Chatterjee's paper. See also Meredith Borthwick, *The Changing Role of Women in Bengal, 1849–1905* (Princeton, N.J.: Princeton University Press, 1984); and Lata Mani, "Contentious Traditions: The Debate on *Sati* in Colonial India," *Cultural Critique* 7 (1987): 119–156.

39. For a study of the author of one of the most influential of these works, the *Treatise of Domestic Economy,* see Kathryn Kish Sklar, *Catharine Beecher: A Study in American Domesticity* (New York: Norton, 1976).

40. See Chiragh ʿAli, *Proposed Political, Constitutional, and Legislative Reforms in the Ottoman Empire and Other Mohamedan States* (Bombay: Educational Society Press, 1883); and Syed Ameer Ali, *The Spirit of Islam* (1922; reprint, London: Methuen, 1965).

41. For a particularly insightful and nuanced treatment of the intellectual context of the modernist argument—and of reformist issues related to women generally—see Faisal Devji, "Introduction to the Sexual History of Islamic Reform in India," esp. pp. 38–41.

42. Although the Jamaʿat is often referred to as "fundamentalist," I prefer to use the term "Islamist." The term "fundamentalist" has numerous problems. For example, it is used to blanket movements as diverse as—in the Indian case—the nineteenth-century militant jihad on the frontier, the Deobandis, and the Jamaʿat. Also, with its American associations, the term carries too many linked meanings—reactionary, obscurantist, intolerant—and is often pejorative.

43. Papanek, "Afterword," pp. 78–79.

44. The forthcoming work of Aihwa Ong on Malaysia is particularly illuminating on the relation between state policy and a capitalist economy, on the one hand, and the formulation of a "counterhegemonic" Islamic discourse concerning women, on the other. For the central importance given to women's place in the recent writings of the Jamaʿat-i Islami, see Barbara Metcalf, "Islamic Arguments in Contemporary Pakistan," in *Islam and the Political Economy of Meaning,* ed. William R. Roff (Berkeley and Los Angeles: University of California Press, 1988), pp. 132–159.

45. General Zia ul Haq, who favored what he called "Islamicizing policies," recommended the *Bihishti Zewar* (*Dawn* [Karachi], 22 November 1987); cited in Mubarak Ali, "*Bahishti Zewar* and the Image of Muslim Women," p. 59.

46. Concerning this concept in another Muslim culture, see James T. Siegel, *The Rope of God* (Berkeley and Los Angeles: University of California Press, 1969).

47. For a discussion of this concept in the context of the Punjab, see Richard Kurin, "The Culture of Ethnicity in Pakistan," in *Shariʿat and Ambiguity in South Asian Islam,* ed. Katherine P. Ewing (Berkeley and Los Angeles: University of California Press, 1988), pp. 220–247. In this case, Punjabi culture is seen as more impulsive, more childlike than the culture symbolized by Urdu. See also Annemarie Schimmel, *The Triumphal Sun: A Study of the Works of Jalaloddin Rumi* (Boulder, Colo.: Great Eastern, 1978), in which one symbol of the *nafs* is the Hindu, and the world of clay and darkness (contrasted to Turkestan) is Hindustan.

48. Indeed, I encountered an example of this view in March 1985 in conversation with one of Maulana Thanawi's grandsons (a son of his adopted daughter), Maulana Musharraf Thanawi, a respected Deobandi scholar himself, whom I had the privilege to meet at his *madrasa* in Lahore.

49. Although the core of knowledge is absolute, the Deobandis continued the inherited tradition of limiting discussion of some issues or permitting some practices only to the initiated, the *khwas,* in contrast to the "ordinary" people, the ʿam.

50. The *'ulama* associated with this reform, known as the Farangi Mahallis, have been studied by Francis Robinson. See, for example, Robinson, "The *'Ulama'* of Farangi Mahall and Their *Adab*," in *Moral Conduct and Authority: The Place of Adab in South Asian Islam*, ed. Barbara Metcalf (Berkeley and Los Angeles: University of California Press, 1984), pp. 152–183; also see Robinson's forthcoming monograph.

51. Ralph Russell and Khurshidul Islam, eds. and trans., *Ghalib: 1766–1869*, vol. 1: *Life and Letters* (London: Allen & Unwin, 1969), pp. 30, 33–34.

52. See, for example, the evocative vignette of the north Indian villagers gathered to hear the *Taqwiyatu'l-iman* in the 1820s, in Metcalf, *Islamic Revival in British India*, p. 201. See also the discussion of the Bengali *puthi* literature, which disseminated Islamic teachings, in Rafiuddin Ahmad, *The Bengal Muslims, 1871–1906: A Quest for Identity* (Delhi: Oxford University Press, 1981).

53. Hazrat Qutbe-Alam Mohammad Abdullah, introductory comment in Thanawi, *Bahishti Zewar: Heavenly Ornaments*, trans. Saroha, enl. Abdullah, unnumbered page. As noted above, Thanawi's followers contributed to these writings. In the opening pages of this work, for example, Thanawi himself gives credit to Maulawi Ahmad 'Ali.

54. See Metcalf, *Islamic Revival in British India*, pp. 205–206, for a first-hand description of the lack of texts in pre-Mutiny Delhi.

55. These terms are used by Louis Brenner in his discussions of educational change in Africa (personal communication).

56. Translated by C. M. Naim ("How Bibi Ashraf Learned to Read and Write," *Annual of Urdu Studies* 6 [1987]: 102).

57. Roy Mottahedeh, *The Mantle of the Prophet: Religion and Politics in Iran* (New York: Simon & Schuster, 1985), p. 38, describing education in a secular primary school. See also Mottahedeh's description, in chap. 3, of *madrasa* education.

58. One critique of the "fundamentalist," or Islamist, movements today is that their "lay" leadership has been educated through publications and not through training by traditional scholars.

59. See Metcalf, *Islamic Revival in British India*, p. 243, for a description of such efforts by Maulana Muhammad Ahsan Nanautawi.

60. For discussion of written texts in nonliterate society and the transition from orality to literacy, see Amin Sweeney, *A Full Hearing: Orality and Literacy in the Malay World* (Berkeley and Los Angeles: University of California Press, 1987).

61. See Roger Chartier, *The Cultural Uses of Print in Early Modern France* (Princeton, N.J.: Princeton University Press, 1987). Chartier points out the extent to which the nonliterate depend on written texts that are read aloud to them, texts that form part of ritual, serve as legal documents, and so forth.

62. The analysis of silent reading is taken from Chartier, *Cultural Uses of Print*.

63. See Metcalf, *Islamic Revival in British India*, chap. 6, for a discussion of written and oral debate among religious groups in the late nineteenth century.

64. Dennis Hudson, for example, in his "Arumuga Navalar," shows that Navalar (1822–1879), who was educated in mission schools and assisted in

preparing a Tamil translation of the Bible, was deeply influenced in his view of Shaivite texts and of Hinduism by this contact with Protestant missionaries.

65. See Gail Minault, "Saiyid Ahmad Dehlavi and the Delhi Renaissance," in *Delhi Through the Ages*, ed. Frykenberg, pp. 287–298. Dehlavi (or Dihlawi) wrote on letter writing, etiquette, family relations, and household customs. Far from discouraging custom, he wrote the *Rusum-i dihli*, cataloguing the very customs the reformers opposed. See also Minault's *Voices of Silence* (Delhi: Chanakya, 1986), a translation of Altaf Husain Hali's *Majalisu'n-nisa* (1874), encouraging the education of women to enhance their domestic role. A third important Delhi writer, discussed in Book Ten, was Deputy Nazir Ahmad. See also Minault's work on the Lahore-based couple Sayyid Mumtaz 'Ali (1860–1935) and Muhammadi Begum (1878?–1908), who in 1898 began the *Tahzibu'n-niswan*, a weekly Urdu journal for women (Minault, "Making Invisible Women Visible: Studying the History of Muslim Women in South Asia," *South Asia* [Australia] 9, no. 1 [June 1986]). See also Minault's "Shaikh Abdullah, Begam Abdullah, and *Sharif* Education for Girls at Aligarh," in *Modernization and Social Change Among Muslims in India,* ed. Imtiaz Ahmad (New Delhi: Manohar, 1983), pp. 207–236; and Minault, "Purdah's Progress: The Beginnings of School Education for Indian Muslim Women," in *Individuals and Ideas in Modern India,* ed. J. P. Sharma (Calcutta: K. L. Mukhopdhyaya, 1982), pp. 76–97.

66. Maulana Muhammad Khalil Khan Qadiri, *Sunni bihishti zewar* (Lahore: Farid Book Stall, n.d.). My thanks to Dr. Khalid Masud, Islamabad, for providing me with a copy of this book.

67. M. Nazif Shahrani, "Tradition and Social Discourse in the Cultures of Afghanistan and Turkestan in the Modern Period" (Paper delivered at the School of American Research seminar, "Greater Central Asia as a Cultural Area," 14–19 April 1985, Santa Fe, New Mexico). See also Simon Digby, "The *Tuhfa-i nasa'ih* of Yusuf Gada: An Ethical Treatise in Verse from the Late Fourteenth-Century Delhi Sultanate," in *Moral Conduct and Authority,* ed. Metcalf, pp. 91–123.

68. Naim, "How Bibi Ashraf Learned to Read and Write," pp. 112–113. The genre of books of *adab* continues. See, for example, Marwan Ibrahim Al-Kaysi, *Morals and Manners in Islam: A Guide to Islamic* Adab (Leicester: Islamic Foundation, 1986); this work presents rules of *adab,* with justification in the light of modern science, medicine, psychology, and sociology. See also *Etiquettes of Life in Islam,* trans. Riaz Husain, rev. Abdul Waheed Khan (Lahore: Islamic Publications, 1979); here, teachings are presented with extensive quotations from the *hadis.*

69. The line "to call the day night" is from a well-known Persian couplet of Sa'di. The comments on hierarchy that follow in the text summarize points made in Book Four, not included in the translation here.

70. See Cora Vreed de Stuers, *Parda* (Assen, The Netherlands: Van Gorcum, 1968); Patricia Jeffery, *Frogs in a Well: Indian Women in Purdah* (London: Zed Press, 1979); and Hanna Papanek and Gail Minault, eds., *Separate Worlds: Studies of Purdah in South Asia* (Columbia, Mo.: South Asia Books, 1982).

71. One need not be astonished at the ease with which some wellborn women in the subcontinent have moved into public political and economic roles; they are used to giving orders. The Oxbridge-intoned words of Begam Isfahani in the recent debate in Pakistan over the law of evidence drove this point home: "You suggest *I* am only equal half my manservant?"

72. The terms used are *be-mel* (unharmonious or inappropriate) and *be-jor* (unsuited)—both, needless to say, widely open to interpretation.

73. Norbert Elias, *The History of Manners,* trans. Edmund Jephcott (New York: Pantheon, 1982).

74. The concept of "sanskritization" was developed by M. N. Srinivas, *Social Change in Modern India* (Berkeley and Los Angeles: University of California Press, 1966).

75. I owe this interesting observation to Dr. Muhammad Afzal, Islamabad (from a personal communication).

76. William A. Graham, "Islam in the Mirror of Ritual," in *Islam's Understanding of Itself,* ed. Richard G. Hovannisian and Speros Vryonis, Jr. (Malibu, Calif.: Undena Publications, 1983), pp. 53–71.

77. For a discussion of the meaning of reason or intelligence in Western culture, see C. S. Lewis, *The Discarded Image: An Introduction to Medieval and Renaissance Literature* (Cambridge: Cambridge University Press, 1964).

78. The translation of this Qur'anic verse (4:34) is from Abdullah Yusuf Ali, *The Holy Qur'an: Text, Translation, and Commentary* (Lahore: Sh. Muhammad Ashraf, 1973), p. 190. In the translation, the words "the husbands' " are in brackets. The commentary adds: "The meaning is: the good wife is obedient and harmonious in her husband's presence, and in his absence guards his reputation and property and her own virtue, as ordained by God."

79. See in contrast Fatna A. as-Sabbah, *Woman in the Muslim Unconscious,* trans. Mary Jo Lakeland (New York: Pergamon Press, 1984). See also Nawal El Saadawi, *The Hidden Face of Eve: Women in the Arab World* (London: Zed Press, 1980), for an argument that Islam oppresses women and perpetuates a vision of them as "a lower species" (pp. 4–5).

80. The opponents of the reformers took a stand on hierarchy, too, and accused the Deobandis and those like them of showing disrespect for prophets and saints by eliminating ceremonies related to them. Reformers and opponents shared a common assumption that hierarchy defined relationships; they differed only in its interpretation.

81. *Bahishti Zewar (Requisites of Islam),* trans. Rahm Ali al-Hashmi (Delhi: Dini Book Depot, 1973); *Bahishti Zewar: Heavenly Ornaments,* trans. Saroha, enl. Abdullah; *Bahishti Zewar: Heavenly Ornaments,* trans. Mohammad Masroor Khan (Lahore: Al-Kitab, 1979); and a forthcoming translation by Tayyab Bakhsh Budayuni (Delhi).

Chapter 1
Translator's Introduction to Book One

1. Opposition to jewelry came to be an issue taken up by women themselves. In the early twentieth century, Rokeya Sakahawat Hossain, for exam-

ple, considered jewelry as a symbol of slavery to women's customary role, as she argued in her essay "Maticura" (The pearl bracelet). See Roushan Jahan, ed. and trans., *Inside Seclusion: The Avarodhbasini of Rokeya Sakahawat Hossain* (Dacca: Women for Women, 1981).

2. C. M. Naim, "How Bibi Ashraf Learned to Read and Write," *Annual of Urdu Studies* 6 (1987): 110.

3. For discussion of the concept of education as wealth ("cultural capital"), following Pierre Bourdieu, see Dale F. Eickelman, "Islamic Education and Its Social Reproduction," *Comparative Studies in Society and History* 20, no. 4 (1978): 485–516.

Book One

1. The first *hadis* in this section is recorded in the classical *hadis* collections of Bukhari and Muslim, the second in that of Ibn Majah (attribution in notes of *Akhtari bihishti zewar* [Saharanpur: Kutubkana Akhtari, 1388/1968–1969], p. 2 [hereafter cited as *ABZ*]). The Qur'anic citations are 66:6 and 33:34.

2. By calling himself "contemptible," Thanawi uses the humble form conventional in written self-description. Note that he identifies himself with only one title, Hanafi, indicating his fidelity to the school of Sunni law predominant in India. He thus asserts his scholarly credentials for writing a book like this and specifically dissociates himself from the rival school of reformist *'ulama*, the Ahl-i Hadis, who rejected the law schools, basing themselves directly on the Qur'an and *hadis*.

3. *Mufsid:* corrupt in the sense of being rebellious against the *shari'at*.

4. See Book Six for an extended discussion of the practices that encourage these sins and Book Seven for ways to root out vices.

5. The idea that things are cured by their opposites is not a metaphor but a principle shared with medicine.

6. Note the implication that using Urdu is second-best, although necessary to reach a popular audience.

7. For Maulana Thanawi's opinions of contemporary books, see his lists of approved and disapproved titles in Book Ten.

8. This brief statement on the importance of the *'ulama* points, rather glancingly, to their important new role, discussed in the general introduction to this volume.

9. *Seth:* a merchant; in this case, presumably from the western Indian coastal city of Surat.

10. This formula, in Arabic, is spoken with the name of the deceased.

11. *Hakim:* a doctor in the tradition of Islamic medicine, *yunani tibb*. Danapur, near Patna in Bihar, was a center of support for the *madrasa* at Deoband in the late nineteenth century, thanks largely to the efforts of Hajji Nabi Bakhsh, a trader from Deoband who settled there. See Barbara Metcalf, *Islamic Revival in British India: Deoband, 1860–1900* (Princeton, N.J.: Princeton University Press, 1982), pp. 235–238.

12. *Adab-i din:* those aspects of the *shari'at* whose omission is not punishable but whose performance is commendable.

13. *Makhdum:* one who is served; often used in reference to a sufi leader.

14. This formula is used for a living person regarded as one's superior. *Janab:* sir.

15. The term "Qur'an" is almost always modified by a word of praise or respect: *majid, karim, sharif, hakim,* and so forth.

16. Sura Fatir 35:33.

17. Reported in the classical *hadis* collection of Muslim, from the Companion Abu Huraira (attribution in *ABZ*, p. 5).

18. This weekly paper was published from Ludhiana and had apparently just begun publication in the year this book of the *Bihishti Zewar* was written. Eight pages an issue, it cost two rupees for an annual subscription. In the three-volume history of (often ephemeral) Urdu periodicals, it is described as devoted "to the spread of Islam and refutation of opposition to Islam" (Imdad Sabiri, *Tarikh-i sahafat-i urdu* [Calcutta: Hasan Zaman, 1963?], vol. 2, p. 635).

19. Words underscored in the poem here are written in larger characters in the original; they list the various items of jewelry.

20. John T. Platts's roughly contemporaneous *Grammar of the Hindustani or Urdu Language,* 1st Indian ed. (Delhi: Munshiram Manoharlal, 1967) and his *Dictionary of Urdu, Classical Hindi, and English,* 5th ed. (London: Oxford University Press, 1930; reprint 1960) are useful in studying this section. Platts's *Grammar,* based on consultation with scholars such as Thanawi, provides the kind of rules and organizational principles given briefly here. Later editions of the *Bihishti Zewar* include marginal notes to supplement this rather sketchy instruction. In particular, they discuss methods of learning to write: how to prepare the pen and ink, how to sit with a knee raised as a support for the paper, how to hold the pen, precise instructions on how to draw each letter. See, for example, Ashraf 'Ali Thanawi, *'Aksi bihishti zewar mukammal mudallal muhashsha* (Delhi: New Taj Office, n.d.), pp. 7–14 (hereafter cited as *BZMMM*).

21. Both *ABZ* and *BZMMM* consistently eliminate this phrase of veneration and respect, because apparently it is no longer understood metaphorically but literally, implying that the person addressed is the focus of one's devotions, "the direction of prayer and the Ka'ba." Instead, adjectives of respect are added, supplemented by the preferred Islamic greeting, "*As-salamu alaikum wa rahmatu'llahi wa barkatuhu.*"

22. "Your lofty shadow" implies a shadow as a source of refuge and protection, cast by an elder, a patron, a king, or other such person.

23. The Urdu does not use the first person.

24. A series of footnotes in this section of *ABZ* and *BZMMM* delineates the importance of writing thoughtfully and civilly, never frivolously or sarcastically. For example: "In an answer, if you must refuse something, you must make your excuse in very gentle words that express the constraints on you, so that the heart of the person making the request will not break. Indeed, if it be an important matter, you should write the first time that you will write again.

Then, if you decline in the second letter, the heart will not be broken at once" (*BZMMM*, p. 17, note 7).

25. The words "descendents/dependents" suggest the rhyming prose of the original. Rhymes grew less common in Urdu during the course of the nineteenth century, as the language began to be used for more utilitarian purposes and for a wider audience. There are other examples of such rhyming prose in these letters and elsewhere in the text; only some of them are approximated in the translation.

26. *Janab:* here, madam. Like *hazrat*, it is used for both men and women.

27. Sister: literally, *hamsherah*, she who shares milk.

28. *Jigar:* the liver, understood to be the seat of loving emotions.

29. *Khatun:* a noble woman or lady (from the Turkish and Persian); a common termination of Muslim female names.

30. Thanawi lists this work in Book Ten as suitable for further reading.

31. The father has been addressed by the respectful second-person plural; he addresses the daughter by the familiar second-person plural. In all other instances, however, I have used "you" for both forms rather than "thou," which is archaic in English.

32. *Chikan:* a style of embroidery on muslin or other fine cloth, with open netting and stitching on the reverse side to create raised flowers and leaves. It is a craft particularly associated with Muslims and with the city of Lucknow.

33. *Peshkar:* a deputy or assistant; an officer in a court, ranking below a *sar-rishtadar* (an office superintendent, a court reader).

34. This injunction not to sit in a place higher than where an elder sits is a reference to the elaborate etiquette of space. "Higher" may mean, for example, at the head of a rope cot, rather than at the foot.

35. Only later do various editions suggest writing each component of the address separately and underlining the names of the town and district (e.g., *BZMMM*, p. 22). More information on post office regulations is given in Book Ten. Note that both men addressed in these examples are government servants: one is an inspector of police (or the head of perhaps another office) (*darogha*); the other is a scribe or clerk (*munshi*).

36. Umm Salama was a wife of the Prophet who died in A.H. 59 at the age of eighty-four (*BZMMM*, p. 26). See Book Eight.

37. Hazrat Ibrahim is the biblical Abraham, and these are the archangels Gabriel and Michael.

38. The first of the four stories is a *hadis* reported by the Companion Abu Huraira; the second is also reported by him; the third is from a client of 'Usman; the fourth is from Samura bin Jandub, recorded in Bukhari. *ABZ* and *BZMMM* note these attributions and also the inclusion of all four stories in a compendium of *hadis* widely used in India, the *Mishkat al-Masabih* of Abu Muhammad al-Husain al-Baghawi (d. A.H. 516). The *Mishkat* has been translated by James Robson, in four volumes (Lahore: Sh. Muhammad Ashraf, 1965; reprint 1973). Subsequent references to the *Mishkat* are to this edition. Three of the stories here are found in vol. 1 (p. 397, pp. 397–398, and p. 399); the fourth is from vol. 3 (pp. 964–966). The Urdu versions do not appear to

differ significantly from the original. The morals that appear in the text here were added by Thanawi.

39. Later editions caution that such attribution of meaning should be attempted only by a *maulawi.*

40. The first eleven of these prophets are major figures of the Hebrew Bible: Noah, Abraham, Isaac, Ishmael, Jacob, Joseph, David, Solomon, Job, Moses, and Aaron. The next three are known from the Gospels: Zacharias, John the Baptist, and Jesus. Of the rest, Yunis is identified with Jonah, Lut with Lot; others are also identified with biblical characters, although the names are different (e.g., Shu'aib as Jethro). Others are more tentatively identified with biblical figures, some specifically with Arab prophets.

41. Baitu'l-muqaddas: "the holy house." This is Solomon's temple in Jerusalem, later the site of al-'Aqsa mosque and of Sakhrah, the Dome of the Rock, from which the Prophet is believed to have ascended to heaven on his night journey. By extension, it is also the city of Jerusalem.

42. The numbers have been added to the lists in this section.

43. The possibility of regretting one's faith was a sensitive issue for Muslims, who felt discriminated against in favor of the Hindus, who were a majority in this area.

44. The first two names suggest Shi'a inclinations in favor of reverence for 'Ali and his son Husain; the first three points in the following list, "Reprehensible Innovations, Bad Customs, and Bad Deeds," also include practices associated with the Shi'a.

45. Holi is the spring bacchanalia of the Hindus; Diwali is the autumn festival of lights and new beginnings.

46. *Na-mahram:* marriageable persons, i.e., not of the degrees forbidden by propinquity.

47. *Domni:* a female member of the *dom* caste of Muslims, in which the males are musicians and the women, who perform only for other women, are singers, dancers, and actresses. See Book Six.

48. Current editions use the term "non-Muslims" instead of "Hindus," perhaps to avoid giving offense.

49. This description refers to *kangna,* a custom in which a string is put on the groom's right hand and the bride's left and each then unties the other.

50. *Chauthi:* the custom that takes place when the bride and groom visit the bride's family on the fourth day after the wedding. According to C. M. Naim, the girls on the bride's side and the boys who have accompanied the groom challenge each other with sticks, flowers, fruit, vegetables, cloth balls, and so forth. See the short story by Ismat Chughta'i, "Chauthi ka jora" (The outfit of the fourth), in *Readings in Urdu: Prose and Poetry,* ed. C. M. Naim (Honolulu: East-West Center Press, 1965), pp. 1–34.

51. *Manjhee:* a custom in which the girl is isolated before marriage and rubbed with cosmetics. See Book Six, where the custom is described as "sitting her on a *manjha.*"

52. In the Punjab especially, daughters did not inherit as they should have according to the *shari'at.* Any share came to them in the form of dowry and continued protection by father and brothers.

53. The original title of this final section uses the word *'ibadat,* which is usually translated as "worship," because the primary focus of obedience is to the ritual acts.

Chapter 2
Translator's Introduction to Book Six

1. Three nineteenth-century books in English that have been recently reprinted provide descriptions of some of the customary observances of the time, including many of those Maulana Thanawi discusses. One volume was written in 1832 by an Englishwoman who was married to a Lucknow Shi'a and who was a longtime resident in India: Mrs. Meer Hassan Ali, *Observations on the Mussalmauns of India* (Karachi: Oxford University Press, 1974). The second was originally compiled in 1832 by a Deccani Sunni, a *munshi* in the employ of the British: Ja'far Sharif, *Islam in India, or the Qanun-i-Islam,* ed. and trans. G. A. Herklots, rev. William Crooke (1921; reprint, New Delhi: Oriental Books Reprint Corp., 1972). The subject of the third, written by the wife of a servant of the East India Company who went to India in 1822, is not limited to Muslims: Fanny Parks, *Wanderings of a Pilgrim in Search of the Picturesque,* introduction and notes by Esther Chawner (Karachi: Oxford University Press, 1975); the original title adds: *During Four-and-Twenty Years in the East; with Revelations of Life in the Zenana.*

Closer in period and location to Maulana Thanawi's book is the Urdu work of Saiyid Ahmad Dihlawi, *Rusum-i dihli,* first published in 1905 (reprint, New Delhi: Urdu Academy, Delhi, 1986). The work makes no attempt at reform but rather describes the customs that so troubled Maulana Thanawi. Saiyid Ahmad Dihlawi also wrote the monumental four-volume dictionary *Farhang-i asafiyya,* first published in 1892 (Delhi: National Academy, 1974); it is frequently cited in the notes to Book Six.

2. William R. Roff, "Whence Cometh the Law? Dog Saliva in Kelantan, 1937," and David Gilmartin, "Customary Law and Shari'at in British Punjab"; both in *Shari'at and Ambiguity in South Asian Islam,* ed. Katherine P. Ewing (Berkeley and Los Angeles: University of California Press, 1988), pp. 25–42 and pp. 43–62, respectively.

3. C. M. Naim, "How Bibi Ashraf Learned to Read and Write," *Annual of Urdu Studies* 6 (1987): 118.

4. Zekiye S. Eglar, *A Punjabi Village in Pakistan* (New York: Columbia University Press, 1960); H. A. Alavi, "Kinship in West Pakistan Villages," in *Muslim Communities of South Asia,* ed. T. N. Madan (New Delhi: Vikas Publishing House, 1976), pp. 1–27.

5. See William H. Wiser and Charlotte V. Wiser, *Behind Mud Walls, 1930–1960,* rev. ed. (Berkeley and Los Angeles: University of California Press, 1971); and William H. Wiser, *The Hindu Jajmani System* (Lucknow: Lucknow Publishing House, 1936). The same village studied by the pioneering Wisers has recently been restudied by anthropologists Susan Wadley and Bruce Derr.

6. Gloria Goodwin Raheja, "The Poison in the Gift: Ritual, Prestation,

and the Dominant Caste in a North Indian Village" (Ph.D. dissertation, University of Chicago, 1986).

Book Six

1. Platts suggests a link between the word *domni* and the word for gypsy, "Rom-ni," whom he takes *domni* to resemble (John T. Platts, *A Dictionary of Urdu, Classical Hindi, and English*, 5th ed. [London: Oxford University Press, 1930; reprint 1960], p. 569).

2. *Na-mahram:* those whom it is not forbidden to marry (that is, the relationship is not so close as to prohibit marriage).

3. The *tabla* is a pair of drums played by one person; the *sarangi* is a stringed instrument.

4. Literally, a carat.

5. Mount Uhud is a rugged mountain located about three miles from Medina, celebrated for the battle won there by Muhammad against the Quraish in A.H. 3.

6. *Shatranj:* chess. *Tash:* cards. *Chausar:* a board game like pachisi, played with dice or cowries.

7. *Kankawa:* a square kite flown with silk string.

8. Two terms are used for shaving, *mundwana* and *babari.* Maulana Thanawi's objection, presumably, is to the custom of leaving a tuft of hair (*choti*) on the center of the head, a Hindu practice.

9. *Mushkil kusha:* a title of the Prophet's son-in-law ʿAli; see Saiyid Ahmad Dihlawi, *Farhang-i asafiyya* (1892; reprint, Delhi: National Academy, 1974), vol. 4, p. 389. The image created by placing the grain in the winnowing basket is that negative qualities, the chaff, are thus separated from the life of the child.

10. C. M. Naim comments that, as part of the preparation of these foods, women take a portion to the mosque in a procession. The glossary descriptions of *gulgula* and *batasha* (mentioned later) are also his, based on firsthand experience.

11. *Taka:* a copper coin worth two *paʾi.*

12. The call to prayer is spoken to a new baby, often by a venerable relative.

13. The second word here is not clear; in later editions, *y* becomes *b,* making the word *thanbh,* a pillar-shaped sweetmeat offered at shrines, chiefly by women. *Chhattis* (thirty-six) recalls *chhattis bhojan* or *chhattis vyanjan,* the thirty-six different kinds of food lawful for Brahmins (see Platts, *Dictionary,* p. 459). The dishes fed to menials on this occasion would then represent the kind of ritual inversion common to certain festive occasions.

14. *Dudh dhulaʾi:* "washing the milk," that is, washing the breast of the mother just before the baby is suckled for the first time. In a contemporary case study in Bijnor, the husband's sister is expected to do the work of the new mother while she is confined. She also "washes the milk" and receives *neg* in return. See Patricia Jeffery, Roger Jeffery, and Andrew Lyon, *Labour Pains and Labour Power: Childbearing in Rural North India* (London: Zed Press,

1988), pp. 131–132. This study of two villages, one Hindu and one Muslim, echoes many of the ideas of customary gifts (pp. 134–138), pollution (p. 124), auspicious charms (p. 258, note 14), and so forth discussed here. Villagers even make Thanawi's argument that gifts were once given joyously and voluntarily but are now an obligatory burden (pp. 26–27).

15. Haman was Pharaoh's prime minister, mentioned in the Qur'an. Qarun led a rebellion against Moses, reported in the *hadis.*

16. The mother wears the old shoes presumably because the midwife has taken the new ones.

17. The sandalwood, a cooling substance, is perhaps meant to offset the warmth of new maturity.

18. The literal translation is "to hear the 'wah, wah' of others"; in Urdu this is a cry of approbation.

19. *Niyat bandhna:* to form an intention, as one does according to the *shari'at* in order to make legitimate any ritual observances. This use is made the more ironic by the shift of subject to the prayer in the next sentence.

20. *Manzil-i maqsud:* the intended stage. The metaphor is the final goal of the journey of the sufi.

21. The greetings reflect wishes for fertility, family, or long life. In the hot/cold and wet/dry matrix characteristic of medical—and, indeed, cosmological—thought in this culture, coolness and moisture are associated with fertility.

22. Yajuj and Majuj are the biblical Gog and Magog. These are barbarous people, represented in the Qur'an as having done evil in the historical past; their return is reported in the *hadis* as one of the dread signs of the Last Day, as described in Book Seven of the *Bihishti Zewar.*

23. *Manjha:* a Punjabi localism for a string bed or cot. I have found the second word only in a definition of *manjha,* in which one of its meanings is given as "the yellow outfit of *ma'iyun*" (Ahmad Dihlawi, *Farhang-i asafiyya,* vol. 4, p. 269).

24. Harm might come from *jinn* or others who are attracted by her fragrance and softness.

25. *Baraka:* the blessed power of a saint. Here, the irony draws not on the legal but on the sufi idiom.

26. *Missi:* yellow myrobalan, gall nut, iron filings, vitriol, or other substance used to blacken the teeth.

27. *Halal:* the opposite of the legally prohibited, *haram.* Note the irony of using the legal idiom.

28. *Bhalamanus:* a Hindi term for gentlemen, often used ironically, as it may be here, with the implication of "simpleton."

29. The *shahna'i* is particularly associated with the rejoicing of weddings. Only in recent years has it become an instrument played in concerts and other public performances.

30. *Halwa'i ki dukan aur dadaji ki fatiha.* The implication of this proverb is that one distributes the sweets necessary to performing *fatiha* at the confectioner's expense. The saying is used to describe people who supply their own wants at the expense of others (Ahmad Dihlawi, *Farhang-i asafiyya,* vol. 2, p. 169).

31. The purpose of examining the bedding, of course, is to ascertain whether or not the bride was a virgin, judged by the presence or absence of bloodstains.

32. The part in the hair of a Hindu married woman is reddened with henna or vermilion; it is a sign of being married. Indian Muslims decorate a bride's part by sprinkling it with coarsely powdered gold and silver leaf or with tinsel called *afshaq* (Ismat Chughta'i, "Chauthi ka jora" (The outfit of the fourth), in *Readings in Urdu: Prose and Poetry,* ed. C. M. Naim [Honolulu: East-West Center Press, 1965], p. 25).

33. See Book One, note 50, for a description of this custom.

34. *Daiyus:* "a wittol, a tame cuckold; one who winks at the adultery of his wife or the fornication of his female relations from interested motives" (Platts, *Dictionary,* p. 560). The custom involves making a show of beating one another with sticks covered with flowers.

35. In this custom, the bride's family provides food for the bridegroom and his friends when the bride is about to leave home.

36. Ghee (clarified butter) is used in metaphorical expressions for prosperity. Here, the gifts are given in place of ghee.

37. *A'o bhagat:* come, *bhagat!* Because a *bhagat* is a Hindu holy man who may or may not be sincere, the phrase carries a note of irony in its usage as courtesy, civility, and so on.

38. In "tying the bracelet," a thread or string is tied around the right wrist of the groom and another around the left wrist of the bride. For detail, see Ahmad Dihlawi, *Farhang-i asafiyya,* vol. 3, p. 574.

39. After the marriage contract has been signed, the groom is called into the bride's house, where all the women of the family are gathered. The bride and groom are seated side by side. A red cloth is thrown over the bride's head, and a mirror and a Holy Qur'an (opened to the chapter "Ikhlas") are placed between them. ("Ikhlas" [Purity of faith] is chapter 112 of the Qur'an; it is recited on many different occasions because of its terse and effective statement of the Unity of God. See Naim, *Readings in Urdu,* p. 85.) The bride is cajoled to open her eyes so that the couple will catch their first glimpse of each other in the mirror, sanctified by the Qur'an nearby. The women tell the groom to say, "I am your slave; open your eyes." For more detail, see Ahmad Dihlawi, *Farhang-i asafiyya,* vol. 1, pp. 146–147.

40. *Jahiliyat:* the period before the teachings of the Prophet; hence also the period of time including the present for those who have not accepted those teachings.

41. The marriage portion is the *mahr,* set by the groom. It should not be confused with the *jahez,* or dowry, provided by the bride.

42. It is customary in some Muslim societies for the father to absent himself from a daughter's wedding. Compare contemporary Oman, where the bride's father apparently becomes increasingly shy and embarrassed as the time approaches for the bride to leave with the groom; the father often actually leaves town (Unni Wikan, *Behind the Veil in Arabia: Women in Oman* [Baltimore: Johns Hopkins University Press, 1982]).

43. Qur'an 113:1, 114:1.

44. A *ser* is about two pounds; a *chhatank* is one-sixteenth of a *ser*.

45. *Giyarhwin:* the eleventh, referring to the date of the death of Shah Abdul'l-Qadir Gilani, a greatly revered saint. He died in 1166 on the eleventh day of the eleventh month. His followers observe this occasion with sweets and other items either at his tomb or wherever they may be, in the hope of securing their desires through his intercession or power. His death is remembered by some not only annually but also on the eleventh of every month.

46. The titles, except for the first, refer to official positions in the colonial government.

47. *Ihsan rakhna:* to place an obligation on someone; used ironically.

48. This question refers to the local custom of ritually purifying the floor by daubing it with dung.

49. *Dargah:* a portal, a door, a threshold; a royal court, a palace, a mosque; a shrine or tomb of a reputed saint that is the object of worship and pilgrimage.

50. "Our Revered Lady" refers to Hazrat Bibi, the Prophet's daughter Fatima.

51. *Bibi ki sahnak:* "the dish of our Lady," food prepared in the name of Fatima and eaten only by selected women.

52. *Giyarhwin:* the eleventh; see note 45 above. *Sahmani:* literally, three *man,* a measure roughly equal to eighty pounds; this presumably refers to an amount of food offered on certain occasions. *Tosha:* provisions in general; also, food provided for a funeral, presumably to accompany the deceased during the journey to the other world but usually given as alms to the grave digger or some poor person; also, the food distributed in the name of a saint or elder on the day of the death anniversary (Ahmad Dihlawi, *Farhang-i asafiyya,* vol. 1, p. 239).

53. After the death of a husband or a divorce, a woman is required to wait for a certain period before contracting a new marriage, in order to determine whether she may be pregnant from the original marriage. In Islamic law, this period is set at three months in the case of a divorce and at four months and ten days in the case of a death. If the woman is pregnant, the waiting period extends until the child is born. The common name for this period implies, however, that custom has set a six-month period.

54. *Tarawih:* a prayer performed during Ramazan, at some point in the night after the ordinary prayer at nightfall.

55. The month of Zi-qa'd falls between the festivals of 'Id and Baqr 'Id; it is called empty because no festival occurs during the period.

56. The first thirteen (*tera*) days of Safar are held to be unlucky because the Prophet was seriously ill during those days. *Tezi:* sharpness, intensity.

57. The observance of the Prophet's birthday grew in popularity during the nineteenth century and was fostered by most groups of *'ulama* other than the Deobandi.

58. The fast of Mary took place during her retirement to a distant place when she was about to give birth to Jesus. It is recorded that she heard a voice, either the child in her womb or the Angel Gabriel, telling her that she should find comfort in a rivulet at her feet and dates from the palms above her; should

she encounter anyone, she should say that she had vowed a fast to God and could speak to no one (Qur'an 19:22–28). Her fast (*saum*) is thus a fast of silence. Sufi commentators saw that fast as a withdrawal from all society and absorption in the vision of God, the goal of every fast (V. Courtois, *Mary in Islam* [Calcutta: Oriental Institute, 1954], pp. 20–23, 49–50).

59. *Tabaraka ki rotiyan:* the custom during Rajab of reading the Sura Tabaraka (the sixty-seventh, or "blessed," *sura,* so called from its first word, *tabaraka*) forty-one times and distributing a sweet, rich, seeded bread made of refined flour. This *sura* is said to prevent torments of the grave and encourage intercession at Judgment. See Ahmad Dihlawi, *Farhang-i asafiyya,* vol. 1, p. 590.

60. Thanawi lists this work in Book Ten as suitable for further reading.

61. *'Isawi:* the conventional way of writing common era dates; from 'Isa (Jesus).

Chapter 3
Translator's Introduction to Book Seven

1. See *Moral Conduct and Authority: The Place of* Adab *in South Asian Islam,* ed. Barbara Metcalf (Berkeley and Los Angeles: University of California Press, 1984), for a fuller discussion of these issues. See, in particular, the introduction and the articles by Peter Brown ("Late Antiquity and Islam: Parallels and Contrasts," pp. 23–37) and by Ira M. Lapidus ("Knowledge, Virtue, and Action: The Classical Muslim Conception of *Adab* and the Nature of Religious Fulfillment in Islam," pp. 38–61).

2. See, for example, James T. Siegel, *The Rope of God* (Berkeley and Los Angeles: University of California Press, 1969), for a discussion of similar concepts in Southeast Asia.

3. W. Montgomery Watt, *The Faith and Practice of al-Ghazali* (Lahore: Sh. Muhammad Ashraf, 1963), pp. 79–80.

Book Seven

1. Disease is seen as being caused by imbalances of heat and cold, dry and wet. This injunction against using water warmed by the sun may suggest that such water absorbs heat, which is transferred to the body and manifested in the disease of leprosy.

2. The disciplines, typically including some form of repetition of the name of God, are *wazifa.* A frequent saying of the Deobandi teachers was the rhyming phrase "*Istiqamat karamat see afzal haj*" ("Steadfastness is greater than miracles").

3. Supplication, *du'a,* is prayer other than the required *namaz. Zikr* is the recollection of the name of God as a spiritual exercise.

4. The text gives these prayers in Arabic only, because here, as elsewhere, they are meant to be recited only in that language.

5. Book Five of the *Bihishti Zewar,* not translated here, is devoted entirely to business and financial dealings.

6. Issues related to marriage are discussed in Book Four of the *Bihishti Zewar,* not translated here.

7. Many of the Deobandis participated in the revival of Greco-Arabic medicine during this period. Book Nine of the *Bihishti Zewar,* not translated here, is devoted to the principles of this kind of medicine, *yunani tibb.*

8. *Bi'smi'llah:* see the Note on Translation for the full phrase and its use.

9. *Alhamdu'li'llah:* see the Note on Translation for the full phrase and its use.

10. Lead ore, reduced to a powder, is applied to the eyes in the expectation that it will aid sight.

11. Three charms are listed: *ta'wiz,* often a Qur'anic verse encased in some covering so that it can be worn; *gande,* rings of four cowries or pice used as a charm against evil spirits, or cords of three colored threads worn on the body; and *totka,* a charm, amulet, or philter.

12. Later editions add that one must not use the greetings of infidels. Children in government schools in India are instructed to use neither the English nor the Hindu style of address (Ashraf 'Ali Thanawi, *'Aksi bihishti zewar mukammal mudallal muhashsha* [Delhi: New Taj Office, n.d.], p. 472).

13. South Asians, like many other peoples, consider it offensive to sit in such a way that one's feet are extended toward another person.

14. *Narmi* (softness) and *riqqat* (tenderness) are physical terms that have moral and spiritual implications. The latter conveys tenderheartedness, mercy, ecstasy, religious transport. Note, as discussed above, the physical basis for moral action.

15. No pious action is acceptable without fixing an intention (*niyat*) for the purpose of the act.

16. Platts defines *dhyan* (Sanskrit) in part as "mental representation of the personal attributes of the divinity to whom worship is addressed" (John T. Platts, *A Dictionary of Urdu, Classical Hindi, and English,* 5th ed. [London: Oxford University Press, 1930; reprint 1960], p. 553). One might speculate that this term seems appropriate, given the personal relationship to Allah Miyan, analogous to the relationship to the sufi master, discussed below.

17. One's relationship to a *pir* is described in kin terms, with the master as father, his master as grandfather, his fellow initiates as uncles, the disciple's fellows as sisters and brothers in the *pir,* and so forth.

18. The tooth-stick is a twig of the *nim* tree, used as a dental stimulant and brush.

19. The miraculous *mi'raj,* or night ascension, of the Prophet, via Jerusalem, to the highest heavens.

20. These three letters open six chapters of the Qur'an. They, along with letters opening other chapters, have been much discussed. For comments on these letters (*al-muqatta'at*), see Abdullah Yusuf Ali, *The Holy Qur'an: Text, Translation, and Commentary* (Lahore: Sh. Muhammad Ashraf, 1973), Appendix 1 to Sura 2.

21. *Balist* is the Sanskrit term for the span from the thumb to the little finger; *saton dyip* identifies the seven divisions of the world of Hindu cosmology.

22. Urdu provides more specific kin terms than does English; here, the relatives specified are a husband's younger brother (*dewar*), a husband's older brother (*jheth*), a sister's husband (*bahnui*), the son of a father's brother (*chachazad*), the son of a mother's brother (*mamunzad*), the son of a father's sister (*phuphizad*), and the son of a mother's sister (*khalazad*).

23. Diwali, the Hindu autumnal festival of lights, is celebrated with fireworks and revelry.

24. Every believer is said to be attended by two angels, one to record good deeds and one to record bad.

25. The Muslim day begins at sunset. Hence the Urdu reference to "Friday night," the eve of Friday, is translated into English as "Thursday night."

26. A child whose father has died is considered an orphan here.

27. The word *kho* suggests again the identity of outer behavior and inner self: it is a habit or custom as well as one's nature and disposition.

28. The *hauz-i kausar* is the pool at the center of the garden of paradise.

29. The term "Nazarenes" for Christians became a point of controversy in the late nineteenth century. Saiyid Ahmad Khan, as part of his effort to improve relations between elite Muslims and the British, argued that the term in fact referred not in a derogatory way to the town of Nasira ("Can any good come out of Nazareth?") but rather to the word "help," *nasr* (citing the Qur'an [3:45], in which Jesus asks for helpers and the disciples respond). He tried to show that Christians had indeed helped others. See L. S. May, *The Evolution of Indo-Muslim Thought After 1857* (Lahore: Sh. Muhammad Ashraf, 1970), p. 43. Maulana Thanawi, unlike Sir Saiyid, used the term without apology.

30. Abu Sufyan was an opponent of the Prophet, notable as leader of the Meccans in the Battle of Badr.

31. The emperor is martyred in the Islamic sense, in that any Muslim who dies in a legitimate battle is a martyr.

32. Khaibar is a rich and densely settled valley, populated by Jews at the time of the Prophet and the site of one of his famous successful expeditions from Medina.

33. The *mahdi*, "the guided one," is for many of the Shi'a the twelfth *imam*, but for all he is the ruler who will appear in the final days.

34. The conventional epithets of these two sacred cities, not always translated in the text: *madina al-munawwara, makka al-mu'azzama.*

35. The *abdal* are part of an invisible hierarchy of saints through whom God is said to sustain the world. There are seventy at any given time; when one dies, another takes his place. God alone knows who they are.

36. The black stone, placed in the wall of the Ka'ba, is believed to have been sent from heaven. The Station of Ibrahim is the stone used by Ibrahim when building the Ka'ba.

37. *Bai'a:* the oath of allegiance to a ruler or spiritual guide.

38. Dajjal is the one-eyed imposter who will be mistaken for the messiah at the end of time.

39. This power or effect, *tasir,* is a reversal of the usual Muslim image of Jesus as a reviver of life.

40. Yajuj and Majuj are the biblical Gog and Magog.

41. The mountain of Tur is the biblical Mount Sinai.

42. The month Zi'l-hij, the last month of the year; it is the occasion of the *hajj* and the feast of Baqr 'Id, held in commemoration of Ibrahim's offer to sacrifice his son Isma'il at God's order.

43. Such declarations are not accepted at the time of death.

44. The tenth of Muharram is considered the day of creation; it is also commemorated by the Shi'a as the day of mourning for the death of Imam Husain.

45. Later editions of the *Bihishti Zewar* set this interval at one hundred thirty years.

46. The empyrean is the location of the throne of God.

47. Although marriage is part of the *sunna,* there is a minor strand favoring celibacy in some sufism.

48. Thanawi lists this work in Book Ten as suitable for further reading.

Chapter 4

Translator's Introduction to Book Eight

1. The doctrine of the *nur-i muhammadi* is rooted in the esoteric teachings of Islam. The Shi'a believe that a primordial light is passed from prophet to prophet, and after the Prophet of Islam to the *imam*s. The light makes them sinless and bestows knowledge of divine mysteries. The *imam*s are thus humanity's intermediaries with God. In sufism, a person must similarly become attached to an initiatory chain, which goes back to the Prophet and through which a spiritual presence, much like this light, is passed. (See Seyyid Hossein Nasr, *Sufi Essays* [London: Allen & Unwin, 1972], p. 111.) Here, however, Thanawi implies that the light does not continue beyond the lifetime of the Prophet, an issue of contention between the Deobandis and their opponents.

2. The shape given to these stories in the Qur'an, the main source, can be conveniently found under individual entries in the *Encyclopedia of Islam,* new ed. (Leiden: E. J. Brill, 1960–).

3. Concerning this final essay, see, for example, Ashraf 'Ali Thanawi, *'Aksi bihishti zewar mukammal mudallal muhashsha* (Delhi: New Taj Office, n.d.), esp. pp. 592–596.

Book Eight

1. The Islamic months are taught in Books One and Ten. The year given here is equivalent to A.D. 571.

2. See Book Seven, note 29, concerning use of the term "Nazarenes" for Christians.

3. Hawwa (the biblical Eve) does not appear by name in the Qur'an; see 2:33–37.

4. Nuh is the biblical Noah; see Qur'an 71:27–29, 11:27–50, 11:88. Although the use of the term "Muslim" may seem anachronistic here and in the story of Hazrat Ayyub below, Muslims hold that the earlier prophets and those who followed them were Muslim in the sense that they received essentially the same message as the prophet Muhammad received and, as he did, surrendered their will to God.

5. Sara is not mentioned by name in the Qur'an but is referred to in 11:74. Ibrahim and Ishaq are the biblical Abraham and Isaac, respectively. They are mentioned frequently in the Qur'an; see 2:121–126, 2:260–263, 3:58–60, 6:74–87, 11:72–78, 19:42–51, 21:52–75.

6. Hajira is the biblical Hagar, Isma'il the biblical Ishmael. See Qur'an 28:97–113 for an account of Isma'il. The stories of Hajira are recounted in numerous *hadis*.

7. Namrud—though not this incident—is alluded to in the Qur'an; see 2:260.

8. Lut is the biblical Lot. He is mentioned in the Qur'an in 7:72–82, 21:74, 21:75, 29:27–37, 16:160–175, 27:55–59.

9. Ayyub is the biblical Job. The incident of the broom is referred to in the Qur'an 38:40–44; see also 4:166, 6:184.

10. Yusuf is the biblical Joseph; Ya'qub is Jacob. See Qur'an 12 for the story of Yusuf; the episode concerning his aunt is not mentioned, however.

11. Musa is the biblical Moses. See Qur'an 18:59–81, 28:21–28, 40:27–49.

12. Three terms for rank are used in the *Bihishti Zewar,* apparently interchangeably: *rutba, martaba,* and *darja.*

13. The story is referred to in Qur'an 66:11, although the wife of Pharaoh is not mentioned by name.

14. The book *Rauzatu's-safa* (The garden of purity) is probably one written by Muhammad bin Khavendshah bin Mahmud ("Mir Khwand") (d. 1498). It was translated into English from the original Persian by E. Rehatsek and titled by him *Sacred and Profane History According to the Moslem Belief;* it was edited by E. F. Arbuthnot and published in London by the Royal Asiatic Society between 1891 and 1894. It includes chapters on earlier prophets and kings, on Muhammad, and on the first four caliphs. It is cited in J. F. Blumhardt, *Catalogue of Hindustani Printed Books in the Library of the British Museum* (London: British Museum, 1889).

15. For the account of Khizr killing the young boy, see Qur'an 18:59–81; it is one of three acts of this companion of Moses that appear irrational but are in fact the will of God. Khizr is not mentioned by name, and in general his identity is obscure. In the Indian subcontinent, he is associated with places of water; shrines to his name are found by rivers and bridges.

16. Sulaiman is the biblical Solomon; see Qur'an 21:78–82, 27:15–45, 34:11–13, 38:29–39.

17. Hazrat Bilqis of the country of Saba is the biblical queen of Sheba; see Qur'an 27:15–45.

18. Maryam is Mary, the mother of Jesus; see Qur'an 3:31.

19. For these stories about Maryam, see Qur'an 3:31–44, 19:1–37, 16:12.

20. Zakariya is the biblical Zachariah, the father of John the Baptist.

21. For these stories about Isha', see Qur'an 3:33–37, 19:1–15, and esp. 21:89.

22. Note that the previous husband of each of the Prophet's wives is listed. This is not widely known information, but it is important here because of Maulana Thanawi's emphasis on the importance of the remarriage of widows.

23. See Qur'an 33:37.

24. The reference to "someone from outside" suggests how common it was for wellborn Muslims in this society to marry within their own circle of relatives.

25. The *mahr*, or marriage portion, was the amount set to be paid to the bride by the husband. In India, it was typically deferred, except in the case of divorce, and often excused completely. A marriage is not legitimate without a *mahr* being promised. See the discussion in Book Six.

26. The Ansar, "Helpers," were those residents of Medina who accepted the leadership of the Prophet.

27. The signet ring of the Prophet, with his name and "the Messenger of God" engraved on it, is discussed in the *hadis*.

28. *Hikmat* (wisdom) can refer to philosophy in general, but here it is the equivalent of *tibb,* Greco-Arabic medicine. The revival of medicine in Thanawi's time attempted to disseminate scientific medicine at the expense of local curing practices, which were often in the hands of women. Book Nine of the *Bihishti Zewar* reflects this movement.

29. The late nineteenth century saw a new emphasis on the founding of formally organized religious schools (discussed in the Introduction to the *Bihishti Zewar,* above). Maulana Thanawi himself was actively involved with this development.

30. Rum is the Eastern Roman empire; later, the Ottoman empire. A *qazizada* is an offspring of a family of judges.

31. The pilgrimage proper can be performed only at a fixed time of year; any other ritual visit to Mecca is known as a lesser pilgrimage ('*umra*).

32. This instruction to feign weeping if real tears do not come suggests the importance of outer acts in the shaping of inner attitudes, described in Book Seven.

33. The word for "place" in this sentence, *maqam,* is used specifically for a stage in mystical development.

34. Hajji Imdadu'llah Chishti Sabiri was from the town of Thana Bhawan, Maulana Thanawi's home. He emigrated to Mecca after the Mutiny of 1857, but he kept close ties with his followers, including most of the Deobandi *'ulama*. The book is on the list of approved works cited in Book Ten.

35. Presumably, fever brings forgiveness of sins as does all adversity that is met with patience.

Chapter 5
Translator's Introduction to Book Ten

1. McKim Marriott, "Hindu Transactions: Diversity Without Dualism," in *Transaction and Meaning: Directions in the Anthropology of Exchange and Symbolic Behavior,* ed. Bruce Kapferer (Philadelphia: Institute for the Study of Human Issues [ISHI] Publications, 1976), pp. 109–142.

2. C. M. Naim, "How Bibi Ashraf Learned to Read and Write," *Annual of Urdu Studies* 6 (1987): 103.

3. For current approaches to this problem, see Barbara Metcalf, "An Assessment of Programs and Needs in the Field of Women in Development, Especially in Regard to Education and Training" (typescript prepared for U.S. Agency for International Development, Islamabad, February 1983). The suggestion that women become involved in bookbinding—traditionally a male occupation but ideally suited to women's cottage production—has recently been introduced in Karachi.

4. A summary of the system can be found in Muhammad Abd-al-Rahman Barker, *A Course in Urdu* (Montreal: Institute of Islamic Studies, 1967).

5. The discussion of this and other novels by Nazir Ahmad largely follows the analysis of C. M. Naim, who specifically discusses Thanawi's two lists in "Prize-Winning *Adab:* A Study of Five Urdu Books Written in Response to the Allahabad Government Gazette Notification," in *Moral Conduct and Authority: The Place of* Adab *in South Asian Islam,* ed. Barbara Metcalf (Berkeley and Los Angeles: University of California Press, 1984), pp. 290–314. As Professor Naim notes, the *Taubatu'n-nasuh* was rewarded and patronized by the British, published in an annotated form for British students of Urdu, and translated into English. It has been kept in print to the present. For a general discussion of the novel, see Shaista Akhtar Banu Suhrawardy, *A Critical Survey of the Development of the Urdu Novel and Short Story* (London: Longmans, 1945).

6. On Hali, see Laurel Steele, "Hali and His *Muqaddamah:* The Creation of a Literary Attitude in Nineteenth-Century India," *Annual of Urdu Studies* 1 (1981): 1–45.

7. See Shamsur Rahman Faruqi, "Images in a Darkened Mirror: Issues and Ideas in Modern Urdu Literature," *Annual of Urdu Studies* 6 (1987): 43–54.

8. General surveys of Urdu literature, of course, stress the books that are disapproved here; see Muhammad Sadiq, *A History of Urdu Literature* (London: Oxford University Press, 1964), which has a bias much like that of Hali.

9. For the *qissa* literature, see Frances W. Pritchett, *Marvelous Encounters: Folk Romance in Urdu and Hindi* (Riverdale, N.Y.: Riverdale Co., 1986); chap. 3 of this work analyzes and evocatively retells the *Qissa-yi hatim ta'i.*

10. *Mir'atu'l-'arus* is available in English as *The Bride's Mirror: A Tale of Domestic Life in Delhi Forty Years Ago,* trans. G. E. Ward (London: H. Frowde, 1903).

11. The syllabus of Asghari's school includes the second, fifth, and seventh titles from Thanawi's list of approved books and the fourth and thirteenth from the list of disapproved works. The titles are given in Naim, "Prize-Winning *Adab,*" p. 303.

Book Ten

1. *Ta'wiz* are typically Qur'anic verses encased in a covering and worn on the body; they are considered legitimate by the Deobandis only if properly understood. *Gande,* according to Platts, are charmed cords, generally of three

colored threads knotted together and bound somewhere on the body to avert evil influences (John T. Platts, *A Dictionary of Urdu, Classical Hindi, and English,* 5th ed. [London: Oxford University Press, 1930; reprint 1960], p. 918). These charms are also mentioned in Book Seven in relation to treating illness.

2. The original text in fact says "washerman," but later editions of the *Bihishti Zewar,* attempting to be "proper," make *dhobi* into the feminine *dhobin,* congruent with the "miller's wife" used here.

3. This section on color-coded train tickets was omitted from later editions of the *Bihishti Zewar* when the practice disappeared; presumably, the arrangements for rail journeys had become more familiar to travelers.

4. The reference to sin suggests occasions such as *qiyam,* during *maulid,* when some people customarily stood up, believing that the Prophet was present.

5. *Churan* tablets and Solomon's salt are medications. Both are digestives compounded of ingredients such as ground spices, dried green mangoes, and lime.

6. The list of ingredients at the beginning of each recipe or set of instructions is not always found in the original; it has sometimes been added in this translation for clarity and uniformity of format.

7. The list of utensils originally appeared at the end of the instructions for making soap. In the translation, for clarity, it has been moved.

8. In the original, this paragraph appears after the next paragraph. It has been moved in the translation to make the process more easily understood.

9. Later editions include methods for making soap that are, they claim, simpler, cheaper, and examples of the progress made in household crafts. They offer, in Urdu transliteration, "cold process" for *kacca* soap and "hot process" for *pakka* soap. See Ashraf ʿAli Thanawi, *ʿAksi bihishti zewar mukammal mudallal muhashsha* (Delhi: New Taj Office, n.d.), pp. 716–717.

10. As discussed in the Note on Translation, Urdu has devices to express hierarchy, including causative and double causative verbs, that are unknown in English. In this recipe, suggestive of kitchen hierarchy, the reader herself adds only the color. The usage does not seem consistent with other recipes, however, for simple imperatives are used in the recipe for soap, for example, with its heavy labor and massive amounts of ingredients.

11. These shortcuts (*gur*) are based on the facts that $\frac{1}{40}$ *man* is 1 *ser* and that 16 *ana*s equal 1 rupee. Thus, in the first rule, 2½ *ser* equal $\frac{1}{16}$ of a *man,* just as 1 *ana* is $\frac{1}{16}$ of a rupee. Similarly, a *girih* is $\frac{1}{16}$ of a yard.

12. Daha is taken from the Persian word for ten, referring to the ten days of mourning observed at the beginning of this month.

13. The name Tera tezi is derived from the belief that the first thirteen days of this month are unlucky because the Prophet was ill during those days. See Jaʿfar Sharif, *Islam in India, or the Qanun-i-Islam,* ed. and trans. G. A. Herklots, rev. William Crooke (1921; reprint, New Delhi: Oriental Books Reprint Corp., 1972), p. 186.

14. The Urdu name Bara wafat describes the twelve days of the Prophet's fatal illness. It is held that he was born and died on the twelfth of this month.

15. Platts identifies a saint, Miran, a "miracle monger . . . whose memory

is held in veneration by women, and the lower orders of certain classes of Muhammadans and Hindus." The use of the saint's name for this month, he notes, is limited to women (Platts, *Dictionary*, p. 1105). See also Ja'far Sharif, *Islam in India*, p. 289.

16. Shah Madar is, again, the name of a saint. Platts describes him as "held in great reverence by Bhatiyaras and Kunwar Musalmans; his tomb is at Makanpur, Kanhpur." He also notes the use of the saint's name for this month (Platts, *Dictionary*, p. 1014).

17. Khwajaji is also the name of a saint; in this case, it is the title of the great Chishti saint of Ajmer, Hazrat Mu'inu'd-Din.

18. Maryam roza refers to the fast of Mary. See Book Six, note 58.

19. The month of Sha'ban takes its Urdu name, Shab-i Barat, from the celebration of the eve of the fifteenth day of the month; see Glossary.

20. The month takes its Urdu name, 'Id, from the feast that opens this month and closes the previous month of fasting.

21. The Urdu name Khali describes this month as "empty" of major festivals, particularly because it falls between the months of the two 'Id celebrations.

22. Baqr 'Id, the 'Id of the sacrifice, commemorates Ibrahim's offer to sacrifice his son and is part of the annual pilgrimage to Mecca, which takes place in this month.

23. Some later editions omit this section entirely, to avoid the risk of misleading the reader when postal regulations change; other editions simply bring the information up to date.

24. "Friend" is actually *bha'i* (brother) in the original, but this term is used familiarly to address friends and relatives of both sexes.

25. The format of a numbered list has been added in the translation.

26. This title is noted as a "Hindustani translation by Fakhr al-Din Ahmad of Husain Vaiz's *Tafsir-i Husaini* or Persian commentary on the Koran, Lucknow, 1879–80," in J. F. Blumhardt, *Catalogue of Hindustani Printed Books in the Library of the British Museum* (London: British Museum, 1889), p. 81.

27. "A Muhammadan religious tract," by Munshi Muhammad 'Ali (Lucknow, 1867) (Blumhardt, *Catalogue*, p. 219).

28. "Texts from the Koran with explanations in Hindustani," in the Gujarati character (Bombay, 1881) (Blumhardt, *Catalogue*, p. 177).

29. Blumhardt lists the author of this title as Maulvi 'Abd Allah: "*Hakikatu's-salat . . .* a treatise on prayer, followed by *Risalah i be namazan*, a poem on the same subject by Nizam al-Din, with marginal notes, and translations of Arabic quotations" (Cawnpore, 1872) (*Catalogue*, p. 3).

30. "A treatise on funeral ceremonial observances; compiled from Persian and Arabic sources by Muhammad 'Imran" (Lucknow, 1866) (Blumhardt, *Catalogue*, p. 233).

31. "A work on prayer and ceremonial observances, being a translation by Muhammad Nur al Din of the Persian *Mala i badmanah* of Sana Allah" (Lucknow, 1866) (Blumhardt, *Catalogue*, p. 309).

32. This title is cited as a source in Book Seven of the *Bihishti Zewar*. It is also advertised on the back cover of Book Ten as discussing "necessary issues of *fiqh*, concerning selling and buying, contracts, and so forth." (The books

advertised in Book Ten were listed on a single page; they were available from the book dealers named on the title page.)

33. "A work on the creation of man, death, and the resurrection," by ʿAbbas ʿAli ibn Nasir ʿAli (Lucknow, 1873) (Blumhardt, *Catalogue*, p. 1).

34. This title is by Muhammad Kutb al Din Dihlavi, noted in Blumhardt as "*Tuhfat al zaujain*, or 'The duties of husbands and wives.' Compiled from various Arabic sources and followed by a sermon in Arabic with an interlineary translation" (Lucknow, 1866) (*Catalogue*, p. 241).

35. This work is cited by Thanawi as a source for Book Seven.

36. This work is recommended by Thanawi in Book Seven, at the end of the seventh section. It is also advertised at the end of Book Ten.

37. This work is advertised on the back page of Book Ten as offering "the necessary connection of various rewards to good and bad deeds."

38. "A treatise on the commission and punishment of grievous moral offences," by Muhammad ʿInayat Ahmad (Lucknow, 1872) (Blumhardt, *Catalogue*, p. 233).

39. "A treatise in verse in support of widow marriages," by ʿAbd al Rahim Dihlavi (Delhi, 1873) (Blumhardt, *Catalogue*, p. 13).

40. This work is the source for the account of the Last Judgment at the end of Book Seven.

41. This work is cited as a source in Book Six. It is also advertised on the back page of Book Ten as being specifically concerned with the customs of "Hind."

42. This title is noted in Blumhardt as appended to the *Risalah i benamazan* by Nizam al Din (Bombay, 1877). Also in the edition he notes is the *Nasihat nama* (item 59 on Thanawi's list); Blumhardt describes this particular tract as "a short poem on the necessity of prayer" (*Catalogue*, p. 275).

43. "A work on Muhammadan religious observances according to the school of Abu Hanifah. Translated from the Persian with five additional chapters" (Lucknow, 1871) (Blumhardt, *Catalogue*, p. 332).

44. This title is noted in Blumhardt as "an anonymous publication on the resurrection and Judgment Day" (Lucknow, 1865) (*Catalogue*, p. 38). See also W. W. Hunter, *The Indian Musalmans: Are They Bound in Honor to Rebel Against the Queen?* (1871; reprint, Lahore: Premier Book House, 1964), p. 46. Hunter cites this book among thirteen treasonable works, identifying it as a widely circulated book of poetry by Maulawi Muhammad ʿAli, printed in 1265/ 1849. Hunter unknowingly summarizes the signs of the Last Day (discussed in Book Seven here), taking them for a battle planned at the Khyber Pass on the Punjab frontier, having confused the Khyber with the Arabian *khaibar*.

45. "An account of the Muhammadan paradise from traditions and sayings of the Prophet," by Faiyaz al-Hakk (Delhi, 1873) (Blumhardt, *Catalogue*, p. 80).

46. "Moral advice to women, in verse" (Bombay, 1877) (Blumhardt, *Catalogue*, p. 332).

47. "A work on the social condition of Muhammadan women, based on tradition, being principally a translation of the Persian *ʿUnwan fi suluk al-*

niswan of 'Ali Muttaki," by 'Ali Muhammad ibn Muhammad Mu'in, 2d ed. (Lucknow, 1872) (Blumhardt, *Catalogue,* p. 28).

48. "The duties of Muhammadan women, religious, social, and domestic," by Fatimah Bibi, daughter of Maryam Zahir (Cawnpore, 1871) (Blumhardt, *Catalogue,* p. 83).

49. *Taubatu'n-nasuh* is the famous novel by Deputy Nazir Ahmad, noted in Blumhardt as "a novel on the importance of education and religious training" (Cawnpore, 1869) (*Catalogue,* p. 271). A translation by M. Kempson was published in London in 1884; an edited version, also by Kempson, was published there in 1886. See Translator's Introduction to Book Ten of the *Bihishti Zewar.*

50. The ruling Begam of Bhopal was influenced by her consort to support the legal position of the reformist Ahl-i Hadis, a movement similar to that of the Deobandis in many ways but based on direct use of the sources of Qur'an and *hadis* and opposed to Hanafi law.

51. See Book Eight for the story of Asiya.

52. This title is noted in Blumhardt as a short treatise on the birth, miraculous power, and personal appearance of Muhammad, by Muhammad Salamat Allah, called Kashfi (Cawnpore, 1872) (*Catalogue,* p. 250).

53. A history of the life of Muhammad, by Muhammad 'Inayat Allah Khan (Cawnpore, 1864) (Blumhardt, *Catalogue,* p. 233).

54. The Deobandis opposed the celebration of *maulud-i sharif* on a fixed day, especially when it was linked to customary practices such as distributing sweets. They also opposed *qiyam,* standing during the third part of the poem recounting the Prophet's birth.

55. Blumhardt notes that this work is also known as the *Rauzatu'l-asfiya;* it is a history of the prophets, compiled from Persian and Arabic sources, by Muhammad Tahir (Cawnpore, 1867) (*Catalogue,* p. 252).

56. "A history of the martyrdoms of the two imams, Hasan and Husain; Arabic text, with a Hindustani interlineary translation by Khurram 'Ali; accompanied by notes from Waris 'Ali's *Takriru'l-shahadatain* by Muhammad Salamat Allah and by other notes taken by Mirza Hasan 'Ali from the *Rauzatu'l-ahbab* and various other works," 4th ed. (Lucknow, 1873) (Blumhardt, *Catalogue,* p. 5).

57. A work on Muslim religious obligations and duties; a translation by Fakhru'd-Din Ahmad of the *Kimiya'u's-sa'adat,* a Persian abridgment of Ghazali's *Ihya 'ulum al-din* (Cawnpore, 1866) (Blumhardt, *Catalogue,* p. 209).

58. An account of anecdotes of Muslim saints, translated from the Persian *Hikayatu's-salihin* by Muhammad 'Abdu'r-Rahman Khan (Lahore, 1869) (Blumhardt, *Catalogue,* p. 215).

59. This work and the next one listed (item 55) are both advertised at the end of Book Ten of the *Bihishti Zewar.*

60. This work is cited as the source for the story of Hazrat Tuhfa in Book Eight above; it is written by Hajji Imdadu'llah.

61. A poem on the life of Ibrahim ibn Adham, king of Balkh, by Muhammad Abu'l-Hasan, called Hasan (Lucknow, 1869) (Blumhardt, *Catalogue,* p. 216).

62. See Book Ten, note 42, above.

63. Blumhardt describes this as a poem by Wali Muhammad, called Nazir, published with *Achar chuhon ka* (Pickled rats), by Wajid (Lucknow, 1860) (*Catalogue*, p. 349).

64. This title is noted by Blumhardt as providing directions for leading a holy life. It is a translation with notes by Khurram ʿAli with the Arabic original of the *Kaulu'l-jamil* of Wali Allah ibn ʿAbdu'r-Rahim Dihlawi (Bombay, 1883) (*Catalogue*, p. 349).

65. A treatise on prayer by Hajji Imdadu'llah (Cawnpore, 1879) (Blumhardt, *Catalogue*, p. 132). The author, resident in Mecca after the Mutiny, was the spiritual master of Maulana Thanawi and many of the Deobandis. This work is advertised at the end of Book Ten of the *Bihishti Zewar.*

66. A manual of medicine, by Ihsan ʿAli Khan (Delhi, 1864) (Blumhardt, *Catalogue*, p. 126). *Tibb-i ihsani* and *Makhzanu'l-mufradat* (the next work listed by Thanawi) reflect the Deobandis' interest in the revival of Greco-Arabic medicine at the expense of folk medicine or magic.

67. Instructions for writing letters, with specimens of official documents and correspondence, by Kamaru'd-Din Khan (Bareilly, 1863) (Blumhardt, *Catalogue*, p. 155).

68. *Shikasta* is "broken" script, a shorthand used for rapid writing.

69. An arithmetic book for schools, in four parts. The first and second parts were translated from the Hindi *Ganitaprakasa*, the third and fourth parts from English sources. Various editions were published in Allahabad and Roorkee between 1860 and 1867 (Blumhardt, *Catalogue*, p. 343).

70. Thanawi refers to "*diwans* and books of *ghazals.*" *Diwans* are collections of poetry, in the Persian tradition, arranged in alphabetical order by the final letters of the various end rhymes. The *ghazal* is the most popular verse form in classical Persian and Urdu, a brief lyric poem whose theme is most typically love of a human and/or divine beloved.

71. This well-known and popular work, composed as a drama at the court of Oudh, is noted by Blumhardt as a "fairy tale" in verse, by Amanat ʿAli (Cawnpore, 1853, and many other editions) (*Catalogue*, p. 29).

72. This work was written in the poetic form of a *masnawi* by the celebrated poet Mir Hasan (Shaista Akhtar Banu Suhrawardy, *A Critical Survey of the Development of the Urdu Novel and Short Story* [London: Longmans, 1945], p. 24).

73. A tale in verse of a king of Yemen and of the miracle worked on him by the Prophet (Delhi, 1870) (Blumhardt, *Catalogue*, p. 354).

74. A Persian romance, in four parts, of unknown authorship, containing an account of the life and exploits of Amir Hamza, uncle of the Prophet, translated by Khalil ʿAli Khan (Bombay, 1850, and other editions) (Blumhardt, *Catalogue*, p. 110). Suhrawardy describes it as "the fount and source of most of the romances and tales that are to be found in Urdu and Persian" (*A Critical Survey*, p. 26).

75. This title is described as a Persian tale by ʿIzzat Allah, published in many editions. One edition listed is "A translation into the Hindoostanee tongue, of the popular Persian tales, entitled Goolai Bucawley, by Moonshy

Neehalchund Lahoree, under the superintendent [sic] of John Gilchrist, sixth edition, Bombay, 1843" (Blumhardt, *Catalogue*, p. 144). The first edition was published in 1803. (John Gilchrist at Fort William College was a central figure in encouraging the writing of classical tales in simple Urdu.) This particular work was also translated into English; a translation by Thomas Philip Manuel, for example, was in print in Lucknow at the time Thanawi was writing. It was also known as the *Mazhab-i 'ishq* (Suhrawardy, *A Critical Survey*, p. 20).

76. Many Urdu translations of this work are listed by Blumhardt. An early one was "Hikayautool jaleelah . . . called Arabian Nights; for the use of the College at Fort St. George. Translated by Moonshy Shumsooddeen Uhmed" (Madras, 1836) (*Catalogue*, p. 36).

77. A work on divination, charms, and incantations, by Muhammad Ashraf 'Ali (Lucknow, 1873) (Blumhardt, *Catalogue*, p. 221).

78. A book of fate and interpretation of dreams, by Ja'far Sadiq (Delhi, 1876) (Blumhardt, *Catalogue*, p. 221).

79. A poem on the sanctity of the month of Ramazan, by 'Abdu'llah Khan (Lucknow, 1873) (Blumhardt, *Catalogue*, p. 4).

80. A poem on miracles that are ascribed to the descendents of the Prophet (Blumhardt, *Catalogue*, p. 206). This might well have been a work reflecting what the Deobandis regarded as the errors of the Shi'a.

81. Blumhardt notes the title *Majmu'a-yi chihal risala*, a work devoted to praise of the Prophet (Delhi, 1876) (*Catalogue*, p. 206).

82. A poem on the death of the Prophet "and the miraculous circumstances attending that event," by Nusrat 'Ali (Cawnpore, 1856) (Blumhardt, *Catalogue*, p. 277).

83. Blumhardt notes this as a translation of the Persian story of Hatim Ta'i. It was executed under the direction of John Borthwick Gilchrist by one "Sueed Hydurbux Hydree" (Bombay, 1845) and published subsequently in many editions (*Catalogue*, p. 115). It is by Sher 'Ali Afsos (Suhrawardy, *A Critical Survey*, p. 15; summarized on pp. 18–20). See also the summary and analysis in Frances W. Pritchett, *Marvelous Encounters: Folk Romance in Urdu and Hindi* (Riverdale, N.Y.: Riverdale Co., 1986), chap. 3.

84. Blumhardt notes that this work has also been called the *Fath nama*, an account in verse of the wars of Muhammad Hanif, by Mahmud (Bombay, 1878) (*Catalogue*, p. 191).

85. Blumhardt describes this work as including the Arabic text of the twelfth *sura* of the Qur'an, with a translation and a poem, all on the story of Joseph and Zulaikha (Cawnpore, 1870) (*Catalogue*, p. 177).

86. Selections from the thousand questions put to the Prophet by 'Abdu'l-lah ibn Salam, with the Prophet's replies; a translation from the Arabic (Blumhardt, *Catalogue*, p. 4).

87. Blumhardt describes this title as including answers to difficult questions on Muslim law, translated from the Persian by Ibrahim Husaini (Lucknow, 1873) (*Catalogue*, p. 110).

88. Blumhardt notes two editions, each including poetry in praise of the Prophet (Cawnpore, 1869, 1879) (*Catalogue*, p. 241).

89. "A Hindustani reader containing moral tales and anecdotes, especially

written for Muhammadan women," by Deputy Nazir Ahmad (Lucknow, 1869) (Blumhardt, *Catalogue,* p. 270). See the Translator's Introduction to Book Ten for discussion of this novel and other works by Nazir Ahmad.

90. A tale of Indian life, a sequel to the author's *Mir'atu'l-'arus* (Agra, 1868) (Blumhardt, *Catalogue,* p. 270).

91. A novel by Deputy Nazir Ahmad, also known as *Fasana-i mubtala,* focusing on the pain inflicted on women by the practice of husbands taking a second wife. See Naim, "Prize-Winning *Adab,*" p. 305.

92. A novel by Deputy Nazir Ahmad written to illustrate the evils of prohibiting the remarriage of widows.

Glossary

See also the discussion of terms and Arabic phrases in the Note on Translation. Diacritical marks not included in the text are given here. Capitalization of terms in the text follows conventional English style, not used here.

ābrū   Literally, "brightness of face"; honor; dignity; pride.

adab   Propriety; deportment; civility (pl. *ādāb*, rules of conduct).

'ādat   Custom; usage.

'ālim   See *'ulamā*.

allāh miyāṅ   Our Lord and Master. See the Note on Translation.

allāhu akbar   "God is great," an Arabic phrase used in introducing prayer, when slaughtering an animal, and when expressing surprise or resignation.

ānā   One-sixteenth of a rupee (obs.).

ā'o bhagat   "O come, *bhagat*." A *bhagat* is a Hindu holy man. Expressions such as "to play *bhagat*" are found in Hindi, giving the term the ambiguous connotation of a holy man possibly being a fraud. The phrase is also used as an ironic or sarcastic term for hospitality.

'aql   Intelligence; sense; wisdom.

ashrāf   Gentility among Indian Muslims, including (in the Indian subcontinent) those who trace their lineage to the

	Prophet, his Companions, or to the historic Mughal or Pathan ruling class.
baitu'l-muqaddas	Jerusalem; the mosque of al-Aqṣā.
baqr ʿīd	Also known as *īdu'l-aẓḥa,* this annual festival coincides with the completion of the *ḥajj* and commemorates Ibrahīm's proffered sacrifice of Ismāʿīl (not Isaac, as in the biblical account).
barakat	Abundance; prosperity; blessing; auspiciousness.
barī	The groom's gifts to the bride.
batāsha	A light, crisp sweet made of sugar syrup.
bhangī	A member of a low caste of scavengers and sweepers (fem. *bhangan*).
bidʿat	A reprehensible innovation in religious usage.
bihishtī	Pertaining to paradise.
birādarī	An intermarrying kinship group claiming descent from a common ancestor; kinfolk.
bi'smi'llāh	See the Note on Translation. The phrase is also used as the name of the custom that initiates a child's schooling.
chhaTānk	The sixteenth part of a *ser,* approximately two ounces.
chikan	A particular kind of embroidery including applique and netting, often on muslin, especially associated with the city of Lucknow.
chilla	A period of forty days demarcating such events as a term of mourning, recovery from childbirth, or *sūfī* austerities.
darwesh	A dervish; a *ṣūfī* noted for piety and asceticism; *darweshī,* being a dervish.
Deoband	A town in north India; the site of a reformist theological academy, founded in 1867, where Maulānā Thānawī was trained. A Deobandi, as used here, is a person associated with that academy.
dhyānī	Daughters, or sisters, of a family.
diram	(Persian) or *dirham* (Arabicized). A silver coin that equals twenty to twenty-five *dinar.*
duʿā	A nonritual, personal prayer.
faqīr	A poor person; a mendicant; a *ṣūfī; faqīrī,* poverty, denotes the life of a *ṣūfī* or dervish.
fātiha	The opening chapter of the Qurʾān recited in prayer; prayers, often accompanied by offerings, recited for the dead.

fiqh	Jurisprudence; the discipline of elucidating the *sharī'at;* also, the resultant body of rules.
ghunghnī	Wheat, gram, or pulse boiled whole and in the husk; a sort of stir-about made of grain.
gulgula	Rice or rice flour formed into balls and fried.
hadīs	The reported words, deeds, and occasions of tacit approval by the Prophet Muḥammad, passed on by a chain of reliable authorities.
hāfiz	A person who has memorized the Qur'ān.
hajj	The annual pilgrimage to the *ka'ba* in Mecca, required once of all able Muslims.
hakīm	A doctor in the tradition of Greco-Arabic medicine (*tibb* or *yūnānī tibb*).
halāl	Lawful (in contrast to *harām*); allowable; suitable for eating.
hanafī	Referring to the *sunnī* legal school ascribed to Abū Ḥanīfa (699–767).
haqq	Justice; truth; right; due; obligation (pl. *huqūq*).
hazrat	Presence; dignity; a title used for a great person and benefactor. See the Note on Translation.
henna (*mehndī*)	Leaves ground to a paste and applied in patterns to women's hands and feet; the paste is removed when dry and leaves red patterns on the skin. Henna is essential to a bride's makeup.
hindūstān	The Persian term for India during this period, generally referring to the area between Banaras and the Satlaj, the Indo-Ganjetic plain where Hindi is the dominant language.
'ibādāt	Ritual duties, including performing ablutions, offering prayer, almsgiving, fasting, the *hajj,* reading the Qur'ān, and recollecting God (in contrast to human interactions, *mu'āmalāt*) (sing. *'ibādat*).
'īd	A periodic festival; the two important festivals are *baqr 'īd,* or *'īdu'l-azha,* and *īdu'l-fitr,* the festival of breaking the *ramazān* fast.
ihsān	Benevolent action; kindness; obligation conferred.
imām	A founder of one of the major law schools; a leader of prayer.
'izzat	Dignity; esteem; reputation; honor.

jinn	An order of creatures made from fire, some good, some evil. They are invisible to humans but believed able to possess humans.
ka'ba	The square temple at Mecca enshrining the Black Stone, the goal of the *hajj*.
kalima	The attestation of faith: "There is no god but God, and Muḥammad is the Prophet of God."
karāmat	A miracle; a manifestation of God's grace channeled through a *walī*, as distinct from the miracles (*mu'jiza*) of the prophets.
kashf	An unveiling; a vision of God.
khichaRī	Mixed rice and pulse.
madrasa	A school or college for religious learning.
mahr	The marriage portion; a gift settled on the wife before marriage and claimable upon divorce.
man	A measure of weight, usually 40 *ser*, or approximately 80 pounds, used for bulky items like coal or timber.
māshā	A jeweler's or goldsmith's weight, usually equal to 8 *rattī* or seeds of the *Abrus precatorius*, equal to about 17 grains Troy.
maulānā	"Our lord"; a title used for a learned religious leader.
maulawī	A title used for a learned religious leader; literally, "my tutor or lord."
maulid	A birthday, or nativity; the celebration of the birth of the Prophet.
mazhab	In *sunnī* Islam, one of the four equally legitimate schools of law: *hanafī, hanbalī, shāfi'ī*, and *malikī*.
mu'āmala	Social obligations and interactions; mundane business (in contrast to *'ibādāt*) (pl. *mu'āmalāt*).
muharram	The first month of the Muslim lunar calendar; the first ten days of this month are held as a period of mourning, especially by the *shī'a*, in memory of the deaths of Ḥusain and his companions at Karbala.
munshī	An author or scribe.
murīd	An aspirant or novice on the *ṣufī* path, who undertakes complete obedience to the *shaikh* upon initiation into an order.
nafs	The lower or "animal" faculty of the human being, as opposed to the "angelic" faculty of *'aql*; the lower soul/self.
namāz	The five daily ritual prayers; *ṣalāt*.

neg	Customary gifts, considered perquisites, presented to relatives and dependents on festive occasions. Cf. *purotā*.
ne'otā	An invitation; money collected from those invited to a festive occasion.
niyat	Intention; purpose; the resolve to perform requisite acts of worship, essential to proper completion of the act.
paisā	Coin worth one-fourth of an *ānā* (obs.).
pān	Betel leaf prepared with areca nut, spices, and so forth.
panjīrī	A medicine of five items including flour, sugar, ghee, and cumin, given to puerperal women.
peRā	A sweet made of curd.
pīr	A teacher of the *ṣūfī* path; a *shaikh* or *murshid*.
pīrī-murīdī	The relation of *pīr* and *murīd* (teacher and novice).
purotā	Gifts of sugar, flour, turmeric, and chick-peas given to relatives and servants at weddings in return for small services. Cf. *neg*.
qāẓī	A qualified judge in the Muslim system of *sharī'at* (religious law).
qibla and *ka'ba*	The direction of prayer and the *ka'ba* (a metaphorical title for a revered person).
ramaẓān	The ninth lunar month of the Muslim year, during which the pious fast each day from dawn to sunset.
saiyid	A descendent of the Prophet.
ser	A measure of weight, approximately 2 pounds avoirdupois.
shab-i barāt	The eve of the fifteenth day of the month of *sha'bān*, when a vigil is observed with prayers, feasting, and illuminations, and offerings are made in the name of the dead. Fortunes for the coming year are said to be registered in heaven.
shaikh	An elder or a head; a saint; a descendent of Muḥammad's Companions.
shakarāna	A sweet dish made of sugar, rice, and ghee.
sharāfat	Nobility, associated with birth and with good breeding; respectability.
sharbat	Sherbet; a draft of a mixture of sugar, water, fruit juices, and other ingredients.
sharī'at	A path or road; Islamic law encompassing the ideals of behavior, piety, and virtues provided in the Qur'ān and *sunna*.

sharīf	Noble; of noble birth (pl. *ashrāf*).
shī'a	The minority of Muslims, the "party" of 'Ali, who especially honor the family of the Prophet and the line of *imāms* descended from the family members.
shirk	Partnership; particularly, associating copartners with God; infidelity; polytheism.
siwaiyān	A vermicelli-like noodle, often cooked in a milk syrup as a sweet dish for *'īd*.
ṣūfī	The follower of a path (*ṭarīqa*) of spiritual devotion and discipline; a devotee of a *ṣūfī* master.
sunna	"The trodden path"; the normative practice of the Prophet and the early community, embodied in the *ḥadīs* literature, prescribed for all Muslims (in contrast to *bid'at*, innovation); in a more restricted sense, one of the five categories of actions in Islamic law, those deemed meritorious or recommended (*mandūb*).
sunnī	The majority of Muslims, who accept the authority of the entire first generation of Muslims and the validity of the historical community ("people of custom and community," *ahl as-sunna wa al-jamā'a*).
ṭabī'at	Nature; disposition; constitution.
ṭarīqa	A path or way associated with a *ṣūfī*.
tauba	Vowing to sin no more; repenting; *tauba-tauba*, Fie! Heaven forfend!
tauḥīd	Declaring (God) to be one alone; unity.
ta'ziya	A model of the tomb of Ḥasan, Ḥusain, or others, carried in processions during *muḥarram* by the *shī'a*.
ṭibb	The classical Muslim system of medicine practiced by a *ḥakīm* or *ṭabīb*, often called *yūnānī ṭibb* to indicate its Greek origin.
tolā	A weight of 12 (or 16) *māshā*.
'ulamā	Scholars of Islamic legal and religious studies (sing. *'ālim*).
walī	A friend of God; a saint or holy person.
walīma	The feast given by the groom after the celebration of a marriage.
wazīfa	A pension or stipend; the daily performance of set repetitions as part of pious religious exercises.
yūnānī ṭibb	See *ṭibb*.

zakāt	A religious duty incumbent on free adult Muslims, who are to give a fixed percentage of the value of certain kinds of property to the poor, pious students, and others.
zanāna	Women's apartments, or those areas in which they remain secluded from the gaze of men outside the family.
ẕikr	Remembrance; the recollection of God by pious repetition of his name or set phrases of praise.

Index

Fatima (daughter of Muhammad), 71,
139–141, 242, 254, 255, 273, 281–282,
400nn50,51
Fatima bint Abu Hubaish, 292
Fatima bint Khattab, 287
Fatima Nishapuri, 298–299
Fazil ibn ʿAyyaz, 301
Finance. *See* Monetary transactions
Fiqh, 5, 31–32, 41, 81
Fireworks, 75, 80, 96, 135, 159, 212, 348
Food: and custom, 150–152, 155–159;
and eating habits, 184–185, 189, 334–
337, 352; European, 316; and *fatiha,*
145–151; given as charity, 146–151;
and Hinduism, 84; and ʿId, 157; and
maulid, 158; and minimal transac-
tions, 317; and observance of death,
145–152, 155; and Ramazan, 156; and
ritual, 84, 397n13; and Shab-i Barat,
159; and wedding celebration, 116–
117, 119, 123–124, 130–131, 138, 143.
See also Recipes
Fortune-telling, 218
Fort William College, 325, 413n75
Friendship, 236–238
Funerals. *See* Death

Gaborieau, Marc, 385n13, 386n27
Gambling, 77
Games, 80, 96, 233, 397n6
Geertz, Clifford, 384n1
Gender: bipolar model of, 11; and colonialism, 11–12; hierarchical model of,
2, 11; and language, xiii; and morality, 13; and public/private space, 12;
and sexual difference, 11, 387n35;
and Victorian cult of masculinity, 11;
and virtues, 241–242, 244–245; Western medical views of, 11. *See also*
Men; Patriarchy; Women
al-Ghazali, 167, 323
Ghazals. See Poetry
Ghunghni, 104
Gifts: and custom, 85–87, 98–99, 102,
104, 106, 147, 157, 397–398n14; and
fatiha, 147; and hierarchy, 86–87, 106;
and Hinduism, 85–87, 106; and Islamic culture, 85–87; and minimal
transactions, 317; and shariʿat, 85–86,
99–100, 104; and sin, 106; and wedding celebration, 118–119, 121–122,
126; and women, 387n30. See also
Berghari; Chattis thaniyah; Monetary
transactions; *Neg; Neʾota; Purota*
Gilchrist, John, 325, 413n75
God: anthropomorphization of, 27–28,
67; and Last Judgment, 227–228;
names used for, xii–xiii, 27–28; unity

of (*tauhid*), 2, 26–27, 172; virtuous attitudes toward, 196–198. *See also* Religion, Islamic
Gog and Magog. *See* Yajuj and Majuj
Greeting, 74, 186, 393n21, 398n21,
402n12; prostration as, 263; and sin,
110–111. *See also* Letter writing
Gul-i bakawali, 325, 379

Habits. See *ʿAdat*
Hadis, 28, 39, 50, 62–67, 109–110, 117,
166–168, 177, 190–191, 193, 204–222;
authority of, 204; and critique of custom, 94–96, 98–99, 101, 104–105,
110, 114, 120, 124, 133, 135–139; and
discourse about women, 6–7; and divine punishment and reward, 28–30,
41, 165, 195, 204, 208, 210–211, 227–
230; and family relations, 213; and
faults of women, 245–246, 311–314;
and *fiqh,* 81; and Last Judgment, 30,
109, 165, 169–170, 204, 221–222, 323;
list of fundamental beliefs in, 166,
230–233; and patriarchy, 23, 245; and
praise of women, 308–311, 314; and
prayer, 206–208; and religious knowledge, 205; and remarriage, 145; as
source of correct knowledge, 16–18;
and *sunna,* 97, 105, 139
Hafid ibn Zahra Tabib, female relatives
of, 293
Hafiz ibn ʿAsakir, 293
Hafsa (wife of Muhammad), 254, 274–
275, 281
Haisur, mother of, 268
Haisur, sister of, 267–268
Hajira, 259–261, 405n6
Hajj (pilgrimage), 31, 32, 76, 170, 342,
404n42, 406n31, 409n22
Hala bint Khuwailid, 289
Hali. *See* Altaf Husain Hali
Halima Saʿdiyya, 248, 282–283
Hamna bint Abu Jahsh, 292
Hamza, 290, 412n74
Hanafi Muslims, vii, 81
Handicrafts. *See* Crafts
Hanna (mother of Maryam), 271–272
Haq, Anwarul, 385n14
Haqq, 85–86
Harun (Aaron), 69, 279, 355
Hasan (grandson of Muhammad), 255
Hasan Basri, 295
Hatim Asamm, 307
Hatim Asamm, little girl of, 307
Hawwa (Eve), 241, 244, 246, 258, 404n3
Hazrat, use of term, xii, 394n26
Heart. See *Dil*
Hierarchy: and age, 2; and *Bihishti*

Qur'an: authority of, 204, 231; comprehension of, 180; and critique of custom, 104, 114, 136; and divine punishment and reward, 195, 208; and educational methods, 20; *fatiha* in, 145–
151; and faults of women, 311–312;
as final book from heaven, 70; and
fiqh, 81; and *'ibadat*, 180, 181; and patriarchy, 23; and polygamy, 6; praise
of women in, 308–309, 314; recitation
of, 20, 21, 155–156, 166, 180, 198–
199; *shari'at* based on, 6; as source of
correct knowledge, 16; study of, 108,
351; Sura Tabbat in, 280; Thanawi's
commentary on, 383n2; translation
of, xiv, 222n, 391n78; use of terms
for, 393n15

Rabah Qaisi, wife of, 298
Rabi'a 'Adawiyya (Rabi'a Basriyya),
297, 300
Rab'iyyatu'r-Ra'i, mother of, 295
Rafi'u'd-Din, Shah, 222n, 323
Raheja, Gloria, 86–87
Rahil, 263
Rahman, Fazlur, 385n12
Rahmat (wife of Ayyub), 262–263
Ra'i'a Shamiyya bint Isma'il, 299
Raihana Majnuna, 303–304
Railroads, viii, 4, 316, 344–346
Rajab, 84, 157–158, 401n59
Ramazan, 31, 32, 134, 155–156, 179,
308, 310, 400n54
Raqam, 315, 321, 363
Rauzatu's-safa, 266, 405n14
Ra'za (daughter of Namrud), 262
Reading, 107, 239, 247; of approved
books, 315, 322–323, 352, 376–378;
basic skills of, 40–41, 52–54; benefits
of, 59–61; of novels, 14, 323; and oral
presentation, 21, 389n61; of proscribed books, 315, 322, 324–327,
375–376; and public/private space, 21;
of Qur'an, 20, 21, 155–156, 166, 180,
198–199, 208. *See also* Literacy; Literature; Print media
Recipes, 316, 320–321; for curing tobacco, 360–361; for making chutney,
362–363; for making leaven, 361–362;
for making soap, 357–359, 408nn9,10;
for printing cloth, 359–360
Reformism: and Ahl-i Hadis movement,
22, 392, 411n50; and *Bihishti Zewar*,
vii–2, 5, 7, 9, 22, 38, 41–42, 165, 316–
317, 384n5; and capitalism, 384n10;
and colonialism, 4–5, 7–8, 11–12,
324, 386n27; and correct knowledge,
3, 16, 41, 48, 79, 164; and critique of

custom, 13, 16, 24, 36, 42, 79–88, 172,
324; and critique of Shi'a Muslims, 42;
and Deobandi movement, 3–5, 10, 17,
42, 172, 323, 384n5, 388nn42,48,49,
404n1, 411n54; and divine punishment
and reward, 27, 42; and education, 3,
21–22, 26, 48, 386n27, 389n58; and en-
hancement of female domestic role,
13, 24–26, 37, 40–41; and hierarchy,
2, 82, 391n80; and Jama'at-i Islami
movement, 13, 388n42; and Last Judgment, 68, 285; and literacy, 14, 15, 19,
21, 24; as male intrusion into female
domain, 10, 15; and modernization,
13, 81–82; and moral development,
164, 167, 172, 247–248; and patriarchy, 36–37, 82; and public/private
space, 8; and remarriage, 248, 320;
and ritual, 32; rival schools of, 392;
and self-control, 317–318; and
shari'at, 3, 79–81; and sin, 42; and social change, 4–5, 37, 316; and study of
hadis, 17; and sufism, 5, 42, 172; and
Tablighi Jama'at movement, 5; and urban culture, 324, 385n13; and women,
1–2, 23–24, 247–248, 316, 386n27,
388n41
Relics, 160
Religion, Islamic: and anthropomorphization of God, 27–28, 67; and asceticism, 317; and *bi'smi'llah* (attestation
of faith), xiv, 107; and blessings, xiii–
xiv; and charity, 28; and colonialism,
4, 248; and divine punishment and reward, 27–30, 77–78; and doctrine of
nur-i muhammadi, 243, 253, 404n1;
fundamental beliefs of, 67–72, 166,
230–233; and judgment of dead persons, 71–72; and language, xii–xiii;
and messengers of God, 69; and moral
development, 164; and patriarchy, 23;
and *piri-muridi*, 199–202; and print
media, 19, 21; and public/private
space, 7; and sectarianism, 21; and social identity, 4–5; and *tauhid*, 2, 26–
27, 172. *See also* Angels; Last Judgment; Muhammad, Prophet; Prayer;
Qur'an; Reformism; *Shari'at*
Remarriage, 12, 74, 311, 354–355,
406n22, 414n92; and *hadis*, 145; and
Hinduism, 82–83, 144, 319; and
'iddat, 154; of Muhammad's wives and
daughters, 248, 281–282; and reformism, 248, 320; and *shari'at*, 83, 144–
145; and *sunna*, 83. *See also* Widows
Repentance. See *Tauba*
Reward. *See* Divine punishment and
reward

Shirk (partnership), 36, 84, 204
Shor, Muhammad Ishaq, 348n8
Shu'aib, 69, 264–265, 355
Shukr (gratitude), 197
Sidq (truth), 195, 198
Siegel, James T., 388n46
Sikhs, 386n27
Silsila, 5
Sin, 69, 71; and bodily comportment,
219; and childbirth, 97–103; and conversation, 189–190; dancing as, 93–95,
106; and dress, 108–109, 111, 119,
210–211, 351; and eating habits, 189;
and envy, 191; and fireworks, 96; forsaking of prayer as, 75, 76, 101, 110,
111, 114, 130; fortune-telling as, 218;
games as, 96; and gatherings of
women, 14, 108–112, 116–119, 160;
and gifts, 106; and greed, 191–192; and
greetings, 110–111; guidelines for
avoidance of, 160–161; and hairstyle,
96; list of, 72–77; and marriage customs, 115–139; minor, 212; miserliness
as, 192; and monetary transactions,
100, 113; and music, 125; and oaths,
181–182; and observance of death, 75,
84, 145–155; and observance of
maulid, 157–158; owning images as,
95–96, 218; and owning pet dogs, 95–
96, 218; and owning silver, 107, 135;
and recitation of poetry, 157; and reformism, 42; and singing, 117, 126; and
tauba (repentance), 172, 195; and
travel by women, 14, 108, 110; and
viewing of relics, 160. *See also* Custom;
Shari'at, customs as violation of
Singing, 117, 126, 131, 160, 188, 222
Sirat ibn Hisham, 253
Sittu'l-Muluk, 307
Slave girls, as examples of good women,
269–270, 294, 306, 308
Social change: and *Bihishti Zewar,* 5, 13;
and colonialism, 4–5, 248; and education of women, 247, 316; and morality, 13; and politics, 248; and post offices, 316; and print media, 21; and
railroads, 316; and reformism, 4–5,
37, 316. *See also* Modernization
Social identity: and Islamic religion, 4–5;
and self-control, 317
Social structure: and language, xii–xiii;
and religious universals, 384n9; and
upward mobility, 26. *See also* Class
structure; Hierarchy
Solomon. *See* Sulaiman
Srinivas, M. N., 391n74
Status. *See* Hierarchy
Sufism: and celibacy, 7, 404n47; and fasts,

401n58; and love relationship, 7; and
moral development, 163, 172; and *nafs,*
7; and *piri-muridi,* 200–201; and po-
etry, 7; and reformism, 5, 42, 172; and
shari'at, 163, 172, 201; and women, 7
Sulaiman (Solomon), 69, 226, 244, 268–
269, 355, 405n16
Sulaiman, mother of, 268
Sulaiman Nadwi, Saiyid, 383n2
Sunna, 6, 16, 31, 97; and circumcision,
105; and engagement, 139–140; and
marriage, 404n47; and marriage por-
tion, 139–140; and remarriage, 83;
and wedding celebration, 140
Sunni bihishti zewar, 22
Supplication. *See Du'a;* Prayer
Sura Buruj, 266
Sura Tabaraka, 401n59
Sura Tabbat, 280
Swearing. *See* Oaths
Sweeney, Amin, 389n60

Tabi'at, 33, 189
Tablighi Jama'at movement, 5
Tafsir bayanu'l-qur'an (Ashraf 'Ali
Thanawi), 383n2
Tahir (son of Muhammad), 254, 255
Tahzibu'n-niswan, 22, 323, 377
Ta'i, Hatim, 325
Taiyib (son of Muhammad), 254, 255
Talha, 140
Taqwiyatu'l-imam, 42, 389n52
Tariqa, 5, 83
Tariqa-yi muhammadiyya, 42
Tasawwuf, 163, 165, 238
Tauba (repentance), 172, 244
Taubatu'n-nasuh (Deputy Nazir Ahmad),
323, 325, 377, 407n5, 411n49
Tauhid (unity of God), 2, 26–27, 172
*Ta'ziya*s, 159–160
Teaching. *See* Education
Thanawi, Maulana. *See* Ashraf 'Ali
Thanawi, Maulana
Thousand and One Nights, The, 6, 325,
379
Tithes, 28, 31, 33–34, 76, 179. See also
Zakat
Torah, 70
Truth (*sidq*), 195, 198
Tuhfa, 304–306
Tuhfatu'l-'ushshaq, 306

'Ubaida bint Kilab, 300–301
'Ulama, viii, 4–5, 49, 316, 323, 384n5,
386n27, 389n50, 392n8; of Barelwi,
22; and colonialism, 7–8; and critique
of custom, 81; and educational methods, 19–20; and modernization, 13;

Compositor: Huron Valley Graphics
Text: 10/12.5 Times Roman
Display: Isbell Book
Printer: Princeton University Press / Printing Division
Binder: Princeton University Press / Printing Division